Shakespeare's Theater of Likeness

Shakespeare's Theater of Likeness

R. Allen Shoaf

New Academia Publishing, LLC
Washington, DC

Copyright © 2006 by R. Allen Shoaf

New Academia Publishing, 2006

All rights reserved. No part of this book may be reproduced or transmitted in any form or by any means, electronic or mechanical, including photocopying, recording, or by any information storage and retrieval system.

Printed in the United States of America

Library of Congress Control Number: 2005931973
ISBN 0-9767042-4-2 hardcover (alk. paper)
ISBN 0-9767042-3-4 paperback (alk. paper)

New Academia Publishing, LLC
P.O. Box 27420, Washington, DC 20038-7420
www.newacademia.com - info@newacademia.com

*To the memory of my beloved friend,
Julian Noa Wasserman (1948-2003)*

Language most shewes a man: speake that I may see thee. It springs out of the most retired, and inmost parts of us, and is the Image of the Parent of it, the mind. No glasse renders a mans forme, or likenesse, so true as his speech.

> Ben Jonson, 8 (1947): 620-1

And if then you doe not like him, surely you are in some manifest danger, not to understand him.

> John Heminge / Henrie Condell,
> *The First Folio*, "To the Reader"

Likeness glues love.

> John Donne, *Elegie* 16, line 23

"How hast thou hunger then?" Satan replied,
Tell me, if Food were now before thee set,
Would'st thou not eat?" "Thereafter as I like
The giver," answered Jesus.

> John Milton, *Paradise Regained* 2.319-22

                    Perhaps,
The man-hero is not the exceptional monster,
But he that of repetition is most master.

> Wallace Stevens,
> "Notes Toward a Supreme Fiction"

Contents

A Note on Method   xii
A Note on the Text of Shakespeare   xiii
Preface   xv
Acknowledgments and Permissions   xxii

Introduction: A Theater of Likeness   1
Chronology   13

1. "Since all alike my songs and praises be": Reproducing Likeness in Shakespeare's *Sonnets*   15
2. "Minister the like to you": Metamorphosis and Competition in *The Two Gentlemen of Verona*   23
3. "Sent you hither so unlike yourself": The Truing of the Mate in *The Taming of the Shrew*   35
4. "But thou art neither like thy sire nor dam": Narcissus Disfigured in The First Henriad and *Venus and Adonis*   43
5. "Too like the sire": Likeness and Mutilation in *Titus Andronicus*   53
6. "When they in thee the like offenses prove": The Ruins of Exemplariness in *The Rape of Lucrece*   63
7. "Famous for like victories": Shakespeare's "Mirror for Princes" in *Edward III*   69
8. "These two so like": Error's Error in *The Comedy of Errors*   75
9. "Our love being yours, the error that love makes/Is likewise yours": *L[ike]'s Labours Lost*   85

Contents

10. "I cannot tell vat is 'like me'": Inventing a Likeness in The Second Henriad — 93
11. "I'll look to like": Death and Discourse in *Romeo and Juliet* — 105
12. "All that you are like to know": *A Midsummer Night's Dream* (of Likeness) — 115
13. *King John*: "Liker in feature to his father" — 125
14. "If we are like you in the rest, we will resemble you in that": Likeness, Race, and Gender in *The Merchant of Venice* — 131
15. "An eye to make difference of men's liking": Assimilating Falstaff in *The Merry Wives of Windsor* — 143
16. "To drive liking to the name of love": Much Ado About *Like* in *Much Ado About Nothing* — 149
17. "Every Like Is Not the Same": The Tragedy of Brutus in *The Life and Death of Julius Caesar* — 165
18. *As You Like It*: The Hymen of Likeness in the Forest of Ardenne — 177
19. "A figure like your father": *Hamlet*—Like Mother, Like Son — 187
20. "To like his love": The Violence of Volition in Illyria (Malvolio |Olivia | Viola/Cesario(n) — Or|si|no [Orison]) — 199
21. "That that likes not you pleases me best": The Agony of Reflection in *Troilus and Cressida* — 209
22. "Like as if that God / Owed not nor made not you": The Theater of Likeness in *The Book of Sir Thomas More* — 219
23. "Like doth quit like": The Measure of Likeness — 223
24. "What didst not like?": Othello UnMoored — 235
25. "Hath lost me in your liking [lie, king]": *King Lear* — 251
26. "Do not assume my likeness": *Timon of Athens* — Misanthropy as Unlikeness — 263
27. "Writes them all alike": *Macbeth* — 275
28. "It is shaped, sir, like itself": *Antony and Cleopatra* — 287
29. "To join like likes": All's Will That Ends Ill — 295

30. "Thou show'st/Like one I loved indeed": *Pericles, Prince of Tyre* — 309
31. "What is like me formerly": Coriolanus's Core — 319
32. "Almost as like as eggs": *The Winter's Tale* — 329
33. "The action of my life is like it": The Posthumus Theater of Likeness in *Cymbeline* — 337
34. "Nor can imagination form a shape,/Besides yourself, to like of": The End of Imagination in *The Tempest* — 347
35. "Said I for this the girl was like to him?": Is All True in *All Is True*? — 355
36. "And bear us like the time": The Crisis of Likeness in *The Two Noble Kinsmen* — 361

Notes — 369
List of Works Consulted — 413
Index of Names and Topics — 427

A Note on Method

I call the reading that I have undertaken in this book *micrology*, and I call the method *digitopian*. The reading is not just "close," it is microscopically close, in many cases atomizing the most minimal elements of verbal meaning. The method is digitopian because it would not be possible to undertake such microscopic analysis without digital versions of the literary text that exist in a place (< *topos*) that is unlike any other place in which literature has existed before (which amounts to both utopia and dystopia), effectively a prosthetic memory within which readers can proceed to the kind of analysis undertaken here.

Micrological reading within a digitopian method entails certain differences from several scholarly conventions. Most of these will appear as my study unfolds. But one, in particular, merits special attention here. I quote a good deal more of Shakespeare's poetry than is customary in a traditional scholarly monograph. I do so, in part, because the texts are available in digital form—I have created my own digital archive of many different versions of Shakespeare's texts; also, in part, the type of publication in which my study is appearing—print-on-demand, CD-ROM—alleviates some of the severe constraints encountered in traditional print publication: cost in this format is not the tyrant over books that it is in others.

But I take advantage of the option primarily because the ground of my study is that, within his theater of likeness, Shakespeare's writing is its own most informative context. The cumulative effect of reading/hearing poetry that articulates its structure through repeated contests of likeness and difference is to begin to feel not a theme or an idea but a habit of composition that no amount of assertion or demonstration can convey in the same way as the aural experience of that poetry can and does. It is not enough to say, here is an occurrence of *like*; it is also necessary to say, consider the texture into which the occurrence is woven.

If I here evoke and emphasize the Latin word from which *text* derives—*texere*, "to weave"—I do so, I pause to note, for a number of reasons that will become evident in the course of my study; but my primary motive is to insist that (un)*like*(ness) is woven into Shakespearean composition. We must always be alert to the cross-work of Shakespearean texture. That texture is juxta-form and cruci-lingual, as emerges clearly in digitopia.

A Note on the Text of Shakespeare

Throughout this book, my authority for the text of Shakespeare and all matters related to it is the *Oxford Shakespeare*, 2nd edition (2005). I have paid Oxford University Press the fee they have required of me for permission to use this text as extensively as my study requires.

I make reference throughout the book to other editions: Norton, based on Oxford; Arden; Riverside; Yale; Cambridge. I cite annotations, glosses, introductions, and local arguments from these whenever they are apposite, with full documentation. But my authority is finally Oxford: all quotations, without exception, are from Oxford.

For convenience's sake, I follow (with slight modifications) the traditional abbreviations for works of Shakespeare as found in the *MLA Handbook for Writers of Research Papers* (278-9).

Preface

Consider the following, highly select list of occurrences of the word *like* in various works by Shakespeare (emphasis added):

As You Like It (**a play title**)

CAPULET'S WIFE [*to Juliet*] Speak briefly: can you *like* of Paris' love?
JULIET I'll look to *like*, if looking *liking* move.
Rom. 1.3.98-99

OTHELLO *Thou dost mean something.*
I heard thee say even now thou *liked'st* not that,
When Cassio left my wife. *What didst not like*?
Oth. 3.3.112-14

AREMANTUS Thou hast cast away thyself being *like* thyself.
Tim. 4.3.218; 221

CATHERINE *Pardonnez-moi*, I cannot tell vat is "*like* me."
HV 5.2.108

CITIZEN. Both [France and England] are *alike*, and both *alike* we *like*.
Jn. 2.1.331

TRANIO And tell us what occasion of import
Hath all so long detained you from your wife
And sent you hither so *unlike* yourself?
Shr. 3.2.102-4

HELEN The mightiest space in fortune nature brings
To join *like* *likes* and kiss *like* native things.
AWW 1.1.218-19

DUKE VINCENTIO Haste still pays haste, and leisure answers leisure;
Like doth quit *like*, and measure still for measure.
MM 5.1.407-8

LEONTES Thou want'st a rough pash and the shoots that I have,
To be full *like* me. Yet they say we are
Almost as *like* as eggs.
WT 1.2.130-2.

These and hundreds of others of the nearly 2,400 occurrences of the word suggest that Shakespeare's is a theater of likeness, "as you like it."

All theater is a theater of likeness in that it depends upon imitation. My contention, further, is that this very dependence motivated Shakespeare's remarkable vocabulary of *like*ness. Anxious at all times about copying— in an age that had come, as Adelman, Cave, Fineman, Parker, and others have shown, to re-think *copia* as one of its enduring paradoxes, even as Erasmus perhaps would have wanted done—Shakespeare employs his vocabulary of *like*ness throughout his career to interrogate the dynamic of imitation. *Like* is the marker of the crisis of *imitatio* in Shakespeare's writings, psychological and rhetorical alike.

But, further, and on a larger scale, in the Western philosophical and theological tradition both, likeness is a crisis: for Plato, it is a debased form of knowledge, a copy; for the Judeo-Christian religion, it is a constant threat ("Thou shalt not make unto thee any graven image, or any *likeness* of any thing that is in heaven above, or that is in the earth beneath, or that is in the water under the earth" [Exodus 20:4; emphasis added]), even as Scripture also celebrates that "in His image and *likeness* created He them" (Genesis 2:6), and Jesus emptied himself, being made in the *likeness* of men (Philippians 2:6-7). For Plotinus, "all knowing comes by likeness" (*Ennead* 1.8.1). But St. Augustine found himself in his pre-conversion misery in a "land of unlikeness" (*regio dissimilitudinis*—*Confessions* 7.10.16). Famously, or infamously, the Creed, and the Church that stands by it, teetered on an iota, *homoousion* or *homoiousion*, "one with" or "one like" God—much sorrow for many years from this grave dispute. Language is all but impossible without likeness (simile, assimilation, metaphor); but, perhaps notoriously, Nietzsche shakes his head, "[j]eder Begriff entsteht durch Gleichsetzen des Nicht-Gleichen" ("Every concept arises from a likening of the unlike" [*Über Wahrheit und Lüge im aussermoralischen Sinne*, 1; my translation]), a testier version of Plotinus' point. Against likeness, postmodernism, we know, has leveled the critique that it is logocentrism itself. And everyone who reads this book has looked into the mirror recently, seeing a likeness—whatever exactly that is. The word, as Shakespeare also understood, is so fraught with senses that it seems frequently meaningless (see esp. Siegel 35-71).

But it is not meaningless, not at all. In (human) nature, however anomalously, likes do not repel, they attract. This anomaly may already be implicit in the word's etymology: *like* derives from a root (*lik*) meaning "form" or "shape," and in Anglo-Saxon means "body" (Dutch, Danish, and Swedish instances of the word mean "corpse"). In addition, even more "lawlessly," likes and the shapes that embody them attract especially where difference appears to be most extreme, the most vivid example in Shakespeare's works being Othello and Desdemona—but remember also Romeo and Juliet. Shakespeare pursues insight as compelling as it is (apparently) absurd: where naive perception assumes that there is little or no resemblance, Shakespeare, to the contrary, sees great liking and even love (it is the body's mystery—ultimately, too, the corpse's); where naive perception observes apparent resemblance, Shakespeare, to the contrary, exposes stark *un*likeness and profound resentment (the body's mystery again and, again, ultimately, too, the corpse's).

This latter dimension of the insight is of great importance. It will be found at the center of many of Shakespeare's tragedies: families, where resemblance and thus liking and loving should abound, are actually the seats of terrible unlikeness and tragic antipathy—Lear and his daughters, Hamlet and his uncle and mother, Leontes and Hermione and their son Mamillius, Titus and his sons, Coriolanus and his mother, etc. Shakespeare understood, long before psychoanalysis, that too much resemblance can only breed the inevitable violence of separation and differentiation: too much likeness and the script of your life is only a pre-script, pre-scribed by another in a discourse not your own, from which you *must* escape, which you *must* rescript: "We defy augury…The readiness is all" (*Ham.* 5.2.165-8)—"For he was *likely*, had he been put on, / To have proved most royally" (*Ham.* 5.2. 351-2; emphasis added).

I first began to study the problematic of copying and copies in the 1970s in my early engagement with Ovid's Narcissus, he who falls in love with his own likeness. Narcissus was the central focus of my first book, *Dante, Chaucer, and the Currency of the Word* (published 1983), and studying the figure introduced me to the dilemma of copiousness: if we hoard our likeness, we die of our likeness—"inopem me copia fecit" ("my very copiousness makes me un-copious, impoverished" [*Metamorphoses* 3.466; my translation], and cf. with Sonnet #16, line 12: "To give away yourself keeps yourself still"). Copiousness, in my continuing study, emerges as one of the most deceptively "simple" concepts of human psychology, at once desirable and abhorrent.

To copy seems only natural (children do it all the time, give themselves up to another as likeness); but to refuse to copy (to be individual and independent) also seems only natural—we value originality. The imperative (not) to copy is an exquisitely frustrating double-bind. Narcissus is the symbol of those caught in this double-bind. He refuses to couple his likeness in love with any other ("Ante ... emoriar quam sit tibi copia nostra"—"I will die before my copiousness shall be[long] to you [namely, Echo]" [*Metamorphoses* 3.391; my translation]), and so he wastes away by the pool where he falls in love with his own likeness, a copy of himself (and a parody of originality), realizing the dark etymon of his name, "narx," or "numbness" (as also in "narcotic")—however contradictory it may at first seem, you had better share it or, for sure, you will never be able to spare it.

Think now of Shakespeare's career, he who copied from everybody (but never merely copied), he who, when he was not copying, was collaborating, he who wrote incessantly about disguise, mistaken identities, and twinship (and fathered twins, non-identical copies of each other); and yet he is also the one who is universally recognized as the most distinctive, individual, original genius of his age. What is Shakespeare's likeness? Whom is Shakespeare like? Where is Shakespeare's like? Joyce has it perhaps just right when he calls him "great Shapesphere" (*Finnegan's Wake* 295.3-4). In terms I developed in my book *Milton, Poet of Duality*, Shakespeare's d*ue*ls (with sources and predecessors) always issue in unpredictable d*ua*ls, new likenesses of old texts that show unmistakable signs of imitation *and* innovation, copying *and* creativity.

It was in my work on *Milton, Poet of Duality* that I first began to appreciate the influence that the idea of likeness exerts over early modern writers. In 1980-1981, I undertook a side-by-side reading of *Paradise Lost* and *The Doctrine and Discipline of Divorce*. I observed, for example, such collocations as the following:

> [God] conglobed
> *Like things to like,* the rest to several place
> *Disparted,* and between spun out the Air,
> And earth self-balanced on her centre hung.
> *PL* 7.239-42 (emphasis added); cf. *PL* 3.710

there is a hidden efficacie of love and hatred in man as wel as in other kinds, not morall, but naturall, which though not alwayes in the choyce, yet in the successe of mariage wil ever be most predominant [and this] besides daily experience, the author of *Ecclesiasticus*. . . acknowledges. . . A *man*, saith he, *will cleave to his like.* But what might be the cause, whether each ones alloted *Genius or* proper Starre, or whether the supernall influence of Schemes and angular aspects or this elementall *Crasis* here below, whether all these jointly or singly meeting friendly, or unfriendly in either party, I dare not, with the men I am likest to clash, appear so much a Philosopher as to conjecture. The ancient proverb in *Homer* Iesse abstruse intitles this worke of leading each like person to his like, peculiarly to God himselfe...There is a twofold Seminary or stock in nature, from whence are deriv'd the issues of love and hatred distinctly flowing through the whole masse of created things, and...Gods doing ever is to bring the due likenesses and harmonies of his workes together, except when out of two contraries met to their own destruction, he moulds a third existence.

DD i.10; Yale Edition 2:271-2

God, Milton finds in Homer, is he who "lead[s] each like person to his like" (*Odyssey* 17.218). Over the next five years, as I regularly taught Shakespeare, I became more and more attuned to the word *like* in his writings because of my heightened awareness of its work in Milton, and I began a systematic census of the occurrences of the word in the plays, using the Spevack *Concordance* to corroborate my findings (I drew up my first, partial list, in 1983).

My academic career was interrupted in 1985-1986 (in fact, it almost came to an end), and I did not resume work on Shakespeare again until 1987 when I prepared a plenary address for the 1988 Citadel Conference on Medieval and Renaissance Studies (March 12-14). As I worked on that address, I also was reading Joel Fineman's *Shakespeare's Perjured Eye: The Invention of Poetic Subjectivity in the Sonnets* which had been published in 1986. This book was of immediate help to me. Fineman had clearly grasped the issue of likeness in the *Sonnets*, and although I have come a long way since reading his book, I wish to acknowledge here that his was the last spur that raised my spirit to study the word *like* globally in the Shakespeare canon.

Between 1990 and 1996, I worked on an edition of Thomas Usk's *The Testament of Love* (1385), a work of considerable importance for the study of Chaucer and his contemporaries, and by the time I submitted the final manuscript to the series editor in the late summer of 1996, I had, by dint of reading copiously in editorial theory, become satisfied that editing is a highly subjective enterprise that, however much it strives for accuracy and fidelity, inevitably contaminates the object of its efforts with the interests and the feelings of the editor. When I resumed work on Shakespeare in the fall of 1996, then, drafting the essay "*Hamlet*: Like Mother, Like Son," I understood and premised that subjectivity is also editorial—I am constantly editing my likeness for social and political consumption—and no character in the canon is more excruciatingly aware of this limiting condition of human being than is Hamlet: "I have that within which passeth show—/These but the trappings and the suits of woe" (*Ham.* 1.2.85-86). From that moment to this, my constant professional effort after editorial duties for the journal *Exemplaria* has been to work with the nearly 2,400 occurrences of *like* in the canon.

Following Shakespeare following Ovid, the *Metamorphoses*, in particular, and, most especially, the fable of Narcissus, my book engages the individual psychology of copying and the myriad human problems it provokes. By then turning attention to the Platonic inheritance with its systematic dismay at copying, its thoroughgoing mistrust of all imagery, the book demonstrates how individual psychology flows together with philosophical problematics in Western history. Plato famously complains that "an imitator…is in his nature three removes from…the truth, as are all other imitators" (*Republic* 10.597e; 822-3); all knowledge that depends on copying, in other words, is structurally corrupt—and that is most if not all knowledge, especially *self*-knowledge. Tracing the vexed history of imitation as not just mimesis or pedagogy but *the* problem of epistemology, the book turns to consider why a writer like Shakespeare would return so often in his writings to the word *like*: deeply trained as we now believe he was in Latin (Honan, 43-49, 52-56, 60) and conversant with the Latin transmission of Western thought, he repeatedly positions *like* as a marker of a dilemma at once personal and political, philosophical and theological, logical and poetic—namely, how does any of us answer the question, "whom shall I (be) like?" How does any of us "drive liking to the name of love" (*Ado* 1.1.283)?

My work with *like* and *copia* is closely bound up also with a life-long concern to liberate reading from the fear of apparent coincidence or, the obverse, from the tyranny of the pre-dicted. Very frequently what appears as coincidence upon further examination reveals profound motivation: "Madam, how *like* you this play" (*Ham.* 3.2.218; emphasis added) is usually punctuated with a question mark, but, in light of the word *like* elsewhere in the canon, an exclamation point would be equally justifiable —and that is no "coincidence," although it is coincident. I am at pains to read such moments for their unpredictable juxtapositions, so as to identify the multiple likenesses that compete for the same semantic space and, in doing so, constitute effectively a Shakespearean signature, *like*.

In 1986, Fineman (who died of cancer in 1989), argued that "the sequence [of sonnets] ... manifests itself as a progress from a poetry of likeness to a poetry of difference" (131). In the book that follows, I both agree and profoundly disagree with this position. I think that the poetry of likeness was already a poetry of difference from the very beginning of Shakespeare's writing career—a poetry of (un)likeness, as I would prefer to characterize it—in the "land of unlikeness" (*regio dissimilitudinis*) where human beings invent their likenesses ("fashion" themselves, as Fineman's then colleague at Berkeley, Stephen Greenblatt, would have it); and I hope to show that Shakespeare's theater is also Shakespeare's theory (*theater* and *theory* are from the same Greek word, θέα) of the psychology of likeness and unlikeness in the human striving for that most elusive (and allusive) of all attainments, an individual identity.

"*Pardonnez-moi*, I cannot tell vat is 'like me'."

Acknowledgments and Permissions

The following colleagues, students, and friends have helped me write a better book than I could have written without their contributions. I am grateful to them one and all.

David G. Allen, Harold Bloom, Bruce R. Boehrer, Richard E. Brantley, Patrick Cheney, Ira G. Clark III, Daniel A. Cottom, Mario A. Di Cesare, Kelly M. Dunn, Robert R. Edwards, Cheryl Foodman, William Goodman, Amy Gorelick, Norman N. Holland, Amy Christine Hylton, Ivo Kamps, Heather Lynn Lawson, Jenny Lieberman, Michael W. Muhlhauser, Jessica E. Murray, Rhiannon Price, Alma Elaine Shoaf, Brian D. Shoaf, Judy Shoaf, Kristen D. G. Smith, Mark Taylor, Jonathan Tharin, Adam Vines, J. Whipple Walker, Julian Noa Wasserman (d. 2003), Sandra G. Weems, Naomi Weiss, Robert White, and Despina Williams.

Wallace Stevens. *The Collected Poems of Wallace Stevens*. Copyright © 1954 by Wallace Stevens and renewed 1982 by Holly Stevens. Used by permission of Alfred A. Knopf, a division of Random House, Inc.

Stanley Wells and Gary Taylor. General Editors. Stanley Wells, Gary Taylor, John Jowett, and William Montgomery. Editors. *William Shakespeare: The Complete Works*. 2nd ed. Oxford: Clarendon Press, 2005. Used with permission.

Grateful acknowledgment is also made to the following for permission to use material originally appearing in their publications.

R. Allen Shoaf. "'For there is figures in all things': Juxtology in Shakespeare, Spenser, and Milton." David G. Allen and Robert White, ed. *The Work of Dissimilitude: Essays from the Sixth Citadel Conference on Medieval and Renaissance Literature*. Newark: University of Delaware Press, 1992. 266-85.

R. Allen Shoaf. "*Hamlet*: Like Mother, Like Son." *Journal X* 4.1 (1999): 71-90.

Introduction: A Theater of Likeness

> Examples gross as earth exhort me
> *Ham.* Q2 4.4.37 (Oxford 2ᵉ717J)

Exemplariness is the phenomenon most directly informing Shakespeare's theater of likeness.¹ All cultures depend on copying exemplars or conventional likenesses. Try as you might, you cannot escape likeness—"Le plus profond," says Paul Valery, "c'est le peau" ("The deepest thing, it's the skin").² And however you dress the skin, you're dressing it in a likeness, always. This likeness is also, always, a prescript—it is to one extent or another prescriptive. The prescriptiveness of exemplariness is a constant in early modern culture, and the relationship between exemplariness and drama is unintelligible without recognizing that every example prescribes a likeness you should copy in a rhetoric that is necessarily oriented toward drama, play. Whether you are learning to fence or to parse or to curtsy, you are a player fulfilling a role.

It is very difficult to document an idea and a phenomenon so fundamental to Europe, in particular, for so many generations. (Scholarly punctiliousness would have me "historicize" exemplariness, but I would never live so long.) Stephen Greenblatt attempts to do it with "self-fashioning"; Terence Cave and Patricia Parker, with *copia*, copiousness rhetorical and political; Joel Altman, Norman Rabkin, and others, with a focus on paradox and contrariety (contesting examples) in early modern European culture; materialists, such as Peter Stallybrass, Ann Rosalind Jones, and others, with an insistence on objects, such as clothing (another skin); Harry Berger, Jr. and James Calderwood, with an idea of the meta-fictionality of drama. These are just a few of a very great many. All look toward the same phenomenon of modeling according to an exemplar (which we find everywhere in the works of Shakespeare). Whether we consider the "mirrors for princes" (*Fürstenspiegel*), the numerous conduct and courtesy books of the period (for men, women, and children), the advice to courtiers (Castiglione, for example), the Neo-Platonic (Plotinian) insistence on likeness to God as the supreme human aspiration, or, perhaps most important of all, the ubiquitous *imitatio Christi* fundamental to all Christians of whatever confession, we find in early modern Europe a pedagogy, a rhetoric, a politics, and an ethics of copying exemplars.[3] Nothing is deeper than the skin—you must look like .... Or, to paraphrase George III, in Alan Bennett's play, *The Madness of George III*, it's not about being, it's about seeming (70). It is not enough to be; we must also seem —that is, be *like*—the role we must play.

Examples of exemplarity abound in the period.[4] But consider first Shakespeare himself. The italicized passages in the quotation that follows comprise a lexicon of likeness:

> "And wilt thou [Tarquin] be the *school* where lust shall learn?
> Must *he in thee read lectures* of such shame?
> Wilt thou be *glass* wherein it shall discern
> *Authority* for sin, warrant for blame ...
>
> "Thy princely *office* how canst thou fulfil
> When, *patterned by thy fault*, foul sin may say
> He *learned* to sin, and thou didst *teach the way*?"
> Luc. 617-20, 628-30 (emphasis added)

We may also, for confirmation's sake, listen to Shakespeare's great 17th-century successor meditate the same phenomenon:

> To whom the wilie Adder, blithe and glad.
> Empress, the way is readie, and not long,
> Beyond a row of Myrtles, on a Flat,
> Fast by a Fountain, one small Thicket past
> Of blowing Myrrh and Balme; *if thou accept*
> *My conduct, I can bring thee thither soon.*
> *Paradise Lost* 9.625-30 (emphasis added)

"If you copy my likeness, I can take you there. I can prescribe the way." Milton understands, and exquisitely, the stakes of post-lapsarian pedagogy —we only learn by copying—and Satan calculates precisely:

> Nor hope to be my self less miserable
> By what I seek, *but others to make such*
> *As I* ...
> *Paradise Lost* 9.125-7 (emphasis added)

Copies of himself are his way (he thinks) to ruin God's image and likeness (Genesis 2:6: "imago et similitudo").

If now we consider a common complaint against theater in Elizabethan London, we can see its immediate and far-reaching relevance to the argument:

> We have signified to your Honours many times heretofore the great inconvenience which we find to grow by the common exercise of stage plays. ... specially being of that frame and matter as usually they are, containing nothing but profane fables, lascivious matters, cozening devices, and scurrilous behaviours, *which are so set forth as that they move wholly to imitation* and not to the avoiding of those faults and vices which they represent.... Whereby such as frequent them, being of the base and refuse sort of people, or such young gentlemen as have small regard of credit or conscience, *draw the same into imitation* and not the avoiding the *like* vices which they represent (Aughterson 190-1).

Drama is inseparable from likeness. This of course we already knew. But what must be new is our sense of the pandemic: copying oozes into everything, nothing is immune. And the Mayor and Aldermen of the City of London cannot tolerate this.[5]

The impact of the culture of exemplariness on Shakespeare's theater of likeness is most readily measured in his history plays. Thus, for example, Howard and Rackin (18) observe that

> When apologists for the theater wished to defend it against attacks from critics who saw it as a place of idleness and moral danger, they often held up the history play as an example of theater's value. And they did so in terms that stressed the role of history plays in preserving the memory of English heroes and of encouraging patriotic feelings in the spectators. Thomas Nashe, for example, praised the genre because in it
>
>> our forefathers valiant acts (that have line long buried in rustic brasse and worm-eaten bookes) are revived, and they themselves raised from the Grave of Oblivion, and brought to pleade their aged Honours in open presence.... How would it have joyed brave Talbot (the terror of the French) to thinke that after he had lyne two hundred yeares in his Tombe, hee should triumphe againe on the Stage, and have his bones newe embalmed with the teares

of ten thousand spectators at least (at severall times), who, in the Tragedian that represents his person, imagine they behold him fresh bleeding? (Nashe 1592, in Chambers 1923: 4:238-9).

History plays are, apologists like Nashe claim, exemplary *in a positive sense*, reviving the past for the present to behold.[6] Moralists, we have seen, agree that plays are exemplary, but *in a negative sense*. This conflict, ultimately a political division as much as a moral one, I hope to show, lies behind Shakespeare's gradual disenchantment with history as a genre.[7] Shakespeare comes to think historiographically in terms of likenesses that invariably fall short of their ideal exemplars, produce consequences incompatible with their originals, or issue in copies the imitations of which have been only imprudently (because selfishly) foreseen. History, for Shakespeare, is the history of copies, where copying is always fallible, mortal, interested, and incomplete—or, in the worst case, monstrous. "But thou art neither *like* thy sire nor dam, / But *like* a foul misshapen stigmatic," screams Margaret at Richard Crookback (*3HVI* 2.2.135-6; emphasis added), who in fact boasts that he is *like no one*:

> Then, since the heavens have shaped my body so,
> Let hell make crooked my mind to answer it.
> I had no father, I am *like* no father;
> I have no brother, I am *like* no brother;
> And this word, 'love', which greybeards call divine,
> Be resident in men *like* one another
> And not in me — *I am myself alone*.
> Richard Duke of York (3 Henry VI) 5.6.78-84
> (emphasis added)

It is impossible, Shakespeare learns, to infer character from likeness or likeness from character—except in the case of monsters. As we say, the exception proves the rule. Iago is honest—he acts like an honest man, hardly a monster.[8]

History and history plays are a site where the dynamics of exemplariness—ranging from birth (defects) to cultural (i)cons—are very easily and clearly shown and seen. In history plays, you can see very clearly how prescripts and prescriptiveness fail. History plays are thus also a sight—"theater" derives from Greek θέα, which means "viewing, seeing, a sight."[9] The theater is where the example and the likeness are seen—as the Mayor and Aldermen of London are all too unhappily aware. Theater is the sight as well as the site of likenesses, one important reason *like* occurs nearly 2,400 times in the canon of Shakespeare's writings: theater shows you what something or someone is like. Theater thus shows you a theory of that likeness—"theory" derives from the same Greek word, θέα, having the sense of "that which is contemplated."[10] Theater is a theory of how it happened. Theory is a theater of how it might happen or might have happened. Thus, obviously, all theater is theoretical and all theory is theatrical. We could do with a word like, say, "theatrist." Be that as it may, Shakespeare's theater of likeness, we will see time and again in my book, is also a theory of likeness.[11]

That theory of likeness, assuming exemplariness, is inseparable in Shakespeare's mind (and body, as well, I think) from the primordial datum in human being of sexual division. We are all copyists because we are all divided and, as divided, incomplete, divided first from our mothers at birth and then from each other throughout our lives—by competition, envy, hatred, spite, and love and sex, too (no sex without division, even in masturbation).[12] We are, in fact, so constituted physiologically that copying is inescapable: we can only take our likeness from another, skin to skin. The first other from whom we take our likeness is our mother. (As the anxiety of the patriarchy makes repeatedly clear, it is a certain vexation whether we take our likeness from our father—DNA testing is a *very* recent phenomenon.)[13] Where feminism over the past 30 years has so often seen Shakespeare the misogynist and misogamist, I see Shakespeare the hater of sexual division as such, the man who could imagine (but never attain?) the condition in which

> Either was the other's mine.
>
> Property was thus appalled
> That the self was not the same.
> Single nature's double name
> Neither two nor one was called.
>
> Reason, in itself confounded,
> Saw division grow together
> To themselves, yet either neither,
> Simple were so well compounded
>
> That it cried "How true a twain
> Seemeth this concordant one!
> Love hath reason, reason none,
> If what parts can so remain."
> "The Phoenix and Turtle," lines 36-48

Shakespeare could be misogynistic, I doubt not, nor do I deny it, but, I will argue, what torments him is division itself—I am here, you are there; I am not, unless you are; why *must* this be so?

I assume, axiomatically, that he was wounded in his experience of sexual intimacy by his fortunes with Anne Hathaway (he was eight years her junior and, likely, a virgin), and I am not in any way repulsed by Duncan-Jones's hypothesis that he may have been dying of syphilis at the end of his life, nor would I be in the least surprised to know for a fact that he was the father of a son, christened William, no less (William Davenant), upon his best friend's wife, Jeanette ("'a very beautiful woman,' according to Aubrey, 'of a very good wit and of conversation extremely agreeable'").[14] Sex is a mess. But the case I have to make is of a fundamentally deeper, even rawer, psychopathology: he was hurt to the quick by division itself, and the theater of likeness was his means of reconciling himself to the inescapable dynamic of difference and likeness, likeness and difference— "I'll look to like, if looking liking move," says Juliet to her mother when Lady Capulet asks, "[c]an you like of the county Paris's love?" (*Rom.* 1.3.98). What are we to do?

Torn asunder as we are—from our mothers, from our lovers, from ourselves—we are always looking to like if looking liking move. "Only connect," as Forster's Margaret says in *Howards End* (168). It is, as every one of us knows, very difficult to connect—and a penis inside a vagina or an anus or a mouth is hardly proof of a connection. Shakespeare wrote 40-some major works over 20-some years, call it one every six months, because he was driven, I believe, by a dilemma confronting us all and avoided by almost all of us like the plague, the intolerable question, what am I like? Whom do I like? What do I like? Why am I like this? Who will deliver me from the body of this likeness? Who will deliver me from the likeness of this body?

It would be a mistake to dismiss these questions as adolescent navel-gazing or daytime-TV psychobabble. These questions, the questions of sexual division, are also questions of utmost political moment—who will succeed Elizabeth Tudor to the throne of England? Who will be *like* her? She is childless. More, she is female. Shakespeare's career coincides with the moment in Europe's history of most exquisite anxiety over sexual succession or the uncertainty over the heir to the throne after the reign of Gloriana. Who will be like *her*? For 45 years, against almost unimaginable odds, she reigned gloriously, but she dies childless. In the event the throne will pass to the son whose mother she ordered executed—history beggars irony. Be that as it may, her life and her body insist year in and year out on the intractable and agonizing reality of sexual division: *if* she had married to beget an heir, what would have happened to England under her husband, supposedly her head (St. Paul's argument—e.g., Colossians 3:18)? As troubling as the absence of an heir was, the prospects of a husband for Elizabeth Tudor were more troubling by far. What if he had been a Spaniard? a Catholic? and worse?[15]

Shakespeare is also obsessed with succession, then, I will argue. Thus, for example, we have another way of accounting for his career-long fascination with bastardy, (il)legitimacy, the (un)likeness of offspring to progenitor.[16] Partly, I think this is bound up with Susanna Shakespeare, his first-born, who is also his *daughter*, and with therefore also the patriarchal dilemma he faced of having to accept a daughter as his heir—a dilemma exacerbated beyond endurance by the death of Hamnet, his son, in 1596 (funeral 11 August) at the age of 11.[17] But, important as these biographical facts are, his obsession is not to be reduced to them since legitimacy is *the* canker in all political systems depending upon succession through primogeniture—depending, in other words, upon sex.[18]

They depend on women. They depend on women's bodies. They depend on that over which no man ever felt he had control, at least if he was in his right mind, a woman's genital, her "nothing." They depend upon a "product" (a fetus) no amount of male ingenuity can ever engineer (cloning has yet to work). They depend upon the (so-called) weaker vessel. Something somewhere has to give, doesn't it? I will argue, in my readings of the romances, where the word *he(i)r* is very prominent, and virgin daughters are principal protagonists, that Shakespeare reached some reconciliation with the idea of both Elizabeth and Susanna, not least because Susanna Shakespeare Hall, according to her epitaph, was "witty above her sexe" and "some of Shakespeare was in that" (Honan 400).

If succession and sexual division, engines of exemplariness, drive Shakespeare's constant exploration of the theater of likeness in human being ("That every like is not the same, O Caesar,/The heart of Brutus ernes [grieves] to think upon"—*JC* 2.2.128-9), they also impinge upon his language and his style. Whether we look to his fondness for hendiadys ("one from or by two"), his penchant for compounds, his tendency to generate verbs from nouns, his tireless, restless fascination with neologisms, his extraordinary daring in enjambment or whether, following Joel Fineman, we attempt to summarize his rhetoric by adopting Puttenham's "crossecople" (which is *syneciosis*, συνοικείωσις, or a type of oxymoron), we see, in every instance, how Shakespeare's language drives toward unitary twoness (juxta-form and cruci-lingual), toward likenings that inscribe their differences and differences that inscribe their likenings, inter-relationships that a more quotidian language ignores for the sake of disambiguation[19]; and we can, following Fineman and Puttenham, also see that in the history of *syneciosis*, its etymology, we have a profound introduction to

8   Introduction

Shakespeare's language—"from Gk. *syn*, 'with' and *oikeios*, 'one's own'"— where the word in Greek for "one's own" means "of the household," οἶκος, where one lives and is most like oneself (one's οἰκονομία, one's *economy*). Shakespeare's writing finds, repeatedly, words (ideas and characters, too) that are "with their own" when we, without Shakespeare, would never have thought that they were with their own, at home with each other; without him, we would have mistaken them, misreading them for what they were not—"O, 'tis most sweet / When in one line two crafts directly meet" (*Ham.* Q2 3.4.8-9; Oxford 2ᵉ 717H), but we need him to show us (θεα) their meeting. Shakespeare is the supreme syneciotician (pronounce as if "sin ee see o tishun," on the model of "semiotician") in the English tradition ("great Shapesphere," as James Joyce says [*Finnegans Wake* 295.3-4]).[20] Cross-coupling the least likely couples into likelihoods of unforgettable likenesses—Othello and Desdemona, Hal and Falstaff, Lear and the Fool, Prospero and Caliban, Hamlet and his mother Gertrude— Shakespeare repeatedly utters outrageous "at-home-together-with's" that nonetheless thrill our sensibilities:

> Therefore I lie with her, and she with me,
> And in our faults by lies we flattered be.
>
> Sonnet #138

With a vocabulary exceeding 25,000 words (more than twice that of Milton [Norton 63]), Shakespeare confronted sexual division with verbal division ("lie," e.g.) and changed our understanding of coupling forever.[21]

As mutuality is to the body, so is Shakespeare's rhetoric to language: unlikely likenesses generating unpredictable life. The "cross-cople" is so relevant because every partnership is a kind of oxymoron, *syneciosis*, "together at home with," of two otherwise unlikely individuals bearing no apparent likeness to each other except their membership in the species. Moreover, the player, too, is a couple, of himself and the likeness he represents and performs. The play, then, as well, may be seen and said to couple a form and a performance, an idea and a theory of that idea—this is what it might have looked *like*, here is a theory of Henry V or Othello or Hermione or Juliet or Brutus.[22] Thus, as well, the script is not a prescript but a prompt, the speeches not a formula, to yield the same results every time applied, but a voice, to find its likeness in each new performance. Thus, in our experience of the play, for those two or three hours, we know and do not know at the same time, and this illusion of freedom within necessity gives us pleasure, the pleasure of feeling bounded but not constrained, "cross-cople."

We go to the play to see what we are like. For the Greeks, drama in the beginning was holy, a ritual, for a people must see what they are like else they will not know what it is like to be human—neither gods nor beasts, though perilously near to both.²³ Drama is a spectacle, theater a show, because we must see, we must have a *theory* of what we are like. Since we are going to copy our likenesses regardless, we might copy them in an amphitheater sacred to the gods. This idea did not endure, however. It could not have endured beyond Euripides and Aristophanes anyway—they deconstruct it with almost unerring precision. But the idea nonetheless retains and preserves a truth very hard to deny or suppress (even if you do close the theaters, as in the 1640s)—human beings love to copy and to be copied ("simian" was a favorite image of early modern commentators on the phenomenon²⁴).

In the early modern world, one sphere of human activity in which this proclivity amounted to nearly everything was rhetoric: copying examples is how Shakespeare and every other student of his time learned to read and write.²⁵ All writing was writing after (in every sense that the phrase will bear, as we shall see). Humanism as a culture was a culture of copying, from copying manuscripts in order to preserve them to copying Virgil and Ovid and Cicero to emulate them and, perhaps, achieve a style in Latin not unworthy of being associated with them (if distantly). We are confident that this is how Shakespeare became so intimately familiar with Ovid (even as we are now confident that Shakespeare was a better Latinist than earlier generations allowed—in my opinion, he is an accomplished Latinist).²⁶ Just how inseparable early modern rhetorical training is from copying and copiousness we can measure, too, by the title of Erasmus's influential treatise, *De copia*. And Latin itself, like its cradle, Rome, is a culture of copying: "Graecia capta ferum victorem cepit et artis/intulit agresti Latio" ("Captured Greece took captive her savage conqueror and brought civilization to rustic Latium")—to be a Roman was to have copied the Greeks.²⁷ This *paidea* is part of a vast tradition reaching back into prehistory and taking many forms—perhaps, though, most graphically remembered in the case of Spartan pedagogy, boys copying men in senses that many still find shocking²⁸—and studies of it far exceed any précis I can offer here. But it is still important to stress it, the more so because of Shakespeare's extraordinary devotion to and knowledge of Ovid, the *Metamorphoses* in particular. The Ovidian impulse in the theater of likeness, I have to come to see over the past 25 years, is difficult to exaggerate, and though I acknowledge the importance of Golding's translation of the *Metamorphoses* as much as the next student of English literature, I think Shakespeare liked Ovid's Latin.

With reason. "Ars latet sua arte" ("Art is hidden under his art"—Pygmalion's statue).²⁹ "Legit et silet" ("She reads and is silent"—Procne reading Philomela's tapestry and becoming suddenly as speechless as her violated sister whose tongue Tereus has ripped out [*Metamorphoses* 6.582-3]). Ovid is the syneciotician who taught Shakespeare to be a syneciotician —one master of paradox bequeathing to another master a sense of "couplement" (Sonnet #21.5), of the power of the copula, rhetorical as well as sexual, to show (theatrically and theoretically) things together at home with each other that the rest of us would not even think to consider related, far less at home with each other (*how* can art be hidden under *art*?). If we read the first line of the *Metamorphoses*—"In nova fert animus mutatas dicere formas/corpora" ("Of shapes transformde to bodies straunge, I purpose to entreate" [Golding trans.])—recalling that *like* in Anglo-Saxon is the word for "body" ("corpus"), we can retrieve a sense of how crucial to his theater of likeness Shakespeare found Ovid to be —"Of shapes transformed to *likenesses* strange, I purpose to entreate." In a sense neither trivial nor distorting, Shakespeare's plays can be said time and again to show "shapes transformed to likenesses strange," whether Bottom the ass or Hermione the statue or Lear on the heath with Edgar, Tom o' Bedlam, or Pericles unshorn and unshaven, or Tamora Revenge, et al. In sum, *Metamorphoses* is another name for *Theater of Likeness* and *Theater of Likeness* is another name for *Metamorphoses*.

And both are also, necessarily, a theory of likeness. Ultimately, that theory is Platonic, Neo-Platonic, in particular.[30] Although I have mentioned Neo-Platonism in the Preface to my book, here I need to be more specific. Most scholars and students of early modern culture will have so far missed a central focus on *imitatio* in my Introduction; for many, *imitatio* is what I have been going on about, so to speak.[31] For me, too. That is how I was trained. I still adhere to this training. But if you load the complete works of Shakespeare into your word-processor and search on *imitation* and related forms, you get 22 hits, less than 1% of the occurrences of the word *like*. It is not a theater of imitation; it is a theater of likeness.[32]

I think that this is owing to many factors. Not least among them is Greek *eidos*, Plato's word for *form*, a word also for *idea*, which can bear as well the senses of *likeness, image, shape*.[33] All of these are words that privilege the sense of sight, that which is seen or viewed. Shakespeare through humanists known to him would most likely have been aware of the importance of *like*(ness) to Platonism and Neo-Platonism—the core idea, Plotinian in essence, is that likeness to God is the telos of humanity.[34] It is very likely, however, that Shakespeare himself was well beyond the idealism of Marsiglio Ficino about Platonic forms and Plotinian mysticism, already (as Cavell argues) caught on the cusp of the Cartesian *cogito* and its desperate revolt from likeness (*Cogito* or *dubito, ergo sum* is an argument of a man radically isolated from others).[35] Indeed, Shakespeare could read already in Montaigne (in John Florio's translation published in 1603) that

> The consequence we seeke to draw from the conference of events, is unsure, because they are ever dissemblable. No quality is so universall in this surface of things, as variety and diversity. The Greekes, the Latines, and wee use for the most expresse examples of similitude, that of egs. Some have neverthelesse beene found, especially one in *Delphos*, that knew markes of difference betweene egges, and never tooke one for another. And having divers hennes, could rightly judge which had laid the egge. Dissimilitude doth of it selfe insinuate into our workes, no arte can come neere unto similitude. Resemblance doth not so much make one, as difference maketh another. Nature hath bound herselfe to make nothing that may not be dissemblable (trans. Florio, 322 and Frame, 815).

Here, if I were asked to name "the smoking gun," is the contemporary analog to Shakespeare's theater of likeness: every likeness is also, logically and perforce, an unlikeness, and everything therefore depends for its place in the world on what you liken it to. Both Montaigne and Shakespeare struggle with a Platonic and Neo-Platonic inheritance of immense beauty and power that they know also to be finally, even so, ineffectual in experience (which is the title of the essay by Montaigne from which the quote is drawn). Not only does "the new philosophy call all into doubt" (John Donne, "The First Anniversary: An Anatomy of the World," line 205), even the "old" philosophy understood the paradox and the pain of our appetite for likeness: "nulla duo in universo per omnia aequalia esse possunt simpliciter" (no two things in the universe in every respect can be equal, simply speaking).[36] Nicholas of Cusa in the fifteenth century already clearly understands, though within a different confession, what Montaigne and Shakespeare, among numerous others, also see, all around them, that, to use St. Augustine's oft-cited phrase (itself ultimately Plotinian), we live in a "regio dissimilitudinis," a "land of unlikeness."[37] The new materialism of early capitalism will repeatedly concretize this unlikeness,[38] but it will never cease to be also the intellectual crisis of early modern skepticism. And yet, Shakespeare's skepticism (I agree with Cavell that that is what it is) did not lead him to abandon *like*(ness); to the contrary, he was motivated, I think, all the more to show and examine the very crisis of (un)likeness.

For, in addition to Neo-Platonism, on the one hand, and skepticism, on the other, is Shakespeare's Catholicism. Following Honan and other biographers, I consider Shakespeare to have been emotionally Catholic, though politically and socially Protestant, brought up in a recusant locale and likely close to Catholic sympathizers throughout his youth (see also Marotti 219). Impossible ever to prove definitively, this understanding of his early religiosity helps nevertheless to account for his insuperable sacramentalism throughout his career, even into his senescence of skepticism and, finally, probably, diffidence.[39] He was a man uncannily alive to the sacramentality of nature, its instinct for form and likeness, and this in part derived, I think, from his Catholic, ultimately Roman, sense of the Scriptures as they told him what the world is like: the Genesis case for creation of man in God's "imago et similitudo" (2:6, "image and likeness"); the Gospel's insistence on taking up the cross in *imitatio Christi* and the Eucharistic call to "do this in remembrance of me" (Luke 22:19); and the Pauline emphasis on the *kenosis* or *exinanitio*, the "emptying" of himself by Christ, to assume the *likeness* of man:

> 6: Who, being in the form of God, thought it not robbery to be equal with God: 7: But made himself of no reputation [ἀλλ᾽ ἑαυτὸν ἐκένωσεν], and took upon him the form of a servant, and was made in the likeness of men [ὁμοιώματι ανθρώπων γενόμενος]: 8: And being found in fashion as a man, he humbled himself, and became obedient unto death, even the death of the cross.

> 6: who, though he was in the form of God, did not count equality with God a thing to be grasped, 7: but emptied himself, taking the form of a servant, *being born in the likeness of men*. 8: And being found in human form he humbled himself and became obedient unto death, even death on a cross.
>
> Philippians 2:7
> (I cite the KJV first, then the RSV)

Paul's argument that "the invisible things of him from the creation of the world are clearly seen, being understood by the things that are made" (Romans 1:20; KJV) also meant much to Shakespeare and his theater of likeness, I assume, but the argument from *kenosis* to *homoiomati anthropon genomenos* (in the Latin, *in similitudinem hominum factus*) was, I speculate, the more compelling impetus toward the theater of likeness.[40] If even the Son of God would submit to being made in "the likeness of men," then the most fundamental question of human being is, what is "the likeness of men"? What shall I (be) like?

All of Shakespeare's writings strive to address if not answer this question, for women as well as for men, and the book that follows attempts to see and show this theater of likeness.

Chronology of the Shakespeare Canon Followed in this Book

First, let me state that the argument of my book does not depend upon this or any other chronology. Second, I should note that any chronology is speculative. Third, at this point, I do not address issues of collaboration, textual transmission, etc. But, fourth, I do accept *Edward III* as Shakespeare's, as I also accept Hand D in *The Book of Sir Thomas More* as Shakespeare's. Fifth, and finally, I assume that Shakespeare's plays were not written by committee.[1]

Over the past decade of intensive focus on this book, I have gradually come to see that the chronology posited by the Oxford editors coheres with a postulate of a gradually intensifying commitment on Shakespeare's part to the theater of likeness. In all likelihood, Shakespeare encountered the crisis of likeness first in the Sonnets, the bulk of which are early in his career, and began in his early plays exploring it, to arrive, I think by *Richard III*, at a conscious awareness of the work that the word *like* could perform in his drama, if not yet of the immense power it would release over the course of his career —

> **MARCELLUS** Is it not like the King?
> **HORATIO** As thou art to thyself.
> ...
> **HORATIO** A figure like your father,
> ...
> It would have much amazed you.
> **HAMLET** Very like, very like.
>
> *Ham.* 1.1.57-58; 1.2.199; 1.2.234-5

As the theater of likeness much amazes us.

In the remainder of my book, then, I follow the chronology set forth below, and I hope that it helps my reader as much as it has helped me to see cumulatively how a man of enormous gifts could (just so) make astounding use of so seemingly simple a word.

The Two Gentlemen of Verona (1589-91)
The Taming of the Shrew (1590-1)
The First Part of the Contention of the Two Famous Houses of York and Lancaster (1590-1)
The True Tragedy of Richard Duke of York and the Good King Henry the Sixth (1591)
The First Part of Henry the Sixth (1592)
The Most Lamentable Tragedy of Titus Andronicus (1592)
The Tragedy of King Richard the Third (1592-3)

Venus and Adonis (1592-3)
The Rape of Lucrece (1593-4)
The Reign of King Edward the Third (1594)
The Comedy of Errors (1594)
Love's Labour's Lost (1594-5)
Love's Labour's Won (1595-6) [not extant]
The Tragedy of King Richard the Second (1595)
The Most Excellent and Lamentable Tragedy of Romeo and Juliet (1595)
A Midsummer Night's Dream (1595)
The Life and Death of King John (1596)
The Comical History of the Merchant of Venice, or Otherwise Called the Jew of Venice (1596-7)
The History of Henry the Fourth (1596-7)
The Merry Wives of Windsor (1597-8)
The Second Part of Henry the Fourth (1597-8)
Much Ado About Nothing (1598-9)
The Life of Henry the Fifth (1598-9)
The Tragedy of Julius Caesar (1599)
As You Like It (1599-1600)
The Tragedy of Hamlet, Prince of Denmark (1600-1)
Twelfth Night, or What You Will (1601)
Troilus and Cressida (1602)
Sonnets (1593-1605) and "A Lover's Complaint" (1603-4)
Various Poems (1593-1616)
The Book of Sir Thomas More (1603-4)
Measure for Measure (1603-4; adapted 1621)
The Tragedy of Othello, the Moor of Venice (1603-4)
The History of King Lear (1605-6) [Quarto]
The Life of Timon of Athens (1606)
The Tragedy of Macbeth (1606; adapted 1616)
The Tragedy of Antony and Cleopatra (1606)
All's Well That Ends Well (1606-7)
Pericles, Prince of Tyre (1607)
The Tragedy of Coriolanus (1608)
The Winter's Tale (1609-10)
The Tragedy of King Lear (1610) [Folio]
Cymbeline, King of Britain (1610-11)
The Tempest (1610-11)
Cardenio (1612-13) [not extant]
All Is True (1613)
The Two Noble Kinsmen (1613)

1
"Since all alike my songs and praises be": Reproducing Likeness in Shakespeare's *Sonnets*

Perhaps the truest thing a reader can say about Shakespeare's *Sonnets* is that they presuppose a likeness of the other, the partner or the dual. Whether young man or dark lady, whether real (i.e., historical) or fictional, whether homo- or hetero-erotic, there is an addressee in the *Sonnets*:

> #16
> But wherefore do not you a mightier way
> Make war upon this bloody tyrant, time,
> And fortify yourself in your decay
> With means more blessèd than my barren rhyme?
> Now stand you on the top of happy hours,
> And many *maiden gardens* yet unset
> With virtuous wish *would bear your living flowers*,
> Much *liker* than your painted *counterfeit*.
> So should the lines of life that life repair
> Which this time's pencil or my pupil pen
> Neither in inward worth nor outward fair
> Can make you live yourself in eyes of men.
>   *To give away yourself keeps yourself still,*
>   And you must live drawn by your own sweet skill.
>   (emphasis added)

No reading of the *Sonnets* can go far without accommodating this basic datum. But almost as basic, I think, is the crisis of likeness that is thus provoked: *what* is "liker than your painted counterfeit"?

Following current findings about the dating of the *Sonnets*, one of the thornier problems in Shakespeare studies (to put it mildly), I would like to suggest that there is a rough—and *rough* is all I can claim—correspondence between the early development of the theater of likeness and the probable composition of sonnets #1-60 and #127-54. Colin Burrow summarizes these findings as follows (105):

> 1-60   composed *c*. 1595-6 (possibly revised thereafter)
> 61-103   composed *c*. 1594-5
> 104-26   composed *c*. 1598-1604
> 127-54   composed *c*. 1591-5

It is perhaps prudent if I go on to cite his several cautions (105):

> There are many grey areas in these approximate findings, and the greyest areas are the most critical: there is no certainty when Shakespeare began to write sonnets, and there is no certainty that his revisions and rewritings continued beyond about 1604-5. Many individual sonnets contain neither early nor late rare words. This means that there are some sections of the sequence, and many individual poems, which cannot be firmly allocated to a particular period for any other reason than their contiguity with poems which do contain stylistic indicators of their date. The groups are therefore best thought of as sections which may contain greater or lesser concentrations of early and late periods of work on the sequence, rather than as definitive means of dating individual poems.

With these cautions in mind, I would suggest, tentatively, that the five years between 1591 and 1596[1] see Shakespeare compose perhaps as many as 130 sonnets (a very "grey" number) even as he is also composing some 14 plays and two long poems (numbers not quite as "grey") in which we can chart the development of the theater of likeness and the style of *syneciosis* ("crosse-cople"). As rough and "grey" as this picture must necessarily be, it nonetheless affords us the following view. The earliest sonnets, exquisite poems of sexual disillusionment (supremely #129: "Th'expense of spirit in a waste of shame"), give way, possibly around 1595-6, to sonnets that, as one would predict, I argue, from developments in the theater of likeness in the concurrently composed plays, absorb themselves in the question, what is "liker than your painted counterfeit"? — a child of your body (sex)? or a "child" of the poet's imagination (art)?

> #3
> Look in thy glass, and tell the face thou viewest
> Now is the time that face should form another,
> Whose fresh repair if now thou not renewest
> Thou dost beguile the world, unbless some mother.

Reproducing Likeness in Shakespeare's *Sonnets*

For where is she so fair whose uneared womb
Disdains the tillage of thy husbandry?
Or who is he so fond will be the tomb
Of his self-love to stop posterity?
Thou art thy mother's glass, and she in thee
Calls back the lovely April of her prime;
So thou through windows of thine age shalt see,
Despite of wrinkles, this thy golden time.
  But if thou live remembered not to be,
  Die single, and thine image dies with thee.

This wonderful poem, one of the more beautiful in English, I believe, is also possibly one of the more devious: "Die single, and thine image dies with thee"—does it? or is it alive, here and now, in this poem, as it could never be in an offspring of the body, who would not survive to 400 years of age, even if we knew everything conceivable about the historical identity of his forbear (see also, e.g., #63, #74, or #101)? The word *seed* embedded in the enjambement in lines 11 and 12, "*see*/Despite," suggests, as many devices in many other sonnets also suggest, that, powerful as sex is, words have their power, too. Words, too, couple, and the likenesses they reproduce are also fertile:

#123
No, time, thou shalt not boast that I do change!
Thy pyramids built up with newer might
To me are nothing novel, nothing strange,
They are but dressings of a former sight.
Our dates are brief, and therefore we admire
What thou dost foist upon us that is old,
And rather make them born to our desire
Than think that we before have heard them told.
Thy registers and thee I both defy,
Not wond'ring at the present nor the past;
For thy records and what we *see d*oth lie,
Made more or less by thy continual haste.
  This I do vow, and this shall ever be:
  I will be true despite thy scythe and thee.

                                                    (emphasis added)

What we see/d does lie, if only because it dies eventually, "[m]ade more or less by [time's] continual haste," and it does lie also because it is *like*, and therefore different, *change[d]* by the process of sexual generation (which is to "die" in orgasm); only the poet can boast "I will be true," but only at the price, which is huge, of the irony of admitting that we "rather make them born to our desire/Than think that we before have heard them told"—his poem, too, in other words, is "but [the] dressing[...] of a former sight," just another li(k)e in Time's "continual haste" that "we before have heard ... told."

If it is true that "Shakespeare often experimented with new words and rhymes in non-dramatic verse before letting them loose on the stage" (Burrow 105), he may also, reciprocally, have tested ideas from the stage in his non-dramatic verse, to weigh their implications in a context of greater intimacy, to hear their innuendoes in a mood more confessional and private. This, I propose, is what he did with the theater of likeness in the *Sonnets*. Note that I am not claiming that the *Sonnets* are "about" the theater of likeness or that the theater of likeness is their theme or subject—any such global appropriation of the *Sonnets* will inevitably collapse in totalizing reduction; I am simply, rather, calling attention to those sonnets where a case can be made that some of the concerns of the theater of likeness are also being tested in them, notably succession and duality or coupling (mutuality, if you prefer—Sonnet #8), on the assumption that both they and the theater of likeness can be better understood when this relationship is demonstrated and analyzed. Thus, for example, I think Sonnets #11 and #84 are certainly involved in more than the theater of likeness, and yet, at the same time, in their use of the word "copy" (the only two occurrences of the word in the *Sonnets*), they foreground issues that are crucial to the dramas that Shakespeare is writing as he experiments in the theater of likeness:

#11
She carved thee for her seal, and meant thereby
Thou shouldst print more, not let that *copy* die.

#84
But he that writes of you, if he can *tell*
That you are you, so dignifies his story.
Let him but *copy* what in you is writ,
Not making worse what nature made so clear,
And such a *counterpart* shall fame his wit,
Making his style admirèd everywhere.

(emphasis added)

All theater is copying. Is all copying theatrical ("counter*part*")? even sexual copying? or, most of all, sexual copying? If so, is all copying also and necessarily self-conscious? If not, as seems the case, most especially in much sexual intercourse, why not? Why do we not know until we know that we know (and then feel shame)?[2] And by what means do we come to know that we know (and learn the use and the limit of our shame)?[3]

"Mark how one string, sweet husband to another,/Strikes each in each by *mutual* ordering" (#8; emphasis added). Self-consciousness is alter-consciousness—"To give away yourself keeps yourself still": I am not, unless you are.[4] Many sonnets suggest this insight, as basic to the theater of likeness as it is to the sequence and to individual sonnets, but I find particularly moving #29:

> When, in disgrace with fortune and men's eyes,
> I all alone beweep my outcast state,
> And trouble deaf heaven with my bootless cries,
> And look upon myself and curse my fate,
> Wishing me *like* to one more rich in hope,
> Featured *like* him, *like* him with friends possessed,
> Desiring this man's art and that man's scope,
> With what I most enjoy contented least:
> Yet in these thoughts myself almost despising,
> Haply I think on thee, and then my state,
> *Like* to the lark at break of day arising
> From sullen earth, sings hymns at heaven's gate;
>   For thy sweet love remembered such wealth brings
>   That then I scorn to change my state with kings'.
>   (emphasis added)

This sonnet contains more instances of the word *like* (4 total) than any other single sonnet in the collection. The four instances do important work, I think. They suggest first and foremost how dependent on likeness identity is—"Wishing me *like* ..." I am not, unless you are. I must (be) like someone, even if, in a rage of misanthropy (Timon-like), I insist on being like (and liking) no one (since I am in that case still involved in liking). Next, they also suggest that when I do "come to myself," it is because "haply I think on thee." And then, they further imply, I, having come to myself, liken myself, almost instinctually, to a new and different likeness, "[l]ike to the lark at break of day arising." I feel like a new creature, and "I scorn to change my state with kings'." The point here is that this sonnet and, in many different ways, the entire collection, chart the paradoxicality (*syneciosis*) of identity: I can exist without consciousness of self (eat, drink, sleep, copulate, excrete, etc., etc.), but I cannot *be* without somebody (to) like (me). And herein lies, as every one of us knows, a world of hurt.

20   "Since all alike my songs and praises be"

The *Sonnets*, to be sure, sing about that hurt, most memorably; but we must not forget that they also sing about the likening:

> #36
> Let me confess that we two must be twain
> Although *our undivided loves are one;*
> ...
> Though *in our lives a separable spite*
> ...
>   I love thee in such sort
> As, thou being mine, mine is thy good report.
>
> #39
> O, how thy worth with manners may I sing
> When *thou art all the better part of me?*
> What can mine own praise to mine own self bring,
> And *what is't but mine own when I praise thee?*
> Even for this let us divided live,
> And *our dear love lose name of single one,*
> ...
>   thou teachest how to make one twain
> By praising him here who doth hence remain!
>
>   (emphasis added)

The couplet in each case, especially in #39, invites us to the irony of the situations, no doubt, but at the same time, we are reading texts of likeness that revel in praise of subjectivity-via-objectivity: the beloved, by making me *object* (noun and verb) to myself, makes me a self in ways I could not otherwise be—

> #62
> Mine own self-love quite *contrary* I read;
> Self so self-loving were iniquity.
>   'Tis thee, my self, that *for myself* I praise,
>   Painting my age with beauty of thy days.
>
>   (emphasis added)

The beloved makes me *like myself* just in the measure to which s/he makes me *not* like myself, for thereby s/he makes me know I am and have a self, object to my subject:

#49
Against that time — if ever that time come —
When I shall see thee frown on my defects,
...
Against that time do I ensconce me here
Within the knowledge of mine own desert,
And *this my hand against myself uprear*
To guard the lawful reasons on thy part.
  To leave poor me thou hast the strength of laws,
  Since why to love I can allege no cause.

#89
Thou canst not, love, disgrace me half so ill,
To set a form upon desirèd change,
As *I'll myself disgrace,* knowing thy *will.*
...
  For thee, against myself I'll vow debate;
  For I must ne'er love him whom thou dost hate.
                                    (emphasis added)

This it is to have a self at all: "against [it to] vow debate." In this sense, the *Sonnets* are pre-eminently the poems of a dramatist, a writer who starts from dialogue, from vectors of personal interaction, you over against me. But, it is also true to say, by the same token, that the plays are pre-eminently the poems of a poet, a writer who starts from the copula, sexual and rhetorical alike (simile, metaphor, metonymy, paradox, et al.), you and I, I as you.

I have no brief for a global interpretation of the *Sonnets*, as I have already said. I am also keenly aware of the immensity of commentary on them. I am not anxious to say something "new." I seek, instead, to combine what all commentary known to me recognizes with what I have been able over the past two and a half decades to learn about the theater of likeness in Shakespeare's plays. In this limited scope, I conclude, simply, that the same poet wrote the sonnets as wrote the plays and vice-versa. This, of course, was never in dispute historically. But, theoretically, it is a case worth making nevertheless, by no means a trivial observation. Both plays and poems admit the style of *syneciosis*. They are the work of the cross-coupler, "[m]aking a couplement of proud compare" (#21.5) even when he is insisting that "I will not praise that purpose not to sell" (#21.14). It is the *cross* of the couple (juxta-form and cruci-lingual) that matters, in poems and plays alike, for at the couplement of the cross, where the cross crosses, Shakespeare negotiates the difficulty of difference:

#105
Let not my love be called idolatry,
Nor my belovèd as an idol show,
Since *all alike my songs and praises be*
To one, of one, still such, and ever so.
Kind is my love today, tomorrow kind,
Still constant in a wondrous excellence.
Therefore my verse, to constancy confined,
One thing expressing, leaves out difference.
"Fair, kind, and true" is all my argument,
"Fair, kind, and true" varying to other words,
And *in this change is my invention spent*,
Three themes in one, which wondrous scope affords.
   Fair, kind, and true have often lived alone,
   Which three till now never kept seat in one.

                                                     (emphasis added)

It is the poet practiced in "couplement" who can best imagine his "verse to constancy confined" just because he knows language is always "varying to other words" unless invention "spend" itself "in this change": such expenditure is necessary to "leave[...] out difference" and "express[...] one thing." Otherwise, language, cross-coupling, includes difference as the inevitable residue of expression.[5] No one grasped this liability of writing like Shakespeare. (And Joyce never leaves out difference—one reason his work is so "difficult" to read.) Because he understood so primordially how laborious and expensive it is to express one thing, Shakespeare can be trusted—generations have trusted him—to "leave out difference" (it is not gone, just left out, for us to bring back in) in "couplements" of characters, images, ideas, words like none that anyone else has ever shown us (Othello and Desdemona, say) "[s]ince mind at first in character was done" (#59.8).[6]

2
"Minister the like to you": Metamorphosis and Competition in *The Two Gentlemen of Verona*

The Two Gentlemen of Verona is a play that already bears the stamp of Shakespeare's theater of likeness. Not only does the word *like* itself occur frequently and in crucial contexts, but the constellation of ideas and anxieties that marks the theater of likeness is already abundantly evident, ranging from evocations of Narcissus to elaborate discourses on psychic division to explicit moments of metadrama, complete with the inevitable vocabulary of disguise. At perhaps so young an age as 25 or 26, Shakespeare already sees the crisis of likeness as the subject (and subjectivity) of drama. Emotionally Catholic (I hypothesize) but politically Protestant, sexually disillusioned, prodigiously verbal (in Latin as well as English), imaginatively kenotic (not just sensitive but self-emptyingly sensitive), financially unsatisfied (though remembering when his father, John, was successful and prominent), Shakespeare in his mid-twenties is alive to the whirligig of likeness and difference in the most mundane to the most sublime human endeavor.

As we turn from the *Sonnets* to *The Two Gentlemen of Verona*, we also turn to the word *sonnet* therein. Relatively late in the play and in a scene that might at first blush appear less than momentous, a powerful clue occurs as to the involvement of *The Two Gentlemen of Verona* in Shakespeare's emerging theater of likeness:

> **THURIO** I have a *sonnet* that will serve the turn
> To give the *onset* to thy good advice.
> 					*TGV* 3.2.92-3 (emphasis added)

The anagram *sonnet/onset* alerts us to at least two key characteristics of Shakespearean style at the beginning of his career. One, he is already willing to abide by the dictum he expresses in his own *Sonnets*: "To hear with eyes belongs to love's fine wit" (#23.14). Two, he is already, perhaps we should say, preternaturally, sensitive to the manipulability of words, their lability and liability, to cross each other and mingle with each other in ways not only unpredictable and seemingly coincidental but also syneciotic. In Shakespeare's theater of likeness, we see, it is more than an accident that *sonnet* and *onset* are anagrammatically related; we are invited, rather, to see and understand that words harbor relationships that undermine any assumption that language is simply mine: Thurio says far more than he knows.

It is this extraordinary sensitivity to language that led Shakespeare to his uncanny comprehension of internal self-division in character after character that he invents.[1] Proteus is a prototype of this comprehension and its consequences on the stage. Aptly named, Proteus ("he who changes, adopts many shapes") is an early study in the unreliability of the subject inasmuch as the subject is subject to language. Immediately upon seeing Silvia, Proteus is thrown back upon the resources of a medium that surprise him with their debility:

> Is it mine eye, or Valentine's praise,
> Her true perfection, or my false transgression
> That makes me, *reasonless, to reason thus*?
> She is fair, and so is Julia that I love —
> That I did love, for now my love is thawed,
> Which like a waxen image 'gainst a fire
> Bears no impression of the thing it was.
> 					TGV 2.4.194-200 (emphasis added)

And then, only a short while later, in a speech crucial for understanding the emerging theater of likeness in Shakespeare's career, Proteus soliloquizes:

> Love bade me swear, and love bids me forswear.
> O sweet-suggesting love, if thou hast sinned
> Teach me, *thy tempted subject*, to excuse it.
> ...
> Fie, fie, unreverent tongue, to call her bad
> ...
> I cannot leave to love, and yet I do.
> But there I leave to love where I should love.
> Julia I lose, and Valentine I lose.
> *If I keep them I needs must lose myself.*
> If I lose them, thus find I by their loss
> For Valentine, myself, for Julia, Silvia.
> *I to myself am dearer than a friend,*

For love is still most precious in itself,

...

I cannot now prove constant to myself
Without some treachery used to Valentine.

...
TGV 2.6.6-8; 14; 17-24; 31-32
(emphasis added)

Here, under the title "love," Shakespeare begins to inscribe a lifelong fascination with the paradox of language, that however much it may unite, it also and always divides, most especially "me" into *I* and *me* and *mine*, as opposed to *you* and *them* and the *others* ("competitor[s]"). Love may well be our first consciousness of language's inhering divisiveness, but once we have become conscious of it, we can never again, as the entire canon of Shakespeare's plays so stunningly demonstrates, completely trust language and those who use it, including each of us ourselves:

VALENTINE   *Banished from her* [Silvia]
Is self from self, a deadly banishment.

...

She is my essence, and *I leave to be*
If I be not by her fair influence
Fostered, illumined, cherished, kept alive.
TGV 3.1.172-3; 182-4 (emphasis added)

If I can talk to myself about myself, for or against myself, then I am by definition not at one with myself. And if this it is to be human, not all one in myself, then to be human, as Shakespeare has taught us so deeply as well, is also to be alone in the world—

VALENTINE   Proteus,
I am sorry I must never trust thee more,
But *count the world a stranger for thy sake.*
TGV 5.4.68-70 (emphasis added)

—constantly seeking another who may (be) like me and thus make me all one with myself, at one with myself and atoned with myself. This quest, however, is ever fraught with peril. As Valentine says in the next breath, "[t]he private wound is deepest" (*TGV* 5.4.71).

It is fitting that it should be Valentine who acknowledges this sorrow. He began in the play as a version of Narcissus, scornful of love (*TGV* 1.1.29-35; 45-50). Although less absolute than Ovid's self-enamored boy

(*Metamorphosis* 3.391), Valentine still assumes a posture toward love for which he will eventually pay dearly:

> Ay, Proteus, but that life is altered now.
> I have done penance for contemning love,
> Whose high imperious thoughts have punished me
> With bitter fasts, with penitential groans,
> ...
> Now can I break my fast, dine, sup, and sleep
> Upon the very naked name of love.
>
> TGV 2.4.126-9; 139-40

If less absolute than Narcissus, Valentine suffers punishment also less severe, though severe enough in the event. He does not waste away in death into a flower, but he must for a while suffer exile and its sorrowful isolation. Still, because he loves, he does not die; he undergoes a different *metamorphosis* (*TGV* 1.1.66; 2.1.29):

> **SPEED** Marry, by these special marks: first, you have
> learned, *like* Sir Proteus, to wreath your arms, *like* a
> malcontent; to relish a love-song, *like* a robin redbreast;
> to walk alone, *like* one that had the pestilence; to sigh,
> *like* a schoolboy that had lost his ABC; to weep, *like* a
> young wench that had buried her grandam; to fast,
> *like* one that takes diet; to watch, *like* one that fears
> robbing; to speak puling, *like* a beggar at Hallowmas.
> You were wont, when you laughed, to crow *like* a
> cock; when you walked, to walk *like* one of the lions.
> When you fasted, it was presently after dinner; when
> you looked sadly, it was for want of money. And now
> you are *metamorphosed* with a mistress, that when I
> look on you I can hardly think you my master.
> **VALENTINE** Are all these things perceived in me?
> **SPEED** They are all perceived without ye.
> **VALENTINE** Without me? They cannot.
> **SPEED** Without you? Nay, that's certain, for without you
> were so simple, none else would. But you are so without
> these follies that these follies are within you, and shine
> through you *like* the water in an urinal, that not an
> eye that sees you but is a physician to comment on
> your malady.
>
> TGV 2.1.17-39 (emphasis added)

Metamorphosis and Competition in *The Two Gentlemen of Verona*

In this dancing exchange, the word *like* does work we must recognize as especially Shakespearean. All 12 occurrences of *like* insist on the metamorphosis of Valentine into lover. So like a lover is Valentine now that "not an eye that sees [him] but is a physician to comment on [his] malady" (but for a letter, note, also "my lady," and see also the next line: "But tell me, dost thou know my lady Silvia?" — *TGV* 2.1.40). "One touch of love makes the whole world like" is hardly un-Shakespearean even though it was not literally written by Shakespeare.[2] One touch of love makes without within and within without.

Proteus, perhaps as his name predicts, was earlier metamorphosed and deeply aware of it: "Thou, Julia, thou hast *metamorphosed* me" (*TGV* 1.1.66; emphasis added). And it may be Proteus's precocity that, at least partly, contributes to his subsequent metamorphosis under the influence of Silvia, who "shows Julia but a swarthy Ethiope" (*TGV* 2.6.26). At any rate, when finally confronted with his treachery, his "inconstancy" (*TGV* 5.4.111), he displays a new likeness that could only be won of metamorphosis:

> Forgive me, Valentine. If hearty sorrow
> Be a sufficient ransom for offence,
> I tender't here. *I do as truly suffer*
> *As e'er I did commit.*
>
> *TGV* 5.4.74-77 (emphasis added)

Proteus, I assume, can only "as truly suffer/As e'er [he] did commit" because he sees in Valentine his victim the likeness of the suffering he has perpetrated, now reflected back upon him in "shame and guilt": the "shame and guilt" are the image in him of the offence he committed against Valentine, and he suffers it. If we are persuaded of the integrity of Proteus's "ransom," as Valentine obviously is, then our accord, like his, emerges from the proof before our eyes that to be one, each must first be two. Valentine is not alone; nor is Proteus.

This conclusion, although obviously provisional, will nonetheless meet with unhappiness and displeasure among those readers who share in the now centuries-old disquiet and unease at the conclusion of *Two Gentlemen* (Norton registers some of this [77 and 83]), with its repulsive image of threatened rape and its account of the callous disposal of women without regard to their own feelings or minds. But I suggest that Shakespeare's theater of likeness accounts for the troubling conclusion of *Two Gentlemen* and that, further, once we have understood the logic of likeness in the play, we can also understand why it must conclude in the way that it does, even though — indeed, perhaps just because — we do not like it.

Initially, the most important consideration for this argument is the fact that there are *two* pairs of lovers in the play as a result of Shakespeare's alterations of and additions to his sources (Norton 78). The summary effect of Shakespeare's interventions was to generate several sets of pairs:

Valentine :: Silvia | Proteus :: Julia | Speed :: Lance

It is important not to underestimate this effect; it is integral to Shakespeare's representation of human psychic reality. Without these sets of pairs, the play would be much more a coarse farce than the romantic comedy that, however complex, it is. The sets of pairs enable Shakespeare to develop strategies of doubling, mirroring, repetition, and likening that govern the overall structure of the play and its final unfolding. In effect, I propose, we are meant *not* to like the final scene's implications of rape and traffic in women as part of our emerging awareness of the logic of likeness in the theater of likeness: our dislike, precisely intense, teaches us what it is to (be) like another whom we, at best, will ever only partly know.

Julia emerges as the crux of the "competition." When Proteus calls himself Valentine's competitor (*TGV* 2.6.35), we know that the word bears its 16th-century sense of "one who seeks with another a common goal" (*OED* II *sub voce*), more nearly synonymous with "partner" than with "competitor" in the later, our contemporary, sense of the word. The "competitor" in the 16th and early 17th centuries is the one who "seeks together with." Without Julia, Proteus and Valentine would be merely competitors in our contemporary sense, each struggling to overcome the other in claiming a prize, Silvia, solely for himself. With Julia, however, Shakespeare balances and distributes the competition so that the logic of likeness may proceed to its conclusion. In effect, Julia, and to a lesser extent the clowns, are the monitors of likeness in the play: they measure each likeness for its relationship to the (fictional) real of the play and thus repeatedly register for us, the audience, the degree of distortion in a given likeness, so that we are always aware, as indeed we should be in a comedy (as distinct from a tragedy), that no likeness is going to usurp the posited real.[3] A real rape of Silvia by Proteus is not possible, in effect, just because Proteus *says*

> I'll woo you *like* a soldier, at arm's end,
> And love you 'gainst the nature of love: force ye.
>
> *TGV* 5.4.57-58 (emphasis added)

In the comedic theater of likeness, as Shakespeare understands it, this likeness exists so as *not* to be performed.[4] The very utterance, "I'll woo

Metamorphosis and Competition in *The Two Gentlemen of Verona*   29

you like a soldier," interposes sufficient division and thus distance for the likeness to be interrupted, initially by Valentine and subsequently, more definitively, by Julia, whose disguise is the separable, unreal likeness that perforce chastens and exposes the presumptive likenesses that it encounters.

> **HOST** How now, are you sadder than you were before?
> How do you, man? The music *likes* you not.
> **JULIA** You mistake. The musician *likes* me not.
> **HOST** Why, my pretty youth?
> **JULIA** He plays false, father.
> *TGV* 4.2.53-57 (emphasis added)

Julia, in a false likeness, recognizes the musician playing false, that "likes [her] not." She is in effect a talisman in whose presence likeness discloses itself.

Through the logic of likeness, once we see it, neither Proteus's threat of rape nor Valentine's attempted traffic in Silvia's person for Proteus's benefit can, we understand, be real; they are, at most, likenesses for which our own dislike is a measure of their falling-off—even as we recoil from them, we see them disappear in Julia's dis/guise.

> **JULIA** O Proteus, let this habit make thee blush.
> Be thou ashamed that I have took upon me
> Such an immodest raiment, if shame live
> In a disguise of love.
> It is the lesser blot, modesty finds,
> Women to change their shapes than men their minds.
> **PROTEUS** Than men their minds! 'Tis true. O heaven, were man
> But constant, he were perfect. That one error
> Fills him with faults, makes him run through all th' sins;
> Inconstancy falls off ere it begins.
> What is in Silvia's face but I may spy
> More fresh in Julia's, with a constant eye?
> *TGV* 5.4.103-14

In just the measure to which, in comparing her "blot" (and "lot") to his, Julia *names* Proteus—"women *to change their shapes*"—she holds his likeness before him in her action—*change their shapes*—so that he may see himself what he is like, his own *habit*. And seeing himself what he is like, he can then affirm: "What is in Silvia's face, but I may spy/More fresh in Julia's with a constant eye?"; where we may be certain Shakespeare also heard "What is in Silvia's face, but *eye* may spy/More fresh in Julia's with a constant *I*?" Such is the logic of likeness: to be one I must be two (Shoaf, *Milton* xxiv).

But I must also *know* it and never forget it, that I must be two; otherwise, I may make the potentially fatal mistake of assuming I am alone like no one but myself, to do just as I like—the error of Narcissus, the type of psychosis. In all of Shakespeare the most horrific realization of this psychosis is Iago:

> **IAGO** Demand me nothing. *What you know, you know.*
> From this time forth I never will speak word.
> *Oth*. 5.2.309-10 (emphasis added)

—as if he were crowing, "there is no difference between us, we are just alike, so shut up: what you know, you know, just like me." Inasmuch as Julia interrupts the false likeness of Proteus and, for that matter, Valentine as well, she is, unlike Iago, the saving identity saving identity.

✄

Shakespeare's achievement within the theater of likeness in *Two Gentlemen* is also apparent in the two clowns, Speed and Lance, perhaps the first of his memorable clown inventions. In particular, in the hilarious exchange on Lance's wife, we find the logic of likeness no less at work than elsewhere in the play.

Our point of entry can usefully be another anagram:

> **SPEED** "*Item*, she hath no teeth."
> **LANCE** I care not for that, neither, because I love *crusts*.
> **SPEED** "*Item*, she is *curst*."
> **LANCE** Well, the best is, she hath no teeth to bite.
> *TGV* 3.1.331-4 (emphasis added)

The anagram *crusts/curst* alerts us to the doubling and the crossing and the double-crossing (juxta-form and cruci-lingual) in the scene (Lance delays Speed from joining Valentine and plans to "rejoice in the boy's correction" [*TGV* 3.1.372]). The exchange is a concatenation of units across a given key repetition: for example,

> **SPEED** How now, Signor Lance, what news with your *mastership*?
> **LANCE** With my *master's ship*? Why, it is at sea.

Metamorphosis and Competition in *The Two Gentlemen of Verona* 31

> **SPEED** Well, your old vice still, mistake the word. What
>   news then in your paper?
> **LANCE** The *blackest news* that ever thou heard'st.
> **SPEED** Why, man, how '*black*'?
> **LANCE** Why, as *black* as ink.
>   *TGV* 3.1.276-83 (emphasis added)

As this concatenation proceeds, we become aware of the mirroring and likening that compose the exchange:

> **SPEED** "*Item*, she doth *talk* in her *sleep*."
> **LANCE** It's no matter for that, so she *sleep* not in her *talk*
>   *TGV* 3.1.322-3 (emphasis added),

or, perhaps more telling,

> **SPEED** "*Item*, she is not to be broken with *fasting*, in
>   respect of her *breath*."
> **LANCE** Well, that fault may be mended with a *breakfast*.
>   Read on.
>   *TGV* 3.1.316-19 (emphasis added),

where the near homophony between *breath* and *break*, in tandem with *fast, -ing*, trains our ears to anticipate likenesses beyond the expected in ordinary stichomythia. The forging (in all senses) of identities through concatenated, mirroring likenesses will lead in Shakespeare's career to thrilling moments—Falstaff and Hal, Romeo and Mercutio, Othello and Iago—but we see again, and already, in *Two Gentlemen*, possibly his first play, that fundamental inclination to let like(ness) lie as it will.

> **LANCE** Nay, I remember the
> trick you [his dog, Crab] served me when I took my leave
> of Madam Silvia. Did not I bid thee still *mark me, and do as I do*?
> When didst thou see me heave up my leg and make
> water against a gentlewoman's farthingale? Didst thou
> ever see me do such a trick?
>   *TGV* 4.4.33-38 (emphasis added)

Here, to be sure, we read *as* rather than *like*, but the theater of likeness still shows us the lie of the like(ness): Lance so likes his dog that he is so like the dog that

> Nay, I'll be sworn I have sat in the
> stocks for puddings he hath stolen, otherwise he had
> been executed. I have stood on the pillory for geese he
> hath killed, otherwise he had suffered for't.
>
> *TGV* 4.4.29-32

and thus he expects the dog to "mark [him] and do as [he] do[es]" as if, indeed, he and the dog were just alike, despite their wholly different speciation. Everywhere in this early play, we find Shakespeare exploiting the logic of likeness within the theater of likeness: "all knowing," as Plotinus says, "comes by likeness," even when it's knowing your dog, your Crab from his *barc* (as it were).

✻

We find the logic of likeness also at work in one of the other, highly memorable clown scenes in the play, Speed's attempt to let Valentine in on Silvia's joke:

> What need she, when she hath made you write to
> yourself? Why, do you not perceive the jest?
>
> *TGV* 2.1.143-4

If Valentine writes to himself for Silvia's sake, a letter of love, then he writes also for his sake: her sake ("cause" — *OED* II *sub voce*) is also his. They are just alike, the same cause, the same sake. He is then the beneficiary of his labor:

> **SILVIA** And when it's writ, for my sake read it over,
> And if it please you, so. If not, why, so.
> **VALENTINE** If it please me, madam? What then?
> **SILVIA** Why, if it please you, take it for your labour.
>
> *TGV* 2.1.122-5

This logic enables Shakespeare to craft a scene that in an earlier tradition would have been an allegory, a psychomachia, between Valentine and his *Expeditio*, where "Speed" (in the word's widely attested sense of "to prosper") is rather the clown who now embodies (and far extends) this particular psychic quality of the lover, seeking to speed or prosper in his, the lover's, ambition for his lady, to *expedite* his wooing of her. What in the psychomachia would have been an internal debate between *Ratio* and *Expeditio*, in Shakespeare's play is a lively and charming dialogue between

Metamorphosis and Competition in *The Two Gentlemen of Verona*

Valentine the lover and Speed the clown-servant, which gradually leads to the illumination of Valentine's improbable if not absurd obtuseness and, by the way, to a realization of the relationship between rhyming and reasoning: "Nay [says Speed], I was rhyming. 'Tis you that have the reason" (however slow Valentine is to realize it [*TGV* 2.1.135]).

In the scene so understood what we hear and see is verbal; the action of the scene is speech. Valentine, obtuse in his dizzy infatuation with Silvia, only gradually learns what Speed grasps so speedily, that love—as distinct from rape, bestiality, brutality, animality—is a matter (and a *mater*) of discourse, and (Speed observes)

> [Silvia] in modesty
> Or else for want of idle time could not again reply,
> Or fearing else some messenger that might her mind discover,
> Herself hath taught her love himself to write unto her lover.
> *TGV* 2.1.155-8,

where the reduplications in "Herself hath taught her love himself to write unto her lover" insist on the mutual implication of love and discourse. The members of the sentence—

Herself *hath taught* <u>her love</u> >< >< >< **himself** *to write* <u>unto her lover</u>

—couple by reflection ("bending back") to reproduce a meaning otherwise impossible than between them (1 + 1 = 3). At the same time and in the same way, the reduplications show Shakespeare's mastery (and mystery), however youthful, of the discursivity of love, "excellent device" (*TGV* 2.1.131): the lover, "being scribe, *to himself*...write[s] the letter" (*TGV* 2.1.132; emphasis added) *always*, inasmuch as he fantasizes the Other of the beloved. Indeed, Speed rightly corrects himself—"Why, she woos you by a *figure*...*By a letter*, I should say" (*TGV* 2.1.139-41)—not only because it is a letter Silvia has "jest"-ed (*TGV* 2.1.144) Valentine into writing but also because it is not figurative but literal wooing, wooing *of words*:

> **VALENTINE** That's the letter I writ to her friend.
> **SPEED** And that letter hath she delivered [viz., to you], and there an end.
> *TGV* 2.1.150-2

Q.E.D., as we might say. Or, preferable, Speed's exact summation, "[a]ll this I speak in print, for in print I found it" (*TGV* 2.1.159), where the idiom, "in print" ("with exactness or preciseness; to a nicety" [*OED* II *sub voce*]),

34 "Minister the like to you"

also insists on the discursivity of it all—Speed is not without Deeps in his (dis)course—as if it were typeset and type-set. And there an end.

3
"Sent you hither so unlike yourself": The Truing of the Mate in *The Taming of the Shrew*

The Taming of the Shrew is a play inseparable from, unthinkable without, the dynamics of disguise, pretense, and imposture. Narrowly, from this perspective, it would appear to be the most calculated, the least spontaneous and most predictable of Shakespeare's comedies: once you grasp that hardly anybody is what he or she seems, the play seems to be little more than variations on a theme.

And yet, as the popularity of the play, on the one hand, and its extraordinary rhetorical panache, on the other, affirm, the play is hardly reducible to such calculation. The disconnect between the play's thematic and its rhetoric asks for an interpretation that can somehow account for the curious combination of obviousness and unexpectedness. At times the play seems little more than machinery, if certainly entertaining machinery; at other times, though, the play shows a verbal wit, a fund of invention, that is all but breathtaking, as if the very obviousness of the machinery had served Shakespeare as an occasion of liberty to test the limits of his rhetorical gift. We know instinctively that there is something more than the bawdy about "What! With my tongue in your tail?" This writing is inspired—as we grasp, even if we do not proceed beyond the remarkable pun in *tail/tale*.

The theater of likeness, I propose, offers a possibility of interpreting *The Taming of the Shrew* that goes some way toward explaining the play's anomalousness. The play is certainly rich in occurrences of the word *like*. Many of them are arresting in their relevance. But beyond the quantitative impact that they have, there is a qualitative transformation of scene and character that they import into the play, helping to give it that distinctive edge which carries it beyond predictability and which we rightly call Shakespearean. Within the theater of likeness, we see that the play is an unusually searching examination of what it means to answer for oneself the question, whom shall I (be) like? As such an examination, the play is a remarkable achievement.

The play depends on outlandishness: "Of all mad matches never was the *like*" (*Shr.* 3.3.114); "Such a mad marriage never was before" (*Shr.* 3.3.55). Or, to make the point in a different, more telling way, the play proposes improbable mating as well as improbable taming. It yokes together by violence (often real violence) the most heterogeneous of things.¹ The anagram *taming/mating* introduces us to one of the engines of the play, its insistence on comparisons that challenge our sense of propriety and logic alike. Sometimes these are wildly comical, as when Petruccio demands that Kate take Vincentio for a fair young virgin:

Tell me, sweet Kate, and tell me truly too,
Hast thou beheld a fresher gentlewoman,
...
Sweet Kate, embrace her for her beauty's sake.
...
KATHERINE Young budding virgin, fair, and fresh, and sweet,
Whither away, or where is thy abode?
Happy the parents of so fair a child,
Happier the man whom favourable stars
Allots thee for his lovely bedfellow.
PETRUCCIO Why, how now, Kate, I hope thou art not mad.
This is a man, old, wrinkled, faded, withered,
And not a maiden as thou sayst he is.
KATHERINE Pardon, old father, my mistaking eyes ...
Shr. 4.6.29-30; 35; 38-46

Sometimes they are quietly disorienting: "A woman moved is *like* a fountain troubled," where we feel there is a term, or there are terms, of similarity not immediately evident or emergent from what we think has been developing:

KATHERINE A woman moved is like a fountain troubled,
Muddy, ill-seeming, thick, bereft of beauty,
And while it is so, none so dry or thirsty
Will deign to sip or touch one drop of it.
Shr. 5.2.147-50

When we remember that the proper name Katherine derives from the Greek word for "pure" or "clean" (καθαρός), we realize that the simile expresses a profound *mating* between Kate and her new identity, which she understands, being as she is a very smart woman, in ways that reconfigure her image of her body—

> Why are our bodies soft, and weak, and smooth,
> Unapt to toil and trouble in the world,
> But that our soft conditions and our hearts
> Should well agree with our external parts?
> *Shr.* 5.2.170-3

I am not concerned here either to condone or to condemn the masculinist ideology informing this conventional description of women's bodies, but rather to understand Kate's new understanding of likeness, similitude, assimilation, or, to use her word, "agree(ment)." Kate is now a fountain *un*troubled. She has found a likeness that agrees with her. If she has been *tamed*, it is because she has also been *mated*.

This conclusion is not trivial. *The Taming of the Shrew* is a play very much about the truing of the mate. Tranio asks Petruccio

> what occasion of import
> Hath all so long detained you from your wife
> And sent you hither *so unlike yourself*?
> ...
> See not your bride in these unreverent robes.
> *Shr.* 3.2.102-4; 112 (emphasis added)

But Petruccio refuses all anxiety about his apparel:

> To me she's married, not unto my clothes.
> Could I repair what she will wear in me
> As I can change these poor accoutrements,
> 'Twere well for Kate and better for myself.
> *Shr.* 3.2.117-120

The taming, Petruccio understands, is really about mating ("re-*pair*[ing]") inner and outer, so that one is truly not "so unlike [one]self," whatever apparel one may be wearing: there can be no taming or mating of Kate until Kate and Petruccio both are tamed and mated within—like himself, like herself. And if he seems farther along in this process of such self-repair than she, that is in part because he knows what a formidable task it is—"*Could* I repair what she will wear in me."

Here, I think, is why the first exchange between Kate and Petruccio (*Shr.* 2.1.182) is so important, even beyond the universally admired wit of it. In it, two very intelligent persons take each other's measure and find each his and her match, his and her mate. They find, in Shakespeare's theater of likeness, that they (are) like each other (although Kate cannot yet afford to relax in the likeness).

> KATHERINE If I be waspish, best beware my sting.
> PETRUCCIO My remedy is then to pluck it out.
> KATHERINE Ay, if the fool could find it where it lies.
> PETRUCCIO Who knows not where a wasp does wear his sting? In his tail.
> KATHERINE In his tongue.
> PETRUCCIO   Whose tongue?
> KATHERINE Yours, if you talk of tales, and so farewell.
> PETRUCCIO What, with my tongue in your tail?
>
> *Shr.* 2.1.210-16

What matters in the stichomythia is the balance, the parallelism, the symmetry—in sum, the *like*ness between the two of them. In a very important sense, each gives as good as each gets. And Petruccio clearly knows his audience when he begins his praise of her,

> No, not a whit. I find you passing gentle.
> 'Twas told me you were rough, and coy, and sullen,
> And now I find report a very liar ....
>
> *Shr.* 2.1.237-9

Kate, in turn, knows *her* audience,

>   one half-lunatic,
> A madcap ruffian and a swearing Jack,
> That thinks with oaths to face the matter out.
>
> *Shr.* 2.1.282-4

And she suspects she can well be the other, answering "half lunatic." Nor does Petruccio disappoint her:

> And to conclude, *we have 'greed so well together*
> That upon Sunday is the wedding day.
>
> *Shr.* 2.1.292-3 (emphasis added)

Nor does she disappoint him:

> KATHERINE I'll see thee hanged on Sunday first.
>
> *Shr.* 2.1.294

And to this (between them) perfectly reasonable riposte, Petruccio offers an equally reasonable counter:

> *I choose her for myself.*
> If she and I be pleased, what's that to you?
> 'Tis bargained 'twixt us twain, being alone,
> That she shall still be curst in company.
> I tell you, 'tis incredible to believe
> How much she loves me. O, the kindest Kate!
> Shr. 2.1.298-303 (emphasis added)

If Petruccio has a wife, Kate has a voice, at last, in the masculine world—she can "be curst in company" all she likes.

Certainly, she is not therefore enfranchised; that is not possible in the world she inhabits. She must submit. *That* is the world she inhabits. But she knows now that she is not doomed to submit to a mindless, tongueless, witless, feelingless inferior. She knows now that it is her mate who will tame her.

And so the importance in the play of *meat*, the next anagram after *tame* and *mate*. In starving Kate of meat, as part of his design to tame (and mate) her, Petruccio thinks of her as a falcon:

> My falcon now is sharp and passing empty,
> And till she stoop she must not be full-gorged,
> For then she never looks upon her lure.
> ...
> She ate no *meat* today, nor none shall eat.
> Last night she slept not, nor tonight she shall not.
> As with the *meat*, some undeservèd fault
> I'll find about the making of the bed.
> Shr. 4.1.176-8; 183-6 (emphasis added)

Figuring the desired and desirable female as a falcon is a venerable convention in European poetry: Chaucer's Criseyde, for example, is "as fressh as faukoun comen out of mewe" in *Troilus and Criseyde* (3.1774). Shakespeare, like many others, sees in the figure, among many other implications, the underlying image of change, *molting*, which is so crucial to the health and the life of the falcon—clearly, Kate must molt, must change her "feathers," even as a falcon must do (Shoaf, "Falcon"). But the falcon imagery also serves the rhetoric of *tame*, *mate*, and *meat* in the play, for not only are we what we eat (assimilation, likening), we also eat what we are—we feed on likeness—and *meat* is not our only likeness.

"Sent you hither so unlike yourself"

> **PETRUCCIO** 'Tis burnt, and so is all the *meat*.
> ...
> You heedless jolt-heads and unmannered slaves.
> What, do you grumble? I'll be with you straight.
> *He chases the servants away.*
> **KATHERINE** I pray you, husband, be not so disquiet.
> The *meat* was well, *if you were so contented*.
> **PETRUCCIO** I tell thee, Kate, 'twas burnt and dried away,
> And I expressly am forbid to touch it,
> For it engenders choler, planteth anger,
> And better 'twere that both of us did fast,
> *Since of ourselves ourselves are choleric,*
> Than feed it with such overroasted flesh....
> **NATHANIEL** Peter, didst ever see the *like*?
> **PETER** *He kills her in her own humour.*
> Shr. 4.1.147; 152-61; 165-6 (emphasis added)

Kate must feed on a different meat if she is to be tame and enjoy a mate. She must feed on her likeness—"didst ever see the *like*?"/*He kills her in her own humour*"—until she realizes who she has been ... like.[2] "Since, of ourselves ourselves are choleric," Kate must eat her choler, must be fed upon it, until she is fed up with it.

> **KATHERINE** Go, get thee gone, thou false, deluding slave,
> *(Beating him)* That *feed'st me with the very name of*
>   *meat*.
> Sorrow on thee and all the pack of you,
> That triumph thus upon my misery.
> Go, get thee gone, I say.
> Shr. 4.3.31-35 (emphasis added)

At last, then, she can give thanks:

> **KATHERINE**   I pray you, let it [the meat] stand.
> **PETRUCCIO** The poorest service is repaid with thanks,
> And so shall mine before you touch the meat.
> **KATHERINE** I thank you, sir.
> Shr. 4.3.44-47 (emphasis added)

Kate has begun to feed on a new likeness, one that encourages Petruccio that *she might love* him—*amet*, the remaining anagram (3rd person singular subjunctive of the Latin verb *amo*, "I love").

Not infrequently in Shakespeare's plays, love proves impossible until and unless the lover comes to *like* the would-be beloved (see, e.g., chapter 20 on *Twelfth Night*; also, chapter 29 on *All's Well That Ends Well*). This process reveals that the lover and the beloved are—and, indeed, have been all along—alike without, usually, having known it until much action has passed. Part of the genius (I mean the word with something also of its sense of "geniality") of Shakespeare's dramatic art is its capacity, its copiousness (also a kind of patience), for showing (theater and theory) the canniness of liking in the mystery of love. It is probably a miracle that any two of us come together in the first place (although we have forgotten how to cherish the miracle); but the miracle, if that is what it is, indisputably depends upon our bodies which are the likes of us, even "a joint-stool" (/"joints-tool").

4
"But thou art neither like thy sire nor dam": Narcissus Disfigured in the First Henriad and *Venus and Adonis*

If the Oxford chronology is correct (a big *if*, of course), then the fourth play that Shakespeare wrote (that we know of, at least), and the second in time, in 1591, of the three *Henry VI* plays, entitled *The True Tragedy of Richard Duke of York and the Good King Henry the Sixth* or *3 Henry VI* (as it is commonly designated from the 1623 Folio), foregrounds the character, Richard Gloucester, known as Crookback, who focuses for Shakespeare the crisis of likeness as a generational or genealogical crisis. Considering succession as one of the most intimate anxieties of monarchy led Shakespeare, in part, to his uncanny sensitivity to likeness as such. You cannot infer character from likeness, as of son to father, and you thus discover that neither can you infer truth or, in many cases, reality from likeness, and this epistemological crisis, a serious human deficit, repeatedly confronted Shakespeare in writing the history plays.

Margaret, with her characteristic fury, scathingly brands Richard as she also defines the genealogical crisis for us:

> But thou art neither *like* thy sire nor dam,
> But *like* a foul misshapen stigmatic,
> Marked by the destinies to be avoided.
>   3HVI 2.2.135-7 (emphasis added)

It is in the profoundest sense ironic that in *1 Henry VI*, written third of the four plays in the First Henriad[1], in 1592, perhaps a year after *3 Henry VI* and a year before *Richard III*, Shakespeare (perhaps, but it is also possible that another hand wrote the scene, although I myself do not think so—but see Oxford 2ᵉ 125) has Suffolk declare,

> ... Henry, son unto a conqueror,
> Is *likely* to beget more conquerors
> If with a lady of so high resolve

"But thou art neither like thy sire nor dam"

> As is fair Margaret he be linked in love
>
> *1HVI* 5.7.73-76 (emphasis added),

since not only does the audience know that Henry VI did not leave behind him more conquerors, the audience also knows that Richard Gloucester, Crookback, is soon to be on the scene, chronologically (already on the scene in the earlier plays' chronology), to make a horrific, bloody mockery of any putative rule that fathers beget sons who are *like* them.

To be sure, Henry VI was himself already a notorious exception to this putative rule, since in no way was he *like* his father Henry V, but, I speculate, it was not until Shakespeare began to imagine the character of Richard Crookback that he also began to see and understand this deep flaw in patriarchal monarchy, namely, that succession to the father's throne by the son can in no way count on the *like*ness of the son to the father (or of the daughter, even if "she have the heart and stomach of a king").[2] Succession through sexuality is a system, in other words, devoid not only of political but also epistemological certainty—epistemologically, Elizabeth I was unthinkable until, spectacularly, she proved otherwise. I speculate that the theater of likeness emerged fully into view for Shakespeare in writing and contributing to writing the first three plays of the First Henriad (1590-2) as he was also writing *Titus Andronicus* (1592) and then *Richard III* (1592-3), the culmination of the first Henriad and of the first experimentation with the theater of likeness in histories.

Shakespeare, I propose, first *felt* the seismic skepticism of the early modern world not by intellectualizing—by reading Montaigne, for example—but by observing and experiencing the impossibility of inferring likeness from generation and genealogy:

> Thy mother felt more than a mother's pain,
> And yet brought forth less than a mother's hope—
> To wit, an indigested and deformèd lump,
> *Not like the fruit of such a goodly tree.*
>
> *3HVI* 5.6.49-52 (emphasis added)

Here is one deep explanation for Shakespeare's characterization of Richard Crookback (in addition to others, such as morality plays and their Vices): Shakespeare needed the physical deformity of a monster to represent the monstrosity of a culture of presumed likeness—let me show you what power by succession really looks *like*. And what *will* we do when Elizabeth dies? Richard Crookback (as distinct from Richard III) never existed except as Shakespeare's early, youthful imagination of the crisis of likeness:

> Then, since the heavens have shaped my body so,
> Let hell make crooked my mind to answer it.
> I had no father, I am *like* no father;
> I have no brother, I am *like* no brother;
> And this word, "love," which greybeards call divine,
> Be resident in men *like* one another
> And not in me — *I am myself alone.*
> 3HVI 5.6.78-84 (emphasis added)

It is a matter neither of the morality Vice nor yet the Freudian case history (Garber, *Ghost Writers* 28-51). It is rather a matter of a being so *un*like all others that he betrays by his very language of unlikeness the terrible folly of trusting *like*ness(es), most of all trusting the likenesses of rhetoric that liken ugliness to beauty, lies to truth, hatred to love:

> And I no friends to back my suit withal
> But the plain devil and dissembling looks—
> And yet to win her, all the world to nothing? Ha!
> RIII 1.2.223-5

The first Henriad is Shakespeare's first exploration of the first, the primordial, darkness in the theater of likeness: "I am not what I am" (*Oth.* 1.1.65).

✺

But before Iago and before Richard is Titus. Shakespeare wrote *Titus Andronicus* in between the 3 *Henry VI* plays and *Richard III* doubtless under many impulses but also because he was in the process of liberating himself from any faith in historical typologies. I believe that this intellectual development also lies behind his work on *Edward III*, soon to follow (1594), for this play, although in a different mode, shows the same process, a weaning from the *Fürstenspiegel* tradition and its premise of princes likening themselves to great predecessors in the "mirrors" of their former accomplishments.

No inference can be made from past likenesses to present conditions that is epistemologically secure. Typologically, Tamora's sons treat Lavinia like Philomela; typologically, Titus treats Saturninus and Tamora like Tereus and he treats Lavinia like Virginia. If you are going to account for history by the prescripts of typological exempla/likenesses, you have no guarantee that the typological likeness chosen for the account will not itself prompt and promote an interpretation of self-serving violence, mutilation, homicide, and ruthless exploitation. Similarly, the focus in *Edward III* on the Black Prince's education and on the trials he must endure insists on an interrogation of the value of exemplariness, the more searchingly insofar as, early in the play the prime mirror, his father, Edward III, all but commits heinous adultery in complete deviation from and degradation of princely pedagogy. Hence, I believe, *Richard III* follows *Titus Andronicus* and anticipates *Edward III* with compelling internal logic—Richard Crookback reduces to mockery every prescript or typology, whether it be of royalty, or nobility, or honor, or, finally, even humanity itself. Shakespeare is learning not to trust history—to this lesson *King John* will be the exclamation point (and the Bastard Falconbridge the exception that proves the rule, through and because of his bastardy). And the five history plays that remain—*Richard II, 1 & 2 Henry IV, Henry V,* and *All Is True (Henry VIII)*—will be, even more than the First Henriad, *Edward III*, and *King John*, not so much history as metadrama unraveling the claims of alleged historicity and its putative historiography.

If "all knowing comes by likeness" (Plotinus), all knowing is not merely inadequate; it is also corrupt, structurally corrupt, before it is corrupted through individual malice. We live in a world of lies. But the world of lies is not merely mendacity; it is a world of forgetting:

> Every word instantly becomes a concept precisely insofar as it is not supposed to serve as a reminder of the unique and entirely individual original experience to which it owes its origin; but rather, a word becomes a concept insofar as it simultaneously has to fit countless more or less similar cases [*zugleich für zahllose, mehr oder weniger ähnliche*]—which means, purely and simply, cases which are never like [*gleich*] and thus altogether unequal [*ungleiche*]. Every concept arises from the likening of unlike things [*Jeder Begriff entsteht durch Gleichsetzen des Nicht-Gleichen*]. Just as it is certain that one leaf is never totally the same [*gleich*] as another, so it is certain that the concept "leaf" is formed by arbitrarily discarding these individual differences and by forgetting the distinguishing aspects.[3]

But the poet in this world of lies and forgetting can distinguish, at least some of the time, the lies that tell the truth, or the fictions, without which we would perish from the truth that there is no truth.

> What then is truth? A movable host of metaphors, metonymies, and anthropomorphisms: in short, a sum of human relations which have been poetically and rhetorically intensified, transferred, and embellished, and which, after long usage, seem to a people to be fixed, canonical, and binding. Truths are illusions which we have forgotten are illusions—they are metaphors that have become worn out and have been drained of sensuous force, coins which have lost their embossing and are now considered as metal and no longer as coins.... to be truthful means to employ the usual metaphors. Thus, to express it morally, this is the duty to lie according to a fixed convention, to lie with the herd and in a manner binding upon everyone. Now man of course forgets that this is the way things stand for him. Thus he lies in the manner indicated, unconsciously and in accordance with habits which are centuries' old; and precisely by means of this unconsciousness and forgetfulness he arrives at his sense of truth.[4]

The poet can disturb this fossilized "truth" by "hold[ing] as 'twere the mirror up to nature" (*Ham.* 3.2.22), which reminds it again, being so *unlike* nature, how much it depends upon fiction, how great a debt it owes to metaphor, and therefore how important it is *not to forget* so as, in fact, to remember to renew the truth, to participate resolutely in its constant construction, lest power wrest the truth to its own private, psychotic, and murderous illusion.

Which is the lust of the politician in this world of lies, of whom Richard III is the archetype in the history plays. Relentlessly and ruthlessly the politician (b)locks our vision so that the only truth we ever see is that there is no truth—no fiction, no like, but what its lie preponderates, even to the voiding of nature herself (as in Hitler's "Final Solution")—and hence we can trust nothing; we are always insecure of any truth, which is the exquisitely terrible lot of the characters in *Richard III*, who are systematically destroyed by Richard just because they trusted some seeming truth of his, forgetting that, as coiner (to use Nietzsche's analogy), he can stamp any value he likes on any metal at any time: "Thus *like* the formal Vice, Iniquity,/I moralize two meanings in one word" (*RIII* 3.1.82-83). Richard kings it up as he goes so that no one can be sure what they see: "What of his heart perceive you in his face/By any *like*lihood he showed today?" (*RIII* 3.4.54-55, Stanley speaking; emphasis added). He lords it as he likes it: "I am not in the giving vein today" (*RIII* 4.2.119):

> **BUCKINGHAM** And is it thus? Repays he my deep service
> With such contempt? Made I him king for this?

> ...
> Thus doth he [God] force the swords of wicked men
> To turn their own points in their masters' bosoms.
>
> *RIII* 4.2.122-3; 5.1.23-24

The profound pathos of Buckingham's lot, to which he remains oblivious, mocks him in his own question—"*Made* I him king for this?" (*RIII* 4.2.123; emphasis added): if even Buckingham can "make" a king, then the "truth" of *king* is but an impression upon metal, waiting to be scraped off by the next liar, who will replace it with an image more to his own li*king*.

Richard III is also the play in which Shakespeare exploits his instinct for the divided personality. This instinct had been at work in the earlier plays, especially in *Henry VI*, Part 3, but it is in *Richard III* that he makes the instinct conscious and drives toward a realization of a character so far abstracted from social obligation that he can literally act upon the psychotic impulse, "I am myself alone" (*3HVI* 5.6.84). If Richard is the monster he is fabled to be, his monstrosity is first and foremost his aloneness. As his standard was the boar, *synguler*, so he is singular, relentlessly and ruthlessly.[5] His isolation, as unnatural as his deformed body, is the necessary precondition of all the monstrous acts that he commits. He is not only, as he says, "*like* no brother" (*3HVI* 5.6.81), he is *like* no other, *like* no one at all. If we remind ourselves that the word *like* derives from the Anglo-Saxon word that means *body*, we may reason that Richard's deformed, "bunch-backed" (*RIII* 4.4.81), "toad"-like (*RIII* 4.4.81) body, is itself, in a *literally metaphoric* way, his unlikeness to any other human being. It is as if Shakespeare had asked himself, how would I best incarnate unlikeness itself so as to test its being and doing in a world of likenesses? Before the political, before the sexual, before gender- and body-constructedness, it is the epistemology of likeness and unlikeness that mobilizes the language of *Richard III*.

If Richard is the monster of unlikeness, his language is also deformed, but its deformity is strangely recognizable, even reassuringly familiar:

> Richard loves Richard; that is, I am I.
> Is there a murderer here? No. Yes, I am.
> Then fly! What, from myself? Great reason. Why?
> Lest I revenge. Myself upon myself?
> Alack, I love myself. Wherefore? For any good
> That I myself have done unto myself?
> O no, alas, I rather hate myself
> For hateful deeds committed by myself.
> I am a villain. Yet I lie: I am not.
> Fool, of thyself speak well. — Fool, do not flatter.

> ...
> I shall despair. There is no creature loves me,
> And if I die no soul will pity me.
> Nay, wherefore should they? — Since that I myself
> Find in myself no pity to myself.
>
> RIII 5.5.137-46; 154-7

This is the language of the "double man," that is, man divided against himself in two: "we are, I know not how, *double in ourselves, which is the cause that what we believe we do not believe*, and cannot disengage ourselves from what we condemn" (Montaigne, *Essais* 9 "Of Glory"). This is the language of self-examination, of elementary reflexivity—it is, in short, the language of *self*, as such.[6] Imagine for a moment that Richard is Narcissus by the pool interrogating his image as to why it does not reciprocate his love and then recall Teiresias's answer to Liriope, Narcissus's mother, when she asked if her son would live a long life, "Si, se non noverit" ("Yes, if he does not know himself"—*Metamorphoses* 3.348). Richard is the deformed Narcissus, "Richard loves Richard," who now knows himself, "I am I," and is shortly to die.

Imagining Richard III as Narcissus disfigured enabled Shakespeare to fold together history, fable, and rhetoric in a single character of enormous fascination. The disfigured Narcissus, an ugly and repulsive Narcissus, is an unparalleled occasion to probe the darkest recesses of self-love. Take away Narcissus's soul-arresting beauty and what remains is "one false glass,/That grieves me when I see my shame in him" (*RIII* 2.2.53-54), as Richard's mother expresses it, a mirror that distorts and destroys all that passes before it. They who look into Richard see not just their death but their degradation as well into the sub-human, creatures worth so little why not drown them in a butt of malmsey. Richard is no *sun* of York—no life emanates from him, only death, the death of self-love, minus even a flower to grace it.

✳

If the Oxford editors are correct in their chronology that *Venus & Adonis* is the next work in Shakespeare's canon, we do well to reflect for a moment on the extraordinary connection between the poem and *Richard III* inasmuch as it also depends so heavily on Ovid's account of Narcissus. Adonis is also a version of Narcissus, if one very different in features and comportment, and here, too, Shakespeare is drawn to, cannot rest from, the drama of self-knowledge. As different as Richard and Adonis obviously are, they share a likeness with Narcissus that has already become a part of Shakespeare's rhetorical ethics—action in the world cannot finally be understood apart from action with the word, and action with the word cannot be understood apart from the passion (and the pathologies) of love.

Adonis rejecting Venus's embraces is just like Richard insisting "I am myself alone"; both refuse, as did Narcissus, too, the elementary condition of belonging—belonging is repugnant to them. They are, each in his different way, creatures of the boar. The boar is Richard's heraldic device; the boar is Adonis' doom. The boar in its savagery marks the inhumanity of both. Men who prefer the boar to Venus are the bad-mates of death, whether they are hideously ugly or supernally beautiful.

Singularity is a throbbing nerve in Shakespeare's poetry. Freud analyzed Richard III in terms of the narcissist who thinks of himself as the "exception" (*SE* 14: 314-15). And the "exception" cannot help but also think of himself as singular (*synguler*, the boar), not merely detached, nor only unattached, but, if you will, *dys*attached (as in, *dys*functional). This nonce word serves well enough if it conveys the sense prominent throughout the play that Richard attaches himself to others only to make the attachment destructive. His is the boar's touch, the tusk of mutilation and death.

> Thou elvish-marked, abortive, rooting hog,
> Thou that wast sealed in thy nativity
> The slave of nature and the son of hell,
> Thou slander of thy heavy mother's womb,
> Thou loathèd issue of thy father's loins,
> Thou rag of honour, thou detested —
>
> *RIII* 1.3.225-30

Margaret's curse, especially the pun/anagram "*abor*tive" (note also *elvish*: *evil* -sh), names Richard's monstrosity with precision attainable only in figurative discourse: the boar aborts everything he touches, rooting (rutting, rotting) it up and out of life (where *root* parallels *fetus*, the young that is being *abor*ted). Only so can he feed his hunger to be singular/ *synguler*.

Adonis hunts the boar that aborts his youth. He dies of the boar's tusk, is boar-ed as well as aborted, because he too insists on singularity, *dys*attachment. When Venus remonstrates with Adonis about his selfishness, she identifies precisely what drives him to the boar:

> "Is thine own heart to thine own face affected?
> ...
>   *Narcissus* so himself himself forsook,
>   And died to kiss his shadow in the brook.

Narcissus Disfigured in The First Henriad and *Venus and Adonis*

> *Things growing to themselves are growth's abuse.*
>   Seeds spring from seeds, and beauty breedeth beauty:
> *Thou wast begot; to get it is thy duty.*
>
> By law of nature *thou art bound to breed,*
> That thine may live when thou thyself art dead;
>   And so in spite of death thou dost survive,
>   In that thy *likeness* still is left alive."
>
>   *Ven.* 157; 161-2; 166-8; 171-4 (emphasis added)

Adonis, Venus argues, must be *just like all other men*, breeding to survive in spite of death by leaving his likeness still alive after his death. Any singularity Adonis may attain will be cancelled in the moment of copulation when he will be like any man, every man, groaning in sex. Thus, he insists, appalled:

> "I know not love," quoth he, "nor will not know it,
> *Unless it be a boar*, and then I chase it.
> 'Tis much to borrow, and I will not owe it.
> *My love to love is love but to disgrace it;*
>   For I have heard it is *a life in death,*
>   That laughs and weeps, and all but with a breath."
>
>   *Ven.* 409-14 (emphasis added)

It is not that Adonis hunts the boar, as such; it is that he chases it *for* love, in all senses of the word *for*. He chases the *synguler* to be singular, thus to claim, "I will not owe it"—he who is in debt is *not* singular. The only love he bears for love is his love of disgracing it, but he cannot hear how then his is already "a life in death," for he has not escaped love, rather fallen already under its spell, obeying urges that make him just *like* every man, "[t]hat laughs and weeps, and all but with a breath." For all that he understands of what he is saying or proposing to do, he might as well declare, "I know not love .. unless it be *abor*(tion), and then I chase it," chas(t)e only chasing death in a boar(tion).

It is possible that Shakespeare wrote *1 Henry VI*, *Titus Andronicus*, *Richard III*, and *Venus and Adonis* in the years 1592-3.[7] *The Rape of Lucrece* may follow closely upon them. And he was writing several score sonnets during the same period, we currently think. I will proceed now to separate chapters on *Titus*, *Lucrece*, and then *Edward III*, an important culmination in this early phase of the theater of likeness, as the next steps in the argument I have begun to unfold in this chapter. My reader should bear in mind, therefore, that there is a loose but important connection among these chapters, tying them to the crisis of likeness as in part the problem of generational succession which I propose is one of the paradigmatic problems of the theater of likeness in Shakespeare's drama. I also propose that by the time we reach 1595, *annus mirabilis,* as I now think of it, with *Richard II, Romeo and Juliet,* and *A Midsummer Night's Dream,* we will meet a theory of the theater of likeness, at work in every play written thereafter until Shakespeare ceases writing in 1613.

5
"Too like the sire": Likeness and Mutilation in *Titus Andronicus*

Titus Andronicus[1] is a play important for our consideration of Shakespeare's theater of likeness in the measure to which it is concerned with the likeness between children and parents.[2] Repeatedly in the play, characters comment upon generational likeness or unlikeness in ways that suggest that *Titus* is an early, crucial study by Shakespeare of a problematic that will emerge over the course of his career as inseparable from his understanding and representation of human tragedy. Parental, filial, and sibling likenesses are rooted so deeply in human experience that they are not only ineradicable, they are also always potentially fatal, even as they are inescapably mortal. When Lucius declares of Aaron's bastard that he is "too like the sire for ever being good" (*Tit.* 5.1.50), we recognize language that is effectively a Shakespearean signature, even as we also recognize once more the tyranny of resemblance over the mind—the bastard is but a few days old and already condemned as people behold his *likeness* to his father.

At this point, I think it useful simply to list the occurrences of the word *like* in those passages of the play that contribute to its analysis of generational likeness and the tragic consequences that flow from it.[3] The list is an abstract of the crisis:

> **LAVINIA** When did the tiger's young ones teach the dam?
> O, do not learn her wrath! ...
> Yet every mother breeds not sons a*like*.
> *Tit.* 2.3.142-3; 146 (emphasis added)

> **AARON** Not far, one Muliteus my countryman
> His wife but yesternight was brought to bed.
> His child is *like* to her, fair as you are.
> Go pack with him, ...
> *Tit.* 4.2.151-4 (emphasis added)

LUCIUS Say, wall-eyed slave, whither wouldst thou convey
This growing *image* of thy fiend*like* face?
...
And by his side his *fruit* of bastardy.
> *Tit.* 5.1.44-5; 48 (emphasis added)

AARON Why, she was washed and cut and trimmed, and 'twas
Trim sport for them which had the doing of it.
LUCIUS O barbarous beastly villains, *like* thyself!
AARON Indeed, I was *their tutor to instruct them*.
> *Tit.* 5.1.95-98 (emphasis added)

TITUS Good Lord, how *like* the Empress' sons they are,
And you the Empress! But we worldly men
Have miserable, mad, mistaking eyes.
...
Rapine and Murder, you are welcome, too.
How *like* the Empress and her sons you are!
Well are you fitted, had you but a Moor.
> *Tit.* 5.2.64-66; 83-85 (emphasis added)

TITUS Look round about the wicked streets of Rome,
And when thou find'st a man that's *like* thyself,
Good Murder, stab him; he's a murderer.
[*To Chiron*] Go thou with him, and when it is thy hap
To find another that is *like* to thee,
Good Rapine, stab him; he is a ravisher.
[*To Tamora*] Go thou with them, and in the Emperor's court
There is a queen attended by a Moor.
Well shalt thou know her by thine own proportion,
For up and down she doth *resemble* thee.
I pray thee, do on them some violent death;
They have been violent to me and mine.
> *Tit.* 5.2.98-109 (emphasis added)

We need hardly do more than to scan this list in order to see that *like*ness drives the play's relentless inquisition of human depravity toward the limit of concluding that all are a*like* bestial in their treatment of their fellow human beings—none is unlike this likeness of inhumanity, as if all were descended from the same tiger (*Tit.* 2.3.142). It is a matter of degree and not of kind, where Aaron and Tamora occupy the extremest degree of bestiality—

> As for that ravenous *tiger*, Tamora,
> No funeral rite nor man in mourning weed,
> No mournful bell shall ring her burial;
> But throw her forth to beasts and birds to prey:
> *Her life was beast-like*, and devoid of pity,
> And being so, shall have *like* want of pity.
>
> The First Folio *TA* 5.3.194-9 (emphasis added)

—but everyone else can be positioned alongside them on the same axis, if at a lesser point of degree. Time and again, the play resists such a conclusion, trying to represent a moment or an occasion where prevailing precedent likeness does not prescript the devastating conclusion that the human family itself is all alike "beast-*like*," but the evidence overwhelms the representation and repeatedly returns it to another scene of carnage.

The dynamic I am describing finds its prescriptive likeness in revenge tragedy and the "fathers" thereof—Kyd and Marlowe, above all, presumably—from which, and from whom, Shakespeare would spend much of the 1590s finding ways to differentiate himself and his playwriting (see, e.g., Norton 371-2). *Titus* is very much a play bound to its prior likenesses. Even so, it already demonstrates unmistakable signs of the independence and originality that would come to mark the mature Shakespeare. One of these signs is the word *like*.

Deep in the Shakespearean imagination lies an angst over the discrepancy between a man's likeness and his inwardness (cf. Posthumus's "less without and more within" [*Cym.* 5.1.33]).[4] What interests me and, I believe, interested Shakespeare, too, is the inexhaustible plasticity of the word *like* to represent and measure the trauma of perpetually dis/covering the inadequacy of every covering even to hide, much less to knit up, the inner riven fragments of human being.

> **MARCUS** You sad-faced men, people and sons of Rome,
> By uproars severed, *as* a flight of fowl
> *Scattered* by winds and high tempestuous gusts,
> O, let me teach you how *to knit again*
> This *scattered* corn into *one mutual sheaf*,
> These broken limbs again into one body.
>
> *Tit.* 5.3.66-71 (emphasis added)

For the moment, think of this speech as applicable also to the individual, scattered (as in an Orphic *sparagmos*, being ripped asunder) so as never to know a self that is "one mutual sheaf," never to "knit.../These broken limbs again into one body." Here is the trauma, the pain, that defines

Shakespeare, I think. What *like*ness will make me whole? *Integer vitae, scelerisque purus?* (Horace, quoted at *Tit.* 4.2.20)? Whence can I take my likeness such that I know who I am? "Intact of life and pure of crime"?

So hard does this angst drive Shakespeare that we often see it most clearly in his villains where fashions of compromise and temporizing are discarded as the niceties of those without the raw animal will, the villainy, to lord it over their fellows: "Aaron will have his soul black *like* his face" (*Tit.* 3.1.204). Aaron is the very likeness of those who would be one, whole, integral, undivided, relentlessly singular and contained, using the weakness, "conscience" (*Tit.* 5.1.75), of others to tear them asunder so that he is never asunder (from) himself (it is obviously useful at this point to recall Richard III also). It is by the perfidy of Shakespeare's villains that we are able to measure the inappropriateness of wholeness to human being—a whole human being is (a) total(itarian) madness. It is by the weakness of Shakespeare's tragic heroes, above all Hamlet, that we are able to appreciate conscience and the unlikeness that it makes between the human and the bestial.

Where conscience fails to intervene, likeness is not interrupted. With no conscience, an individual subject may glue a likeness to himself with an (e)pox(y) of the will. This, I take it, helps to account for the occasions on which Aaron insists that he would ever be even more wicked than he is if only he could be:

AARON I am no baby, I, that with base prayers
I should repent the evils I have done.
Ten thousand worse than ever yet I did
Would I perform if I might have my will.
If one good deed in all my life I did
I do repent it from my very soul.

Tit. 5.3.184-9

AARON (*Aside*) Their heads, I mean. O, how this villainy
Doth fat me with the very thoughts of it!
Let fools do good, and fair men call for grace:

Tit. 3.1.201-3

LUCIUS Art thou not sorry for these heinous deeds?
AARON Ay, that I had not done a thousand more.
...
And nothing grieves me heartily indeed
But that I cannot do ten thousand more.

Tit. 5.1.123-4; 143-4

Shakespeare realizes in the character of Aaron the relentless drive of the will somehow to impress itself on reality such that reality could never prove to the will that it is anything but unified, total, and in control of its life. The fissures that make the human human—doubts, misgivings, re-considerations, scruples—fill Aaron with a disgust so vehement that it renders him, in the precise etymological sense of the word, a caricature, that is, a figure so burdened, so weighted down, with a single characteristic that it distorts his appearance utterly.[5] We hear in Aaron's speeches the discourse of the madness of wholeness with no holiness. (Hence, too, the form of his execution—slow death by starvation in absolute isolation within a premature grave, hole in the ground.)

Titus and Tamora both are like Aaron, but the likeness is not absolute, not an identity, although Shakespeare, I am confident, saw the telling confusion of the name *Aaron* in the name *Tamora*—T/aarom(n)—which is the more ironic because of the presence in her name of *mo(o)r* and *amor* as well. The most obvious difference between them, we know, is race, black and white. But I think it would be a mistake to reduce the representation to racism, since Shakespeare, it seems to me, clearly imagines a blackness within that is color, the color of evil, and not of a particular race. Certainly, Titus shows black within, perhaps most vividly in the slaying of his son over the fate of Lavinia (*Tit.* 1.1.289). But this example is in fact very instructive. Titus is here motivated, unlike Aaron, not by a malice as pure as can be willed, but by a sense of honor which is in turn the likeness of a good that his entire culture endorses and acknowledges. The difference between Titus and Aaron is just the choice of likenesses, Aaron choosing unlikeness to anything humane and Titus choosing likeness to his culture's deepest norms of humanity. That such a difference should nonetheless coincide with results of both men's actions that are identical in cruelty is, I take it, part of what moves Shakespeare's prosecution of the play. In the moment when Titus slays his son or severs his own hand, however different we know him to be from Aaron, he is all the same acting *like* Aaron (and thus "fat[ting]" [*Tit.* 3.1.202] Aaron's lust to make others *like* him).

As I understand Shakespeare's theater of likeness, this truth haunts it as well as him. Exemplariness is a two-edged sword—you follow the example, the example follows you. We are so constituted that we can only take our likeness from another. The first other from whom we take our likeness is our mother; and here we need pause only long enough to think of Tamora and her sons. But eventually we adopt other likenesses from elsewhere, and, clearly, the warrior Titus has adopted his likeness from the martial identity of Rome. This likeness, however, has cost him the many likenesses of all the sons he has had to bury, dead in his wars in behalf of Rome. It is no small part of the tragic irony of the play that the killing of sons so dominates its opening scenes. But it is the killing of the daughter, Lavinia, that most instructs us in the wretched intricacy of exemplariness. Faithful adherence to exemplary likenesses is no guarantee of righteousness and its solaces.

Titus is one in a long line of Shakespearean heroes who slowly come to realize the drastic consequences of the likenesses that they have chosen for themselves or that they have had thrust upon them and over which they have at best only limited control. Hence the importance, I think, of the reference to Virginius and Virginia. At the moment of the final crisis in the play, Titus adduces their example as the pattern for his action:

> **TITUS** My lord the Emperor, resolve me this:
> Was it well done of rash Virginius
> To slay his daughter with his own right hand
> Because she was enforced, stained, and deflowered?
> **SATURNINUS** It was, Andronicus.
> **TITUS**   Your reason, mighty lord?
> **SATURNINUS** Because the girl should not survive her shame,
> And by her presence still renew his sorrows.
> **TITUS** A reason mighty, strong, effectual;
> *A pattern, precedent, and lively warrant*
> *For me, most wretched, to perform the like.*
> Die, die, Lavinia, and thy shame with thee,
> And with thy shame thy father's sorrow die.
>   *He kills her.*
> **SATURNINUS** What hast thou done, unnatural and unkind?
> **TITUS** Killed her for whom my tears have made me blind.
> I am as woeful as Virginius was,
> And have a thousand times more cause than he
> To do this outrage, and it now is done.
>   *Tit.* 5.3.35-51 (emphasis added)

Although a feminist critique might claim that this is a moment as unspeakably misogynistic as the earlier rape of Lavinia, it is also true that in dramatizing this intensely conscious imitation by Titus of Virginius, Shakespeare is also dramatizing an equally intensely conscious choice by Titus of a likeness—"to perform the like"—that sets the final seal on his assimilation of himself and his fate to figures and characters of horror with whom, beyond any conscious control that he could exercise, he had become associated as a consequence of his martial Roman likeness. In other words, if Titus is to be assimilated to, likened to, tragic figures of the historical and/or mythological past, he now, in this paroxysm of revenge, deliberately chooses a likeness that provides his final actions with a story. And, I propose, it is as much this story as it is his own courage or desperate resolve that enables him to carry out his vengeance upon Tamora. He had not only to find the occasion but also to invent the language—i.e., likeness —of this action of revenge upon his enemies. And this, as I understand the writings, is fundamental to the Shakespearean effect: the story must precede the action, else no action can or will be taken.[6]

We see this effect also in the banquet itself: its story or pre-script is, of course, Procne (adduced explicitly by Titus at *TA* 5.2.194), Philomela, and Tereus (with Thyestes as well)—Titus at the end of his life assimilates himself to those stories that give shape to, if they hardly make sense of, the horrors that have befallen him. He copies these stories in(to) his own life. And it is this copying, as much as the life itself of Titus, that, I want to propose next, fascinated Shakespeare. For copying is as inseparable from mutilation as was the life of Titus Andronicus.

To dramatize the life of Titus is also to dramatize the scandal of copying. Every copy that is not a forgery is necessarily a mutation of some original.[7] If it is a commonplace that Shakespeare's *Titus* copies liberally from numerous literary sources—especially Ovid's *Metamorphoses* and Seneca's tragedies—it perhaps should also be commonplace that such copying is integral to Shakespeare's early development as a tragedian: tragedy is always in part the tragedy of a copy gone awry.

The family is the site of tragedy because reproduction is the ur-type of copying and its all too often fatal consequences. Just as there can be no reproduction without the prior mutilation of the hymen, so there can be no copying without mutation of the original. As every son is a mutation of his father and his mother, so every son is a mutilation of his mother and his father—hence the enduring ubiquity of Oedipus and his story. Oedipus is the type of mut(il)ation of his progenitors. In *Titus*, the mut(il)ation of children (subjective genitive as well as objective genitive) becomes for Shakespeare the very scene of writing tragedy: raping and hacking Lavinia is also raping and hacking the *Metamorphoses*. To write tragedy, Shakespeare learns very early on, is to participate in the tragedy of writing, that it always entails taking life from another as if it were your own (and the guilt that this bequeaths you leads to bizarre excesses— murder and bake two children, for example, not just one, like Procne).[8]

Fathers appear more often, and more often as victims, in tragedies because fathers unlike mothers are not ripped by their children at birth. Fathers for a while can more easily afford the delusions of reproductive copying. Sooner or later, though, they too are ripped by their children. Then they know that the copy is imperfect and they must somehow learn to accept as much. The most tragic fathers are those, like Lear, who learn too late. Perhaps the most fortunate fathers are those, like Leontes and Pericles, who are given a second chance—although such felicity may indeed exist only in romance.

Certainly Titus experiences no such felicity. For Titus, as we are now positioned to see and to say, began by repudiating maternity:

> **TAMORA** [*kneeling*] Stay, Roman brethren! Gracious conqueror,
> Victorious Titus, rue the tears I shed —
> A mother's tears in passion for her son —
> ...
> Thrice-noble Titus, spare my first-born son.
> **TITUS** Patient yourself, madam, and pardon me.
> These are their brethren whom your Goths beheld
> Alive and dead, and for their brethren slain
> Religiously they ask a sacrifice.
> To this your son is marked, and die he must
> T'appease their groaning shadows that are gone.
>
> *Tit.* 1.1.104-6; 120-6

Not only a mother's love but also a mother's knowledge Titus repudiates here—and repudiates precisely in the name of the Father, i.e., religion and its sacrifice. There is no place in Titus's world—the world of the state, the world of war, the world of the patriarchy—for the knowledge of sons that Tamora has and that he does not have: for her, the son was first a fetus tearing through her cervix; for him, he is another corpse to add to the family vault. He will soon learn to think and feel differently.

So did Shakespeare, I believe, learn to think and feel differently. The paradoxes and the scandals of copying, I suggest, early in his career left an impression on him that contributed greatly to the mark of difference he bears. He learned early that to be unlike those who were his rivals, and occasionally his enemies, he must be *more like* them and, by extension, their fellow men than they themselves were capable of conceiving.

John Keats called it "negative capability" (letter of 21, 27 [?] December 1817). I would like to call it—not as an improvement on Keats, which is impossible, but merely as a supplement to his insight—"genitive capability,"[9] the capability of re-producing a likeness that is greater, or more, or intenser, or "'dpi'-er" ("more 'data per insight'"), or, simply, *of*-er (and thus also *over*), what other writers are capable *of*. Shakespeare as negative is genitive (or, in terms I suggested in the Introduction, Shakespeare as kenotic [empty] is full). And each of us gets to be what he begets (consider how many have fantasized being Hamlet or Romeo or

Ophelia or Juliet at some time in their lives). Here too is the origin(ality) of Shakespeare's style: it is abundant, prolific, copious, or, if you prefer, over the top, just because it is endlessly begetting, always genitive, never sterile (not even Joyce's abundance is as fertile as Shakespeare's). It is full with the fullness of a man capable of emptying himself (is the archetype of such a man the player, the actor?).

We could put it this way. When Keats describes Shakespeare's "negative capability," he is deliberately excluding passivity from Shakespeare's gift — he does not mean "passive capability." Indeed, there is nothing passive at all about Shakespeare's writing. Keats rather means that Shakespeare is negating, actively negating, that "irritable reaching after fact and reason" that would, in Keats's view, diminish the power of poetry:

> at once it struck me what quality went to form a Man of Achievement, especially in Literature, and which Shakespeare possessed so enormously—*I mean Negative Capability, that is, when a man is capable of being in uncertainties, mysteries, doubts, without any irritable reaching after fact and reason*—Coleridge, for instance, would let go by a fine isolated verisimilitude caught from the Penetralium of mystery, from being incapable of remaining content with half-knowledge (emphasis added).

The pressure of this negation, I am proposing, is like a birthing, a receptivity followed by an expressivity so nearly complete that the final effect is like nothing, "negative capability."

This that I write, "like nothing," is more than a play on words. I do not intend it as a witticism (although I recognize the polysemy of *nothing* in Shakespeare's English). I am, to the contrary, attempting to write criticism as serious as I have ever written. I am trying to let the word *like* do the work that I think Shakespeare felt it to do. To be original is to be like nothing, but to be like nothing is, paradoxically, to be like everything, which, being finally impossible, means "being in uncertainties, mysteries, doubts, without any irritable reaching after fact and reason ... being ... capable of remaining content with half-knowledge." Likeness is at best half-knowledge. And it is most of the time the best we have (a fact that Coleridge and other compulsive Platonists cannot abide—they are not empty men).

So it is that humans universally seek likenesses or models or patterns by which to organize and govern their lives in the absence of complete knowledge. So Titus, for example, is thoroughly, indeed remorselessly, a Roman, modeling everything he does on the likeness of a Roman. But such insistent, even desperate, copying cannot escape the mut(il)ation of the copy. The copy can only be a likeness, a part-knowledge and apart-knowledge. Blocked by his entire heritage from understanding this, Titus possesses no "negative capability," or, say rather, tragically, he gains it only at the end when the likenesses remaining to him (with which to fill his terrible emptiness) are Procne, Thyestes, and Virginius—murder, cannibalism, filiacide.

Rome, we may now pause to reflect, is *the* culture of copying, of imitation. Ancestors, traditions, and, of course, Greece, all are likenesses the Roman citizen was expected to copy, imitate, and emulate. Rome and her greatness would have been unthinkable without the discipline of imitation—and we should remember that the discipline was always harsh, frequently cruel. I think we have here one key to Shakespeare's fascination with Rome, to why he wrote so many Roman works (at least six), and to why, contrary to one strand of interpretation, we must rigorously *include Titus* in the canon.[10] Rome was the literary site of one of Shakespeare's deepest anxieties, or the invention of likenesses.[11]

Ultimately, my concern here encompasses the relatively startling fact that there is no secure source for *Titus Andronicus*; there are many identifiable sources *in* the play but no known source *of* the play (Dobson and Wells 478). It would appear to be Shakespeare's invention. If indeed this is the case, I would hazard that the argument I have put forward in this chapter contributes at least a robust conjecture as to why Shakespeare invented it. Before he could begin a career of copying (Holinshed, Saxo, Chaucer, the Brut, et al.), Shakespeare had to confront and examine, on his own terms, the dynamic of likeness and mut(il)ation. He had to convince himself that he was not (like) a Titus Andronicus, that, if anything, he was more (like) an Aaron. Shakespeare was not a man, nor a writer, to stack his sons in the family vault; he was rather a man and a writer to love the child of his "genitive capability," no matter what the bastard might look like.

6
"When they in thee the like offences prove": The Ruins of Exemplariness in *The Rape of Lucrece*

The Rape of Lucrece is an important poem in the history of English literature from many different perspectives. Recently, most especially, it has been a lightning rod for feminist issues, for obvious reasons.[1] For understanding Shakespeare's theater of likeness, the poem is crucial because of its insistence on exemplariness—modeling or patterns—and the failure of exemplariness to function as either education or admonition. Exemplariness itself is also violated in the poem and, like Lucrece, lies in ruins at the end (lines 1850-1). In writing the poem Shakespeare takes a major step toward understanding the crisis of likeness in human comportment.[2]

The tradition of the *Fürstenspiegel*, or "mirrors for princes" (see above Introduction 1-2) includes the celebrated *Mirror for Magistrates*, compiled/edited by William Baldwin between 1555 and 1559, but is actually far more compendious, going beyond the *de casibus* tradition, associated especially with Boccaccio, to the Latin tradition of high scholasticism, represented most importantly by the *De regimine principum* of Aegidius Romanus, which in turn is indebted to the classical tradition that extends as far back, at least, as Aristotle's tutelage of Alexander. Throughout this vast tradition, the basic goal of all "mirrors" is to show the prince what he should be *like*. The mirrors for princes are treatises on princely comportment, aimed at educating the prince in behavior becoming to him in all his various offices or, we may say, likenesses. In this most comprehensive perspective, Machiavelli's *Il Principe* is but one, if a very famous one, of many "mirrors," all of which essay to show the prince his likeness.

Exemplariness is explicitly topical in *The Rape of Lucrece* and in a way that directly links it to the *Fürstenspiegel* tradition:

"This deed will make thee only loved for fear,
But happy monarchs still are feared for love.
With foul offenders thou perforce must bear
When *they in thee the like offences prove.*

If but for fear of this, thy will remove;
For princes are the glass, the school, the book
Where subjects' eyes do learn, do read, do look.

"And wilt thou be the *school* where lust shall learn?
Must *he in thee read lectures* of such shame?
Wilt thou be *glass* wherein it shall discern
Authority for sin, warrant for blame,
...

"Thy princely office how canst thou fulfil
When, *patterned by thy fault*, foul sin may say
He learned to sin, and thou didst teach the way?"
Luc. 610-20; 628-30 (emphasis added)

I quote at length here, initially, to make as clear as possible the extent to which Shakespeare is examining the structure and the process of learning by example: in the crisis of likeness, as he is coming to understand it, humans can not rely on "pattern" ("the like") to effect meaningfulness in their lives. Pattern may be pattern of evil as well as of good, and of itself compels likeness indifferently. Thus, Tarquin will not school his subjects in the good because he is himself not schooled even by "counsel" much less by the good—and, indeed, he admits as much:

"I see what crosses my attempt will bring,
I know what thorns the growing rose defends;
I think the honey guarded with a sting;
All this beforehand counsel comprehends.
But will is deaf, and hears no heedful friends.
  Only he hath an eye to gaze on beauty,
  And dotes on what he looks, 'gainst law or duty."
Luc. 491-7 (emphasis added)

Neither law nor duty is a powerful enough example, a brilliant enough mirror, to show Tarquin a different likeness, one of honor and dignity, say—"Only he hath an eye to gaze on beauty,/And dotes on what he looks":

"I have debated, even in my soul
What wrong, what shame, what sorrow I shall breed;
...
  Yet strive I to embrace mine infamy."
Luc. 498-9; 504 (emphasis added)

Tarquin knowingly proceeds to be like and look like his infamy, examples to the contrary be damned.

The fate of Lucrece chillingly illustrates that it is not only futile but also fatal to count on the power in exemplariness; no argument *from* or *to* exemplariness can constrain a will hell-bent that "thou yoke thy *liking* to my *will*" (*Luc.* 1633; emphasis added).³ Such a will wills another's "liking" to disappear in it, consumed by its ravenous appetite to possess that liking as its own likeness: "The fault *is thine*,/For those thine eyes betray thee unto mine" (*Luc.* 482-3; emphasis added)—Lucrece "is" Tarquin as far as Tarquin cares, his fault or her fault just alike, it makes no difference, and he will use her not only as if she were his but also as if she were he, as he would use himself. Hence, precisely, there can be no appeal to that "self," that "likeness":

> "In *Tarquin's likeness* I did entertain thee.
> *Hast thou put on his shape to do him shame?*
> To all the host of heaven I complain me.
> ...
> "How will thy shame be seeded in thine age
> When thus thy vices bud before thy spring?
> *If in thy hope thou dar'st do such outrage,*
> *What dar'st thou not when once thou art a king?*
>   *Luc.* 596-8; 603-6 (emphasis added)

This is an extraordinary moment in Shakespeare's theater of likeness, I think. It is an epitome of the crisis of likeness. "In Tarquin's likeness": everyone, anyone, is separable from his or her likeness—"Hast thou put on his shape to do him shame?" Likeness is no more fixed than language is and is no more trustworthy. Lucrece's helplessness is the helplessness of all victims of total(-izing) power: she does not even know what her persecutor looks like—"Hast thou put on his shape"? Nazis raping and gassing Jews looked like humans, after all; Klansmen castrating young African-Americans after hanging them looked like humans, too.

Hence the importance in the poem, and for the theater of likeness, of the figure of Sinon in the painting of Troy's destruction:

> This picture she advisedly perused,
> And chid the painter *for his wondrous skill,*
> Saying *some shape in Sinon's was abused,*
> So fair a form lodged not a mind so ill;
> And still on him she gazed, and gazing still,
>   Such *signs of truth* in his plain face she spied

"When they in thee the like offenses prove"

> That she concludes the picture was belied.
> ...
> "It cannot be, I find,
> But *such a face should bear a wicked mind*.
>
> "For even as subtle Sinon here is painted,
> ...
> As Priam him did cherish,
> So did I Tarquin, so my Troy did perish."
>
> *Luc.* 1527-33; 1539-41; 1546-7 (emphasis added)

The scene of Lucrece's "reading" the painting (a moment of ekphrasis) is itself an interrogation of exemplariness: does the painting provide "means to mourn some newer way" (*Luc.* 1365)? or does it instead merely delude her with "the painter's...wondrous skill" which can "abuse" some "shape" in Sinon's?—

> *She tears the senseless Sinon with her nails,*
> Comparing him to that unhappy guest
> Whose deed hath made herself herself detest.
>   At last she smilingly with this gives o'er:
>   "Fool, fool," quoth she, "his wounds will not be sore."
>
> *Luc.* 1564-8 (emphasis added)

So much for exemplariness: in a "passion" (*Luc.* 1562) one attempts to punish an image in a painting, "[c]omparing him ...." The grapes of Zeuxis are no argument to the contrary, for if the birds attempt to eat the painted grapes,[4] Lucrece, being conscious, unlike birds, knows that "his wounds will not be sore" no matter how "wondrous" the painter's skill—"The painter was no god to lend" (*Luc.* 1461) him (or her) that. Yet again, Shakespeare demonstrates the limits of likeness and likening even as he also, simultaneously, demonstrates our ineradicable need for likenesses:

> On this sad shadow Lucrece spends her eyes,
> And shapes her sorrow to the beldame's [Hecuba's] woes,
> Who nothing wants to answer her but cries
> And bitter words to ban her cruel foes.
> The painter was no god to lend her those,
>   And therefore Lucrece swears he did her wrong
>   To give her so much grief, and not a tongue.
>
> *Luc.* 1457-63

At one and the same time, we cleave to art and berate it—the ruins of exemplariness.

Hence the inescapable burden of the controversial conclusion to the poem:

> When they had sworn to this advisèd doom
> They did conclude to bear dead Lucrece thence,
> *To show her bleeding body thorough Rome,*
> And so *to publish Tarquin's foul offence;*
> Which being done with speedy diligence,
>   The Romans plausibly did give consent
>   To Tarquin's everlasting banishment.
> *Luc.* 1849-55 (emphasis added)

With an irony almost too exquisite to bear, the poem concludes showing Lucrece being "shown" as an example, a likeness, "to publish Tarquin's foul offence." The only good woman is a dead woman. A poem about the failure of exemplariness concludes with an example of exemplariness constructed of and from the corpse of a victim of failed exemplariness who becomes forever after nevertheless the example or likeness of "loyal wife" (*Luc.* 1048) by killing herself to beget that exemplariness, even though "Of that true *type* hath Tarquin rifled [her]" (*Luc.* 1050; emphasis added). The mise en abîme is truly abyssal, the specularity a hell of mirrors. And Shakespeare has taught himself as well as us just how cross-coupled, paradoxical, and indeterminate the work of art is—it is only like life, which is only like it.

7
"Famous for like victories": Shakespeare's "Mirror for Princes" in *Edward III*

> Let Edward be delivered by our hands
> And, still in danger, he'll expect the *like*.
> But if himself himself redeem from thence,
> He will have vanquished, cheerful, death and fear...
> *EIII* Sc. 8. 48-51 (emphasis added)

The editors of the Oxford Shakespeare wrote in the first edition of their work that

> ...the consensus of investigators [is] that *Edward III* deserves a place in the Shakespeare canon. ... The stylistic evidence for Shakespeare's authorship of *Edward III* is greater than that for the additions to *Sir Thomas More* (excluding the palaeographical argument); if we had attempted a thorough reinvestigation of candidates for inclusion in the early dramatic canon, it would have begun with *Edward III*.
> *Textual Companion* 136-7

Similarly, in 1994, Jonathan Hope concluded that *Edward III* is "the best candidate from the apocryphal plays for inclusion in the canon" (154). And, in 2005, Oxford 2[e] included the play as part of the canon (257-83). My own, independent study of the theater of likeness in Shakespeare's works corroborates these various findings: I believe Shakespeare wrote the play and either wrote all of it or was responsible for the final copying of it.[1] My conviction stems from and continues my investigation into exemplariness and the *Fürstenspiegel* tradition in Shakespeare's early work. *Edward III* is, I suggest, like a "mirror for prince" Edward, the Black Prince, and in writing the play, dated to 1594, Shakespeare, I propose, is working out terms of the theater of likeness that he had begun to develop in the First Henriad and that emerge convincingly in the nearly contemporary *Richard III* and *The*

Rape of Lucrece. In many ways, *Edward III* is a culmination in Shakespeare's early career: as the work of the word *like* in this play will show us, he has by this point become master of a vocabulary of likeness and exemplarity that will continue to serve him the remainder of his career.

Consider initially the passage appearing as an epigraph to this chapter:

> Let Edward be delivered by our hands
> And, still in danger, he'll expect the *like*.
> But if himself himself redeem from thence,
> He will have vanquished, cheerful, death and fear...
>
> *EIII* Sc. 8. 48-51 (emphasis added)

It is, I think, self-evident how this speech coheres with the tradition of "mirrors for princes," both within the play, where the instructional tractate is actually the battlefield, and through the play, which becomes in effect an exemplum of princely behavior for all Englishmen.[2] And central to the effect of the passage is the work of the word *like*. The king must be careful as to what he accustoms his son, the Black Prince, for "he'll expect the like" afterwards. If he sees deliverance by others in his "mirror," he will not see himself redeeming himself from danger in future.

We may now consider the thesis that the play is a play about the prince's likeness. (I will use "prince" generically, as in the *Fürstenspiegel* tradition.) Immediately, I would observe that such an argument is certainly consistent with the representation of Edward III's lascivious assault on the Countess of Salisbury's sex (*EIII* Sc. 2.361ff.): here we see what a prince should *not* be like and we also see, as the plot unfolds, how Edward III has reflected back to him by the Countess this obnoxious likeness so that he may be repulsed by it and thus eschew it. I quote liberally but selectively to show, so to speak, as it is happening, her reflection of Edward's detestable likeness:

> **COUNTESS OF SALISBURY** O, were it painted I would wipe it off
> And dispossess myself to give it thee!
> But, sovereign, it is soldered to my life:
> Take one, and both, for, *like* an humble shadow,
> It haunts the sunshine of my summer's life —
> ...
> He that doth clip or *counterfeit* your *stamp*
> Shall die, my lord: and will your sacred self
> Commit high treason 'gainst the king of heaven
> To *stamp* his *image* in forbidden metal,

Forgetting your allegiance and your oath?

...

KING EDWARD Their opposition is beyond our law.
COUNTESS OF SALISBURY So is your desire. If the law
Can hinder you to execute the one,
Let it forbid you to attempt the other.

...

KING EDWARD Even by that power I swear, that gives me now
The *power to be ashamèd of myself*,
I never mean to part my lips again
In any words that tends to such a suit.
Arise, true English lady, whom our isle
May better boast of than ever Roman might
Of her, whose ransacked treasury hath tasked
The vain endeavor of so many pens.
Arise, and *be my fault thy honor's fame*
Which after-ages shall enrich thee with.
I am awakèd from this idle dream.
        EIII Sc. 2.397-401; 423-7; Sc. 3.142-5; Sc. 3.186-96
                            (emphasis added)

This selection of passages demonstrates the way in which the Countess of Salisbury is a "mirror for the prince," that is, King Edward: time and again, she shows him the likeness of himself as a *counterfeit* prince, not a true and honorable king, but a traitor, to himself as well as to the highest King. And she is willing to fix the likeness forever in place by committing suicide in front of him (*EIII* Sc. 3.172-85) only to relent in the last possible moment when he has "awakèd from this idle dream," which, without violence to the text, we could also paraphrase as "idle likeness."

I contend, from this demonstration, then, that the entire episode of the Countess of Salisbury is a crucial moment in the development of Shakespeare's theater of likeness. Although doubtless many motives impel him to construct the episode, I think it is also arguable that among them is his growing sense of likeness and of human dependency on likeness. The episode affords him the opportunity, within the tradition of *Fürstenspiegel*, to explore the dynamic of likeness as it plays out in the sensitive and dangerous psychology of educating a prince—in this regard, Edward III is the countertype to Richard III who is "not made to sport before an amorous looking glass" and sees no reflection anywhere other than his own monstrosity.

This reading of the episode of the Countess of Salisbury delineates and sharply focuses other moments in the play where the theater of likeness can be seen to draw on and modify the *Fürstenspiegel* tradition; these moments, I suggest, strengthen further the ascription of the play to Shakespeare—they bear his signature of likeness.

Consider, first, for example, the episode of Copland's apparent disobedience to Queen Phillipa in not surrendering his royal captive to her in her capacity as Edward's representative during his absence in France:

> **COPLAND** No wilful disobedience, mighty lord,
> But my desert, and public law at arms.
> I took the King, myself, in single fight,
> And, *like a soldier*, would be loath to lose
> The least pre-eminence that I had won.
> ...
> **QUEEN PHILIPPA** But, Copland, thou didst scorn the King's command,
> Neglecting our commission in his name.
> ...
> **KING EDWARD** I pray thee, Phillip, let displeasure pass.
> This man doth please me, *and I like his words*.
>
> *EIII* Sc. 18.72-76; 84-85; 89-90 (emphasis added)

When King Edward concludes, "I like his words," we hear more than just royal approbation; in the theater of likeness, we also see the mirror of likeness for princes at work ("like a soldier"): Edward sees in Copland what he would have Copland see in him—

> Kneel therefore down.
> *He knights him*
> Now rise, King Edward's knight.
> And to maintain thy state, I freely give
> Five hundred marks a year to thee and thine.
>
> *EIII* Sc. 18.95-97

In making Copland his knight, "King Edward's knight," he is ceremonializing and officializing a likeness that is indispensable to his monarchy and its theater—Copland is a "mirror for his prince," and his prince is, in effect, proclaiming that the two of them do, indeed, look alike ("I like his words"). This mirroring, in the *Fürstenspiegel* tradition, serves Shakespeare also in the theater of likeness: as he works his way through the implications of genealogical succession, narcissism, exemplariness, and playing, he can intensify his focus on the dynamic of copying that underlies so much of human culture, especially culture predicated upon class and primogeniture. And he is thus that much closer to the "mirror [held] up to nature" (*Ham.* 3.2.22).

Another example, more important, is apposite here. Following his victory, Edward the Black Prince lifts up a prayer:

> ... that many princes more,
> Bred and brought up within that little isle,
> *May still be famous for like victories.*
> And for my part, the bloody scars I bear,
> ...
> I wish were now redoubled twentyfold,
> So that *hereafter ages, when they read*
> The painful traffic of my tender youth,
> *Might thereby be inflamed with such resolve.*
>   *EIII* Sc. 18.221-4; 229-32 (emphasis added)

In addition to the echo of *The Famous Victories of Henry V* (performed first ca. 1586, published 1598), we have here a palpable conflation of the *Fürstenspiegel* tradition and the theater of likeness. The prayer for "many princes more" to "be famous for *like* victories" rises simultaneously with the prayer that "hereafter ages, when they read" about the Black Prince "might thereby be inflamed"—his life become, in effect, the text of a "mirror for princes." This, the very ending of the play, seals both the signature of likeness and the idea of the mirror in a way that, I suggest, is indisputably Shakespearean: he thinks them together in this fashion.[3]

❦

One argument often adduced against Shakespearean authorship of *Edward III* is that Shakespeare does not write history the way history is written in this play: (relatively) unambiguous, overtly moralistic, admitting of facile closure, patriotic to a simplistic extreme (Shakespeare, *Riverside* 1733). I believe these characteristics are justly adduced of the play, but I do not believe that they amount therefore to a brief against Shakespeare's authorship—to the contrary, they may well be a powerful case *for* it.

The key, I think, is the theater of likeness. As I have tried to show, and as I will continue to argue throughout this study, the theater of likeness is a site of contest between prescript and script, between dictation (and dictatorship) and creative play allowing of spontaneity and improvisation. Shakespeare the player and playwright explores throughout his career the dynamic of this contest and its implications for understanding human being. We must copy in order to survive; we must transcend copying in order to live: we are irreducible combinations of derivativeness and originality. We need both prescripts and scripts. Hence, in terms of the theater of likeness, *Edward III* is crucial, and definitely Shakespearean, insofar as it is the history play of his that most depends upon prescripts and prescriptiveness even as it exploits that dependency to examine the limits on prescripts and prescriptiveness. Those limits, like the limits of the "mirrors for princes," are severe: you can only tell a prince so much before he is like to chop off your head. History seen as a series of prescripts leads in Shakespeare's case to an acute suspicion of prescriptive historiography. The histories that follow *Edward III* are the histories of a writer who has got *Edward III* out of his system; they are the work of a man who will go on incessantly to interrogate the exemplariness of history, showing the likes of history to be all too often dark and distorting mirrors we may trust only at our peril.

KING HARRY Do you like me, Kate?
CATHERINE *Pardonnez-moi*, I cannot tell vat is "like me."
HV 5.2.107-8

Which, as far as history and historiography go, may just be the human condition.

8
"These two so like": Error's Error in *The Comedy of Errors*

A key statistic of Shakespeare's theater of likeness, which we will meet again in the chapter on *A Midsummer Night's Dream*, is that it, *A Midsummer Night's Dream*, and *The Comedy of Errors* contain the lowest incidences of the word *like* in the canon—27 for *Errors* and 29 for *MND* (as opposed to a numerical average of 60 across the entire canon). I propose that in each case, the theater of likeness accounts for the statistic by the readily observable fact that no other plays in the canon, including especially those in which mistaken identity is an issue, foreground the crisis of likeness in their dramatic situations as these two plays do. The word *like* occurs less frequently in them because it is less needed: scene, circumstance, and event do much of the work of *like* in these two plays. But also, relative to later comedies, these two early comedies find Shakespeare still developing the vocabulary of likeness for the comedies, and the sophistication he attains in the theater of likeness in *Much Ado About Nothing*, *As You Like It*, and *Twelfth Night*, especially in the rhetoric of likeness, is still in the future. If the turning point, as I think it is, was *Richard III*—if, that is, *Richard III* is the play in which the theater of likeness first became consciously theoretical in Shakespeare's thought, became what we today might call a generative metadramatic structure—then, the two years that separate *Richard III* from *Errors* and *MND* are still formative years in which, especially, the poems, *Venus and Adonis* and *The Rape of Lucrece*, and the Sonnets find Shakespeare analyzing the crisis of likeness as theory as well as dramaturgy, as an *idea* of poetry as well as a mechanics for the theater. This analysis—or, say, perhaps better, exploration—continues through *Love's Labour's Lost*, *Richard II*, and *Romeo and Juliet*, until it culminates in the astonishingly articulate and self-assured theater of likeness that we encounter in *A Midsummer Night's Dream*, most especially in Bottom's dream and in the "rude mechanicals'" performance of "Pyramus and Thisbe," where the "actors… show…all that [we] are like to know" (*MND* 5.1.116-17), a phrase, I will argue, indispensable to the theater of likeness:

in Shakespeare's theater, we are indeed *like* to know.

Another key statistic, but specific to *Errors*, is Shakespeare's addition of the twins, the servants, Dromio, to the plot he takes from Plautus's *Menaechmi*. Shakespeare doubles the doubles, reduplicates the duplication (two sets of twins and not just one), and the theater of likeness accounts for this by observing the *meta*-duplicative effect Shakespeare thus achieves (an effect I try also to convey in the title to this chapter), whereby doubling becomes not just stage business but thematic, even theoretical, since two sets of twins are, so to speak, more like a geometric than they are like an arithmetic progression, and, as such, they foreground the crisis of likeness—"these two so like" (*Err.* 5.1.349)—as *the* concern of the play: if one flesh can be "these two so like," can two so like—say, husband and wife—be one flesh?

Here, of course, is the Pauline subtext of the play, recognized by all students of Shakespeare, on which Shakespeare insists by transferring the action to Ephesus (it is Paul's Epistle to the Ephesians that so insists on marriage and its definition, as we know, especially 5.22ff.). And this subtext is crucial to the play, as it is pivotal to this moment in Shakespeare's career, the theater of likeness suggests, because Shakespeare, wounded in his experience of intimacy in his own marriage and ever deeper in doubt about the prospects of genealogical succession, is more and more restlessly examining and interrogating the possibility of there *ever* being "these two so like." For all that the play is a comedy, it is also the tragedy of error's error: once error has precipitated, you can hardly ever *get it* right, it only sometimes happens that it *falls out* right. Everything else is "fool-begg[ing]":

> **ADRIANA** So thou, that hast no unkind mate to grieve thee,
> With urging helpless patience would relieve me.
> But if thou live to see *like right bereft*,
> *This fool-begged patience in thee will be left*.
>   *Err.* 2.1.38-41 (emphasis added)

Reduplicating right and left as simultaneously both spatial (natural) and legal (conventional), Shakespeare can insist on the uneasy marriage between the two: legal right can deteriorate into spatio-local left because finally "fool-begg[ing]" is all that is between them—that is, *language*, "begg[ing]," is all that is between them, keeping them together but also keeping them apart. When the marriage collapses, it is not only union but also separation that suffers (witness Adriana and the "wrong" Antipholus abusing each other). When you lose the like right, in you will be left this fool-begged patience because the like right and the left patience are only conventions in the first place; they are not absolute (hence the right can be bereft) and they depend necessarily on position. You will find out how useless patience is when you have changed positions with me. And you will see that the right is only *like*, not an essence but a convention, a figure (of speech—in this case, legal speech).

Error's error is to lead us to think we can escape error when all we can do is (try to) correct it—and hope for the best. We are immersed in error, wandering (and wondering), just because we are *homo viator* or *peregrinus*, in exile in the land of unlikeness, *regio dissimilitudinis* (Introduction note 37) no matter where in space we are. Error's error is the "fool-begged" transcendence of division, which can never be transcended, let the fool beg never so hard and long. In division is our (un)likeness, and in (un)likeness is our error. It is not women, I have argued, that grieve Shakespeare, it is not women he hates, but division itself, of which sex is the root, from which root division suppurates like a miasma to contaminate everything human. You and I are not one, at best we are just alike:

ANTIPHOLUS OF SYRACUSE
He that commends me to mine own content
Commends me to the thing I cannot get.
I to the world am *like* a *drop of water*
That in the ocean *seeks another drop*,
Who, falling there to find his fellow forth,
Unseen, inquisitive, *confounds himself*.
So I, to find a mother and a brother,
In quest of them, *unhappy, lose myself.*

...

ADRIANA ...
Ah, do not tear away thyself from me;
For know, my love, as easy mayst thou fall
A drop of water in the breaking gulf,
And take unmingled thence that drop again
Without addition or diminishing,
As take from me thyself, and not me too.
                    Err. 1.2.33-40; 2.2.127-32 (emphasis added)

The Pauline sublimity (Ephesians 5:22-33) of Adriana's plea is beli(k)ed by Antipholus of Syracuse's desperate, illusionless consciousness; and Shakespeare asks us to understand as much by the crucial repetition of "drop of water." However we desire to be mingled ("undividable, incorporate"—*Err* 2.2.125), we are but "*like* a drop of water" (in reality, "unmingled") and are each who he or she *is as* a *drop* of water, *not* the whole water (in the whole water, we are simply lost). This is what hurts: I am here, you are there.

"Known unto these, and to myself disguised!" (*Err.* 2.2.217), Shakespeare has come in the early years of his poetic career to understand, is the human condition. It may be even that "[w]e came into the world like brother and brother" (*Err.* 5.1.429), but each to himself is still disguised. As Achilles says to Ulysses, in a passage I will analyze at considerable length later, in my chapter on *Troilus and Cressida*,

> This is not strange, Ulysses.
> The beauty that is borne here in the face
> The bearer knows not, but commends itself
> To others' eyes. Nor doth the eye itself,
> That most pure spirit of sense, behold itself,
> Not going from itself; but eye to eye opposed
> Salutes each other with each other's form.
> For speculation turns not to itself
> Till it hath travelled and is mirrored there
> Where it may see itself.
>
> *Tro.* 3.3.97-106

We are, like it or not, Aristophanic halves in need of other halves (Introduction note 12), or we have not. Marriage, we try to convince ourselves, should be some salve to being halved, but all too often it is not:

LUCIANA
> And may it be that you have quite forgot
>   A husband's office?
> ...
> If you *like* elsewhere, do it by stealth:
> ...
>   *Apparel vice like virtue's harbinger.*
> ...
> Shame hath a bastard fame, well managèd;
>   *Ill deeds is doubled with an evil word.*
>   *Err.* 3.2.1-2; 7; 12; 19-20 (emphasis added)

How easy it is to "like elsewhere" since everywhere we see our likeness and even (another) one whom we may like:

ANTIPHOLUS OF SYRACUSE
>Are you a god? *Would you create me new?*
>>Transform me, then, and to your power I'll yield.
>But *if that I am I,*
>...
>>Far more, far more, to you do I *decline.*
>...
>>>No,
>It is thyself, *mine own self's better part,*
>Mine eye's clear eye, my dear heart's dearer heart.
>>>>*Err.* 3.2.39-41; 44; 60-62 (emphasis added)

In the plot, this exchange, to be sure, is the result of a comedy of errors, and rectification is close to hand. But insofar as the plot is a mimesis, if not of life then of life's not being like a play (that is, the error of comedy), this exchange between Luciana and Antipholus of Syracuse is proof of Luciana's lament, "Ill deeds is *doubled* with an evil word," and the double, as Shakespeare so cannily discerned, has a life and a like of its own, waiting in the wings.

We understand, then, why Shakespeare reduplicates the doubles: I am always here as my like(ness); I am never not what I am like, although I may be, true, like many likenesses at once—I am always at least my double. The play literally enacts this psychic contingency in the twin twins and examines how a man fares when one of his likenesses, as it were, goes free of him, disconnected from him.

>**ADRIANA** I see two husbands, or mine eyes deceive me.
>**DUKE** One of these men is *genius* to the other:
>And so of these, which is the natural man,
>And which the spirit? Who deciphers them?
>>>>*Err.* 5.1.333-6 (emphasis added)

It is Shakespearean precision, exactly, that has *Sol*-inus ask: "Who deciphers them?" He who is "sol[e]" and who must sustain the integrity of the law, its unity (however illusory that may be), is he who asks for the cipher to be *solved*, so that each *one* can be (ac)counted (for) in the bookkeeping of the State, which cannot otherwise do business—it is very difficult to tax a man's "genius" (although that has never stopped the State from trying). The State, Solinus, must cense each man as an individual integer, circumscribe him with a putative identity, lest confusion undermine State control. To Shakespeare, already in 1594, at about 29-30 years of age, this exigency has become a career-defining anxiety: years later, when Lear cries out, "[w]ho is it that can tell me who I am?" (*Lr.* [1610] 1.4.212) and the Fool replies, "Lear's shadow" (*Lr.* [1610] 1.4.213), Shakespeare is still sounding the crisis of likeness, "which is the natural man, / And which the spirit?" In the end, the very end, in *The Two Noble Kinsmen*, when Theseus concludes

> Let us be thankful
> For that which is, and with you [the gods] leave dispute
> That are above our question. Let's go off
> And bear us *like* the time,
>
> *TNK* 5.6.134-7 (emphasis added)

Shakespeare,[1] I think, has decided it is the best any of us can do, "bear us like the time," in a theater of likeness that is no more (but also no less) than a likeness of theater.

Within this theater we can also see that *The Comedy of Errors* already enacts as well how Shakespeare writes. The syneciotician couples (and uncouples) words that we without him would have mistaken, misreading them for what they were not, as if they were twins in confusion when in fact they are likenesses in profusion:

> **ADRIANA** How ill a*grees* it with your *gravity*
> To counterfeit thus *grossly* with your *slave*,
> Abetting him to thwart me in my mood!
> Be it my *wrong* you are from me exempt,
> But *wrong* not that *wrong* with a more contempt.
> Come, I will fasten on this sleeve [*this leave*, not *s/lave*] of thine.
> Thou art an elm, my husband; I a vine,
> Whose weakness, married to thy *stronger* state,
> Makes me with thy *strength* to communicate.
> If aught po*ss*ess thee from me, it is dross,
> Usurping ivy, brier, or idle moss,
> Who, all for want of pruning, *with intrusion*
> *Infect thy sap, and live on thy confusion.*
> **ANTIPHOLUS OF SYRACUSE**
> (*aside*) To me she speaks, she moves me *for her theme.*
> What, was I married to her in my dream?
> Or sleep I now, and think I hear all this?
> *What error drives our eyes and ears amiss?*
> Until I know *this sure uncertainty,*
> I'll entertain *the offered fallacy.*
>
> *Err.* 2.2.171-89 (emphasis added)

Shakespeare's language functions in this way—"slave,""sleeve"; antiphony of "g's"; chorus of "s's" as an exact reflex of the theater of likeness, a language of likeness in a theater of likeness where the same is also different (juxta-form and cruci-lingual)—"It shall be called, 'Bottom's Dream,' because it hath no bottom" (*MND* 4.1.212-13).

We all live and like "in these contraries" (*Err.* 4.4.80) because we are all alike which means also we are all different. In *Errors* Shakespeare invented a plot and a structure that enabled him, by *meta*-duplication, to represent contraries in their contrariety, a literal "crosse-cople," or *syneciosis*, where apparent differences are alike and apparent likenesses are different (especially Antipholus of Syracuse in contrast to Antipholus of Ephesus, the former being far more introspective and melancholy than his twin brother). *Errors*, therefore, is a crucial play in the development of the theater of likeness, for it shows us maturing Shakespearean style as well as deepening Shakespearean thought, even in the smallest detail —e. g.,

> **EGEON** Our helpful ship was splitted in the midst,
> So that in this *unjust divorce* of us
> Fortune had left to both of us *alike*
> *What to delight in, what to sorrow for*
>
> *Err.* 1.1.103-6 (emphasis added)

—where, although the passage is little more than narrative plot summary, it nonetheless resonates with the economy (οἰκονομία < "law or rule of the household") of Shakespeare's geminative, and germinative, style, a style prolific in couplings that would never cross the mind of a less robust imagination.

As a final example of Shakespeare's robust imagination in *Errors*, and as an important, further step in understanding the theater of likeness, Abbess Emelia's concluding speech repays close examination:

> Renownèd Duke, vouchsafe to take the pains
> To go with us into the abbey here,
> And hear at large discoursèd all our fortunes,
> And all that are assembled in this place,
> That by *this sympathizèd one day's error*
> Have suffered wrong. Go, keep us company,
> And we shall make full satisfaction.
> Thirty-three years have I but gone in travail
> Of you, my sons, and till this present hour

> My heavy burden ne'er deliverèd.
> The Duke, my husband, and my children both,
> And you the calendars of their nativity,
> Go to *a gossips' feast*, and joy with me.
> After so long grief, such festivity!
> Err. 5.1.396-409 (emphasis added)

"This sympathizèd one day's error" is exquisite Shakespearean writing, where "sympathizèd" ("shared") is "at home with" its context in ways that only he could school us to see and hear. Further, "a gossips' feast," embedded in alliteration (on *g*) and internal assonance (feast/grief; me/festivity), suggesting a christening as well,[2] closes the play with an intimation of naming that will correct errors of confusion by supplying needed distinctions. But it is Abbess Emelia's account of her "travail" that most arrests our attention and confirms for us that we are reading Shakespeare.

The Comedy of Errors is an essay in parturition, the mystery by which one becomes two (or three or more) only to become one again. If *Errors* is more Pauline than Plautine, if it overgoes Latin farce and at least skirts the edges (I think it does more than that) of profound human contingencies, it does so, at least in part, by meditating on parturition, specifically on what it might mean to be re-born—"Are you a god? Would you create me new?" (Antipholus of Syracuse, *Err.* 3.2.39). St. Paul may be the Apostle to the Gentiles, but he is also, equally, the Apostle obsessed with death and re-birth: "O, who shall deliver me from the body of this death?" (Romans 7:24). *Errors* is an Epistle *from* the Ephesians (so to speak) in which Shakespeare examines not only the sacrament of marriage but also explores the curse of death, which is the dissolution and confusion of all distinctions, all individuality (which means "*un*dividedness"—death divides the undivided individual). In this Epistle *from* the Ephesians, Shakespeare imagines that, though a man may not be able to "enter the second time into his mother's womb, and be born" (quoting Nicodemus to Jesus, in John 3:4), he may even so, as it were, remain in his mother's womb until he is ready to be born *as who he is*, like himself. Abess Emelia's speech recognizes that, although she has not literally, physically carried two fetuses for 33 years (which is also the age of Jesus at his death), her sons were still undelivered until this moment when each knows what he is like, by seeing his like, so as thus to differentiate himself as who he is. This is not immortality but it may be "the death of death" (1 Corinthians 15:55) for which St. Paul longed—"not I but Christ lives in me" (Galatians 2:20). Because I am not unless you are, I must be known to know, recognized to cognize, seen to see—I must be *Anti*-pholus (and I need Antipholus, my brother) else I am only a centaur (Pholus, host of Heracles), half-horse, half-human, unable ever to escape my likeness to the beasts.[3]

9
"Our love being yours, the error that love makes/Is likewise yours": *L[ike]'s Labours Lost*

Itself as much a comedy of errors as the play that probably precedes it, *Love's Labour's Lost*, even in a canon vexed by some of the most formidable cruces in English literary history, is a most vexed and vexatious play. For starters, how do we punctuate the title? An essay hangs on that question alone. Next, to which character do we assign what speeches?[1] Next, in the absence of a source, itself a notable fact ("Shakespeare seems ... to have invented the plot himself" [Oxford 2ᵉ 307]), is the play as topical as it seems (Norton 733-4)? Or, again, does the riot of sexual punning in the play all but justify Dr. Johnson's dismissive snort at Shakespeare's fondness for "quibbles" (*Selections* 21-22)? To answer these and similar questions would need another book. Still, the theater of likeness can contribute at least somewhat to our comprehension of the play by accounting for its place in Shakespeare's developing sense of the crisis of likeness in human affairs: well before love's, like's labors are lost when sexual division goes disguised in the rhetoric of conformity, courtly or otherwise—no one can behave his way out of, there is no valid prescript for excusing him from, being sexed, any more than she can jump over her own shadow.

And, just so, the theater of likeness recognizes, first, that there is no source for the play. It is largely Shakespeare's invention, possibly highly topical—i. e., based in historical reality to a great extent—and thus already, just here, begs the question of the prescript. Shakespeare proceeds without a prescript on a script that explores the consequences of attempting life on a prescript:

> QUEEN We have received your *letters* full of love,
> Your favours the *ambassadors* of love,
> And in our maiden council *rated them*
> At courtship, pleasant jest, and courtesy,
> As bombast and as *lining to the time*.
> But more devout than this in our respects

> Have we not been, and *therefore met your loves*
> *In their own fashion, like a merriment.*
>
> LLL 5.2.769-76 (emphasis added)

As always, Shakespeare is precise. The ladies have construed "letters" and "ambassadors" of love as prescripts of "merriment" and have "therefore met [the] loves / In their own fashion, *like* a merriment." Hence, the futility, not to mention belatedness, of the rejoinders,

> **DUMAIN** Our letters, madam, showed much more than jest.
> **LONGUEVILLE** So did our looks.
>
> LLL 5.2.777-8

Hence, too, the exactitude of Rosaline's reply to the rejoinders: "We did not *quote* them so" (*LLL* 5.2.778), where "quote" should be heard as *quote* —i. e., the prescript was *not* quoted "correctly," according to the desires of those prescribing it, but according to the will of those who were (so to speak) transcribing it:

> **ROSALINE** A jest's prosperity lies in the ear
> Of him that hears it, never in the tongue
> Of him that makes it.
>
> LLL 5.2.847-9

If your audience doesn't like it, your labor is lost: "A jest's prosperity li[k]es in the ear / Of him that hears it" even as it also lies there.

A script is superior to a prescript just because it allows for improvisation, for the *un*predictable. A script, as Shakespeare so very well knew, is not under the dictation of "the tongue / Of him that makes it"—lots of other tongues, attached to bodies with ears, have a say in it: collaborators, directors, managers, etc. The playwright is frequently more an arbitrator than he is arbitrary. He is a critic *in order* to be a writer. *Love's Labour's Lost*, in this regard, is a play of criticism, literary criticism in the precise sense.

"Our wooing doth not end *like* an *old play*" (*LLL* 5.2.860) is just the point of Shakespeare's criticism. It can*not* end "like an old play"—as a later character will observe,

> **LYSANDER** Ay me, for aught that I could ever read,
> Could ever hear by tale or history,
> The course of true love never did run smooth
>
> MND 1.1.132-4

—because wooing never obeys a prescript, other than, perhaps, that it always takes its own course (script), which never does run smooth (especially when the prescript is a father's tyrannical insistence that a daughter marry a man she loathes). But also it can*not* end "like an old play" because *it has not yet been written*. And no amount of conventional, courtly rhetoric can make it that it has "always already" been written:

> **KING** Now, *at the latest minute of the hour*,
> Grant us your loves.
> **QUEEN**   *A time, methinks, too short*
> *To make a world-without-end bargain in.*
>   ... go with speed
> To some forlorn and naked hermitage
> Remote from all the pleasures of the world.
> There stay until the twelve celestial signs
> Have brought about the annual reckoning.
> If *this austere, insociable life*
> Change not your offer made in heat of blood.
>   *LLL* 5.2.779-81; 786-92 (emphasis added)

Just this *"insociable life"* is what is needed to teach those who woo by the book that wooing cannot end "like an old play." It can only end like a *new* play, the new play of the new couple acting out *their* script, not a predecessor's prescript.

This is the new play that Shakespeare wants to write (the first exemplar, I think, is *A Midsummer Night's Dream*), a play that cannot be "dash[ed] ... like a Christmas comedy" (*LLL* 5.2.462) because no one can tell its "intents before":

> **BIRON** Some carry-tale,
> ...
> *Told our intents before*, which once disclosed,
> The ladies did change favours, and then we,
> Following the signs, wooed but the sign of she.
>   *LLL* 5.2.463; 467-9 (emphasis added)

However recognizable, like a Christmas comedy, it may be, the new play is cognizable only in its own terms: "The best in this kind are but shadows, and the worst are no worse if imagination amend them" (*MND* 5.1.210-11). "It must be your imagination, then," rejoins Hippolyta, the audience's, "not theirs [the players']" (*MND* 5.1.212-13), which is Rosaline's point again:

> A jest's prosperity lies in the ear
> Of him that hears it, never in the tongue
> Of him that makes it.
>
> LLL 5.2.847-9

You cannot *dictate* your art to your audience. If you do, they will dash it.

The mystery of art that endures is that it is both form[ed] and form-less: highly structured, it nonetheless admits, simultaneously and paradoxically, of spontaneity, improvisation, ambiguity, multiplicity, in a word, contingency. *Love's Labour's Lost* probes this mystery by pushing form to the limit—convention, conceit, quibbling, fashion, etc.—so that our experience of the play is somewhat like feeling stuffed into the small world of the present stage: either we're in or we're out. Thus, when this world collapses, when contingency does erupt into it, it is no less than the contingency of death, the shocking and, for the audience, seemingly incommensurate, death of the King of France:

> **PRINCESS** Welcome, Mercadé,
> But that *thou interrupt'st our merriment*.
> **MERCADÉ** I am sorry, madam, for the news I bring
> Is heavy in my tongue. The King your father —
> **PRINCESS** *Dead*, for my life.
> **MERCADÉ** Even so. My tale is told.
> **BIRON** Worthies, away. *The scene begins to cloud.*
>
> LLL 5.2.709-14 (emphasis added)

Shrewdly, Shakespeare elects to shatter the form(s) with the one experience art can never circumscribe with form, death—"Dead, *for my life*" (emphasis added). Death has no likeness unless it be life itself.

Hence, the extraordinary—I would say, personally, improbably courageous—decision on Shakespeare's (p)art to send Biron to jest in hospitals:

> **ROSALINE** ...
> And therewithal to win me if you please,
> Without the which I am not to be won,
> You shall this twelvemonth term from day to day
> *Visit the speechless sick and still converse*
> *With groaning wretches*, and your task shall be
> With all the fierce endeavor of your wit
> To enforce the painèd impotent to smile.
> **BIRON** *To move wild laughter in the throat of death*? —

It cannot be, it is impossible.
Mirth cannot move a soul in agony.
ROSALINE Why, that's the way to choke a gibing spirit,
Whose influence is begot of that loose grace
Which shallow laughing hearers give to fools.
A jest's prosperity lies in the ear
Of him that hears it, never in the tongue
Of him that makes it. Then if sickly ears,
Deafed with the clamours of their own dear groans,
Will hear your idle scorns, continue then,
And I will have you and that fault withal.
But if they will not, throw away that spirit,
And I shall find you empty of that fault,
Right joyful of your reformation.
BIRON A twelvemonth? Well, befall what will befall,
I'll jest a twelvemonth in an hospital.

LLL 5.2.834-57 (emphasis added)

To understand Shakespeare, in about 1595, we must, I think, take the measure of what he imagines here: he imagines the limits of art, he confronts himself with "[t]he undiscovered country from whose bourn / No traveller returns" (*Ham.* 3.1.81-82), even if it is not yet *Hamlet* that he is writing, and thus acknowledges what it will be like to write the new play.

Here emerges, I think, the importance of the topicality of *Love's Labour's Lost*. For efficiency's and convenience's sake, I quote the summary in the Norton edition (733-4):

> A similar mixture of levity and gravity characterizes the contemporary political events that lie behind the play, events that assume importance given the virtual absence of literary sources for the plot. The comedy's King of Navarre is partly based on King Henry of Navarre, who established a philosophical academy, had been accused of withdrawing from life, and became King Henry IV of France in 1589. His three courtiers are named for three of the historical king's aristocratic contemporaries, two of whom (Biron and Dumaine in the play) served him. The figure of the Princess may draw on a French princess, Marguerite de Valois, daughter of King Henry II of France. Marguerite was already Henry Navarre's estranged wife when she led an embassy of reconciliation to him in 1578, accompanied by her famous ladies-in-waiting. As in

Love's Labour's Lost, one topic of discussion was "Aquitaine, a dowry for a queen" (2.1.8).

The negotiations between Henry and Marguerite proceeded amid pastoral aristocrat festivity combined with rampant adultery that made a mockery of the vows of reconciliation. Contemporaries believed that this oath-breaking caused the renewal of France's Wars of Religion (1562-98), the long-running bloody conflict between rival Protestant and Catholic aristocratic factions alluded to in the play's martial imagery, its "civil war of wits" (2.1.225). Among the characters *of Love's Labour's Lost,* not only the King and his courtiers, but also Boyet, Mercadé, and perhaps Mote have prominent namesakes from these civil wars. To end the religious antagonisms and to secure his claim on the French throne, Henry converted to Catholicism in 1593, a further oath-breaking that produced harsh, if temporary, criticism in Protestant England, where he had been extremely popular. These, then, are the play's historical roots.

As if he had set himself the challenge to transmute history into play, Shakespeare assumed a notorious circumstance of recent events in France as a test for how far art may go in the metamorphosis of history into language for language's sake. Note that I am not arguing that the play is an allegory or a *roman à clef* or any type of covert tract. I am arguing rather that it is topical for topicality's sake, that is, to have topicality to experiment with (the play after next, in the Oxford chronology, *Richard II,* will demonstrate just what Shakespeare has learned with his experiment).[2] The new play, Shakespeare concluded, I think, will usually insult the prescriptive line between history and art, showing again and again how like each other they are and, at the same time, how treacherous that likeness can be. "A speaks not *like* a man of God his making" (*LLL* 5.2.523), for all that it appears in a highly wrought comedy, almost a farce, is still one of Shakespeare's most sobering observations about humanity and language — indeed, more than sobering, almost terrifying, when we consider the legions who have been slain in human history for, allegedly, "speak[ing] not like a man of God his making."[3]

Love's Labour's Lost is a difficult play, challenging any normative interpretation, just in the measure to which it overlays historical circumstance with improbable rhetorical excess and shows, thus, their near intimacy. What troubles us is not the play's apparent *silliness* but its *apparent* silliness. It is, Shakespeare helps us to see, surprisingly easy to imagine nobility behaving as silly as the nobles do in *Love's Labour's Lost*.

Perhaps they and only they would swear an oath, pledge themselves to a prescript such as Navarre and his lords do, only to play out, and in, the contortions that they must then undergo to "negotiate" (their way out of) such oaths. It is perhaps only death that is *un*like enough to "interrupt… [such] merriment."[4]

Understood in this way, the play is not only a critique of prescriptiveness, it is also a rational assessment of the cost thereof: love's labors are lost. If every likeness you can imagine likening yourself to is already prescribed, if spontaneity is impossible, so that you cannot suddenly, fortuitously (and felicitously?) like someone or something that is new on your horizon, the loss of like's labors will surely lead to the loss of love's, too. The play demonstrates that spontaneity *is* possible:

> **BOYET** If my observation, which very seldom lies,
> By the heart's still rhetoric disclosèd with eyes,
> Deceive me not now, Navarre is infected.
> **PRINCESS** With what?
> **BOYET** With that which we lovers entitle 'affected'.
> **PRINCESS** Your reason?
> **BOYET** Why, all his behaviours did make their retire
> To the court of his eye, peeping thorough desire.
> *His heart like an agate with your print impressed,*
> Proud with his form, in his eye pride expressed.
> His tongue, all impatient to speak and not see,
> Did stumble with haste in his eyesight to be.
> …
> **PRINCESS** Come, to our pavilion. Boyet is disposed.
> **BOYET** But to speak that in words which his eye hath disclosed.
> I only have made *a mouth of his eye*
> By adding a tongue, which I know will not lie.
> LLL 2.1.228-39; 250-3 (emphasis added)

Here the word *like* functions with utmost Shakespearean precision to inform us that the inescapable mystery has transpired again: "His heart *like* an agate with your print impressed"—likeness is laboring in behalf of love and its labors. And the fruit of that labor is an unambiguous, though rhetorically ornate, acknowledgment of mutuality:

> **BIRON** Which parti-coated presence of loose love
> Put on by us, if in your heavenly eyes
> Have misbecomed our oaths and gravities,
> Those heavenly eyes that look into these faults

> *Suggested us to make them. Therefore, ladies,*
> *Our love being yours, the error that love makes*
> *Is likewise yours.* We to ourselves prove false
> By being once false for ever to be true
> To those that make us both — fair ladies, you.
> *And even that falsehood, in itself a sin,*
> *Thus purifies itself and turns to grace.*
>
> LLL 5.2.758-68 (emphasis added)

Perhaps not too little, it is still too late, as the Queen insists in the next breath, at least for now, but it is nonetheless a clear articulation of a position that Shakespeare will keep in view his entire career. Thus, for example, Isabella, in *Measure for Measure*, laments

> Ignominy in ransom and free pardon
> Are of two houses; lawful mercy
> Is nothing kin to foul redemption.
>
> MM 2.4.112-14

only to learn in the course of this vexed and vexatious play the exquisite Shakespearean lesson, the lesson of the syneciotician, that she is mistaken —apparent opposites are frequently very close kin. It is, in fact, the position from which Shakespeare will be able eventually to write "[t]he readiness is all" (*Ham.* 5.2.168), and "[r]ipeness is all" (*Lr.* [1610] 5.2.11), *the prescript-less scripts of his art.*

10
"I cannot tell vat is 'like me'": Inventing a Likeness in The Second Henriad

> And make high majesty look like itself.
> *RII* 2.1.297

> Your majesty came not like yourself.
> *HV* 4.8.51

Between 1595 and 1599 (we think), Shakespeare wrote four plays, among others, now commonly referred to by professional Shakespeareans as the Second Tetralogy or the Second Henriad: *Richard II* (1595); *1 Henry IV* (1596-7), *2 Henry IV* (1597-8), and *Henry V* (1598-9).[1] Two of these plays are among the most famous in world drama: *1 Henry IV* and *Henry V*. And they and *2 Henry IV* contain one of the most unforgettable characters in world drama, Sir John Falstaff. For the Second Henriad (my preferred designation), Shakespeare's theater and theory of likeness are crucial intellectual structures, indispensable, I think, to the realization, above all, of the relationship between Hal and Falstaff, one of the most improbable, and (as Hal finally believes) ultimately impossible, couples ever imagined.

All four plays, but especially *1HIV* and *HV*, depend upon binarism; Shakespeare exploits doubling and likening throughout the plays. In corroboration, consider the following, partial list:

> **SIR JOHN** Thou hast the most unsavoury *similes*, and art indeed the most *comparative*, rascalliest, sweet young Prince.
> *1HIV* 1.2.79-81 (emphasis added)

> **SIR JOHN** O, thou hast damnable *iteration*, and art indeed able to corrupt a saint.
> *1HIV* 1.2.90-91 (emphasis added)

94   "I cannot tell vat is 'like me'"

> **PRINCE HARRY** And *like* bright metal on a sullen ground,
> My reformation, glitt'ring o'er my fault,
> Shall show more goodly and attract more eyes
> Than that which hath no *foil* to set it off.
> 1HIV 1.2.209-12 (emphasis added)

> **SIR JOHN** 'Sblood, you starveling, you elf-skin, you dried
> neat's tongue, you bull's pizzle, you stock-fish — O, for
> breath to utter what is *like* thee! — you tailor's yard,
> you sheath, you bow-case, you vile standing tuck —
> **PRINCE HARRY** Well, breathe awhile, and then to't again,
> and when thou hast tired thyself in base *comparisons*,
> hear me speak but this.
> 1HIV 2.5.248-54 (emphasis added)

These and other passages suggest that the Second Henriad is a group of plays about comparison itself, how it works and in what it results. More specifically, the group is about the function of comparison in inventing a likeness, "to utter what is like thee!" And when, near the very end of the group (*HV* 5.2.106-8), Katherine replies to Hal's, "[d]o you like me?" with "I cannot tell vat is 'like me'," Shakespeare is ready to imagine Brutus, Hamlet, Troilus.

One of the more memorable moments of binarism and comparison in *Henry V* is a famous speech, often discussed, in act 4 by Fluellen:

> **FLUELLEN** ... what call you the town's name where Alexander the
> Pig was born?
> **GOWER** Alexander the Great.
> **FLUELLEN** Why I pray you, is not "pig" great? The pig or
> the great or the mighty or the huge or the
> magnanimous are all one reckonings, save the phrase
> is a little variations.
> ...
> I tell you, captain, if you look in the maps of the
> world I warrant you sall find, in the *comparisons*
> between Macedon and Monmouth, that the situations,
> look you, is both *alike*...'tis *alike* as my fingers is to my fingers,...
> If you mark Alexander's life well,
> Harry of Monmouth's life is *come after it indifferent*
> *well. For there is figures in all things*...
> I speak but in the *figures and comparisons* of
> it. As Alexander killed his friend Cleitus, being in his

ales and his cups, so also Harry Monmouth, being in
his right wits and his good judgements, turned away
the fat knight with the great-belly doublet ...
I have forgot his name.
> HV 4.7.12-18; 22-25; 29; 30-32; 42-48 (emphasis added)

Fluellen is an eloquent, if not exactly elegant, spokesman for the exemplarity of history (see the Introduction 3-4), "[f]or there is figures in all things." Reading King Henry's life as a copy of Alexander the "Pig"'s ("the situations, look you, is both alike"), Fluellen represents a historiography that Shakespeare is on the verge of abandoning, never to return to it again — exemplarity is more complicated than it appears in the "mirrors for princes" and likeness is not as "alike as my fingers is to my fingers." To the contrary, likeness is more like the phoneme, as in "b" and "p," or the minimal distinctive unit of sound, where, crucially, both likeness and difference cohere together in a binary or differential relationship.[2] Shakespeare brilliantly exploits Fluellen's pronunciation gaffes to call attention to the problem of comparison and the crisis of likeness—comparison and likeness function *because of* difference (as in the phoneme), because " 'tis [*not*] alike as my fingers is to my fingers." There is no escaping the operation, logical or physical, of difference:

> The consequence we seeke to draw from the conference of events, is unsure, because they are ever dissemblable. No quality is so universall in this surface of things, as variety and diversity. The Greekes, the Latines, and wee use for the most expresses examples of similitude, that of egs. Some have nethelesse beene found, especially one in *Delphos*, that knew markes of difference betweene egges, and never tooke one for another. And having divers hennes, could rightly judge which had laid the egge. Dissimilitude doth of it selfe insinuate into our workes, no arte can come neere unto similitude. Resemblance doth not so much make one, as difference maketh another. Nature hath bound herselfe to make nothing that may not be dissemblable.
> Montaigne, "Of Experience" (Florio 322; Frame 815)

To say that any two things are alike is also to say that they are unlike —"no arte can come neere unto similitude."

The fatal mistake of Richard II was to neglect that "[r]esemblance doth not so much make one, as difference maketh another. Nature hath bound herselfe to make nothing that may not be dissemblable."

> For you have but mistook me all this while.
> I live with bread, *like* you; feel want,
> Taste grief, need friends. Subjected thus,
> How can you say to me I am a king?
> RII 3.2.170-3 (emphasis added)

Too little, too late. Richard cannot now plead likeness (similitude), having so prodigally and arrogantly traded for so long on difference (especially the divine sanction that, as he insists, distinguishes him—*RII* 3.2.50-53, e.g.). Everyone knows he is "dissemblable." His pun, "*subject*ed thus," which signals the difference of his wit and his breeding, betrays him: he knows (very well) the difference between a subject and a king—his question, in the worst sense applicable, is rhetorical, aimed at no one but himself.

The difference between a subject and a king, as Richard well knows, is place or position: the subject knows his place; the king (supposedly) knows his. But Richard neglected to remember that place is largely a fiction (if, admittedly, an enforced fiction), a fact that Henry V, to the contrary, never lets out of his sight:

> **WILLIAMS** Your majesty came not *like* yourself. *You appeared to me but as a common man*. Witness the night, your garments, your lowliness. And what your highness *suffered under that shape*, I beseech you take it for your own fault, and not mine, for had you been *as I took you for*, I made no offence.
> HV 4.8.51-56 (emphasis added)³

Henry's is the genius to know when to come "not like him[self]," when to change the fiction. Henry is like the unnamed king whom Montaigne describes in his *Essays*—in Florio's words, "[t]he likeliest a man may one day conclude of him, shall be that he affected and laboured to make himselfe knowne *by being not to be knowne*" (336; Frame, 825; emphasis added). Henry knows, what Richard acknowledges only too late, that no man is like himself except as and because he is different from himself. Indeed, it is this knowledge that enables him to disguise himself and pose to Bates, Court, and Williams the night before St. Crispin's day that "I think the King is but a man, as I am. ... His ceremonies laid by, in his nakedness he appears but a man" (*HV* 4.1.101-2; 104-5). This pose is obviously the pose of a man who has not forgotten his place (only changed his cloak)—

> And what have kings that privates have not too,
> Save ceremony ...?
> O ceremony, show me but thy worth.
> What is thy soul of adoration?
> Art thou aught else but *place, degree, and form,*
> Creating awe and fear in other men?
>
> HV 4.1.235-6; 241-4 (emphasis added)

Henry V is never not conscious of "place, degree, and form," however he may for the moment lament the lot of kings, which is why he can "lay [them] by"—unlike Richard, who assumes that they are his by divine right and cannot therefore lay them by until they are forcibly reft from him. When Henry rewards Williams after the latter's plea in his defense (*HV* 4.8.46-51), he gives him crowns, but the crowns do not crown Williams, they do not change his place; to the contrary, they merely reinforce the ceremony, the fiction, of Henry's place—

> Here, Uncle Exeter, fill this glove with crowns
> And give it to this fellow. — Keep it, fellow,
> And wear it for an honour in thy cap
> *Till I do challenge it.* — Give him the crowns.
>
> HV 4.8.58-61 (emphasis added)

Perhaps, it should be emphasized that they thus also, in Henry's thought, at least, reinforce the place of fiction.

Famously, Elizabeth I objected to the performance of *Richard II*; Richard was childless like her and also deposed, as she feared she might be (Norton 943-4). But unlike her, Richard was unable to persuade his people that he loved them.[4] Richard was always too different (and, unlike Elizabeth, could not exploit the difference of gender, at which she was expert, especially when it came to dallying with suitors). The historical Richard, evidence suggests, harbored absolutist, tyrannical designs (Saul 366, e.g.), but Shakespeare's Richard is absolutist in his very being. And this absolutism is nowhere so evident as it is in his obsession with the ceremony, the ritual, of his kingship—for example,

> Not all the water in the rough rude sea
> Can wash the balm from an anointed king.
> The breath of worldly men cannot depose
> The deputy elected by the Lord.
>
> RII 3.2.50-53 (see also RII 3.3.76-89)

98   "I cannot tell vat is 'like me'"

Richard thinks he *is* what he is but like. He is (con)fused, and has let himself be so, with the likenesses in which he appears. In him Shakespeare imagines, as he does in other characters, too (Angelo, in *Measure for Measure*, for example), a character who would *be* what in reality he can only be *like* (see *MM* 3.1.474-5). Richard deliberately ignores and has become oblivious to the fiction of his reality until Bolingbroke compels him to confront the reality of his fiction:

> I have no name, no title,
> No, not that name was given me at the font,
> But 'tis usurped. Alack the heavy day,
> That I have worn so many winters out
> And know not now what name to call myself!
> O, that I were *a mockery king of snow*,
> Standing before the sun of Bolingbroke
> To melt myself away in water-drops!
> Good king, great king — and yet not greatly good —
> An if my word be sterling yet in England,
> Let it command a mirror hither straight,
> That it may show me what a face I have,
> Since it is bankrupt of his majesty.
>   *RII* 4.1.245-57 (emphasis added)

Only when it can serve him no purpose at all can Richard acknowledge that his name, all names, are *given*, conventional, and, as conventional, mutable utterly.

Hence, the importance of the justly famous scene with the mirror that follows:

> **RICHARD** They [the Commons] shall be satisfied. I'll read enough
> When I do see *the very book indeed*
> Where all my sins are writ, *and that's myself.*
>   *Enter one with a glass*
> Give me that glass, and therein will I read.
>   *Richard takes the glass and looks in it*
> No deeper wrinkles yet? Hath sorrow struck
> So many blows upon this <u>face</u> of mine
> And made no deeper wounds? O flatt'ring glass,
> *Like* to my followers in prosperity,
> *Thou dost beguile me!* Was this <u>face</u> the <u>face</u>
> That every day under his household roof
> Did keep ten thousand men? Was this the <u>face</u>

That *like* the sun did make beholders wink?
Is this the <u>face</u> which <u>face</u>d so many follies,
That was at last out<u>face</u>d by Bolingbroke?
A brittle glory shineth in this <u>face</u>.
As brittle as the glory is the <u>face</u>,
    He shatters the glass
For there it is, cracked in an hundred shivers.
Mark, silent King, the moral of this sport:
How soon my sorrow hath destroyed my <u>face</u>.
                    RII 4.1.263-81 (emphasis added)

Here is the theater of likeness as Shakespeare has come by 1595 to understand and practice it: seeing his likeness in the mirror,[5] Richard knows it for a likeness, and nothing more (the *ploce* on <u>face</u> [10 repetitions] exquisitely emphasizes the point—whatever the face may be, the "face" has no certain, fixed meaning). And, as he admits a few lines later (*RII* 4.1.289-92), Bolingbroke also teaches him as much: "The shadow of your sorrow hath destroyed / The shadow of your face" (*RII* 4.1.282-3).

Richard, famously in Shakespeare's writings, laments:

Thoughts tending to content flatter themselves
That they are not the first of fortune's slaves,
Nor shall not be the last — *like* seely beggars,
Who, sitting in the stocks, refuge their shame
That many have, and others must, set there;
And in this thought they find a kind of ease,
Bearing their own misfortunes *on the back*
Of such as have *before endured the like*.
Thus play I in one person many people,
And none contented. Sometimes am I king;
Then treason makes me wish myself a beggar,
And so I am. Then crushing penury
Persuades me I was better when a king.
Then am I kinged again, and by and by
Think that I am unkinged by Bolingbroke,
And straight am nothing. But whate'er I be,
Nor I, nor any man that but man is,
With nothing shall be pleased till he be eased
With being nothing.
                    RII 5.5.23-41 (emphasis added)

Some of the most moving poetry in English, this speech also, I think, continues Shakespeare's farewell to exemplariness ("on the back/Of such as have before endured the like") and marks his increasing acceptance of the theatricality of human likeness—"Thus play I in one person many people." And yet, Richard learned too late that

> All the world's a stage,
> And all the men and women merely players.
> They have their exits and their entrances,
> And one man in his time plays many parts.
>
> *AYL* 2.7.139-42

He learned too late to "sit upon the ground/And tell sad stories of the death of kings" (*RII* 3.2.151-2), examples of no avail to him at all in a "mirror for princes" he largely ignored.[6] He learned too late that

> ... nothing can we call our own but death,
> And that small *model* of the barren earth
> Which serves as paste and cover to our bones.
>
> *RII* 3.2.148-50 (emphasis added)

He learned too late the trick of

> ... perspectives, which, rightly gazed upon,
> Show nothing but confusion; eyed awry,
> Distinguish form.
>
> *RII* 2.2.18-20

Thinking the king (himself) exempt, he denied that every subject is a "perspective" that must be "I'd" awry to "[d]istinguish form" since "rightly gazed upon," he or she "[s]how[s] nothing but confusion."[7] But Shakespeare learned, and with astonishing speed, when we stop to think about it, how to write, for example,

> But whate'er I be,
> Nor I, nor any man that but man is,
> With nothing shall be pleased till he be eased
> With being nothing
>
> *RII* 5.5.38-41,

where the coupling and the crossing (juxta-form and cruci-lingual) of the synecioticians shows us (we see [θεα]) the theater and the theory of likeness:

"nothing...be pleased...be eased...being nothing" — words so alike, nearly mirroring each other, that yet bear such a differential of meaning.[8]

※

If Richard learns only too late the play of difference in likeness, Henry V never forgets this datum so differential to his play for ascendancy to the throne:

> *Percy is but my factor*, good my lord,
> To engross up glorious deeds *on my behalf*;
> And I will call him to so strict account
> That he shall *render every glory up*.
> *1HIV* 3.2.147-50 (emphasis added)

> I am the Prince of Wales; and *think not, Percy,*
> *To share with me in glory any more.*
> Two stars keep not their motion in one sphere,
> Nor can one England brook *a double reign*
> Of Harry Percy and the Prince of Wales.
> *1HIV* 5.4.62-66 (emphasis added)

Indeed, Hal is a student of difference:

> The Prince but studies his companions,
> *Like* a strange tongue, wherein, to gain the language,
> 'Tis needful that the most immodest word
> Be looked upon and learnt, which once attained,
> Your highness knows, comes to no further use
> But to be known and hated; so, *like* gross terms,
> The Prince will in the perfectness of time
> Cast off his followers, and their memory
> Shall as *a pattern or a measure* live
> By which his grace must *mete the lives of other*,
> Turning past evils to advantages.
> *2HIV* 4.3.68-78 (emphasis added)

Hal studies what it would be like to be like other men, but only so as to be different from them — only so as finally to be a student of difference itself (and not just a reveler in it, like Richard). For only thus can he finally achieve that tautology which secures his identity as king: "Not Amurath an Amurath succeeds [says Hal to his brothers when Henry IV has died],/

But Harry Harry" (*2HIV* 5.2.48-49), where the syntax of succession barely conceals the paradigm of tautological equivalence—"Harry Harry"—which is then repeated by the Chorus in the opening of *Henry V*, "warlike Harry, like himself" (*HV* Prol 5). Now like himself, warlike Harry knows that there must be no double, no rival, no repetition of himself except himself. He does not make Richard's mistake, of leaving a double (Bolingbroke, Hal's father) with enough power to take his place.[9] If there is no one like him but himself, if no one can imitate him though he can imitate anyone, if no one can represent him though he can represent anyone, then Henry V is king indeed, one and singular, without peer—he is, in effect, God (nor was godhead from his thought).

But this is a perilous condition, for his body is a man's, and will die therefore like any man's. Hence there must be a son, to continue the succession or, much more precise, to secure and preserve the tautology.[10] Hence also the final act of *Henry V*, the act that subverts Fluellen's peroratorical exemplariness and its would-be final evocation of Alexander the Pig (in Act 4). The play cannot close here where a certain generic expectation would be satisfied, as though Alexander were the "mirror" for Prince Hal. Rather it must close with a marriage, or the embodiment of comparison, comparison of man and woman, which satisfies a different and ultimately more problematic expectation. How does the peerless, singular and one, king without rival, represent himself? how does he reproduce himself? can he escape from the process of comparison and become (the) transcendental?

"Do you like me, Kate?" asks Harry. "*Pardonnez-moi*, [she responds] I cannot tell vat is 'like me'" (*HV* 5.2.106-8). So Shakespeare dissolves the tautology of Harry the Fifth. Of course, Kate means that she does not understand the English words "like me," but Shakespeare, in addition, means that Harry's question is a massive self-subversion and ultimately a self-betrayal. No one likes the king because no one is like the king—after all, did not the king break the heart of "the fat knight with the great-belly doublet ... I have [says Fluellen] forgot his name" (*HV* 4.7.46-48)? Did not the king destroy his likenesses, Falstaff and Hotspur? Indeed, the king has no likeness, as history will only too bitterly prove when Henry VI ascends the throne and helps to plunge England into the crisis of the Wars of the Roses. The king is so different that no one can tell, recall now Falstaff's breathless harangue, what is "like [him]" (*1HIV* 2.5.250). The king is alone.

This, I take it, is a major part of the Hal-Falstaff subplot. For all the wonder, the humane expanse, of Falstaff, Shakespeare is also interested in the paradox Falstaff coupled with Hal represents. When Hal stands between the bodies of Hotspur and Falstaff, thinking them both dead, we may see an early modern "mirror" of princely moderation, how the prince should steer between two forms of excess or immoderation, but in this *Fürstenspiegel* exemplum, Shakespeare also sees (and shows) the solitariness of the prince, his separateness from the likes of his fellow men. And he also sees and shows, in the same exemplum, how constructed that separateness is, how much it depends upon fiction and the power that enforces fiction. What Richard thought was divine right, sanctioned by chrism, Hal knows is a function of language and its manipulability, its difference:

> O, I should have a heavy miss of thee,
> If I were much in love with vanity.
> Death hath not struck so fat a deer today,
> Though many dearer in this bloody fray.
>
> 1HIV 5.4.104-7

Hal's puns are exactly what he thinks not only of Falstaff but also of power —it's all in how you trope it. Little wonder he finds it so easy to banish Falstaff:

> I know thee not, old man. Fall to thy prayers.
> How ill white hairs becomes a fool and jester!
> I have long dreamt of such a kind of man,
> So surfeit-swelled, so old, and so profane;
> But being awake, I do despise my dream.[11]
> ...
> Presume not that I am the thing I was,
> For God doth know, so shall the world perceive,
> That *I have turned away my former self*;
> So will I those that kept me company.
>
> 2HIV 5.4.47-51; 56-59 (emphasis added)

Hal can "turn" (the basic sense of "trope") anyway anything anytime, from words (puns) to Falstaff to his former self. Today we call it "spin" —Shakespeare's Hal was one of its first great "doctors":

> And *like* bright metal on a sullen ground,
> My reformation, glitt'ring o'er my fault,
> Shall show more goodly and attract more eyes
> Than that which hath no *foil* to set it off.
>
> 1HIV 1.2.209-12 (emphasis added)

But the "spin" is wobbly. To be king, Hal must be singular. But to be king, Hal must have not only a "foil" but also an heir. The contradiction is non-negotiable. Because he must marry he is therefore not singular and, precisely, not king—he will, in time, be replaced, having (been) reproduced. The transcendental is almost achieved but cannot in the end escape comparison and its materiality, the materiality in particular of genealogical succession. We may, if we like, call such a situation as this ironic. Certainly, irony is an applicable term when Isabella of France concludes the final act, saying:

> As man and wife, being two, are one in love,
> So be there 'twixt your kingdoms such a spousal
> That never may ill office or fell jealousy,
> Which troubles oft the bed of blessèd marriage,
> Thrust in between the paction of these kingdoms
> To make divorce of their incorporate league;
> That English may as French, French Englishmen,
> Receive each other.
>
> HV 5.2.356-63

Just a few years hence, catastrophic wars will none the less "make divorce of their incorporate league." But I think it is also true that we feel something here that is more complex than irony. The rhetorical effect is one of a coupling of differences—Harry and Kate, England and France—so irremediably different that every alleged effect of that coupling can only be its opposite. And the explicit figure in Isabella's speech of sexual violence only deepens the complexity. The phrase "[t]hrust in between" is a choice of words that helplessly evokes the *in*escapable "[t]hrust[ing] in between" of sex (if there is to be a marriage at all) which foreshadows the "[t]hrust[ing] in between" of the wars between France and England. "Thrust[ing] in between" is "together at home with" (*syneciosis*) both sex and war and contaminates each with the other—the difference becomes the likeness. Shakespeare the syneciotician both acknowledges the greatness of the warrior-king Henry V and at the same time knows that he will not live long (he died at 35). And the style of the syneciotician exactly answers to this knowledge, thrusting in between likeness and difference (juxta-form and cruci-lingual).

11
"I'll look to like": Death and Discourse in *Romeo and Juliet*

> Till we can clear these ambiguities.
> *Romeo and Juliet* 5.3.216

Romeo and Juliet is a play not only of, but also about, ambiguity. Not in the sense that some might chastise as "new-critical" or "Empsonian," nor even, at least exclusively, in the sense of "in utramque partem," but in a robust and philosophically non-trivial sense of epistemological crisis, occasioned, at least proximately, by early modern skepticism; we can see that this early tragedy already demonstrates Shakespeare's concern with problems of knowing and, especially, of knowing by *like*ness (Cavell 1-37). What in the mature tragedies—say, *Hamlet* or *Othello*—will emerge as despair of certitude and refusal of the world appears already in *Romeo and Juliet*, if only proleptically, as retreat into intimacy and nearly complete eroticization of discourse. Since no one can be a self in the world without submitting to the conventions of the world, a being-spoken-by-the-world, Romeo and Juliet choose instead to be subjects of love by subjecting their language and, ultimately, their lives to a discourse that is effectively intercourse and an intercourse that aspires to the condition of discourse, a "concrete universal," that defies conventionalization, that refuses any and all being-spoken-by.[1] That the consequence of this choice should finally bear the likeness of death (*Rom.* 4.1.104) must come as no surprise to the student of Western thought who has observed the tradition of that thought repeatedly frustrated by what Heidegger, for example, calls "Das Man."[2] The likeness of unity costs also the unity of one's likeness: Romeo and Juliet cannot both and at the same time love each other to the exclusion of the world ("the they") and remain in the world Montague and Capulet, Veronese and Italian—the "concrete universal," if "concrete," is not universal; if "universal," is not concrete.

We may see the problem initially in the famous first scene of act 2:

> **ROMEO** *Had I it* [viz., my name] *written, I would tear the word.*
> **JULIET** My ears have not yet drunk a hundred words
> Of thy tongue's uttering, yet I know the sound.
> Art thou not Romeo, and a Montague?
> **ROMEO** Neither, fair maid, *if either thee dislike.*
>
> *Rom.* 2.1.99-103 (emphasis added)

Romeo would disassimilate himself—un*like*n himself—from his names "if either [Juliet] dislike." Here is Shakespeare's theater of likeness, in the exquisite ambiguity of the syntax: "if either displease thee" *or* "if either dis/like thee," that is, if either name interferes with the likeness to Juliet such that he may not (be) like Juliet and she may not (be) like him. The names "Romeo" and "Montague" bind Romeo to a time and a place and a history that, with the force of "the they" ("Das Man"), dis/like Juliet. Had he written it, he declares, with ominous insight, he would tear either word, but, and again Shakespeare's theater of likeness thrills our attention, it is *not* he who has written the pre-scripts (and prescriptives) by which he enters into the world with a family, a home, a city, a country, etc, already constituted. No one has written the word of his own origin, though every one sooner or later must tear the word of her origin *as if* s/he had written it—thus Hamlet, an obvious example as well.[3]

Shakespeare's theater of likeness dramatizes first and foremost the crisis of likeness, or the choice of the other by which I will seek, or invent, my likeness, or both. Whom shall I (be) like? is the question driving all of Shakespeare's characters at some point or other. Hence the importance of the early exchange between Lady Capulet and Juliet from which I draw the title of this chapter:

> **CAPULET'S WIFE** *(to Juliet)* Speak briefly: can you *like of* Paris' love?
> **JULIET** I'll *look to like, if looking liking move*;
> But no more deep will I endart mine eye
> Than your consent gives strength to make it fly.
>
> *Rom.* 1.3.98-101 (emphasis added)

Note first that Juliet's response acknowledges the prescript and the prescriptive, "your consent," that binds her choice: her parents, and especially her father, soon to be enraged at her independence, dictate and prescribe her "liking"—her choice is not free. Note next the extraordinary eroticism of "endart," as if her eye were penile to penetrate an object of liking, already an omen of her burgeoning sexuality and her willfulness, her transgressiveness. And, finally, note the work of *like*. Her mother's "like of," no doubt unwittingly, marks already the fissure, the gap, that will betray her and Juliet alike: Juliet cannot (be the) like of Paris; at most, she can look to like, and if looking inspire liking, then she may to a certain depth endart her eye, but not otherwise.

We must, I think, pause over the precision of Shakespeare's vocabulary of likeness. If we learn to listen for *like*, we hear a lifelong sounding of the problem of identity in a world of copies (/*copia*). We become conversant in a vocabulary that subtly but insistently alerts us to the threat of duplication, reductive reiteration:

> **CHORUS** *Two* households, both *alike* in dignity
>   In fair Verona, ...
> From forth the fatal loins of these *two* foes
>   A *pair* of star-crossed lovers take their life.
> Prologue 1-2; 5-6 (emphasis added)

> **CAPULET** But Montague is bound as well as I,
> In penalty *alike*...
> *Rom.* 1.2.1-2 (emphasis added)

It is the *like*ness, not the difference, of the houses of Montague and Capulet that brings tragedy down upon them. But the theater of likeness also shows us always that likeness is *not* identity—where there is likeness, there is also, necessarily, difference.[4] Hence, if their likeness penalizes Montague and Capulet, this is also to say and to see that it does so by obscuring their difference from each other. Shakespeare's art is concerned with the emergence of difference from likeness and the cost, often tragic in its proportions, of such an emergency. Friar Laurence provides us a working vocabulary for the thesis:

> The earth, that's nature's mother, is her tomb.
> What is her burying grave, that is her womb,
> And from her womb children of divers kind
> We sucking on her natural bosom find,
> Many for many virtues excellent,
> None but for some, *and yet all different*.
> O mickle is the powerful grace that lies
> In plants, herbs, stones, and their true qualities,
> For naught so *vile* that on the earth doth *live*
> But to the earth some special good doth give;
> Nor aught so good but, strained from that fair use,
> Revolts from true birth, stumbling on abuse.
> *Rom.* 2.2.9-20 (emphasis added)

Shakespeare's theater of likeness time and again sorts (and stor[e]s) these reciprocities (juxta-form and cruci-lingual): it sees and says, for example, that –v-i-l-e– and –l-i-v-e– are, anagrammatically, *alike*, made of the same letters (which also spell –e-v-i-l–), "and yet all different."[5] Required is an intelligence of distinction, to "choose" or "select" (ultimately the root meanings of "intelligence"[6]) the differences within likenesses, which, note well, implies having recognized the likenesses already. But such intelligence is also finally no guarantee of success, much less happiness. If "[m]y grave is *like* to be my wedding bed" (*Rom.* 1.5.134; emphasis added), if "[m]y only love [is] sprung from my only hate" (*Rom.* 1.5.137), if "[m]y life is my foe's debt" (*Rom.* 1.5.117), how can I possibly "select" or "sort" the parts of such a confusion, even if "passion ... [should]/Temp[er] extremities with extreme sweet" (*Rom.* 2.0.13-14)? To separate a part of such confusion apart from the lump is possible in some cases perhaps—

> **BENVOLIO** While we were interchanging thrusts and blows,
> Came more and more, and *fought on part and part*
> Till the Prince came, *who parted either part*.
>   *Rom.* 1.1.110-12 (emphasis added)

—but there are other cases too hard for any authority, prince or poet, to sort.

And yet the imperative *is* to sort, to distinguish—to render each her due, if we should elect to express it in juridical terms. Hence the extraordinary emphasis on comparing and contrasting in the early scenes of the play:

> **ROMEO** Show me a mistress that is passing fair,
> What doth her beauty serve but as a note
> Where I may read who *passed that passing fair*?
>   *Rom.* 1.1.231-3

> **BENVOLIO** Go thither, and with unattainted eye
> *Compare* her face with some that I shall show,
> And *I will make thee think thy swan a crow*.
>   *Rom.* 1.2.87-89

> **BENVOLIO** Tut, you saw her fair, none else being by,
> *Herself poised with herself in either eye*;
> But in that crystal scales let there be *weighed*
> Your lady's love against some other maid
> That I will show you shining at this feast,
> And she shall scant show well that now seems best.
>   *Rom.* 1.2.96-101 (emphasis added)

The play establishes very early on that the dilemma is one of distinguishing, separating, sorting, so that we do not—ought not?—confront the case of "[h]erself poised with herself in either eye [I]." From the beginning of his career, Shakespeare relentlessly demands that poetry, verbal art, manage to name not just, or even most importantly, properly, but also inw*o*rdly:

> **JULIET** *What's in a name?*
> ...
> Romeo, doff thy name,
> And for *thy name* — *which is no part of thee* —
> Take all myself.
> **ROMEO** *(to Juliet) I take thee at thy word.*
> *Call me but love* and I'll be *new baptized.*
> Henceforth I never will be Romeo.
> *Rom.* 2.1.85; 89-93 (emphasis added)

If "[t]hat which we call a rose/By any other word would smell as sweet" (*Rom.* 2.1.85-86), then *rose* is not the inward word (the inw*o*rd *name*⁷) of the flower. What, after all, does a –n-a-m-e- -m-e-a-n- ? Why is –r-o-s-e- *not* –e-r-o-s- ? What if -R-o-m-e-o- were –(H)-o-m-e-r-o- ? (He speaks in poetry, does he not?) His name is precisely "no part of" him since any man could be named "Romeo." "Romeo," then, is not his inw*o*rd name. "I take thee at thy word./Call me but love and I'll be new baptized." But, immediately we hear him speak this, we know that neither is "love" his inw*o*rd name since it, too, may be predicated of anyone. The inw*o*rd name, then, the name which truly and definitively distinguishes one from many, must be a name we do not yet comprehend.

Possibly, it is a name that does not exist. Possibly, it is the fate of every name, every word, to be only ab–out that of which it is predicated. "The worst is not / So long as we can say 'This is the worst'" (*Lr.* [1610] 4.1.28-29), since, if we can still say "this is the worst," we are still ab–out, mediated to, the worst, and do not yet actually feel the worst that, presumably, would strike us dumb, hopelessly mute, once we had felt it. If Romeo can exclaim (*Rom.* 3.3.104-7),

> O tell me, friar, tell me,
> In what vile part of this anatomy
> Doth my name lodge? Tell me, that I may sack
> The hateful mansion,

he cannot, at the same time, or so it appears, comprehend that if the "hateful mansion" can be sacked, another name can find another lodging easily enough in him—if, that is, names are not inw*o*rd, but merely wandering travelers colonizing property and persons as they go.

What, then, does a |n|a|m|e| |m|e|a|n|? In this question, we discover, I suggest, one reason, not the least important one, why Shakespeare's language is so restlessly self-referential, paranomasian, devious, adventitious, and syneciotic: he never tires of seeking the inw*o*rd name. *Romeo and Juliet* is notorious for its pyrotechnical verbal displays, especially in the early scenes (Romeo and Juliet speak to each other in an exquisite Shakespearean sonnet in the fourteen lines between 1.5.92 and 105). Most famous, perhaps, is Mercutio's Queen Mab speech, which is certainly appropriate (inw*o*rd?) to a character named after the Greco-Roman god of eloquence, Mercury; moreover, Mercutio utters, after receiving his mortal wound, one of the most memorable, if also (apparently) *in*appropriate, puns in the entire play: "Ask for me tomorrow, and you shall find me a grave man" (*Rom.* 3.1.97-98). If Romeo cannot quite match (copy?) Mercutio, he nevertheless holds his own (as we say):

> Why then, O brawling love, O loving hate,
> O anything of nothing first create;
> O heavy lightness, serious vanity,
> Misshapen chaos of well-seeming forms,
> Feather of lead, bright smoke, cold fire, sick health,
> Still-waking sleep, that is not what it is!
> This love feel I, that feel no love in this.
> ...
> Tut, I have lost myself. I am not here.
> This is not Romeo; he's some other where.
>
> *Rom.* 1.1.173-9; 194-5

Sounding like Jean de Meun and Francesco Petrarch, Romeo indulges paradoxes and oxymora until he has lost himself, "[t]his is not Romeo, he's some other where," anticipating the flight from his name to some as yet unknown inw*o*rdness that will dominate his behavior later in the play.[8] Nor is the pyrotechnical display restricted to male characters alone. Juliet exclaims, when her Nurse refuses to speak directly to the point:

> What devil art thou that dost torment me thus?
> This torture should be roared in dismal hell.
> Hath Romeo slain himself? Say thou but "Ay,"
> And that bare vowel "I" shall poison more
> Than the death-darting eye of cockatrice.
> I am not I if there be such an "Ay,"

Or those eyes shut that make thee answer "Ay."
If he be slain, say "Ay"; or if not, "No."
Brief sounds determine of my weal or woe.

Rom. 3.2.43-51

The changes she rings on "I" reverberate like a death-knell in the cold air of our anticipation. And when, later in the same scene (*Rom.* 3.2.124-6), she cries out,

"Romeo is banishèd" —
There is no end, no limit, measure, bound,
In that word's death. No words can that woe sound,

the pun in "sound" and the reversibility of the syntax of "[n]o words can that woe sound" ("no words can utter that woe"/"that woe can utter no words") convince us that she, as much as Romeo, has understood how inw_o_rd her love is.

But if we want to appreciate fully Shakespeare's restless inw_o_rdness in *Romeo and Juliet*, we perhaps do best to listen to the virtuoso exchange between Romeo and Mercutio after Romeo has fallen in love with Juliet:

MERCUTIO Signor Romeo, *bonjour*. There's a French
salutation to your French slop. You gave us the
counterfeit fairly last night.
ROMEO Good morrow to you both. What counterfeit did I
give you?
MERCUTIO The slip, sir, the slip. Can you not conceive?
ROMEO Pardon, good Mercutio. My business was great, and
in such a case as mine a man may strain courtesy.
MERCUTIO That's as much as to say such a case as yours
constrains a man to bow in the hams.
ROMEO Meaning to curtsy.
MERCUTIO Thou hast most kindly hit it.
ROMEO A most courteous exposition.
MERCUTIO Nay, *I am the very pink of courtesy*.
ROMEO Pink for flower.
MERCUTIO Right.
ROMEO Why, then is my pump well flowered.
MERCUTIO Sure wit, follow me this jest now till thou hast
worn out thy pump, that when the single sole of it is
worn, the jest may remain, after the wearing, solely
singular.

> **ROMEO** *O single-soled jest, solely singular for the singleness!*
> **MERCUTIO** Come between us, good Benvolio. My wits faints.
> **ROMEO** Switch and spurs, switch and spurs, *or I'll cry a match.*
>
> ...
>
> **MERCUTIO** Why, is not this better now than groaning for love? Now art thou sociable, now art thou Romeo, *now art thou what thou art by art* as well as by nature.
>
> Rom. 2.3.41-65; 81-83 (emphasis added)

The dizzying tick-tock of this exchange obviously arouses wonder and admiration and delight. It also, however, provides deep insight into Shakespeare's theater of likeness. "I am the very pink of courtesy"—i.e., incomparable; and this boast helps us hear the competition (comparison, likening) between Mercutio and Romeo; but once we have heard it, we also comprehend that adventitious invention deflects rivalry into more, and more creative, discourse, so that Romeo's "match," in "O single-soled jest, solely singular for the singleness," is discourse more intercourse than contention, more du*a*l than du*e*l—to use terms I have developed in my study of Milton, *Paradise Lost*, in particular (Shoaf, *Duality* 3ff.)— and the result is a certain "sociable[ness]." But we must not under-read Shakespeare's meaning or think automatically we know where we are and have everything under our purview. Of "sociable" Romeo Mercutio can say "now *art* thou Romeo, now *art* thou what thou *art* by *art*," where the fourfold repetition of "art" in two different senses teaches us that the inw*o*rdness of a name depends on art as well as nature, on a conscious and resolute praxis/poiesis of *like*ning oneself to one's name by all the resources of language available. Anything less and one falls into "the they," "Das Man."

If death and the language of death are so pervasive in *Romeo and Juliet*, the discourse of "the they"—family, state, church, institutionality itself—is, in great measure, to blame. Since there can be no discourse or intercourse totally private — the one would be incomprehensible, the other sterile—the children of Montague and Capulet can either deceive their families or die. Deceit having failed, they die, but their death, transpiring in Shakespeare's theater of likeness, reveals intricate relationships among death, discourse, and likeness, relationships that Shakespeare will examine again on more than one occasion in his career.

It is important first to recognize and understand that Juliet "dies" *before* she dies:

> **FRIAR LAURENCE** If, rather than to marry County Paris,

> Thou hast the strength of will to slay thyself,
> Then is it *likely* thou wilt undertake
> A thing *like* death to chide away this shame,
> That cop'st with death himself to scape from it.
>
> *Rom.* 4.1.71-75 (emphasis added)

FRIAR LAURENCE No warmth, no breath shall testify thou livest.
The roses in thy lips and cheeks shall fade
To wanny ashes, thy eyes' windows fall
Like death...

Rom. 4.1.98-101 (emphasis added)

FRIAR LAURENCE Each part, deprived of supple government,
Shall, stiff and stark and cold, *appear like death;*
And in *this borrowed likeness of shrunk death*
Thou shalt continue two-and-forty hours.

Rom. 4.1.102-5 (emphasis added)

Juliet dies *first* in language, as here in Friar Laurence's discourse. She "lives" in "this borrowed likeness of shrunk death/... two-and-forty hours" and thus looks like death as in a rehearsal of and for death. The genius of the play within Shakespeare's theater of likeness is to insist time and again on the likeness of Romeo and Juliet's lives to theater—everything is either rehearsal or performance, until death actually, literally, stops the show. Even Capulet, hardly sensitive to or conscious of his daughter's theater, contributes to it when he cries, "[d]eath *lies on her like* an untimely frost" (*Rom.* 4.4.55; emphasis added), where the pun in *lies* (one of the most exquisite in Shakespeare's entire theater of likeness, in my opinion) continues the insistence on fiction and drama. Discursive death precedes carnal death, and "lies on" Juliet, so as to propose that erotic intercourse like Juliet's and Romeo's is always discourse, too—it can only be inw*o*rdly.

In the ordinary world in which we live of cynicism, lust, spite, meanness, murder, envy, and revenge, such "adolescent" intensity, consuming mutual absorption, cannot exist, of course—all of us good little adults know that. Few of us actually consummate our eros—it requires discourse, imagination, attention, solicitude, humanity. Romeo and Juliet's eros can only exist in fiction—in theater, specifically—and Shakespeare so constructs the play that we may never *not* see the theater within the drama, the theater by which and within which Romeo and Juliet would invent a world *like* their love, a world necessarily of words, an inw*o*rd world. If the play is a pyrotechnical display of wordplay, it is because a love like Romeo and Juliet's can only exist in such a word play. So fragile is

114   "I'll look to like"

such an invention, however, so delicate an art, that it cannot endure, and it is merely mocked by the gold statues, lifeless and inert likenesses, that the two fathers pledge to erect each to the other's child at the end of the play (*Rom.* 5.3.297-303)—universals concrete merely.

But, perhaps, a yet crueler mockery can be detected at the end: "[Romeo c]ame to this vault to die, and *lie* with Juliet" (*Rom.* 5.3.289; emphasis added). Here *lie* can bear no pun but only one meaning, "stretched out supine beside her in death" (the *fault* of the *vault*). Here *lie* cannot lie: there is nothing else it can be(-)li(k)e, unless it be the corpse in Ju*liet*. And that is mortal—this corpse the end of discourse.

Against the end of discourse Shakespeare struggled throughout his career (this is what Joyce so beautifully comprehends in his great pun, "[a]s great Shapesphere puns it"—*Finnegans Wake* 295.3-4), and his "early retirement" may well be a final admission of defeat. But until that time, he was tirelessly inw*o*rd:

> For never was a story of more woe
> Than this of Juliet and her Romeo.
>
> *Rom.* 5.3.308-9

The astonishing final, anagrammatic rhyme—

> more woe ● Romeo
> |r|o|m|e|o|w|e| ● |m|o|R|e|(w)|o|

—is the work of a man who had "fall[en] into so deep an O" (*Rom.* 3.3.90) that he could only go on creating wor(l)ds upon wor(l)ds.

12
"All that you are like to know": *A Midsummer Night's Dream* (of Likeness)

> Love looks not with the eyes, but with the mind,
> And therefore is winged Cupid painted blind.
> Nor hath love's mind of any judgement taste.
> *MND* 1.1.234-6

> The actors are at hand, and by their show
> You shall know all that you are like to know.
> *MND* 5.1.116-17

A key statistic of Shakespeare's theater of likeness, discussed already in the chapter on *The Comedy of Errors*, is that *A Midsummer Night's Dream* and that play contain the lowest incidences of the word *like* in the canon— 27 for *Errors* and 29 for *MND*. I have argued that in each case, the theater of likeness accounts for the statistic by the readily observable fact that no other plays in the canon, including especially those in which mistaken identity is an issue, foreground the crisis of likeness in their dramatic situations as these two plays do. The word *like* occurs less frequently in them because it is less needed: scene, circumstance, and event do much of the work of *like* in these two plays. But also, relative to later comedies, these two early comedies (1594 and 1595, according to the Oxford chronology) find Shakespeare still developing the vocabulary of likeness for the comedies, and the sophistication he attains in the theater of likeness in *Much Ado About Nothing*, *As You Like It*, and *Twelfth Night*, especially in the rhetoric of likeness, is still in the future. If the turning point, as I think it is, was *Richard III*—if, that is, *Richard III* is the play in which the theater of likeness first became consciously theoretical in Shakespeare's thought, became what we today might call a generative metadramatic structure— then, the two years that separate *Richard III* from *Errors* and *Dream* are still formative years in which the Sonnets, the poems *Venus and Adonis* and *The Rape of Lucrece*, and the tragedy *Romeo and Juliet*, find Shakespeare analyzing the crisis of likeness as theory as well as dramaturgy, as an *idea* of theater as well as a mechanics for the stage. In this genealogy as well as chronology of the plays, MND, especially since it follows *Romeo and Juliet*, whose story it re-tells in comedic mode, is a crucially developmental play in its experimentation with transforming likenesses without the use of twins (*Errors*) as well as without coterie rhetoric (*Love's Labour's Lost*): MND uses "rude mechanicals" and fairies to stage the crisis of likeness as a function of the poet's I and

> The poet's eye, in a fine frenzy rolling,
> [That] Doth glance from heaven to earth, from earth to
>   heaven,
> And as imagination bodies forth
> The forms of things unknown, the poet's pen
> Turns them to shapes, and gives to airy nothing
> A local habitation and a name.
> Such tricks hath strong imagination
> That if it would but apprehend some joy
> It comprehends some bringer of that joy;
> Or in the night, imagining some fear,
> How easy is a bush supposed a bear!
>
> MND 5.1.12-22

This, I think, is the first theorization of the theater of likeness that Shakespeare composes. And "[a] local habitation and a name" is probably hereafter his working definition of theatrical likeness, what imagination *bodies* [> Anglo-Saxon *likam* > *like*] forth. Henceforth, whenever the word *like* works in a play or poem within the theater of likeness, it may be assumed—axiomatically, I think—to bear this much as a minimum.

> **OTHELLO**   Thou dost mean something.
> I heard thee say even now thou *liked'st* not that,
> When Cassio left my wife. What didst not *like*?
>
> *Oth*. 3.3.112-14 (emphasis added)

And "how easy is a" remorseful lieutenant, Cassio, "supposed" an adulterer cuckolding him, by Othello who is "imagining some fear" out of what Iago "did[...] not like" but thereby, just so, "bodied forth," an "airy nothing"—a not-like begetting a like(ness):

> Such tricks hath strong imagination
> That if it would but apprehend some [horror]

It comprehends some bringer of that [horror].
MND 5.1.18-20 (modifications mine)

And, although I will dwell on it at greater length later in my book, here I would be remiss not to observe that the name *Iago* (*Jacopo, Jacobus*) is also the proposition "I ago," that is, "I act or perform or play ... like" (see chapter 24 below).

Although less work is required of *like* in *MND*, Shakespeare stations the word nonetheless at key positions in the play's unfolding. Probably most important is its work in Helena's pained recrimination of Hermia:

> We, Hermia, *like* two artificial gods
> ...
>   grew together,
> *Like* to a double cherry: *seeming parted,*
> *But yet an union in partition,*
> Two lovely berries moulded on one stem.
> So, *with two seeming bodies but one heart,*
> Two of the first — *like* coats in heraldry,
> Due but to one and crownèd with one crest.
> MND 3.2.204; 209-15 (emphasis added)

Characteristic Shakespearean rhetoric of division is abundant here, but the three occurrences of *like* also mark the speech and deepen that rhetoric in the theater of likeness. Helena pleads that she and Hermia were once just alike, a reflex of Shakespeare's uncanny sensitivity to heteroerotic interruption of homoerotic affection, especially among women (see, e. g., later, Rosalind and Celia's "thou and I am one," in *As You Like It* 1.3.96). And this former likeness, "a double cherry, seeming parted, / But yet an union in partition," is the crux of the drama's action: Helena and Hermia *must* be parted, separated, for any resolution to transpire that the play can compass within its premises. So also Lysander and Demetrius, Titania and the boy, Titania and Bottom, Pyramus and Thisbe and their parents, Hippolyta and Amazonia (and, in *The Two Noble Kinsmen*, at the end of his career, collaborating with John Fletcher, Shakespeare will add Emilia and her childhood friend, Flavina, to this long list). *MND* is the story of the parting of these likes — Wall must be, precisely, ambulatory and itinerant in human relationships, like a (Snout, the) tinker, moving from one couple to another in the constant realignment of erotic and social relationships on which human culture depends (see *OED* II *sub voce* "tinker," 1a).

No walls, no culture. Every relationship builds walls, to the effect: we are like this, unlike that. (No doubt this is why the Pyramus and Thisbe fable is so enduringly popular—it is always relevant.) As feminism has insisted for nearly three generations now, the most fundamental wall erected by the patriarchy is that separating a woman from her father and communicating her to her husband, the two men who "traffic" (Rubin 157-210) in her; the wall of the incest taboo blocks her father's penis *from* her allegedly intact genital and facilitates her husband's penis *to* her allegedly intact genital (aided by her dowry, her father's debt for the wall, in return for which he acquires an interest in her husband's family and its treasure)—this wall says, in effect, our two families (are) like each other. This is the wall and the law that Egeus seeks to defend and to uphold, having appointed Demetrius his choice for his daughter Hermia's husband, although it is Lysander whom she prefers. The principal conflict of the play resides here, in Hermia's refusal to abide by the wall.

> **EGEUS** ...
> *As she is mine, I may dispose of her,*
> Which shall be either to this gentleman
> Or to her death, *according to our law*
> Immediately provided in that case.
> **THESEUS** What say you, Hermia? Be advised, fair maid.
> *To you your father should be as a god,*
> One that composed your beauties, yea, and one
> To whom you are but as a form in wax,
> By him imprinted, and *within his power*
> *To leave the figure or disfigure it.*
> Demetrius is a worthy gentleman.
> **HERMIA** So is Lysander.
> **THESEUS**   In himself he is,
> But in this kind, *wanting your father's voice,*
> *The other must be held the worthier.*
> **HERMIA** I would my father looked but with my eyes.
> **THESEUS** Rather your eyes must with his judgment look.
>   *MND* 1.1.42-57 (emphasis added)

If we return for a moment to *Romeo and Juliet* and recall Juliet's response to her mother ("I'll look to like, if looking liking move"—*Rom.* 1.3.99), we could, without violating Shakespeare's meaning, paraphrase Hermia, "I would my father *liked* but with my eyes" and Theseus, "[r]ather your eyes must with his judgment *like*." Be that as it may, what we not only can but also must say is that Hermia is *un*like her father to an extreme that the patriarchal law and wall of Athens cannot tolerate:

HERMIA So will I grow, so live, so die, my lord,
Ere I will yield my virgin patent up
Unto his lordship whose unwishèd yoke
My soul consents not to give sovereignty.

MND 1.1.79-82

Hermia refuses to abide within the wall or the law of "his lordship['s]... yoke" — she does not like him and, moreover, is not like him. Her *difference* is the motive of the conflict.

LYSANDER You have her father's love, Demetrius;
Let me have Hermia's. Do you marry him.
EGEUS Scornful Lysander! True, he hath my love,
And what is mine my love shall render him,
And she is mine, and all my right of her
I do estate unto Demetrius.

MND 1.1.93-98

Shakespeare exposes just what the difference of the female means: the likeness of her father and her father's choice ("You have her father's love, Demetrius;/... *Do you marry him*"; emphasis added) implodes, and this homogamy is a threat to the State (*MND* 1.1.119-21), for if the father cannot reproduce his likeness in the one he chooses to reproduce likenesses in his daughter's genital, then he cannot be "as a god,

One that composed your beauties, yea, and one
To whom you are but as a form in wax
By him imprinted and within his power
To leave the figure or disfigure it.

He cannot be lord and master of his theater of likeness.

Hence, though in a different key and a modulated structure, the conflict between Oberon and Titania over a boy, son and likeness of Titania's "vot'ress" (*MND* 2.1.123): in refusing to relinquish the boy to Oberon, Titania undermines his theater of likeness, too (the more so if it should be Oberon who impregnated the votaress, herself a mortal [*MND* 2.1.135], with his own likeness in the son of her body). This "injury" (*MND* 2.1.147) is intolerable to Oberon just in the measure to which fairyland is his kingdom, where his law should be absolute and yet clearly is not. Hence, when he applies the juice of love-in-idleness to Titania's eyes, he is effectively treating her as if she were a daughter, or property he can alienate, to the first candidate that appears:

> **OBERON** And with the juice of this I'll streak her eyes,
> And make her full of hateful fantasies.
> ...
> What thou seest when thou dost wake,
> Do it for thy true love take;
> Love and languish for his sake.
>
> MND 2.1.257-8; 2.2.33-35

Under the influence of the baneful juice, Titania is even more constrained to masculine will than is Hermia: "Titania waked and straightway loved an ass" (*MND* 3.2.34), which ass, in turn, she would make like a fairy:

> And I will purge thy mortal grossness so
> That thou shalt *like* an airy spirit go
>
> MND 3.1.152-3 (emphasis added),

oblivious to the way in which Oberon and Robin have made her (to) like an ass.

When Bottom wakes from his dream that "hath no bottom" (*MND* 4.1.213), he tells us that "[m]an is but an ass if he go about t'expound this dream" (*MND* 4.1.204), but I must run the risk of bearing this likeness to say that part at least of the bottomlessness of the dream is its enactment of the irrationality and inexplicableness of likes and dislikes, whether in the world of fairies or of mortals—Shakespeare is well on his way to *As You Like It* and *Twelfth Night, or What You Will*, to his mature understanding of the arbitrariness of human likes and dislikes. If *de gustibus non disputandum*, it is also true to say, especially after Bottom's dream, *de consimilibus non disputandum*.[1] No one can predict, and it is hard to account for, how we weave our likenesses from the stuff of our lives.

> I have had a most rare vision. I have had a
> dream past the wit of man to say what dream it was.
> Man is but an ass if he go about t'expound this dream.
> Methought I was — there is no man can tell what.
> Methought I was, and methought I had — but man is
> but a patched fool if he will offer to say what methought
> I had. The eye of man hath not heard, the ear of man
> hath not seen, man's hand is not able to taste, his
> tongue to conceive, nor his heart to report what my
> dream was. I will get Peter Quince to write a ballad of
> this dream. It shall be called "Bottom's Dream," because
> it hath no bottom.
>
> MND 4.1.202-13

Even as Bottom the Weaver weaves patches of Scripture into a crazy quilt of expounding, so Shakespeare weaves a text, juxta-form and cruci-lingual (cross-work)—

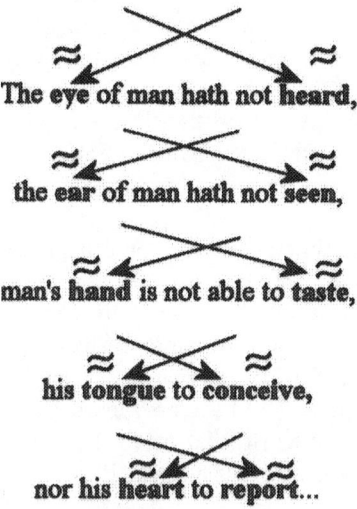

($\approx$ i.e., almost equal to)

—of what we look like when we try to expound our dreams.[2] We look like *both* an ass and a reasonably good man trying his best:

> QUINCE ... You have *not a man in all*
> *Athens able* to discharge Pyramus but he.
> FLUTE No, he hath *simply the best wit of any handicraft-*
> *man in Athens.*
> QUINCE Yea, and *the best person, too*; and he is a *very*
> *paramour for a sweet voice.*
> FLUTE You must say "paragon." A paramour is, God bless
> us, a thing of naught.
> MND 4.2.7-14 (emphasis added)

Flute might be surprised at what Bottom could tell him about paramours and paragons: sometimes they are more alike than one would like to imagine—it is hard to get to the bottom of the weave.

And that is part of the point of it all, the limits on imagination. If *de consimilibus non disputandum*, this means that the imagination is unpredictably capacious. When Titania is relieved of the effects of love-in-idleness, she wakes to loathe the thing she has loved: "O, how mine eyes do loathe his visage now!" (*MND* 4.1.78). But so "translated" by the juice of Oberon's flower was she earlier that she yielded the boy to him that had been like a wall between them—her imagination was filled with Nick Bottom the Athenian weaver, and the boy was no longer a factor.

> Love looks not with the eyes, but with the mind,
> And therefore is winged Cupid painted blind.
>
> *MND* 1.1.234-6

It really is not possible, when love (in- or out-of-idleness) is at play, to legislate likes and dislikes. Like Bottom's dream, they have no bottom.

So it is that in fairyland Oberon's law triumphs. Love is just like that. He is now lord and master of his theater of likeness. His is no longer a *regio dissimilitudinis* ("land of unlikeness" [Introduction note 37]); all is like itself again—"Now thou and I are new in amity," as he coos to Titania (*MND* 4.1.86). Not so in the world of mortals, however. Here, Egeus is still enraged at the injury to his likeness and his likes:

> **EGEUS** Enough, enough, my lord, you have enough.
> I beg the law, the law upon his head. —
> They would have stol'n away, they would, Demetrius,
> Thereby to have defeated you and me —
> You of your wife, and *me of my consent,*
> *Of my consent that she should be your wife.*
>
> *MND* 4.1.153-8 (emphasis added)

But to Egeus's aggrieved demand for the law (remember Shylock: "I crave the law"—*MV* 4.1.203), Theseus replies otherwise:

> Egeus, I will overbear your will,
> For in the temple by and by with us
> These couples shall eternally be knit.
>
> *MND* 4.1.178-80

The world of mortals is still a land of unlikeness. The "country proverb .../That 'every man should take his own,' ... /Jack shall have Jill" (*MND* 3.3.42-43; 45) does not favor Egeus or the law. Indeed, "*like* in sickness" (*MND* 4.1.172), Demetrius had "loathe[d] this food [Helena]," but now, "come to [his] natural *taste*," he "wish[es] it, love[s] it, long[s] for it,/And will for evermore be true to it" (*MND* 4.1.172-5). So much for

Egeus. So much for the law, beg and crave it as we will. *De gustibus non disputandum. De consimilibus non disputandum.* In the imagery of food and sickness, Shakespeare maps taste and likeness onto a scene of human incomprehension—

> **DEMETRIUS** These things seem small and undistinguishable,
> Like far-off mountains turnèd into clouds.
> **HERMIA** Methinks I see these things with parted eye,
> When everything seems double.
> **HELENA**   So methinks,
> And I have found Demetrius like a jewel,
> Mine own and not mine own.
> **DEMETRIUS**   It seems to me
> That yet we sleep, we dream.
>
> *MND* 4.1.186-92

—in which we observe and learn that whenever one of us finds her beloved, he is, very likely, to be "like a jewel,/Mine own and not mine own." Only so

> ... comes this gentle concord in the world,
> That hatred is so far from jealousy
> To sleep by hate, and fear no enmity
>
> *MND* 4.1.142-4,

for it is unpredictable, un-prescriptable, and without rational accounting for.

Hence fiction. Shakespeare would likely have said, "playing." Playing is a lie that tells you what you are like, maybe. Playing is a li(k)e that enjoys a certain privileged access to the life you'd like to imagine you might live. Playing is not a rational accounting for, and it is not a (scientific) tool for prediction (the only weather reports it can give you are internal "whether reports"). But even mighty, rational Theseus (his name is the same Greek word that gives us *thesis*) will concede that "[o]ur sport shall be to take what they mistake," which is, when we stop to think about it, what every theatergoer does no matter what company is performing. "The best in this kind are but shadows, and the worst are no worse if imagination amend them" (*MND* 5.1.210-11). So oft-quoted as this line is, I think it is misquoted without what follows:

> **HIPPOLYTA** It must be your imagination, then, and not
>   theirs.

"All that you are like to know"

> **THESEUS** If we imagine no worse of them than they of themselves, they may pass for excellent men.
>
> *MND* 5.1.212-15

This is where playing may rightly claim

> The actors are at hand, and by their show
> You shall know *all that you are like to know*
>
> *MND* 5.1.116-17 (emphasis added)

—about your likeness, anyway, that is.

13
King John: "Liker in feature to his father"

For purposes of studying Shakespeare's theater of likeness, *King John* is a remarkably important play since the crisis of likeness disturbs its surface practically everywhere, from its scenes consumed with bastardy and (il)legitimacy, which is the crisis of likeness in terms of patrilinear succession, to its scenes insisting on the non-differentiation of England and France—"Both are *alike,* and both *alike* we *like*" (*Jn.* 2.1.331)—to the Bastard's great discourse on commodity, the leveler—"this same bias, this commodity,/This bawd, this broker, this all-changing word" (*Jn.* 2.1.582-3)—that always succeeds in making one thing like another thing. The work of the word *like* in the play is so visible, so palpable, that it is as if Shakespeare had decided (for reasons we will see later) to come right out with it (*King John* is in most respects a very unsubtle play) and show even the groundlings how treacherous the ground of likeness is. If "all knowing comes by likeness" (Plotinus) and if "like will to like" (Ulpian Fulwell), then all knowledge is bastard, base, and commodified:

> Well, whiles I am a beggar I will rail,
> And say there is no sin but to be rich,
> And being rich, my virtue then shall be
> To say there is no vice but beggary.
> Since kings break faith upon commodity,
> Gain, be my lord, for I will worship thee.
>
> *Jn.* 2.1.594-9

When the Bastard is (*like* the) poor, he will acknowledge that to be rich is the only sin; when he is (*like* the) rich, he will acknowledge that beggary is the only vice. His "knowledge" is as illegitimate as he is, changing with "this all-changing word" that com-*modifies* one likeness into another likeness like a "bawd" or a "broker." Commodity we may think of as the commercial equivalent to metaphor (Shoaf, *Currency* 34ff.). If we assume this analogy for the moment, we can propose that, after *Romeo and Juliet* and *A Midsummer Night's Dream*, plays of exquisite metaphoric transformations, Shakespeare sees and shows the other side, so to speak, the brutally material side, of transformations in the world of reälpolitik:

> **BASTARD** ...
> Commodity, the bias of the world,
> The world who of itself is peisèd well,
> Made to run even upon even ground,
> Till this advantage, this vile-drawing bias,
> This sway of motion, this commodity,
> Makes it take head from all indifferency,
> From all direction, purpose, course, intent;
> And this same bias, this commodity,
> This bawd, this broker, this all-changing word,
> Clapped on the outward eye of fickle France,
> Hath drawn him from his own determined aid,
> From a resolved and honourable war,
> To a most base and vile-concluded peace.
>
> *Jn.* 2.1.575-87

An unforgettable speech by a master of unforgettable speeches, this discourse is also a measure, I suggest, of how far the theater of likeness has developed by the eve of *The Merchant of Venice* and *1 Henry IV*. Shakespeare understands that the modus of anything—its modality and its modesty as well—all are subject to "this all-changing word" that "[m]akes it take head from all indifferency" (i.e., abandon impartiality) just because it is a word that can pretend, produce the fiction, that the modus can be modified, commodified. Plenty will buy dirt that has been commodified as the soil where so-and-so trod: give it a new *like*ness and charge what the market will bear. Whether we like it or not, this is how it goes, how it circulates. And, in fact, this will even work with human "identity."

The opening scene of *King John* is notorious for its disquisition on sex and bastardy. The word *like*, as the following list of examples demonstrates, focuses the issue and identifies the crisis (emphasis added):

> **BASTARD** Compare our faces and be judge yourself.
> If old Sir Robert did beget us both
> And were our father, and this son *like* him,
> O old Sir Robert, father, on my knee
> I give heaven thanks I was not *like* to thee.
>
> *Jn.* 1.1.79-83

BASTARD Because he hath a half-face *like* my father!
Jn. 1.1.92

QUEEN ELEANOR Whether hadst thou rather be: a Falconbridge,
And *like* thy brother to enjoy thy land,
Or the reputed son of Cœur-de-lion,
Lord of thy presence, and no land beside?
BASTARD Madam, an if my brother had my shape,
And I had his, Sir Robert's his *like* him,
...
I would give it [land] every foot to have this face;
It would not be sir Nob in any case.
QUEEN ELEANOR I *like* thee well.
Jn. 1.1.134-9; 146-8

Eleanor and the Bastard make a new commodity, the illegitimate son of Richard I; they "build" this commodity right on the spot ("I like thee well") out of "a trick of Cœur-de-lion's face" (*Jn.* 1.1.85) apparent in the Bastard and, lo!, we have "the *reputed* son of Cœur-de-lion,/Lord of [his] presence" (*Jn.* 1.1.136-7), or, at least, owner of that commodity.

If next we adduce Constance defending her son's right,

My bed was ever to thy son as true
As thine was to thy husband; and this boy
Liker in feature to his father Geoffrey
Than thou and John in manners, being as *like*
As rain to water, or devil to his dam.
Jn. 2.1.124-8 (emphasis added)

we can hardly avoid the depressing realization that, even if "this boy/[is] Liker in feature to his father," that hardly makes him a viable commodity —indeed, the less so in that his mother's language about him, "being as *like / As rain to water, or devil to his dam*," leaves perhaps something to be desired in the boy's likeness, reduces his marketability or his exchange value, so to speak.

It is clear by now, especially with the work of the word *commodity*, that *like*ness is the crisis driving the play's unfolding story of (il)legitimacy. Nor does the word's work stop with the past or the present, it extends also to the (proposed) future:

BLANCHE My uncle's will in this respect is mine.
If he see aught in you that makes him *like*,

> That anything he sees which moves his *liking*
> I can with ease translate it to my will;
> Or if you will, to speak more properly,
> I will enforce it easily to my love.
> ...
> **KING PHILIP** It *likes* us well. — Young princes, close your hands.
>
> *Jn.* 2.1.511-16; 534 (emphasis added)

Throughout the play, the word *like* marks Shakespearean questions. What, how much, and how reliably can you infer of reality from likeness? What kind of knowledge is knowledge of likeness? If knowledge of likeness depends on the likenesses of language (tropes, figures, puns, syllepses, synecioses, etc.), that (com)modify realities, is knowledge ever more than a construct subject to enforcement, or destruction, by current hegemony? For, if the king says, "[i]t likes us well," the king may just as well say, "[w]e *like* not this. Thou dost forget thyself" (*Jn.* 3.1.60).

Shakespeare focuses his questions to their intensest point in the scene of Arthur's pleading for his life with Hubert:

> **HUBERT** Well, see to live. I will not touch thine eye
> For all the treasure that thine uncle owes.
> Yet am I sworn, and I did purpose, boy,
> With this same very iron to burn them out.
> **ARTHUR** O, *now you look like Hubert*. All this while
> You were *disguisèd*.
>
> *Jn.* 4.1.121-6 (emphasis added)

All of Shakespeare's questions may be thought to gather here, what is the relationship between your likeness and the disguise you wear? Since you can always only "look like" yourself (Arthur does *not* say, "O, now you *are* Hubert"), the likeness you choose may be more or less close, but either way is no proof against disguise—as Valery says: "Le plus profond, c'est le peau" ("the deepest thing, it's the skin"). Since everything else is invisible in the depths of your skin, that constant disguise, *you* have to *choose* the likeness you're going to look like, more or less close(d); you have to regulate the degree of your disguise—as Arthur says to Hubert, "*only you* do lack / That mercy which fierce fire and iron extends" (*Jn.* 4.1.118-19; emphasis added). You have to decide how you will (com)modify yourself.

Considering genealogical succession as one of the most intimate anxieties of both patriarchy and monarchy led Shakespeare, I conjecture, in part, to his uncanny sensitivity to likeness as such. You cannot infer character from likeness, as of son to father. The Bastard Falconbridge may have "a trick of Cœur-de-lion's face" and you may "read some tokens of [Eleanor's] son/In [his] large composition" (*Jn.* 1.1.87-88), but you cannot therefore infer that he is *like* Cœur-de-lion—if nothing else, half of him is his mother (and, while we're at it, which half?). And yet, even so, at times in the play he appears more like Cœur-de-lion than John or any other character. The point is, certainty about likeness is not possible. If, as, for example, the Norton edition posits, *King John* is, to some extent, "a defense of illegitimacy" (1019) and if, "[i]n *King John*, the gods stand up for bastards" (1018), and if, to continue for a moment with this particular edition's case, Shakespeare in this play shows "an impulse toward undermining ideological certainty" (1017) and a "skepticism about the meaningfulness of historical process" (1020), all of these features (and many claim them to be true of the play) derive from the crisis of likeness as Shakespeare explores it within the theater of likeness. Legitimacy, which is nothing more than a legal fiction, just another commodity, in fact, that can be bought and sold every day, can legitimate, warrant, and authorize the unlike as well as the like, and the illegitimate may authorize itself as more like its predecessor or prescript than the legitimate (as in a very real sense did Elizabeth Tudor).[1] To trust likeness, then, is a mistake, even if "[l]iker in feature to [its] father." This is the lesson Shakespeare learned from writing history plays and that he used to brilliant effect in the Second Henriad he was about to complete (*I Henry IV*, 1596-7; *2 Henry IV*, 1597-8; *Henry V*, 1598-9, with *Richard II* preceding King John by about one year, in 1595). Since everything is a commodity and can be bought and sold, exchanged at will, why not slum with Falstaff for a while? After all,

> ... *like* bright metal on a sullen ground,
> My reformation, *glitt'ring o'er my fault*,
> *Shall show more goodly and attract more eyes* [be a "sexier" commodity]
> Than that which hath no foil to set it off.
>
> 1HIV 1.2.209-12 (emphasis added)

And why not, come to think of it, demand as bond a pound of a man's flesh, just another commodity in the market place of human exploitation of other humans?

14
"If we are like you in the rest, we will resemble you in that": Likeness, Race, and Gender in *The Merchant of Venice*

The Merchant of Venice is a grievously vexed work of art. Containing some of Shakespeare's most memorable and exalted writing—"The quality of mercy is not strained" (*MV* 4.1.181); "The man that hath no music in himself .../Is fit for treasons, stratagems, and spoils" (*MV* 5.1.83-85); etc. — it also is openly inhumane in its treatment of Shylock and Jews; and there can be no return from the play that is not mingled with grief as well as sublimity. This is how we are, the play proposes, a rarely tolerable contradiction of creativity and cruelty, which, for the most part, we have difficulty recognizing let alone amending. "Nothing is good, I see, without respect" (*MV* 5.1.99). We see the good in nothing "without respect"—that is, without perspective, or basis of comparison (likening) in context, but also, re-spect, a "looking again" (< "to look [back] at, regard, consider, *respectare*" [*OED* II *sub voce* "respect" v]). We must look again to see "[h]ow many things by season seasoned are/To their right praise and true perfection!" (*MV* 5.1.107-8), or we will never know what they are *like*— what season seasons them, what likeness likens them, "[t]o their right praise and true perfection."

> **PORTIA** So doth the greater glory dim the less.
> ...
>   I think
> The nightingale, if she should sing by day,
> When every goose is cackling, would be thought
> No better a musician than the wren.
>   *MV* 5.1.93; 103-6

A nightingale singing by day when the goose is cackling may seem like the goose, for that matter, like any bird, "[n]o better a musician than the wren."

Everything depends on what you liken it to. Depending on what you liken it to, it will seem banal and quotidian or unique and marvelous. Depending on what you liken it to, with respect, it will seem human or ... a Jew:

> **SHYLOCK** ... and what's his reason? — I am a Jew. Hath not a Jew eyes? Hath not a Jew hands, organs, dimensions, senses, affections, passions; fed with the same food, hurt with the same weapons, subject to the same diseases, healed by the same means, warmed and cooled by the same winter and summer as a Christian is? If you prick us do we not bleed? If you tickle us do we not laugh? If you poison us do we not die? And if you wrong us shall we not revenge? *If we are like you in the rest, we will resemble you in that*. If a Jew wrong a Christian, what is his humility? Revenge. If a Christian wrong a Jew, what should his sufferance be *by Christian example*? Why, revenge. The villainy you teach me I will execute, and it shall go hard but I will better the instruction.
>
> MV 3.1.53-68 (emphasis added)

In Shakespeare's theater of likeness, this speech, surely one of the most memorable he wrote, is also one of the most revelatory of the crisis of likeness: since Shylock is incontrovertibly right on both counts, "[i]f we are *like* you in the rest, we will resemble you in that"—that is, in being human and in exacting revenge—the only way we can make him (appear) *unlike* a Christian is to demonize him, dehumanize him, and denature him (castrate him, as psychoanalysis would argue). With such a "Christian example" (i.e., likeness) to instruct him, little wonder he learns so well: "The villainy you teach me I will execute, and it shall go hard but I will better the instruction." Shylock and his Christian adversary are, it turns out, just alike; and the only means to separate them is fiction—"... the devil ... here he comes in the *likeness* of a Jew" (*MV* 3.1.19; 21).

This last quotation emerges, we know, from the scholar's punctiliousness: I am citing my source, my evidence, practicing my profession. All too easy is it, behind the aura of scholarly method, to fail to hear what the text is saying—here comes the devil in the likeness of a Jew. Here comes a slut in the likeness of a woman; here comes a nigger in the likeness of an African-American; here comes a gook in the likeness of a Japanese. Shakespeare's play, if we respect it, unhesitatingly shows us the mechanics of racism, namely, likeness, the particular reflex of likeness that functions in and as categorization—here comes the devil in the likeness of a Jew. It seems, as one learns more history and more, that it is nearly impossible for humans to overcome categorial thinking in its numerous manifestations, racism or sexism or statism or jingoism or classism or…a host of -ism's one might name (see *Being and Time*, § H44, 54). Since "all knowing comes by likeness" (Plotinus), we can hardly even begin to think without category or classification, and yet if we suspend thinking at the level of category or classification, we can hardly avoid prejudice either since category and classification structurally entail pre-judging, that decision by which an entity is said to belong to this, that or the other class. But to suspend thinking at the level of category and classification is nevertheless very tempting since prejudice then does the hard, laborious work of thinking, forestalling the attention one otherwise owes the individual in his or her historical predicament. Besides, it is so much easier to hate a class than it is to hate an individual.

The class of Venetian patricians cannot bear the thought that they have created Shylock (the only profession open to him is loaning money at interest), that he is but a copy of them (they would do it if they could), made in their likeness, and so they perforce demonize him as Jew, loading onto him every possible punitive likeness they can cull from the class of Jew. This is to behave "without respect," and little wonder "[n]othing is good." For them, the man Shylock has no identity other than the epithets of race and racism. *His* identity in *his* context is "without respect" because beneath the threshold of Venetian tolerance. They can only "re-spect" him from their vantage of Venetian law wherein he has a position and is visible because he is a category, "Jew," that that law recognizes and accommodates for purposes of business, i.e., money-lending. Hence, with typical breathtaking precision, Shakespeare has Shylock repeatedly confront the Venetian patricians with arguments not only from but also of radically subjective individuality:

SHYLOCK I have possessed your grace of what *I purpose*,
And by our holy Sabbath have I sworn
To have the due and forfeit of my bond.
If you deny it, let the danger light
Upon your charter and your city's freedom.
You'll ask me why I rather choose to have
A weight of carrion flesh than to receive
Three thousand ducats. *I'll not answer that,*
But say it is my humour. Is it answered?
What if my house be troubled with a rat,
And *I be pleased* to give ten thousand ducats

> To have it baned? What, are you answered yet?
> Some men there are love not a gaping pig,
> Some that are mad if they behold a cat,
> And others when the bagpipe sings i'th' nose
> Cannot contain their urine; *for affection,*
> *Mistress of passion, sways it to the mood*
> *Of what it* likes *or* loathes. Now for your answer:
> *As there is no firm reason to be rendered*
> Why he cannot abide a gaping pig,
> Why he a harmless necessary cat,
> Why he a woollen bagpipe, but of force
> Must yield to such inevitable shame
> As to offend *himself being offended,*
> *So can I give no reason, nor I will not,*
> More than a lodged hate and a certain loathing
> I bear Antonio, that I follow thus
> A losing suit against him. Are you answered?
>
> MV 4.1.34-61 (emphasis added)

I quote this speech in its entirety because, in the theater of likeness, it is as important as Shylock's more famous speech I quoted earlier. It is impossible in this speech to avoid Shakespeare's staging of the intolerable and unmanageable epistemological conflict of individual taste over against categorial reason: "for affection,/Mistress of passion, sways it [passion] to the mood/Of what it *likes* or loathes." Out of all nearly 2400 occurrences of the word *like* in the Shakespearean canon, no other, I think, could *more* forcefully demonstrate the crisis of likeness in the theater of likeness as men play their likenesses upon the stage of the world. I like it. Or I loathe it. Leave me alone.

Shakespeare here brings us to the outer limit of any human socius: *de gustibus non disputandum est* or *chacun a son goût*. The best that can be done, as was tried in our nation, is a Bill of Rights, which was written *after* history proved that "certain inalienable rights" were *not* self-evident to George III of England. Indeed, to this day they are not self-evident to most of the world and especially those who rule the world, who have nothing but scorn for "life, liberty, and the pursuit of happiness," unless it be their own. Shylock enjoys no bill of rights; he has only the law, and, as he repeatedly declares, he *will* have the law—"I crave the law" (*MV* 4.1.203). But the law, operating as it does in and by categories, exists to constrain and, if need be, restrain the individual in behalf of the socius—in law, it is the People versus such-and-such an individual. Most of the time the law is precisely disputing *de gustibus* no matter what the public rhetoric may claim to the contrary.

Hence the importance of mercy. Mercy, and its corollary forgiveness, make room for individual vagaries, idiosyncrasies, differences. Mercy "seasons" the law: "earthly power doth then show *likest* God's/When mercy *seasons* justice" (*MV* 4.1.193-4), argues Balthasar(/Portia) in her speech, among Shakespeare's most enduringly famous speeches. If "many things by season seasoned are/To their right praise and true perfection," mercy is perhaps the most savory season since it *sows* (the root of *season*) the possibility of a future, a release from the past into a future where praise, which is *price*, and perfection, which is *made through to completion* have a chance to continue (in) human com*merce*, which, as we know, shares also the same root as *mercy*, perhaps an Etruscan word that means basically "market," "merchant," "pay," "reward," "price." When I have mercy on you or you have mercy on me, we are merchandising with each other; when I forgive you or you forgive me, we are *giving*. Finally, Shylock is guilty of bad business practice, as he himself clearly knows (*MV* 4.1.39-42) because his "affection, mistress of passion" (*MV* 4.1.49-50), has corrupted his self-interest; if only he had remained true to his likeness as a merchant, the whole issue could easily have been resolved with mercy, or lots and lots of ducats.

But humans don't function that way. No human is ever finally true to a likeness, least of all perhaps the likeness he or she is *supposed to* adhere to by some external compulsion, for every human feels that she or he is unique, important, privileged, special. I crave *my* law; concerning *my* tastes there can be no disputing. I choose my likeness, and if I don't like the likeness I choose, I discard it and choose another.

Or, do I?

> **PORTIA** If to do were as easy as to know what were good
> to do, chapels had been churches, and poor men's
> cottages princes' palaces. It is a good divine that follows
> his own instructions. I can easier teach twenty what
> were good to be done than to be one of the twenty to
> follow mine own teaching. The brain may devise laws
> for the blood, but a hot temper leaps o'er a cold decree.
> Such a hare is madness, the youth, to skip o'er the
> meshes of good counsel, the cripple. But this reasoning
> is not in the fashion to choose me a husband. O me,
> the word "choose"! I may neither choose who I would
> nor refuse who I *dislike*; so is the will of a living
> daughter curbed by the will of a dead father. Is it not
> hard, Nerissa, that I cannot choose one nor refuse
> none?
>
> *MV* 1.2.12-26 (emphasis added)

The speech should not be skimmed. The play is careful—as only, I have come to believe, a Shakespearean play can be careful—to set the wager at the maximum, as here for example. Portia is not a Jew, but every bit as much as Shylock, she is constrained and indeed restrained to a likeness—this is indeed her portion, the part (likeness) that she has been prescribed, the role she must play, the category she must fit, the class to which she must willy-nilly belong. Jessica, too, is similarly constrained to a likeness, the Jew's daughter, perhaps as valuable to him as his ducats, but finally Jessica is Shakespeare's foil to Portia simply to show through her actions the comparative ease with which she, Jessica, escapes the paternal and paternalistic likeness: she elopes, but also

> **LORENZO** ... she is wise, if I can judge of her;
> And fair she is, if that mine eyes be true;
> And true she is, as she hath proved herself;
> And therefore *like herself*, wise, fair and true,
> Shall she be placèd in my constant soul.
>
> *MV* 2.6.53-57 (emphasis added)

Jessica is "like herself" in more senses than Lorenzo considers—she has freely chosen her likeness:

> Alack, what heinous sin is it in me
> To be ashamed to be my father's child!
> But though I am *a daughter to his blood,
> I am not to his manners.* O Lorenzo,
> If thou keep promise I shall end this strife,
> Become a Christian and thy loving wife.
>
> *MV* 2.3.16-21 (emphasis added)

It is Portia who cannot choose "whom [she] would nor refuse whom [she] dislike[s]." It is Portia whose gust is "curbed by the will of a dead father" who disputes from the grave her right to her palate. It is Portia who is condemned to a prescribed and prescriptive likeness as much as Shylock is (cf. Berger 8-9).

Hence, I believe, in spite of all that has been written on it, there is also this to insist on in the caskets scene, that the correct choice, the leaden, contains Portia's likeness:

> *Fair Portia's counterfeit.* What demi-god
> Hath come so near creation?
>
> *MV* 3.2.115-16 (emphasis added)

Here comes Portia in the likeness of a lead casket because inside a lead casket. As far as her sex is concerned, Portia has been dead and buried in a lead casket: her likeness, a "counterfeit ... come so near creation," says as much. Shakespeare deliberately aligns sexism with racism (these are our terms, terms of today) because his concern in the play is categoriality. He drives his language to examine and expose the audible discrepancy grating between categorial likeness and individual likes. As Bassanio observes just before choosing,

> So may *the outward shows* be least themselves.
> The world is still deceived with *ornament*.
> In law, what plea so tainted and corrupt
> But, being *seasoned* with a gracious voice,
> Obscures the show of evil?
> MV 3.2.73-77 (emphasis added)

In this otherwise highly conventional lore, basic stuff of moral satire, the word, occurring yet once more, *seasoned*, should call our attention to what Shakespeare is doing with the conventional: change the category, change the likeness; season corruption with graciousness, and it will taste different, of a different likeness. Everywhere, we see, it depends upon what you liken it to. Portia's father likened her (in several senses) to a lead casket; in doing so, he effectively buried her sex, as the patriarchy would, and if she is re-born by Bassanio, he "that choose[s] not by the view/ [but] Chance[s] as fair and choose[s] as true" (*MV* 3.2.131-2), her re-birth coincides immediately with her re-inscription in patriarchal categories:

> **PORTIA** ... *Myself and what is mine to you and yours*
> *Is now converted.* But now I was the lord
> Of this fair mansion, master of my servants,
> Queen o'er myself; and *even now, but now,*
> *This house, these servants, and this same myself*
> *Are yours, my lord's.* I give them with this ring,
> Which when you part from, lose, or give away,
> Let it presage the ruin of your love,
> And be my vantage to exclaim on you.
> MV 3.2.166-74 (emphasis added)

Portia is now Bassanio's, "converted" to him and his. The crucial difference is Portia's *willingness* to assume this likeness, submit to this conversion, because she *likes* Bassanio.

Within the theater of likeness, Shakespeare's play makes it abundantly clear that this is the difference between Portia and Shylock, that she likes Bassanio and he hates Antonio (*MV* 4.1.59-60), who hates him: "I am as like to call thee so [i.e., a dog] again" (*MV* 1.3.128). Although obviously much else intervenes, the play proposes that all we have, finally, is our *like*ness, our body (*likam*). The Christian does not like the Jew, the Jew does not like the Christian, but in their bodies, the Christian and the Jew are alike — hence the frenzy to categorize, to label, to mark (the Jew with circumcision, the Christian with baptism), any sign that will pretend that these bodies are not alike. History is the disgusting sight of innumerable murders committed in the name of marking one body as not like, as different from and superior to, another body. It would seem that if all we have is our likeness, we haven't much to go on. We are intolerant of likeness when it is different (Jewish, African-American, Asian, etc.), and we are just as rabid that likeness change when it suits our lust—"We all expect a gentle answer, Jew" (*MV* 4.1.33), as if the Jew, like that, could turn "gentle"/Gentile. But ours is such a world that the likeness has already been too deeply rubbed in.

As Shakespeare learned at a young age, God created male and female "in his image and likeness" (Genesis 2:6). This teaching has never deterred anyone from murdering the image and the likeness if hatred grew hot enough. But in the culture he inherited, Shakespeare would have understood clearly the argument that Milton also cites some 50 years later in *The Doctrine and Discipline of Divorce* that the work of God is joining like to like.[1] I have been arguing throughout this book that there was for Shakespeare a peculiar and powerful attraction to such an idea; we see it in "The Phoenix and Turtle," time and again in the Sonnets, in *Othello*, in *Antony and Cleopatra*, and also in *The Merchant of Venice*:

> **PORTIA** ...There's something tells me — but it is not love —
> I would not lose you; and you know yourself
> Hate counsels not in such a quality.
> ...
>   Beshrew your eyes,
> They have o'erlooked me and *divided me.*
> *One half of me is yours, the other half yours —*
> *Mine own, I would say, but if mine, then yours,*
> *And so all yours.* O, these naughty times
> Put bars between the owners and their rights;
> And so, though yours, not yours.
>
>   *MV* 3.2.4-6; 14-20 (emphasis added)

This may well be the best we have to go on, that despite all impediments, from body odor to parental disapproval to religious ideologies, we sometimes manage to like someone who likes us in turn—"if mine, then yours." It is not a lot. It cannot solve most of the world's ills. It may urge daughters to elope and steal from their fathers. It may turn out in someone liking gold more than he likes his daughter. But it still recommends itself, the likeness from which love and mutuality grow, sown in that season.

Its public equivalent is respect. I may not like you, but I respect you: I "look again" at you in your predicament and accord you a minimum right-to-be in the expectation that you will do the like for me. Again, it is not much. It is very fragile, as we all know. But it may be as close to care as most ever come:

> **GRAZIANO** You look not well, Signor Antonio.
> You have too much *respect* upon the world.
> They lose it that do buy it with much *care*.
> Believe me, you are marvellously changed.
> **ANTONIO** I hold the world but as the world, Graziano —
> A *stage* where every man must *play a part*,
> And mine a sad one.
>
> *MV* 1.1.73-79 (emphasis added)

Although we recognize a Shakespearean standard here and although we understand that metatheater is on display, we should also be careful to hear the unmistakable collocation in Shakespeare's language of *respect*, *care*, *stage*, and *play a part*. Antonio speaks from a place that Shakespeare privileged, the theater of likeness, where these four differentia assemble in a particular understanding of what it is like to be human, especially in a world spilling over with prescriptions for what the human should be like. It does seem to me that—this is no news, I readily confess—Shakespeare thought we each play a part on the stage of the world; but, and this may be new if not exactly news, Shakespeare also, I believe, thought every part is a likeness that each of us players must struggle to change from prescript to script, the difference being small but real that, in a script, I may improvise, my part even turning out someday to be other than "a sad one."

And this because it is in the nature of respect—approximating care, at least—to teach me something about *my* likeness:

> **NERISSA** Though not for me, yet for your vehement oaths
> You should have been respective and have kept it [her ring].
>
> *MV* 5.1.155-6

We should be patient so as to hear what Shakespeare has Nerissa say: not for me, but for *your* oaths. The point of respect and care is that if they exist at all between people, then they are mutuality between those people, a minimum no doubt but a minimum still. And thus it is my oath, part of *my* likeness, that I preserve and nourish when I respect and care for the likeness of another. It is myself I care for when I care for you. Not much. But, it is at least arguable that Shakespeare thought we should value it. Otherwise, someone will demand a pound of flesh.

If respect is to the public sphere what liking is to the private, Shakespeare's language of respect and liking also reaches far toward a comprehension of homoeroticism in the play, one that shares in his comprehension of categorial thinking and its discontents. Portia herself sees the issue clearly:

> in companions
> That do converse and waste the time together,
> Whose souls do bear an equal yoke of love,
> There must be needs a *like* proportion
> Of lineaments, of manners, and of spirit,
> Which makes me think that this Antonio,
> Being the bosom lover of my lord,
> Must needs be *like* my lord. If it be so,
> How little is the cost I have bestowed
> In purchasing the semblance of my soul
> From out the state of hellish cruelty.
>
> MV 3.4.11-21 (emphasis added)

First, this is perhaps the diametric opposite of categorial thinking; this is *care*ful thinking that cares for those who are the subjects of the thought. Next, in this careful thinking, re-spect, "looking again," sees that Antonio "must needs be like" Bassanio. Looking again sees a context in which this likeness makes sense, necessarily. But, third, this context includes Portia. Whatever the homoerotic relationship between Antonio, "a tainted wether of the flock" (*MV* 4.1.113), and Bassanio before Portia, even if they had been sexually active together, it is in the context of Portia's liking and love for Bassanio that their likeness one to the other can emerge from the category or class of male sex into the particularity of "[b]eing the bosom lover of my lord." Here, as elsewhere, Shakespeare suggests that the homoerotic is inseparable from the heteroerotic. Because we live in a world of comparison and contrast, at least if we would converse with each other at all, we can never wholly eliminate either pole of a bipolar reality — "Nothing is good, I see, without respect."[2]

And this, ultimately, is why the rings trick in the final scene is so important to the play (*MV* 5.1.142-285). Bassanio and Gratiano must see, to understand, that nothing is good without respect. The good of marriage is different from the good of male bonding; and what Bassanio might do for Antonio—reward his deliverer at law with his wife's ring—he must not do because he is now a man married to a wife who has claims on him that pre-empt (< "buy before") his bonds with his male friends. Bassanio and Antonio may (be) like one another, but their liking may not "[b]e *valued 'gainst* [Bassanio's] wife's commandëment" (*MV* 4.1.448)—merchandising has changed; for "man and wife is one flesh" (*Ham.* 4.3.54), not the same flesh, and requires a different "respective," changed from the categorial to the careful, from the same to the different, "two distincts, division none."[3]

15
"An eye to make difference of men's liking": Assimilating Falstaff in *The Merry Wives of Windsor*

Tradition has it that Queen Elizabeth personally asked for a play showing Falstaff in love (Dobson and Wells 292). If this tradition records actual fact, Shakespeare must have known that he had a "hit on his hands," even as he had already learned that he had invented a character not to the liking of the Cobham family who pressured him to change the name of their relative Sir John Oldcastle in *I Henry IV* before it was printed in quarto in 1598— Sir John Oldcastle became Sir John Falstaff (*Famous Victories* 9-12).[1] These extremes are important, I think, to understanding the theater of likeness in *The Merry Wives of Windsor*. Among the most memorable characters in all European drama, Falstaff is also a historical embarrassment; in his vast imperfection, he is a perfect test case of the intersection between fiction and history: he is a construct if ever there was one.

Many are the peculiarities of this construct, but not least among them is his rhetorical fecundity (see, especially, Parker, *Margins* 116-48). Falstaff talks. His talk is, if anything, bigger than he is, not just in braggadoccio but also in copiousness. He is, in many senses, a figure of copia, a heap of words as well as a heap of grease, who constantly resists assimilation:

> Have I lived to be carried in a basket *like* a barrow of butcher's offal, and to be thrown in the Thames? ...
> you may know by my size that I have a kind of alacrity in sinking. If the bottom were as deep as hell, I should down. I had been drowned, but that the shore was shelvy and shallow — a death that I abhor, for the water swells a man, and what a thing should I have been when I had been swelled? By the Lord, a mountain of mummy!
>
> [...]

> But mark the sequel, Master Brooke. I
> suffered the pangs of three several deaths. First, an
> intolerable fright, to be detected with a jealous rotten
> bell-wether. Next, to be compassed *like* a good bilbo in
> the circumference of a peck, hilt to point, heel to head.
> And then, to be stopped in, *like* a strong distillation,
> with stinking clothes that fretted in their own grease.
> Think of that — a man of my kidney — think of that —
> that am as subject to heat as butter, a man of continual
> dissolution and thaw. It was a miracle to scape
> suffocation. And in the height of this bath, when I was
> more than half stewed in grease *like* a Dutch dish, to
> be thrown into the Thames and cooled, glowing-hot,
> in that surge, *like* a horseshoe.
>
> Wiv. 3.5.4-5; 11-17; 99-112 (emphasis added)

As a student of the word *like* and its work in the canon, within the theater of likeness, I am most interested in the likenesses Falstaff can compare himself to. Mistress Ford is no doubt justified in her conclusion—"I shall think the worse of fat men as long as I have an eye to make difference of men's liking" (*Wiv.* 2.1.53-54)—but she may not grasp the full import of what it is "to make difference of men's liking" since it is more than distinguishing between fat and lean: it is also to make *difference* of men's *liking*. And how if a man's liking is a barrow of butcher's offal, a good bilbo, a strong distillation, a Dutch dish, and a horseshoe (whore's shoe), et alia? What do you do with a man, how do you assimilate him, whose like you've never heard of—at least, not yet, and, maybe, not even then?

Constructed not only *of* language, Falstaff is also constructed *for* language. Both in the *Henriad* and in *Windsor*, he is the site—"Indeed, I am in the waist two yards about" (*Wiv.* 1.3.36-37)—of language. On this site, language constructs. Like a self-replicating like-icon, Falstaff is a machine for likenesses:

> **SIR JOHN** (*showing letters*) I have writ me here a letter to
> her — and here another to Page's wife, who even now
> gave me good eyes too, examined my parts with most
> judicious oeillades; sometimes the beam of her view
> gilded my foot, sometimes my portly belly.
> **PISTOL** Then did the sun on dunghill shine.
> **NIM** I thank thee for that humour.
> **SIR JOHN** O, she did so course o'er my exteriors, with such
> a greedy intention, that the appetite of her eye did

seem to scorch me up *like* a burning-glass! Here's
another letter to her. She bears the purse too. She is a
region in Guiana, all gold and bounty. I will be cheaters
to them both, and they shall be exchequers to me. They
shall be my East and West Indies, and I will trade to
them both. (*Giving a letter to Pistol*) Go bear thou this
letter to Mistress Page, (*giving a letter to Nim*) and thou
this to Mistress Ford. We will thrive, lads, we will
thrive.
Wiv. 1.3.51-68 (emphasis added)

I quote at length in order to draw attention to the self-replicating cascade of likenesses (metaphors, similes, etc.) that pours through this exchange. Parker has shown how translation becomes a subject of the play through such language. I wish to show, in addition, how translation, to use that term for it, becomes an object in such a passage: the objective in such language, the end that is its object, call it "translation" if we like, is more language. And it is, thus, properly endless.

In this sense, by the logic of the supplement, Falstaff is also the site of deconstruction in the play, "a man of continual dissolution and thaw." Exuding likenesses like grease from his pores, Falstaff shows construct after construct in its constructedness: "She is a region in Guiana, all gold and bounty," each one provoking its supplement, "I will be cheaters to them both, and they shall be exchequers to me," which, in its turn, is supplemented again, "[t]hey shall be my East and West Indies, and I will trade to them both," so that, unchecked by circumstance, likenesses would construct themselves and deconstruct themselves and construct themselves again interminably, not to mention cloyingly, in the vast *regio similitudinorum* that is Sir John Falstaff—

MISTRESS FORD
What tempest, I trow, threw this whale, with so many
tuns of oil in his belly, ashore at Windsor? How shall
I be revenged on him? I think the best way were to
entertain him with hope, till the wicked fire of lust
have melted him in his own grease. *Did you ever hear
the like?*
Wiv. 2.1.61-66 (emphasis added)

No. And that is the point. We have never heard the *like*.

Falstaff's importance to Shakespeare's theater of likeness is as great as his fantastic corpulence. Anomalous in every way, Falstaff frees Shakespeare to imagine a character who will "speak like an Anthropophaginian unto thee" (*Wiv.* 4.5.8), a cannibal not only of other human being's substance but of language's substance as well. Falstaff consumes English, digests it, and assimilates it to a body improbably fabular:

> I would all the world might be cozened, for I
> have been cozened, and beaten too. If it should come
> to the ear of the court how I have been transformed,
> and how my transformation hath been washed and
> cudgelled, they would melt me out of my fat, drop by
> drop, and liquor fishermen's boots with me. I warrant
> they would whip me with their fine wits till I were as
> crestfallen as a dried pear.
>
> *Wiv.* 4.5.87-94

It is not just the transformation of Falstaff but the transformation of the language that constructs Falstaff that moves us, even in the throes of laughter, to detect and even, perhaps, tremble at, the assimilation, the likening, of English to a construct after which it will never again be the same. If all writing is writing after, writing after Falstaff Shakespeare writes so prodigally[2] as well as prodigiously that no one writing after Shakespeare can ever do the like. Likening itself has been transformed:

> **SIR JOHN**
> ...I was *like* to be apprehended for the witch of Brentford.
> But that my admirable dexterity of wit, my
> counterfeiting the action of an old woman, delivered
> me, [...]
> I went to her, Master Brooke, as you see, *like*
> a poor old man; but I came from her, Master Brooke,
> *like* a poor old woman...
> he [Ford] beat me grievously in the shape of a woman —
> for in the shape of man, Master Brooke, I fear not
> Goliath with a weaver's beam, because I know also life
> is a shuttle...
> Follow me...Follow.
>
> *Wiv.* 4.5.109-12; 5.1.15-17; 20-23; 26-29
> (emphasis added)

The "voice of the shuttle" (http://vos.ucsb.edu/myth.asp) is new, and the text(ure) of English poetry is never again to be without the beam of Falstaff, whom we do, indeed, follow. When, in the end, Falstaff has been duped by those he would have duped and become their "theme" (*Wiv.* 5.5.159), Shakespeare, with unerring precision, has him nevertheless respond to Evans' torture of the English language: "'Seese' and 'putter'? Have I lived to stand at the taunt of one that makes fritters of English?" (*Wiv.* 5.5.141-2). Falstaff, even "dejected" (*Wiv.* 5.5.160) as he admits he is, has perfect right to this complaint, he knows who he is—Sir John Falstaff would never make "fritters" of English.

To the contrary, his English is one of the glories of human culture. Utterly oblivious to convention, his English nonetheless swells and sweats in a body of unmistakable humor and pathos. Again, to Mistress Ford's question, "[d]id you ever hear the like," we must answer, perforce, no. Assimilating Falstaff is a constant challenge. No one wrote before Falstaff like Shakespeare writing after Falstaff. "Speak scholarly and wisely" (*Wiv.* 1.3.2-3). "Nothing without, and perhaps nothing within, Shakespeare's words could discover the power to withstand the power Shakespeare's words release" (Cavell, *Disowning* 20). To say, then, that Falstaff is unlike any other character in world drama is, I hope, within the theater of likeness, to be understood to say something obvious and yet in no way banal. In his unlikeness Falstaff is a factory of likenesses and teaches us to hear more than Mistress Ford understands when she comments on "an eye to make difference of men's liking": we hear one of the secrets to Shakespeare's craft—

> **SIR JOHN** Sayst thou so, old Jack? Go thy ways! I'll make more of thy old body than I have done. [. . .]
> Good body, I thank thee. Let them say 'tis grossly done; so it be fairly done, no matter.
>
> *Wiv.* 2.2.134-5; 137-9

16
"To drive liking to the name of love": Much Ado About Like in *Much Ado About Nothing*

The word *like* and forms thereof occur over 60 times in *Much Ado About Nothing*. But, even more significant than frequency, is position. As Shakespeare positions the word, his signature, it emerges as the driving motive of the play's action: who likes, and is like, whom?

Consider how the word opens the play (emphasis added throughout):

> **LEONATO** Never came trouble to my house in the *likeness* of your grace.
>
> *Ado* 1.1.94-95

> **DON PEDRO** Truly, the lady fathers herself. Be happy, lady, for you are *like* an honourable father.
> **BENEDICK** If Signor Leonato be her father, she would not have his head on her shoulders for all Messina, as *like* him as she is.
>
> *Ado* 1.1.104-9

> **BENEDICK**...and being no other but as she [Hero] is, I do not *like* her.
> **CLAUDIO** Thou thinkest I am in sport. I pray thee tell me truly how thou *likest* her.
>
> *Ado* 1.1.167-9

> **CLAUDIO** O my lord,
> When you went onward on this ended action
> I looked upon her with a soldier's eye,
> That *liked*, but had a rougher task in hand

> Than to drive *liking* to the name of love.
> But now I am returned, and that war-thoughts
> Have left their places vacant, in their rooms
> Come thronging soft and delicate desires,
> All prompting me how fair young Hero is,
> Saying I *liked* her ere I went to wars.
> **DON PEDRO** Thou wilt be *like* a lover presently,
> And tire the hearer with a book of words.
>
> *Ado* 1.1.279-90

> **CLAUDIO** … lest my *liking* might too sudden seem
> I would have salved it with a longer treatise.
>
> *Ado* 1.1.297-8

We are here *still in the first scene*. And these are only eight of the 14 occurrences of *like* in this first scene. But, more important, each of the occurrences cited is fraught with implications for the remainder of the play. From the bitter irony, if it is eventually only temporary, of "[n]ever came trouble to my house in the *likeness* of your grace," to the exposure of erotic violence in "drive *liking* to the name of love" (made the more troubling because it is allegedly *less* rough a task in hand than war, therefore still rough enough, as the event will prove), to the telltale "[t]hou wilt be *like* a lover presently / And tire the hearer with a book of words," *like* announces and stages (I deliberately deploy this word) the plot that is now to unfold. That plot is much ado about how liking becomes loving within the vicissitudes of history and the prescriptions and the proscriptions of family. *Much Ado About Nothing* may be a comedy, but, as I hope to show, it is a very serious comedy.

And most serious there where it engages the patriarchal crisis of the disposal of daughters. "Truly, the lady fathers herself" may be thought to be followed, in the imaginary of the patriarchy, with, "If only it were so!" If ladies fathered themselves, if ladies were of a separate sexual event entirely unto themselves, a sort of ambi-sexual freaks, and men did not therefore have to be the fathers of ladies, men might enjoy, as Benedick loudly proclaims he wishes for himself, a most healthy quarantine from women and their bodies:

> That a woman conceived me, I thank her. That
> she brought me up, I likewise give her most humble
> thanks. But...
>   Because I will not do them
> the wrong to mistrust any, I will do myself the right

to trust none. And the fine is — for the which I may go
the finer— I will live a bachelor.

Ado. 1.1.223-5; 227-30

Although this is the same Benedick who will shortly exclaim, "[t]he world must be peopled" (*Ado* 2.3.229-30), at the beginning of the play, he represents a tradition of the patriarchy, at most one step from misogyny, which drives relentlessly through Shakespeare's plays, to the effect that intercourse of any sort with a woman is contagion, to be avoided if at all possible, after the necessary contacts of infancy and childhood. Don Pedro may continue, "[t]ruly, the lady fathers herself. Be happy, lady; for you are like an honourable father"[1]; but Benedick conveys a less happy implication of the filial prescript: "If Signor Leonato be her father, she would not have his head on her shoulders for all Messina, as like him as she is" —*if* he is her father, even if she is *like* him, she would still be bearing a different head on her shoulders, and she cannot therefore be trusted to bear his likeness. Indeed, no woman can ever be trusted to bear a man's likeness (however frequently, in fact, she may do so).

Prolix as ever, not to mention malaprop, Dogberry nonetheless speaks to the point in at least one case: "But, God is to be worshipped, *all men are not alike*, alas, good neighbour" (*Ado* 3.5.37-39; emphasis added). Indeed, they are not, and many have been eager to blame women for this, though clearly it takes two to differ. Be that as it may, the unlikeness of men to each other, even of son to father, haunts Shakespeare everywhere, and not least in *Much Ado*:

> **DON PEDRO** Lady Beatrice, I will get you one [a husband].
> **BEATRICE** I would rather have *one of your father's getting*.
>   Hath your grace ne'er a brother *like* you? *Your father
>   got excellent husbands* if a maid could come by them.
> **DON PEDRO** Will you have me, lady?
> **BEATRICE** No, my lord, unless I might have another for
>   working days. Your grace is too costly to wear every
>   day. But I beseech your grace, pardon me. I was born
>   to speak all mirth and no matter.
>
> *Ado* 2.1.301-9 (emphasis added)

Mirth it may be, but as to "no matter," she is mistaken: it is almost the whole matter, as Don John, Don Pedro's *bastard* brother, makes utterly clear. Don Pedro's father did not always get excellent husbands; in the case of Don John he got not only a bastard but a "bastard" as well, a man of energetic malice and spite, hardly husband material:

> it must not be denied but I am
> a plain-dealing villain. I am trusted with a muzzle, and
> enfranchised with a clog. Therefore I have decreed not
> to sing in my cage. If I had my mouth I would bite. If
> I had my liberty *I would do my liking*. In the mean
> time, let me be that I am, and seek not to alter me.
>
> *Ado* 1.3.29-34 (emphasis added)

And so, Don Pedro does not, to answer Beatrice's question, have "a brother *like*" him; more, and worse, he has one very unlike him—or so we must assume. The play unfolds as a hardly cryptic essay in the (un)likeness of men to each other across a wide spectrum of relationships, and if it ends in marriages, as good comedies apparently must, these, like all marriages, will afford no argument against Dogberry's law, "all men are not alike."

To the contrary marriages are certain proof of Dogberry's law. Hence the extraordinary, if also usually clever and witty and occasionally prettied-up, misogamy in *Much Ado*. Misogamy is a venerable pastime in Western patriarchy and the literature it produced, giving misogyny a run for its primacy; we can find versions of it practically everywhere in early modern literature. But the misogamy of *Much Ado* warrants special scrutiny. The play may trot out the conventions, obvious and expected, but as it does so, it alters them for the theater of likeness.

> **LEONATO** Well, niece, I hope to see you one day fitted with a husband.
> **BEATRICE** Not till God make men of some other mettle than earth. Would it not grieve a woman to be overmastered with a piece of valiant dust? — to make an account of her life to a clod of wayward marl? No, uncle, I'll none. Adam's sons are my brethren, and truly I hold it a sin to match in my kindred.
>
> *Ado* 2.1.51-58

> **DON PEDRO** You have put him down, lady, you have put him down.
> **BEATRICE** So I would not he should do me, my lord, lest I should prove the mother of fools.
>
> *Ado* 2.1.264-7

> **BENEDICK** I do much wonder that one man, seeing how much another man is a fool when he dedicates his behaviours to love, will, after he hath laughed at such shallow

follies in others, become the argument of his own scorn
by falling in love. And such a man is Claudio. ...
    He was wont to speak plain and to the
purpose, like an honest man and a soldier, and now is
he turned orthography. His words are a very fantastical
banquet, just so many strange dishes.
Ado 2.3.8-12; 18-21

BEATRICE And, Benedick, love on. I will requite thee,
    Taming my wild heart to thy loving hand.
If thou dost love, my kindness shall incite thee
    To bind our loves up in a holy band.
Ado 3.1.111-14

What these and numerous similar passages abut marriage suggest is that peopling the world is not just fortuitous, which is obvious, I suppose, but that it depends upon (dis)likes that the peoplers themselves are almost the last to hear about—indeed, as many married couples learn, not without pain, it may be decades before they know the (dis)likes of each other. (Many divorces are of those who simply cannot wait, it may be for very good reasons.) The misogamy of *Much Ado* goes beyond the conventional in the measure to which it examines, we might say today, the "chemistry" of love and marriage, where, in our parlance, we mean by "chemistry" just that unpredictability of likes and dislikes behind the ado (it's in the *body*, in other words, which is, recall, *likam* in Old English, the root of *like*). Likes may repel in the world of gravity. But Shakespeare was shrewd enough to know that this law, too, has its exceptions, as Benedick and Beatrice, just alike and apparently repulsive each to the other, are, just so, and absurdly, attracted to each other, nay, even an ideal match for each other. Misogamy, in this perspective, is rational, if also clearly unreasonable, since it simply takes a census of the absurdity.

    At the end of the play, the theater of likeness affords an even sharper view of Shakespeare's examination of the crisis of likeness. The patriarchy succeeds in reuniting itself through the bodies of women—

BENEDICK But for my will, my will is your good will
May stand with ours this day to be conjoined
In the state of honourable marriage,
In which, good Friar, I shall desire your help.
LEONATO My heart is *with your liking*.
Ado 5.4.28-32 (emphasis added)

154   "To drive liking to the name of love"

—and, apparently, therefore, men (are) like each other again in a new sexual/marital dispensation:

> **BENEDICK**   For thy part, Claudio,
> I did think to have beaten thee, but in that thou art
> *like* to be my *kinsman*, live unbruised, and love my
> cousin.
>   *Ado* 5.4.107-10 (emphasis added)

But this new harmony, to call it so, is hardly perfect:

> **CLAUDIO** I had well hoped thou wouldst have denied
> Beatrice, that I might have cudgelled thee out of thy
> single life to make thee a double dealer, which out of
> question thou wilt be, if my cousin do not look
> exceeding narrowly to thee.
> **BENEDICK** Come, come, we are friends...
>   *Ado* 5.4.111-16

But friendship, like man, in Benedick's estimate, is "a giddy thing" (*Ado* 5.4.106-7). It depends upon (dis)likes.

When Claudio prepares to accept his penance and marry the unknown kinswoman of the man whom he has offended, he honors his obligation in the following terms:

> **CLAUDIO** (*to Hero*) Give me your hand before this holy friar.
> I am your husband *if you like of me.*
>   *Ado* 5.4.58-59 (emphasis added)

The locution *like of* is now obsolete, but, as the *OED* II records, it once was common in the senses, "to derive pleasure *of*, occas. *by, with* (a person or thing); to approve *of*, become fond *of*" (*OED* II *sub voce* "like" v 1, #5). Latent in these senses is a genericizing of the object; the object is not liked in itself, directly, rather as one of a kind (genre) that may, as kind, provide pleasure, or it may be approved of as an instance of a kind that provides pleasure. Claudio expresses his submission and capitulation, then, in a locution that subtly but really connotes his loss of individuality in the submission; like every *woman* who is getting married in the patriarchy, he is just one of a kind, of which any one would do (as long as she were a virgin and her dowry were adequate):

> **LEONATO** And since you could not be my son-in-law,
> Be yet my nephew. My brother hath a daughter,
> *Almost the copy of my child that's dead.*
>
> *Ado* 5.1.279-81 (emphasis added)

A copy will do, as far as the patriarchy is concerned, as long as it/she binds men in relationship to each other—if not son-in-law, well, then, nephew, not as good, perhaps, but it will do. Shakespeare in this way prepares for a response from Hero that affirms a certain difference of the woman:

> **HERO** (*unmasking*) And when I lived I was your other wife;
> And when you loved, you were my other husband.
> **CLAUDIO** Another Hero!
> **HERO**   Nothing certainer.
> One Hero died defiled, but I do live,
> And surely as I live, I am a maid.
>
> *Ado* 5.4.60-64

Hero in this exchange is not generic (nor a "copy"). She is not just one more woman being transacted between men, though obviously this is still a transaction between men. She is, rather, and even so, an Other, able to assert her uniqueness, her virginity, *as hers*: "One Hero died defiled, but I do live,/And surely as I live, I am a maid"—in other words, her maidenhood is not merely heroic, it is Hero-ic (and here, obviously, I assume, one must remember and acknowledge that Shakespeare would have heard in her name the anagram *[w]hore*, or that which heroically she is *not*—that is to say, what he also no doubt heard, it is *Her-*O).

We must not, however, stop here. If the play is *Much Ado About Nothing*, arguably the most important occurrence of "nothing" in the play is just here, in Hero's response to Claudio, "[n]othing certainer." Some of the propositions Hero utters here are, "nothing is more certain than my nothing (genital)"; "nothing (my genital) is certainer" than whatever you may think; noting (an attested Early Modern pronunciation of "nothing") certainer have you now, i.e., you now have more certain noting about me; nothing itself is now certainer since the "one Hero" is dead. But these propositions, which depend to a great extent on the consistent pun in Early Modern English literature on "nothing" as the female genital, are hardly the whole story. "Certainer" itself must have its turn. Occurring only this once in all of Shakespeare's plays, the word invokes if it does not provoke the crisis that Stanley Cavell has discussed so eloquently in his writings on Shakespeare, or the chaos of skepticism as it swept through Early Modern Europe in the wake of what John Donne famously christens the "new philosophy [that] calls all into doubt" ("The First Anniversary: An Anatomy of the World"). If, as Cavell argues, especially in the case of *Othello*, certainty about sexual fidelity and performance is the degraded remainder of vanished certainty about the truth of nature in the world at large, and if he is correct that Shakespeare is obsessed with this degraded remainder (above all, I would argue, in *King Lear*), as a man profoundly disappointed in his own experience of intimacy, I would claim, then, *Much Ado About Nothing* is a very serious comedy also for its startling enactment of male anxiety in the face of skepticism—intimacy is not only subject to duplicity and malice, which has always been the case, it is also just as much theatricality as everything else men and women do in the world. Not only can you not be certain that your bride is a virgin, not only can you not be certain that you are pleasuring your wife during intercourse, you cannot be certain that your bride is *not* a virgin, nor can you be certain that you are *not* pleasuring your wife. It's fiction. You cannot know. You are alone. And you cannot know. And the apparatus of authority, ecclesiastical and political, that once secured knowledge for you by the exercise of sheer force is itself disintegrating into the merest police state, which can do nothing but arrest you, which is usually to make certain that you will never know anything certain whatsoever about your condition. In this world of relentless anxiety about intimacy, Hero's "nothing certainer" is at once a beacon of hope for exiled masculinity deprived even of intimacy's promises and a death sentence for masculinity's aspiration to dominance: you may put nature to every conceivable torture of experiment, even to unbinding the nucleus of the atom, but you still cannot know the interiority of the woman enfolding your sex inside her sex—"Le coeur a ses raisons que la raison ne connoist point" (The heart has its reasons of which reason knows nothing—Blaise Pascal, *Pensées* #626). Indeed, for all you know, she may be a revenant whom you once killed; and, for all you know, only her death could ever have convinced you that she is a maiden, and this, you may feel at last, is a miserable state of affairs—"Runs not this speech *like* iron through your blood?" (*Ado* 5.1.237; emphasis added), says the abashed Duke to Claudio when he learns the truth.

As we know, the word *fashion* occurs frequently in *Much Ado*, and it is a play that has meant a great deal to Greenblatt and his followers in understanding "Renaissance self-fashioning." If, as the play seems to suggest, fashion is effectively everything, then perhaps we are near the crux of it all when Borachio explains fashion to Conrad:

> **BORACHIO** That shows thou art unconfirmed. Thou knowest that the *fashion* of a doublet, or a hat, or a cloak is nothing to a man.

CONRAD Yes, it is apparel.
BORACHIO I mean the *fashion*.
CONRAD Yes, the *fashion* is the *fashion*.
BORACHIO Tush, I may as well say the fool's the fool. But seest thou not what a deformed thief this *fashion* is?
...
BORACHIO Seest thou not, I say, what a deformed thief this *fashion* is, how giddily a turns about all the hot—bloods between fourteen and five-and-thirty, sometimes *fashioning* them *like* Pharaoh's soldiers in the reechy painting, sometime *like* god Bel's priests in the old church window, sometime *like* the shaven Hercules in the smirched, worm-eaten tapestry, where his codpiece seems as massy as his club?
CONRAD All this I see, and I see that the *fashion* wears out more apparel than the man. But art not thou thyself giddy with the *fashion*, too, that thou hast shifted out of thy tale into telling me of the *fashion*?
             Ado 3.3.113-20; 126-37 (emphasis added)

But there is in this intelligence a cynicism that is difficult to countenance. It may be, as we feel compelled to tell our students today, that essentialism is evil, or non-PC, or not cool, etc., etc., but relentless and ruthless fashioning, such as is used to dupe Claudio and Don Pedro, also convicts us of lacking the intelligence to understand essences and how they might survive fashions and humanize our lives. To be sure, on the left and the right, there are many who disdain the very thought of a humane life, I am hardly ignorant of these politics. Nor, to be sure, was Shakespeare. A playwright who did not comprehend fashion and its allergy to essence would be a contradiction in terms. But, even so, Hero is heroic, the language Shakespeare gives her implies, and her Hero-ism is essential and, I think, humane as well as human. For that matter, so is, I think, Juliet's, Desdemona's, Cordelia's, Ophelia's, Hermione's, Innogen's, and Marina's.

This list of female characters will have reminded you most of all of the fact that they all die or appear to die or appear to be dead for varying lengths of time. *Over Her Dead Body*, as Elizabeth Bronfen's brilliant book title so efficiently if grimly sums it up. The only good woman is a dead woman, usually after she has been raped or otherwise sexually violated. For a dead woman can herself no longer threaten you with incertitude; she has no mind, no body, no genital with which to be her own or to try to be. She cannot, as men say, "fuck you over," and you cannot respond to her, as did Othello to

(Iago's likeness of) Desdemona, "I will chop her into messes" (*Oth*. 4.1.195).

Many before me have addressed the slaughter of women in Shakespeare, who, let us also recall here, before he was 30 years old probably, wrote a poem, *The Rape of Lucrece*. I do not think to improve on what my predecessors have demonstrated. But I do want to underscore the phenomenon evident throughout Shakespeare's career, and especially vivid near the end, of the woman who comes back to life. Borachio utters more than his cynicism comprehends when he scorns: "Tush, I may as well say the fool's the fool." In Shakespeare, the fool may indeed be the only essentialist, the only character capable of the salvific tautology, "he is he, she is she," but the woman who appeared dead only to come back to life, has a claim on essence, a purchase on existence, that seem to have demanded Shakespeare's attention and commanded his craft. Shakespeare learned something of creative powers and experienced their effects through and, more, on account of, women.

Lest I sound sentimental, or worse, I hasten to admit I have no right to trade in the significance of women and women's bodies. At the same time, I do claim a right to exist and to think about my existence. In existing and thinking about my existence, I find it repeatedly instructive to reflect on Shakespeare's representations of women and on the relationship to women in his own life implied by the representations. I am led to focus, in particular, on those women who (appear to) die only to return to the living, and among them Hero especially frets my imagination. Almost universally contrasted, to her detriment, with Beatrice and usually considered little more than a plot necessity, she is, I would counter, indispensable not only to *Much Ado About Nothing* but also to Shakespeare's developing theater of likeness. She is an early experiment (1598-9) in the character of a woman nearly coincident with herself, of whom Cordelia will prove the ultimate experiment, in my opinion.

Hero is the one who can say, rather than hear said of her,

> **HERO** When I *like* your favour; for God defend the lute
>   should be *like* the case.
> **DON PEDRO** My visor is Philemon's roof. Within the house is Jove.
> **HERO** Why, then, your visor should be thatched.
>   *Ado* 2.1.86-89 (emphasis added)

In her case, the lute *may* be *like* its case: not only is her "case" (i.e., "vagina" [Williams 66]) virgin, not yet opened or penetrated, she herself is also innocent. She is at one with herself, or nearly enough at one with herself, that, by contrast, Beatrice, Benedick, Claudio, Don Pedro, and Don John can be scripted in their non-self-coincidence. In the lines that he assigns Hero,

Shakespeare makes of her character the case for "[n]othing certainer."

His warrant and his prompt to do so is Marlowe's Hero in *Hero and Leander*, published in 1598 but written probably in 1593 and almost certainly circulating widely in the intervening years. Local prompts are easy to find: for example,

> Whose name is it, if she be false or not,
> So she be faire, but some vile toongs will blot?
>
> lines 285-6

Here Leander all but rehearses the main plot of *Much Ado* in two scant lines. But far more important is Marlowe's own investigation of likeness in the poem:

> And one especiallie doe we affect,
> Of two gold Ingots *like* in each respect.
> The reason no man knows, let it suffise,
> What we behold is censur'd by our eies.
> Where both deliberat, the love is slight,
> Who ever lov'd, that lov'd not at first sight?
>
> lines 171-6 (emphasis added)

> Who taught thee Rhethoricke to deceive a maid?
> Aye me, such words as these should I abhor,
> And yet I *like* them for the Orator.
>
> lines 338-40 (emphasis added)

> And what he did, she willingly requited.
> (Sweet are the kisses, the imbracements sweet,
> When *like* desires and affections meet,
> For from the earth to heaven, is *Cupid* rais'd,
> Where fancie is in equall ballance peis'd.)
> Yet she this rashnesse sodainly repented,
> And turn'd aside, and to her selfe lamented.
> As if her name and honour had beene wrong'd
> By being possesst of him for whom she long'd....
>
> lines 512-20 (emphasis added)

> But know you not that creatures wanting sence
> By nature have a mutuall appetence,
> And wanting organs to advaunce a step,
> Mov'd by love's force, unto each other lep?

> Much more in subjects having intellect
> Some hidden influence breeds *like* effect.
>
> lines 539-44 (emphasis added)

Sharing similar Latinity with Marlowe and similar Platonic anxieties of epistemology with him, Shakespeare could read in Marlowe's work with *like*(ness) a certain spur to his own: where for Marlowe, "[t]he reason no man knows" and "[s]ome hidden influence breeds like effect," for Shakespeare the challenge is to wonder after the reason and to draw the influence out of hiding, into the light of the theater of likeness. The publication of *Hero and Leander* in 1598 spurred Shakespeare, I think, to increase his effort to understand and portray what happens "[w]hen *like* desires and affections meet ... [and]/Cupid is rais'd / Where fancie is in equall ballance peis'd" — this, in other words, we recognize, is the Beatrice-Benedick plot, which, we know, additionally, that Shakespeare invented.

He invented it to rise to the challenge with which the publication of *Hero and Leander* presented him. Nothing is more certain than that "[t]here is a kind of merry war betwixt Signor Benedick and [Beatrice]. They never meet but there's a skirmish of wit between them" (*Ado* 1.1.58-61); and nothing is more certain than that they are, just so, ideally suited for each other, "fancie ... in equall ballance peis'd." They are Marlowe's "... subjects having intellect / [In whom s]ome hidden influence breeds like effect." And Shakespeare proposes that the "hidden effect" is, in fact, their "wit," which, in their particular case, is their language. Through their language, and in their wit, Beatrice and Benedick recognize each her and his match, or likeness. Their repulsion is epiphenomenal to a deeper attraction, a paradoxical gravity that attracts by repelling.

> **BENEDICK** By my sword, Beatrice, thou lovest me.
> **BEATRICE** Do not swear and eat it.
> **BENEDICK** I will swear by it that you love me, and I will
>   make him eat it that says I love not you.
> **BEATRICE** Will you not eat your word?
> **BENEDICK** With no sauce that can be devised to it. I protest
>   I love thee.
>
> *Ado* 4.1.275-81

Because they are alike, they like each other. The "effect" is not "hidden." To the contrary, it is palpable and present, which is one reason why they skirmish in wit together, to pause the likeness that otherwise compels them each to the other. *Much Ado About Nothing* is a response to *Hero and Leander* in just the measure to which Shakespeare takes Marlowe at his word: "Love deeply grounded, hardly is dissembled" (line 184) however we answer the question, "[w]ho ever lov'd, that lov'd not at first sight?" (line 176). The play imagines dissembling love, in both the Hero-Claudio plot and the Beatrice-Benedick plot, and in both, different as they are, love proves deeply grounded enough to survive dissembling.² "Nothing certainer." But when Shakespeare comes again to imagine a couple so different in appearance but so alike in essence, nothing will be certain, for Othello kills himself as well as Desdemona, and Iago vows, "[w]hat you know, you know./From this time forth I never will speak word" (*Oth.* 5.2.309-10).

If *Much Ado* is a prolepsis of *Othello* (see, e.g., Norton 1387), this is a way we have of understanding why the comedy is in some sense so serious, even as it is incontestably comic. Darkness hovers over it broodingly. It will be followed shortly by major tragedies. Shakespeare is changing. The change, expressed in terms of the theater of likeness, is in his increasing sensitivity to the ways in which an individual is deluded, or deludes himself, about his (dis)likes and his likeness—two plays from *Much Ado*, for example, Shakespeare will portray Brutus, in *The Life and Death of Julius Caesar*, thinking to make the conspirators *like him* when, in fact, he winds up, tragically, becoming all too *like them*. The problem, in terms specific to *Much Ado*, is twofold, not only how does one "drive liking to the name of love" but also, why must one *"drive* liking to the name of love"?

If Marlowe asserts that "[l]ove deeply grounded, hardly is dissembled," he also, famously, asks, "[w]ho ever lov'd, that lov'd not at first sight?" Shakespeare's Claudio is, in the theater of likeness, a meditation on this question:

CLAUDIO   O my lord,
When you went onward on this ended action
I looked upon her with a soldier's eye,
That *liked*, but had a rougher task in hand
Than to drive *liking* to the name of love.
But now I am returned, and that war-thoughts
Have left their places vacant, in their rooms
Come thronging soft and delicate desires,
All prompting me how fair young Hero is,
Saying I *liked* her ere I went to wars.
                              Ado 1.1.279-88 (emphasis added)

One can presume that Claudio "lov'd at first sight"—the text does not technically deny it—but one must also concede that first sight was subject

"To drive liking to the name of love"

to delay, the interruption of "war-thoughts." We recall that Benedick complains of Claudio that

> He was wont to speak plain and to the
> purpose, like an honest man and a soldier, and now is
> he turned orthography. His words are a very fantastical
> banquet, just so many strange dishes.
>
> *Ado* 2.3.18-21

Besides the obvious humor, this statement also notes the division in Claudio, between the soldier and the lover-orthographer. This division, even in comedy, is not trivial to Shakespeare. It informs, I believe, the stress (and distress) in *"drive* liking to the name of love." When war, politics, power, what have you, divide men from their (dis)likes and likenesses—when they are, in short, alienated from their likenesses—the result is violence, perhaps muted but nonetheless violence, capable at any instant of becoming loud, of howling.

But the violence is not merely that, nor is it all that preoccupies Shakespeare. Liking must pass to love through the name thereof. This even deeper division, in the tragedies, becomes the psychopathology of carnality itself:

> **KING LEAR**   Ay, every inch a king.
>   [*Gloucester kneels*]
> When I do stare, see how the subject quakes!
> I pardon that man's life. What was thy cause?
> Adultery? Thou shalt not die. Die for adultery?
> No, the wren goes to 't, and the small gilded fly
> Does lecher in my sight. Let copulation thrive,
> For Gloucester's bastard son
> Was kinder to his father than my daughters
> Got 'tween the lawful sheets. To 't, luxury, pell-mell,
> For I lack soldiers. Behold yon simp'ring dame,
> Whose face between her forks presages snow,
> That minces virtue, and does shake the head
> To hear of pleasure's name.
> The fitchew nor the soilèd horse goes to 't
> With a more riotous appetite. Down from the waist
> They're centaurs, though women all above.
> But to the girdle do the gods inherit;
> Beneath is all the fiend's. There's hell, there's darkness,
> there is the sulphurous pit, burning, scalding, stench,

consumption. Fie, fie, fie; pah, pah! Give me an ounce of civet, good apothecary, to sweeten my imagination. There's money for thee.
GLOUCESTER O, let me kiss that hand!
KING LEAR Let me wipe it first; it smells of mortality.
GLOUCESTER O ruined piece of nature!

Lr. [1610] 4.5.107-30

The ruined piece of nature must first wipe from his hand the smell of mortality, that which every name, all names, any name, can only cover up, never sanitize, even the name of love. As I have noted, the word *like* derives from an etymon that means *body*. Every body is a likeness; every likeness is some type of body. To drive liking, the body, to the name of love, Shakespeare is learning, is a task that burdens the human with more than it can bear—"Ay, every inch a king," every inch aching, every inch. For this aching, from which no one is exempt, death is the only relief. But if humans look for more than relief, if they look to try, in spite of everything, to endure the driving of liking to the name of love, they finally, I think Shakespeare understands, have no alternative but that inwarding and inw<u>o</u>rding that, in the culture in which he lived, is the terrible gift of Incarnation: the poet politically Protestant but emotionally Catholic, as I intuit him to have been, must answer that if the Word became flesh, the flesh must become word, but let no one mistake the cost—much ado about nothing.

17
"Every Like is not the Same":
The Tragedy of Brutus in
The Life and Death of Julius Caesar

> He will be found *like* Brutus, *like* himself.
> JC 5.4.25 (emphasis added)

It is self-evident that, though the title of the play in the Table of Contents of the First Folio is *The Life and Death of Julius Caesar*,[1] Shakespeare's play is really *The Tragedy of* Brutus. Far more than Caesar, Brutus is the chief protagonist of the play, and of him, much more than of Caesar, it is possible to say that his play is a tragedy (cf. Oxford 2ᵉ 627). Caesar's death is not tragic, though it is criminal and an egregious waste, because Caesar is, was, and always will be *Caesar*; Brutus, however, was a man aspiring to virtue whose aspiration destroyed him—this is tragic, even in the measure of Sophocles' *Oedipus tyrannos*, in that a certain good, the aspiration to virtue or, in Oedipus' case, the desire for truth, precipitates a chain of terrible events that issue in death and destruction and the fatal compromise of the certain good. Tragedy must issue from seeds of tragedy that, as seeds, are good but as mature issues are terrible. Hence, for example, Lear's tragedy is his belief that the king's word ought to bring into being what the king envisions. If the king truly were *king*, such would always be the case. But the king is "king" only as and because others *relate* to him *as* king and can, therefore, in the event, change the issue of his words, even, as in the case of Cordelia, out of a just and measured love of the king (the seeds of her, Cordelia's, tragedy).

I speak here not just of "tragic irony," although the *eiron* clearly must inform my thinking. It is not only that the outcome is contrary to its impulse. It is also that the outcome must be the exact distortion of just that impulse, such that we clearly see how that impulse, basically good, in its very good, issues all the same in calamitous and terrible events—it is this that we pity, in this we experience our catharsis, that we see how for all and for each of us, the good impulse imports no guarantee of good

166   "Every Like Is Not the Same"

or just or beautiful results. Each is condemned not only *by* but also *to* his righteousness. After Oedipus it is Hamlet of whom this is most true.

The importance of *Caesar* to Shakespeare's career as a playwright is not its Roman topic nor its analysis of *aemulatio* nor its "theater of envy" (Girard's mistake is to treat all of Shakespeare's plays as if they were *The Life and Death of Julius Caesar*), it is rather the brilliant, early (1599) economy of tragic *like*(ness).

> **LUCILLIUS** When you do find him, or alive or dead,
> *He will be found like Brutus, like himself.*
>
> JC 5.4.24-25 (emphasis added)
>
> **STRATO** *For Brutus only overcame himself,*
> And no man else hath honour by his death.
>
> JC 5.5.56-57 (emphasis added)

He is tragic who "will be found like Brutus, like himself," or "like Hamlet, like himself," or "like Lear, like himself," or "like Othello, like himself," or "like Macbeth, like himself." Tragic *like*(ness), Shakespeare learned, is tragic singularity, "like Brutus, like himself"—radical disconnect from all other likes and likenesses. And Caesar is not tragic because Caesar is like no one, not even "himself."

Just so, it is most fitting that it should be Brutus who laments "[t]hat *every like is not the same*, O Caesar, / The heart of Brutus ernes ["grieves"] to think upon" (JC 2.2.128-9). It is Brutus who understands, and Brutus whose life demonstrates, that only the singular man, like only himself, can (even hope to) guarantee that the "like is the same," so rarely if ever is the like the same. (Here, too, is why Brutus refuses to swear an oath [JC 2.1.113] with the conspirators—their oath would insinuate that their "like" in the plot is not "the same.")

Brutus can be found "like Brutus, like himself" because "Brutus" is a likeness—"This was a man," "the noblest Roman of them all"—that he has spent his entire life alienating himself into, scripting himself as, willing himself to live up to. He is thus the polar opposite of Caesar who invents himself in every moment anew—and every new invention is wildly, indeed improbably, successful. Caesar is so unlike other men that not even tragedy applies to him; Brutus is so like himself that his tragedy is only a matter of time. Caesar, a force of nature, is unlike anyone, including "himself" since his self changes whenever he needs it to do so (Meier, esp. 23-25; 309-10); Brutus, a force of culture, is like no one *but* himself, punctiliously self-scripting Stoic that he is.

The play seems to ask us to accept not just an improbability but an impossibility. Whereas Brutus is one of a kind, man ("This was a man" [*JC* 5.5.74]), Caesar has no kind: "for always I am Caesar" (*JC* 1.2.213). Caesar is para-natural—which is why nature, terrestrial and celestial alike, endures such terrifying upheaval just before the Ides of March (*JC* 2.2.14-26): it is as if another nature were about to die and Nature in sympathy suffers cataclysm upon cataclysm in itself. Here also, we should pause to note, is the exact error of Cassius and the conspirators:

> I had as lief not be, as live to be
> In awe of *such a thing as I myself*.
>
> *JC* 1.2.97-98 (emphasis added)

Caesar is precisely not "such a thing as" Cassius—Caesar has so far exceeded what Cassius, or any other man, could do that it no longer makes any sense to speak of him as "such a thing as I myself." Though reason rejects it, the play demands it: Caesar is beyond nature as he is beyond the human.[2]

Brutus, on the other hand, is within both nature and the human:

> This was the noblest Roman of them all.
> All the conspirators save only he
> Did that they did in envy of great Caesar.
> He only in a general honest thought
> And common good to all made one of them.
> His life was gentle, and the elements
> So mixed in him that nature might stand up
> And say to all the world "This was a man."
>
> *JC* 5.5.67-74

Brutus is the best culture can do with nature's "elements" (hence nature can *say* what culture predicates: "This was a man"). Brutus is one of a kind, but he is *of a kind*. He therefore fits within categories and can be classified. Hence his tragedy—that one of a kind such as Brutus should end his life a suicide, failed in the very virtue he so passionately sought to promote and practice. Caesar, on the other hand, might as well be, what he will quickly become, a god (Suetonius 48 [¶ 88]).

As Cassius is wrong about Caesar, so also is he wrong about Brutus:

> **CASSIUS** Well, Brutus, thou art noble; yet I see
> Thy honourable mettle may be wrought
> From that it is disposed. *Therefore it is meet*

> *That noble minds keep ever with their* likes;
> For who so firm that cannot be seduced?
>
> JC 1.2.308-12 (emphasis added)

Cassius is mistaken. He has not seduced Brutus, who simply proceeds with what he was already considering (JC 1.2.165-6), but he *has* proven "[t]hat noble minds keep ever with their *likes*," which is to say, themselves. There is no one *like* Brutus except Brutus, and, despite his erroneous inference, Cassius is merely the instrument to prove as much. Note here, too, characteristic Shakespearean slyness: "Thy honourable mettle may be wrought/From that it is disposed" is so constructed syntactically that it may also say just the opposite of Cassius's construal: whereas Cassius intends, "your honorable mettle may be turned away from the direction in which it is disposed," the syntax also admits of "your honorable mettle may indeed be made up from that of which it is disposed." Again, and always, the effect is to imply that there is no one like Brutus.

Whereas—crucial difference—Caesar is like no one: "for always I am Caesar" (JC 1.2.213). Caesar is outside the classification system, whereas Brutus is not only inside it but inside it as the paragon establishing the standard for classification—

> **CASCA** O, he sits high in all the people's hearts,
> And that which would appear offence in us
> *His countenance, like richest alchemy,*
> *Will change* to virtue and to worthiness.
>
> JC 1.3.157-60 (emphasis added)

This is why the death of Brutus is tragic: to adapt Cleopatra's lament over the corpse of Antony, "[t]*he odds is gone,*/And there is nothing left remarkable/Beneath the visiting moon" (*Ant.* 4.16.68-70). Similarly, for example, the death of Hamlet is tragic because "what a piece of work" was this "sweet prince." Or, again, the death of Cordelia is tragic because, as she herself says, she was *not like* her sisters (*Lr.* [1610] 1.1.100-3). Shakespeare is moving toward his mature understanding of tragic *like*(ness) as knowable and knowing singularity.

The Life and Death of Julius Caesar is *The* Tragedy *of Brutus*. But if we are in search of the play's most inward (and inw*o*rd) title, we might better consider as the most appropriate candidate, *The Life and Death of Men's Names,* for in this play Shakespeare undertakes one of his most searching examinations of the conventionality of the proper name.

The most obvious dramatization of the problem is the scene of Cinna the Poet's victimization:

> **FIRST PLEBEIAN** What is your name?
>
> ...
>
> **CINNA** What is my name?
>
> ...
>
> **THIRD PLEBEIAN** Your name, sir, truly.
> **CINNA** Truly, my name is Cinna.
> **FIRST PLEBEIAN** Tear him to pieces! He's a conspirator.
> **CINNA** I am Cinna the poet, I am Cinna the poet.
> **FOURTH PLEBEIAN** Tear him for his bad verses, tear him for his bad verses.
> **CINNA** I am not Cinna the conspirator.
> **FOURTH PLEBEIAN** It is no matter, *his name's Cinna. Pluck but his name out of his heart*, and turn him going.
> **THIRD PLEBEIAN** Tear him, tear him! ..
>
> JC 3.3.5; 13; 26-35 (emphasis added)

Because Cinna the Poet shares the name of Cinna the Conspirator, he must die. But to appreciate fully what Shakespeare is writing here we must first recall and comprehend Cassius' long discourse on the two names, "Brutus" and "Caesar":

> Brutus and Caesar: what should be in that "Caesar"?
> Why should that name be sounded more than yours?
> Write them together: yours is as fair a name.
> Sound them: it doth become the mouth as well.
> Weigh them: it is as heavy. Conjure with 'em:
> "Brutus" will start a spirit as soon as "Caesar."
> ...
> When could they say till now, that talked of Rome,
> That her wide walls encompassed but one man?
> *Now is it Rome indeed, and room enough*
> *When there is in it but one only man.*
> O, you and I have heard our fathers say
> There was a Brutus once that would have brooked
> Th'eternal devil to keep his state in Rome
> As easily as a king.
>
> JC 1.2.143-8; 155-62 (emphasis added)

Cassius' sarcasm in the end is not biting enough to cancel the truth he unwittingly utters, that "Caesar" is a different name, as unlike other names as the man is unlike other men. Indeed, because of Caesar, "one only man," *Rome* is now hardly *more* than *room* for this "one only man."

The pun is far more than the dismissive harumph Cassius intends. The pun demonstrates, with characteristic Shakespearean economy in punning, that the man and the name *Caesar* change the operations of words, even as they change the course of human history. The conventions are henceforth different.

Of the greatest importance, then, is the very opening scene of the play, with its magnificent chorus of punning:

> **COBBLER** Truly, sir, in respect of a fine workman I am but, as you would say, a cobbler.
> ...
> **COBBLER** A trade, sir, that I hope I may use with a safe conscience, which is indeed, sir, *a mender of bad soles.*
> ...
> **COBBLER** Nay, I beseech you, sir, be not out with me. *Yet if you be out, sir, I can mend you.*
> **MURELLUS** What mean'st thou by that? *Mend me, thou saucy fellow?*
> **COBBLER** Why, sir, cobble you.
> **FLAVIUS** Thou art a cobbler, art thou?
> **COBBLER** Truly, sir, *all* that I live by is with the *awl*. I meddle with no tradesman's matters, nor women's matters, but *withal* I am indeed, sir, *a surgeon to old shoes*: when they are in great danger I *recover* them. As proper men as ever trod upon neat's leather have gone upon my handiwork.
>   JC 1.1.10-11; 13-14; 16-26 (emphasis added)

Unlike Dr. Johnson (*Selections* 21-22) I do not find Shakespeare's fondness for puns a fault in his writing. To the contrary, it seems to me that throughout his work, and especially here, Shakespeare practices an economy of wordplay that defines his play(s) of words. *The Life and Death of Julius Caesar* opens in the way that it does so as to establish, from the very beginning, that the play is also about the instability and arbitrariness of the signifier, which is, it turns out, a very fragile commodity. For it is possible that a word may be so loose as to become so fixed in meaning that men can "[p]luck but his name out of his heart, and turn him going," but, as the fate of Cinna the Poet, who is not Cinna the Conspirator, shows, this possibility is nothing less than terror.

In the absence of such terror, names are fluid, mobile, and variable, doing different work at different times. But the name of Caesar changes all this. The name of Caesar is the dictator's dictation:

CAESAR But I am *constant* as the Northern Star,
Of whose true *fixed* and resting quality
There is *no fellow* in the firmament.
...
So in the world: 'tis furnished well with men,
And men are flesh and blood, and apprehensive;
Yet in the number I do know but one
That unassailable holds on his rank,
Unshaked of motion; *and that I am he*
Let me a little show it even in this —
JC 3.1.60-62; 66-71 (emphasis added)

After Caesar, the cobbler may never men(d) souls again. To be sure, he may continue to pun, but punning cobbles not Caesar. After Caesar, Cinna must be "Cinna" no matter who Cinna is. After Caesar, there is "one only name" as he is "one only man"; and the conspirators revolt against this tyranny, this dictation.

But they kill only the man, not the name.

CASSIUS Stoop, then, and wash.
They smear their hands with Caesar's blood
                    How many ages hence
Shall this our lofty *scene be acted over,*
In states unborn and accents yet unknown!
BRUTUS How many times shall Caesar bleed in sport,
That now on Pompey's basis lies along,
No worthier than the dust!
CASSIUS   So oft as that shall be,
So often shall the knot of us be called
The men that gave their country liberty.
JC 3.1.112-19 (emphasis added)

The ironies are palpable to the point of making us wince: the very ones who destroy the "one only man" acknowledge the "one only *name*" that will nevertheless endure forever, and Cassius, ever deaf to his own words, admits that they "shall be called" the "(k)not of [them]/The men that gave their country liberty."

Caesar dead, *Caesar* the name lives on. The fatal miscalculation of the conspirators was to fail to realize that they could not kill the name as well as the man. To the contrary, the name becomes immediately and henceforth the title of emperors through many succeeding centuries. Killing Caesar, the conspirators create *Caesar*. And this *Caesar* kills them.

Shakespeare lived his entire life under a monarch—"monos" + "archos," rule by one, one ruler—and though it may have been (becoming) a limited constitutional monarchy, it was still the rule of one: Elizabeth I, then James I. Shakespeare was, I am confident, never not aware of what can happen to words under Caesar: "Come not between the dragon and his wrath" (*Lr.* [1610] 1.1.122). I think that this is why he loved to pun so much. But he who would men(d) souls must be ever wary of man sole, "one only man," lest one only meaning wear out his words and he never recover them withal.[3]

Brutus failed to be an adequate word-cobbler (hence the scene in which he and Cassius so unceremoniously dismiss the poet who would reconcile them—*JC* 4.2.178-90). For, and it should be obvious now how we come to this, he too was "one only man" *but* with one only meaning, or honor. "[F]or Brutus' *tongue*/Hath almost ended his life's history" (*JC* 5.5.39-40; emphasis added) is, tragically, only too true. Brutus was not poet enough to find (*invenire* > invent) another meaning to his life just because he *was* man enough ("This was a man") to constrain his life to the one meaning, honor: "For let the gods so speed me as I love/The name of honour more than I fear death" (*JC* 1.2.90-91).[4] Brutus's innermost condition is to be "with himself at war" (*JC* 1.2.48):

> I turn the trouble of my countenance
> *Merely upon myself.* Vexèd I am
> Of late with *passions of some difference,*
> *Conceptions only proper to myself,*
> Which give some soil, perhaps, to my behaviours...
>   *JC* 1.2.40-44 (emphasis added)

Just because no one else is like Brutus, Brutus "turn[s] the trouble of [his] countenance/Merely upon [him]self"; moreover, he suffers "passions of *some difference*" (emphasis added), just as he is different from other men; he is "with himself at war" (*JC* 1.2.48) just because his "[c]onceptions [are] only proper to [him]self." Brutus is always and everywhere his own text, his own script, and self-referential, because Brutus is determined to write the script of his life according to the intent of honor—honor is his prescript. Honor prescribes his life, and his *like*, to Brutus, and, finally, Brutus cannot deviate from this prescription. He can imagine different scripts but only to dismiss them:

> Brutus had rather be a villager
> Than to *repute* himself a son of Rome

Under these hard conditions as this time
Is *like* to lay upon us.
>   *JC* 1.2.173-6 (emphasis added)

Brutus will be neither a villager nor "a son of Rome/Under these hard conditions as this time/Is like to lay upon us"—Brutus will be, and always, only the Brutus prescribed by honor. Thus, when he appears to rebuff Cassius,

> Into what dangers would you lead me, Cassius,
> That you would have me seek into myself
> For that which is not in me?
>   *JC* 1.2.65-67

we understand that he protests too much: it is in him, all right, else he could not be so prompt(ed) to deny it.

Here we have, I think, an explanation of the mirror imagery in the play (so like the mirror imagery in *Troilus and Cressida*—3.3.97-106) and of the vitriolic stichomythia between Brutus and Cassius in the penultimate act of the play. Mirrors may distort but they distort, if so, only that which is already there.

> **CASSIUS** Tell me, good Brutus, can you see your face?
> **BRUTUS** No, Cassius, *for the eye sees not itself*
> *But by reflection*, by some other things.
> ...
> **CASSIUS** Therefor, good Brutus, be prepared to hear.
> And since you know you cannot see yourself
> So well as *by reflection, I, your glass*,
> Will modestly discover to yourself
> *That of yourself which you yet know not of.*
>   *JC* 1.2.53-55; 68-72 (emphasis added)

Obviously, Shakespeare was fascinated by mirrors and by the relationship of mirroring to self-knowledge, self-awareness. This is also to say that he was fascinated with self-blindness and self-deception—no one can see his face *except* by reflection. Just so, his language in this exchange is startlingly precise: "That of yourself which you yet know not of"—it *is* there, in Brutus, but as yet unknown or, better perhaps, known but not consciously acknowledged.[5] Where Cassius believes himself to be seducing Brutus (*JC* 1.2.306), it is truer to say that Brutus *is seducing himself* by observing "that which is not in [him]" in his reflection in Cassius:

> What you would work me to I have some aim.
> How I *have* thought of this and of these times
> I shall recount hereafter.
>
> JC 1.2.164-6 (emphasis added)

Brutus has already been busy writing his Stoic script of resistance to Caesar, or, as I prefer, taking dictation from his Stoicism as to what his role under Caesar should be. When he looks into Cassius' mirror, he sees "one only man," himself.

Hence the dramatic point of the intense quarrel between them near the end. Their eventual reconciliation serves, ultimately, only to distinguish them more precisely. However alike Brutus and Cassius may seem, even to the point of committing suicide each, it remains the case that there is and can be no one like Brutus:

> **CASSIUS** You love me not.
> **BRUTUS**   I do not *like* your faults.
>
> JC 4.2.143 (emphasis added)

Nor, finally, is Brutus like Cassius, in faults or otherwise. It is Cassius who has "misconstrued everything" (JC 5.3.83):

> **TITINIUS** Alas, thou hast misconstrued everything.
> But hold thee, take this garland on thy brow.
> *Thy Brutus bid me give it thee*, and I
> Will do his bidding.
>
> JC 5.3.83-86 (emphasis added)

It is Brutus who crowns (JC 5.3.96) Cassius, through Titinius (though only in death), for Brutus, truly, would never be crowned, whatever Cassius's earlier construals:

> **ANTONY** All the conspirators save only he
> Did that they did in envy of great Caesar.
> He only in a general honest thought
> And common good to all made one of them.
>
> JC 5.5.68-71

The locution, "[h]e only ... made one of them," is, finally, revelatory but in a very precise way. Not only did he make himself part of their group but he "made one of them": joined them but also made them one, in act (though not in purpose), and made them (a group) with his one, and, even, made himself *like* them. But he could not make (*his*) one of them, he could not make *them* like *him*, for no one is like Brutus ("found *like* Brutus, *like* himself") — tragic singularity, Shakespearean tragedy.

18
As You Like It: The Hymen of Likeness in the Forest of Ardenne

> A more severe
> More harassing master would extemporize
> Subtler, more urgent proof that the theory
> Of poetry is the theory of life,
>
> As it is, in the intricate evasions of as,
> In things seen and unseen, created from nothingness,
> The heavens, the hells, the worlds, the longed-for lands.
> Wallace Stevens, *An Ordinary Evening in New Haven* xviii

Numerous features of *As You Like It* move the play into the foreground of my argument. Not least, of course, is the title itself, since it is the only one of Shakespeare's plays with the word *like* in its title. Moreover, the play is distinguished for its various metadramatic moments, perhaps most famously Jaques' declaration that

> All the world's a stage,
> And all the men and women merely players.
> They have their exits and their entrances,
> And one man in his time plays many parts.
>
> *AYL* 2.7.139-42

However we read the torque in his name (Jaques > "jakes" > outhouse), his utterance seems to escape the torque, at least partially.

The play is also remarkable for its profusion of cross-dressings and gender-bendings, topics of intense critical focus in recent years (e.g., Howard, *Struggle* 118-21). But the feature of the play most demanding of attention in and from my argument is the role of Hymen in the denouement:

> Peace, ho, I bar confusion.
> 'Tis I must make conclusion
>   Of these most strange events.
>
>   *AYL* 5.4.123-25

Hymen, god of marriage, "bar[s] confusion" by sorting out the various couples at the end of the play. I propose that sorting is inseparable from the problematic of *like*ness that elsewhere preoccupies Shakespeare. Furthermore, in particular, if *Hamlet* does indeed follow *As You Like It* in the chronology of Shakespeare's writings, there is, I suggest, a profound connection between the two plays in their interrogation of *like*ness as the basis of (con)sorts.[1] And finally, if *Twelfth Night, or What You Will* follows *Hamlet*, we can, I propose, derive from all three plays taken together a characterization of Shakespeare's dissatisfaction with comedy and his inevitable turn to tragedy as the only vehicle adequate to sustain his vision of the crisis of *like*ness in human being.[2]

The Greek word ὑμὴν meaning "thin skin" or "membrane" (*OED* II *sub voce*) derives from an Indo-European root meaning to "sew" or "bind" (Watkins *sub voce*). This ancient history of the word is instructive. The vaginal orifice is sewn or bound shut to secure a (w)hole. Typically, people recoil from this pun, finding it distasteful or trivial or both. Their recoil, however, I suggest, is a powerfully instructive behavior; it leads us to the dark wisdom of our unconscious, which knows (without telling us) that there is something amiss and awry in a hole that is whole in order to be ruptured and transgressed in the name of life and pleasure. Every fiction we invent to deflect (our knowledge of) our origin in the most animal of functions (Stephen Daedalus calls it "an instant of blind rut" [*Ulysses*, "Scylla and Charybdis"—http://www.online.literature.com/jamesjoyce/ulysses/9/]) serves only and paradoxically to remind us that we are not mind only. The hymen then not only mocks our pretensions to purity, it also mocks our pretensions to (the security of) hard and fast categories.[3]

Shakespeare, I suggest, was keenly aware of the infirmity of Hymen's achievement: "I bar confusion." Barring confusion, Hymen sorts the couples only generic-ly, by genre/gender/generation, according to amorous inclination. Hymen can sort only into consorts. Hymen can establish genealogies. Hymen cannot secure individuality. Hymen can tell Rosalind whose wife she is to be, whose daughter she is, whose mother she may be. Hymen cannot, however, tell her who she *is*—he cannot make her her own.

Comedy is the genre of genealogy. I suspect no playwright ever intuited this more deeply than Shakespeare. But, just so, comedy cannot tell you who you are, only to whom you belong.[4] Only tragedy can tell you who you are—and tragedy most often is the tragedy of *losing* those to whom you belong: Hamlet, his father; Cordelia, her father; Titus, his daughter; Brutus, his Caesar; Othello, his Desdemona. By the time he has written the sequence *As You Like It, Hamlet, Twelfth Night*, Shakespeare will find himself not in the village, or the nearby forest, of comedy but in the city of tragedy (Elsinore, Rome, Venice, Athens), where a new world order—the irony of the title *renaissance* (re-birth) is mordant—will demand a new method for sorting the individual out. Now the way to the individual will be not genealogy but psychology, to *is* not through *of* (this or that family) but through *as* (this or that role or part or construction) and "the intricate evasions of as."

Before proceeding with various particular demonstrations, it may help the more readily to see my argument and its implications if we consider two apparently minor features of the play, the sudden conversion of Duke Frederick at the very end of the play and the personal names of several of the principals of the play. Regarding Duke Frederick's conversion, one may be forgiven for feeling that it is uncommonly convenient, even if in the Forest of Ardenne anything can happen. Still, the more arresting dimension of it is rather its insistence on generality and categoriality. As Jaques observes, "[t]he Duke hath put on a religious life/And thrown into neglect the pompous court.../Out of these *convertites* / There is much matter to be heard and learned" (*AYL* 5.4.179-80, 182-3; emphasis added). The Duke's individuality is wholly subsumed under the category of "convertites"; and note, especially, that the *-ites* suffix (*OED* II *sub voce*, "with the sense '[one] connected with or belonging to', 'a member of'") insists even more emphatically on the membership or the group subsuming the Duke, absorbing his individuality and his identity. In the end, *As You Like It* is very much a play of *it like you is* and so you belong to it.

As for the names of several principals, leaving aside for the moment the *Orlando furioso* and the whole Ariostan element, consider only the suggestion of incestuous duplication in them: Orlando, Ro(w)land, Ro(s)al(i)nd, Jaques, Jaques de Boys, all associated with Duke *Senior*. I infer an insistence on repetition and duplication that serves to underscore the genealogical inwardness of the play's dynamic: so many are of the same name, or are simply senior (and junior) to each other, that sorting, such as Hymen's, will only go so far — it must overlook the individual whom it can only affiliate with the family (name) or the class or the generations.[5] And when, in the next play, Shakespeare plumbs this crisis of sorting and likeness (as it has never before or since been dramatized), the two principals of the *same name*, Hamlet, will descend into arguably the greatest tragedy of paternal-filial likeness ever conceived; and the Prince will only know who "Hamlet" is when he has assented to his (m)other—

acknowledging genealogy but only through (individual) psychology ("in the intricate evasions of as").

Touchstone is the character who best focuses attention on the work of the word *like* in *As You Like It*. Besides being assigned one of Shakespeare's profoundest insights, "the truest poetry is the most feigning" (*AYL* 3.3.16-17), Touchstone the clown time and again reveals, as his name implies, the true mettle(/metal) of those who associate with him (come in touch with him). This is most evident in act 5 in the brief scene leading up to Shakespeare's exquisite celebration of the word *if*:

> JAQUES ... Good my lord, *like* this
> fellow.
> DUKE SENIOR I *like* him very well.
> TOUCHSTONE God'ield you, sir, I desire you of the *like*. I
> press in here, sir, amongst the rest of the *country
> copulatives*, to swear, and to forswear, according as
> marriage binds and blood breaks ...
> DUKE SENIOR By my faith, he is very swift and sententious.
> TOUCHSTONE According to the fool's bolt, sir, and such
> dulcet diseases.
> ...
> TOUCHSTONE *Your "if" is the only peacemaker; much virtue
> in "if."*
> JAQUES (*to the Duke*) Is not this a rare fellow, my lord?
> He's as good at anything, and yet a fool.
> *AYL* 5.4.51-57; 62-64; 100-3 (emphasis added)

When Duke Senior and Touchstone, Jaques mediating, *like* each other, the play realizes a profound philosophical theorem: only when nobility and the clown, the high and the low, *like* each other can Hymen enter the scene (he arrives immediately following Duke Senior's words in response to Jaques' "and yet a fool," at line 106) because only then can "these doubts [be made] all even" (*AYL* 5.4.25).[6] This is the genius of comedy, call it "country copulatives," the expression of the social copula by which the sorting or categorizing of genres and generations (within the village) takes place, by which the *doubles* become even. Comedy oversees the oscillation of the categorial barriers to the generations—it is the genre of the copula—and with compelling logic Shakespeare sees therefore that Duke Senior and Touchstone must *like* each other—this is, we would say, how it works. And Shakespeare further folds into this logic the exquisite celebration of *if* that Touchstone offers Duke Senior and Jaques: "Your 'if' is the only peacemaker; much virtue in 'if'." *If* is the marker of the hypothetical ("If it be..."), of the counter-factual ("If this were the case, then .."), of the optative ("If only it might be...!"):

> I knew when seven justices could not take up a
> quarrel, but when the parties were met themselves,
> one of them thought but of an "if," as "If you said so,
> then I said so," and they shook hands and swore
> brothers.
>
> *AYL* 5.4.96-100

"They shook hands and swore brothers" is the very ground of village (κώμη) being—*if* is the touchstone of *com*edy ("Imagine how it would be in the Forest of Ardenne if..."). When *if* the "peacemaker" is in power, then Hymen, "god of every town," can celebrate that there is "mirth in heaven, /When earthly things made even/Atone together." *If* imagines *different* sorts of *copulatives* that *at-one* together.

If, however, is always the first victim of tragedy.

> **MACBETH** *If* it were done when 'tis done, then 'twere well
> It were done quickly. *If* th'assassination
> Could trammel up the consequence, and catch
> With his surcease success: that but this blow
> Might be the be-all and the end-all, here,
> But here upon this bank and shoal of time,
> We'd jump the life to come.
>
> *Mac.* 1.7.1-7 (emphasis added)

The hairs on the back of our necks tell us that this *if* is all but illusory, fleeting, a disappearing impetus on the way to murder and its gruesome consequences:

> **MACBETH** *If* we should fail?
> **LADY MACBETH** We fail!
> But screw your courage to the sticking-place
> And we'll not fail.
>
> *Mac.* 1.7.59-61 (emphasis added)

So brief is the (candle)power of *if*.

Ultimately, the most pressing definition of tragedy I can imagine is the foreclosure of all options—no more *ifs*. By this definition, the profoundest response to tragedy is probably Hamlet's:

> Not a whit. We defy augury. There's a special
> providence in the fall of a sparrow. *If* it be now, 'tis
> not to come. *If* it be not to come, it will be now. *If* it
> be not now, yet it will come. The readiness is all. Since
> no man has aught of what he leaves, what is't to leave
> betimes?
>
> Ham. 5.2.165-70 (emphasis added)

To be able, after all that he has suffered, to restore the power of *if* to his world this far is, I believe, the touchstone of Hamlet's humanity as well as of *Hamlet*'s greatness. The play, I propose, is *As You Like It* in the tragic mode, the over 90 occurrences of the word *like* in it serving repeatedly to insist on the necessity confronting the individual subject Hamlet to choose his *like*ness himself, "in the intricate evasions of as," as he likes it, assent to it, and embrace the consequences—"the readiness is all."

The clown Touchstone teaches us that the word *like* is a touchstone not only in *As You Like It* but also in Shakespeare's entire dramatic output, which contains nearly 2400 occurrences of the word. Shakespeare's theater of likeness emerges from his incomparable understanding of what it means to say that theater sees and shows what something is like. He who would maintain that "I have that within which passeth show—/These but the trappings and the suits of woe" (*Ham.* 1.2.85-86), is fated to learn that nothing within can ever appear without unless it passes through the likeness of trappings and suits —"[t]he deepest thing, it's the skin" (Valery, above, Introduction page 1). It must be performed: this is the tragedy of the human condition, that the options we can imagine within ("*If* only...") are always limited and curtailed by what we can show without, which, like the performance of a play, can *only* be *a* performance, bound by the limiting conditions of the theater's time, place, and audience. I am always more than I can show you. This reality, however, does not relieve me of the burden of readiness (I must always be ready to show you more).

Like is a touchstone of Shakespeare's drama because every time *like* touches a character it classifies her, correlates him, hierarchizes him or her, maps her or his (e)motions toward or away from each other. As you like it likens you to an *is* and therefore best be careful of your *as*—you may not like it when the play is over. "Do you like me, Kate?" asks Henry V. "*Pardonnez-moi*, I cannot tel vat is 'like me'" (*HV* 5.2.106-8), replies Kate, who must pay a high price for this inability to translate (as she) likes.

As You Like It, the argument positions us to see, is also a play of trappings and suits. Literally, cross-dressing multiplies trappings and suits for Rosalind and Celia, a.k.a. Ganymede and Aliena. But beyond cross-dressing and gender-bending or performing gender are the trappings and the suits of the generational categories or prescribed likenesses that the principals are supposed (lit., "placed underneath") by powerful conventions to wear. Orlando is a junior son; Rosalind, the daughter of a banished Duke; Adam, the aged servant of a deceased knight whose family is out of favor with a tyrannical overlord. Prescribed likenesses abound and characters struggle against them, chiefly by leaving the court to enter the forest, abandoning culture for nature, where *if*, the possibility of options, is not foreclosed—or, at least, so it is hoped. This is pastoral, we recognize, profound liminal space of transformation. But even so, here, Hymen can only "bar confusion." "Much virtue in 'if'" there may be, but when "these doubts [are made] all even," prescriptive likenesses still touch all the characters. Peace and atonement still depend on submission to categories.

I believe that this contingency vexed Shakespeare and pushed him beyond the limits of genre. So much is evident, clearly I think, in the Epilogue:

> **ROSALIND** (*to the audience*)
> *It is not the fashion* to see the
> lady the epilogue; ... 'tis *true that a good play needs
> no epilogue*. Yet ...
> *good plays prove the better by the help of good
> epilogues*. What a *case* am I in then, ...
>   I charge
> you, O women, for the love you bear to men, to *like*
> as much of this play *as please you*. And I charge you,
> O men, ...
>   *If I
> were a woman* I would kiss as many of you as had
> beards that pleased me, *complexions that liked me*, and
> breaths that I defied not. ...
> when I make curtsy, bid me farewell.
>   AYL Epilogue 1-2; 4-7; 7-9; 11-14; 16-19; 21
>   (emphasis added)

The question is, who gets to prescribe the categories to which one submits? Who is *the* scribe? *Who* says that "[i]t is not the fashion to see the lady the epilogue"? What *if* it were best that the lady be the epilogue? Why can't a play or a person be more than and other than the rule? Why must the rule prescribe the event? Who dictates to Shakespeare what he can write?

We have come to the crux of the action in *As You Like It*:

DUKE FREDERICK *Let it suffice thee that I trust thee not.*
ROSALIND Yet your mistrust cannot make me a traitor.
Tell me whereon the *likelihood* depends?
DUKE FREDERICK *Thou art thy father's daughter — there's enough.*
ROSALIND So was I when your highness took his dukedom;
So was I when your highness banished him.
Treason is not inherited, my lord.

AYL 1.3.54-60 (emphasis added)

The likelihood depends on generation: like father, like daughter, the Duke would seem to say. And though Rosalind protest that "[t]reason is not inherited," the Duke is bent on *essentializing* the generational or genealogical "likelihood," and he will not heed her. His motive? The knowledge he secretly (and selfishly) harbors that there is *no essential* and on account of which he upbraids his daughter Celia:

DUKE FREDERICK She is too subtle for thee, and her smoothness,
Her very silence, and her patience
Speak to the people, and they pity her.
Thou art a fool. *She robs thee of thy name,*
And *thou wilt show more bright* and seem more
    virtuous
When she is gone.

AYL 1.3.76-81 (emphasis added)

All appearance is by likeness. If the people have Rosalind to whom to compare Celia, Celia will *show* less bright; with Rosalind banished, Celia will "show more bright"—it's all very simple, not to mention cruel. And the Duke's very next sentence—"Then open not thy lips" (AYL 1.3.81)— only worsens the cruelty by targeting what every misogynist trusts least in woman, her lips ... and her lips; indeed, the "very silence" of her lips (Rosalind's, in this case) is not to be trusted either. And so, to banish Rosalind, which he must do, the Duke pretends to essentialize the real; whereas, to promote his daughter, he presumes that the real is show. (Why not? they are, after all, just girls.) Shakespeare, I propose, invented his theater of likeness to find a way out of such contradictoriness and petty arbitrariness. But the way must pass through the great tragedies—only so can that within which passeth show expect "in the intricate evasions of as" to make up the trappings and suits of woe.

Once we have seen Duke Frederick's hypocrisy, we understand, first that he but advises Celia with the like counsel he followed himself with his brother, Duke *Senior*: banish the likeness (which, moreover, is elder, senior), banish the comparison—supposedly. But we also see, if after some pause, that we here encounter as well one of the deepest motives of Shakespeare's imagination, or the fascination with doubles, twins, iteration, and repetition. Indeed, the particular dramatization of competitive likeness in *As You Like It* leads to similar developments in *Twelfth Night* where twinship and disguise reach very far into a dynamic of revelation that, I think, must properly be called psychological, if not in fact psychoanalytic (Malvolio, "ill will," being the very character of the delusional who protests that he is not mad).

Crucial to this analysis, and where it must begin, is the moment of Celia's rebuke of Rosalind for thinking she alone is banished:

> **CELIA**   Rosalind, lack'st thou then the love
> Which teacheth thee that *thou and I am one*?
> Shall we be sundered? Shall we part, sweet girl?
> No. Let my father seek another heir.
> AYL 1.3.95-98 (emphasis added)

We have here, "thou and I am one," a Shakespearean signature. The plural subject and the singular verb instance a lifelong obsession with "slaying number":

> So they loved as love in twain
> Had the essence but in one,
> Two distincts, division none.
> *Number there in love was slain.*
> "The Phoenix and Turtle," lines 25-28
(emphasis added)

Whether we turn to "The Phoenix and Turtle" or *Romeo and Juliet* or *Antony and Cleopatra*, we find Shakespeare, and find him *always*, seeking "division none" in "two distincts," longing to see "division grow together" ("The Phoenix and Turtle," line 42)—"thou *and* I *am* one." For Shakespeare, the escape from rivalrous likeness is erotic fusion, fusion so complete that "[e]ither was the other's mine" ("The Phoenix and Turtle," line 36). But this condition, we know, as he knew, is impossible of attainment in mortality. Hymen may "bar confusion," but he cannot promise or secure fusion—"man and wife is one flesh," says Hamlet (*Ham.* 4.3.54), yes, but irony is oozing from his lips when he utters the claim. Nor do I think Shakespeare shared one flesh with Anne Hathaway (Honan 231-6). But I also think—and I will risk saying so (I am this much a humanist)—such sharing was his deepest longing, most hurtful ache, least relenting frustration.

It is hardly difficult to understand, then, why Rosalind and Celia, who "am one," become Ganymede and Aliena. Ganymede is the very marker of the homosocial and the homoerotic, the longing for fusion with the divine, and, yet, as we know, Ganymede and fusion both are alike inseparable from alienation (Jupiter abducts the boy). Such are the integrity and the precision of Shakespeare's imagination that even when he breaks the language to his Will—"thou and I am one"—he does not shrink from the terrible truth of sexual division. Long before Lacan, he understood that "il n'y a pas de rapport sexuel" (*L'envers* 134; Evans, *Dictionary* 181): there is never that fusion soul teases body with or body threatens soul with. "We perish, each alone" *(To The Lighthouse* IV) may be just what a man (Mr. Ramsey) would say, but if Shakespeare should be the man who says it, it is difficult to turn a deaf ear—no writer ever dreamed harder of and for an alternative

> that should teach us
> There's a divinity that shapes our ends,
> Rough-hew them how we will —
>
> <div style="text-align:right"><i>Ham.</i> 5.2.9-11</div>

How can we not heed a writer who hears "a div-inity that shapes ou | r | ends /Rough-hew them how we will [as we like it]"?[7]

19
"A figure like your father":
Hamlet—Like Mother, Like Son

> For if the King like not the comedy,
> Why then, belike he likes it not, pardie.
> *Ham.* 3.2.280-1

> **metal**...app. related in some way to μεταλλᾶν to seek after, explore.
> *OED* II M: 667

> As Great Shapesphere puns it.
> James Joyce, *Finnegans Wake* 295.3-4

The logic of likeness in *Hamlet* plays itself out with thrilling and, eventually, terrifying consequences, unparalleled perhaps in Shakespeare's theater of likeness.[1] "Is it not *like* the King?" Marcellus asks Horatio when the ghost appears, and Horatio replies: "As thou art to thyself" (*Ham.* 1.1.57-58; emphasis added).[2] But Hamlet says, only a short while later: "A was a man. Take him for all in all,/I shall not look upon his *like* again" (*Ham.* 1.2.186-7; emphasis added). And his lament can hardly fail to trouble us the more because we have just heard him scorn "mine uncle,/My father's brother, ... no more *like* my father/Than I to Hercules" (*Ham.* 1.2.151-3; emphasis added). Whether too much or too little, *like*(ness), from the beginning, stalks the characters' talk—and thus our response as well.

These instances, with a great many others (*like* occurs over 90 times in the play), suggest the thesis and the argument that I wish to pursue in this chapter—namely, that one discourse for explaining the tragedy of *Hamlet* is that of the crisis of likeness, of which the psychopathology most revulsive, as it is also most recurrent, in Western culture's self-representation, is incest. I argue, in particular, that Hamlet fears most uncontrollably his likeness not with his father, nor with Claudius, nor Horatio, nor Laertes, nor Fortinbras, nor Rosencrantz, nor Guildenstern, nor the players, nor

Osric, nor Polonius, nor Ophelia, nor Yorick, but rather—and it is, after this list, obvious who comes next—with his mother, Gertrude. Hamlet is, indeed, as others have shown, like all these other characters in the play in some particular or particulars; but it is the likeness with Gertrude that he fears the most, not only the likeness with her bespoken by his and her sexual desires but also the likeness bespoken by his and her identities. Incest is not only copulation, incest is also copying. And how if Hamlet should be a copy of Gertrude? How if he should desire his father as she did? How if he should desire Claudius, as she does? (The homoerotic pervades this world, saturated as it may be with the heteroerotic.) How if he desired Hamlet's death (Oedipus' conundrum) as she did? How stands it then in Denmark? How stands it then with Hamlet? How, to be blunt, stands it?

I take it that at least part of Hamlet's crisis, and at least one reason for his (in)famous hesitation, is the question of succession: "A little more than kin and less than kind" (*Ham.* 1.2.65) *and never king*. Hamlet is less than kind toward Claudius because Claudius has made him more than kin, usurping the place of his father as well as the place of his mother's husband, and thus interposed himself between Hamlet and Hamlet. (I will ignore, for reasons that I think are obvious, the distinction between Hamlet, Sr. and Hamlet, Jr.; Ophelia is my witness: "And with a look so piteous in purport /As if he had been loosèd out of hell/To speak of horrors, he comes before me" [*Ham.* 2.1.83-5; emphasis added].) As long as Claudius reigns ("He that hath killed my king and whored my mother,/Popped in between th'election and my hopes" [*Ham.* 5.2.65-66]), Hamlet cannot succeed to his (father's) throne. The sequence *kin* > *kind* cries out the missing graph. And if Hamlet is not to be (*kin, kind,*) *king*, then whom is Hamlet (to) like?

The answer is as strange to him as it is to us, at least at first. In the political logic on which the play insists, he is like Gertrude. He is like Gertrude because, blocked from the succession, he is in the feminine position ("Must, like a whore, unpack my heart with words/And fall a-cursing like a very drab,/A scullion" [*Ham.* 2.2.588-90]). Hamlet (t-h-[e] m-a-l-e^3) is marked feminine. And it is from the feminine position that he must act for almost the rest of his life. Castrated and defective (the misogynist's icon of the despised female ["frailty, thy name is woman" (*Ham.* 1.2.146)]), little wonder he does not like himself, he is not like himself: "For he was *like*ly, had he been put on,/To have proved most royally" (*Ham.* 5.2.351-2; emphasis added). But what "he" would have been put on?—this he or that he, that is the question.[4]

The case I am making can be illustrated in a number of places in the play, but the following cross-section of Act I will perhaps be most helpful (emphasis added).

MARCELLUS   Look where it comes again.
BARNARDO In the same figure *like* the King that's dead.
...
BARNARDO Looks it not *like* the King? — Mark it, Horatio.
HORATIO Most *like*. It harrows me with fear and wonder.
Ham. 1.1.38-39; 41-42

MARCELLUS Is it not *like* the King?
HORATIO As thou art to thyself.
Ham. 1.1.57-58

HAMLET A was a man. Take him for all in all,
I shall not look upon his *like* again.
HORATIO My lord, I think I saw him yesternight.
HAMLET Saw? Who?
HORATIO My lord, the King your father.
Ham. 1.2.186-90

HORATIO   A figure *like* your father,
Armed at all points exactly, cap-à-pie,
Appears ..
The apparition comes. I knew your father;
These hands are not more *like*.
Ham. 1.2.199-201; 211-212

HORATIO It would have much amazed you.
HAMLET Very *like*, very *like*.
Ham. 1.2.234-5

This sample may serve as a guide. It registers the insistence in the play on the almost independent agency of *like*(ness).

If we take this sample as a guide, we will find that the play charges the word *like* with a sometimes almost unbearable predictivity (and productivity):

HORATIO If your mind *dislike* anything, obey it. I will
   forestall their repair hither, and say you are not fit.
Ham. 5.2.163-4 (emphasis added)

I am arguing that only when we have paused, if just a (heart)beat, over the words "if your mind dislike," can we begin to take the measure of what follows:

> **HAMLET** Not a whit. We defy augury. There's a special providence in the fall of a sparrow. If it be now, 'tis not to come. If it be not to come, it will be now. If it be not now, yet it will come. The readiness is all. Since no man has aught of what he leaves, what is't to leave betimes?
>
> *Ham.* 5.2.165-70

We hear, now, how "their re*pair* hither" will actually pair Hamlet and also how it will *spare* him (even a *spar*row), with the likeness in which he will leave this life. We hear how he will leave as ready as a man can be ("since no man has aught [but also: has sought] of what he leaves, what is't to leave betimes?"), and leave, foil now (*Ham.* 5.2.201), likeness even, to Laertes ("This *likes* me well," Hamlet says of his "foil" [*Ham.* 5.2.212; emphasis added]); and we also come to appreciate what he means when he talks of such "foolery ... such a kind of gain-giving as would perhaps trouble a woman" (*Ham.* 5.2.161-2), which he feels "about [his] heart—but it is no matter" (*Ham.* 5.2.158-9), since he is now about to cross the woman, the *mat(t)er*, out,[5] assume his likeness and its awful price, death, as he finally scripts his own story:

> **HAMLET** Was't Hamlet wronged Laertes? Never Hamlet.
> If Hamlet from himself be ta'en away,
> And when he's not himself does wrong Laertes,
> Then Hamlet does it not, Hamlet denies it.
> Who does it then? His madness. If't be so,
> Hamlet is of the faction that is wronged.
> His madness is poor Hamlet's enemy.
>
> *Ham.* 5.2.179-85

If Hamlet now from himself is *not* taken away, then, clearly, such sanity, at least here, is prologue to murder and, perhaps, worse.[6] Laertes responds: "I do receive your offered love *like* love, / And will not wrong it" (*Ham.* 5.2.197-8; emphasis added). The depth of Laertes' hatred presumably we must measure by the likes of the fissure opened in his love by *like*(ness): love *like* love is *not* love.[7]

Like, we know, derives from a root meaning "form" or "shape" and in Anglo-Saxon means "body."[8] I think it would be difficult to exaggerate how important this history is to the tragedy of Hamlet[9]: in a different body (a son's), Hamlet is nonetheless insufficiently different from his father or his mother, too *like* them (especially his mother), to enter into his patrimony or his matrimony; separation in Hamlet and for Hamlet has failed, and thus incest, the scandal of (con)fusion (failure of separation), haunts him throughout the play.[10] Thus, to take one easily overlooked example, the name *Claudius* shares the Latin root *claud-* ("shut," "close"[11]) which produces *claudicare*, "to limp" (Skeat 93; Ayto 118). Oedipus, the club-foot (who limps [Sophocles 14 and 123-4]), shadows Hamlet (*t-h-[e]-l-a-m-e*) in the uncle, Claudius, who commits incest (so Hamlet calls it [*Ham.* 1.2.157; 1.5.83]) with his mother, Gertrude. Everywhere Hamlet is surrounded with too much likeness:

> **KING CLAUDIUS** Thy loving father, Hamlet.
> **HAMLET** My mother. Father and mother is man and wife,
>   man and wife is one flesh, and so my mother.
> *Ham.* 4.3.52-54

Madness, then (or, at least, its simulation), is his one recourse to difference. But he is not mad in the closet scene with his mother (though she thinks he is), where likeness, specifically the body, overwhelms him, confuses him, and destines him to meet his double in Laertes. Here, in a likeness of the Oedipal crisis, a pseudo-Oedipus, in effect, Hamlet kills the wrong father while playing father to his mother with his homily to her of, and from, the realm of the symbolic: "O, throw away the worser part of it,/ and live the purer with the other half!" (*Ham.* 3.4.148-9). Father, husband, son—Hamlet is all and yet none.

The logic of likeness is fierce and intractable. To be like is to be different (enough) to mark the space across which likeness can synapse: too much difference and the space is chasmic, no communication at all obtains; too little difference and the space is chaosmic, (con)fusion threatens to overwhelm communication. Nowhere in art is this terrifying logic more palpable and threatening than in theater, for theater is the space of likeness—without likeness theater is impossible.

Hence *The Mousetrap*, the postscript that is also a prescript (cf. Cavell 189-91):

> **HAMLET**   I'll have these players
> Play something *like* the murder of my father
> Before mine uncle.
> *Ham.* 2.2.596-8 (emphasis added)

> **KING CLAUDIUS** What do you call the play?
> **HAMLET** *The Mousetrap.* Marry, how? Tropically. This play
>   is the *image* of a murder done in Vienna.
> *Ham.* 3.2.225-7 (emphasis added)

"A figure like your father"

The play within the play is the incest of the play (the play playing with its own), the perverse doubling that foregrounds drama's perpetual disruption of the boundaries between self and other, male and female, inner and outer, etc. Beyond the specular *mise en abîme* of post-modernism, this moment, when the tropical is the trapical, is anamnesic, a recalling of the forgotten that is remembered *as* forgotten (Plato's Socratic reverie— *Meno*, 368-71). For this is what is trapped and troped in the play within the play, where the mouse that is trapped is not Claudius, not Claudius at all (cf. Adelman, *Mothers* 24-25; Parker, *Margins* 265), but rather her whom Hamlet calls Claudius' "mouse," his mother Gertrude (*Ham.* 3.4.167)— that soft, round, furry thing.[12] And, just so, Hamlet knew already but had "forgotten" that the guilty mouse was his mother: "Madam, how *like* you this play?" may just as pertinently be punctuated with an exclamation point—"Madam, how *like* you this play!" And thus, just so, Gertrude's reply: "The lady protests too much, methinks" (*Ham.* 3.2.218-19; emphasis added). "The Queen, the Queen's to blame" (cf. *Ham.* 5.2.273; Adelman, *Mothers* 30). Exactly. So what more does Hamlet need?

Of knowledge, nothing, of course. But knowledge is not enough. If knowledge were enough, who of us would not be (thin)king (cf. *Ham.* 2.2.251-2)? No, Hamlet needs difference. Which is to say, identity. He needs to I.D. the culprit else his own I.D. will never become an I.[13] And so he waits for Claudius, to con*claud* his trap. And at the moment of closure, he observes,

> if the King *like* not the comedie,
> Why then, *belike* he *likes* it not, pardie.
>
> *Ham.* 3.2.280-1 (emphasis added)

The misprision is exact: it is not a "comedie" (rather a "tragedy" [*Ham.* 3.2.142]), but it is (an invitation) to *come die* (I retain F's spelling of *comedie*) and so the king likes it not, pardie ("I *like* him not, nor stands it safe with us" [*Ham.* 3.3.1; emphasis added]). No, Hamlet's hesitation is not a problem of knowledge, it is a problem of I.D.-ing, of becoming able, finally, to say: "This is I, / Hamlet the Dane" (*Ham.* 5.1.253-4) — which amounts to saying (let us not flinch from admitting it): "I did it, I am to blame."[14] Every child bereaved of a parent "knows," at some level, that s/he killed that parent (herein, for me, lies the genius of Cavell's reading of *The Mousetrap* [179-91]); and (dis)owning that "knowledge" (which is false but feels, all the same, very real) can be so great a burden the child does not, cannot survive it: "How stand I, then, / That have a father killed, a mother stained" (*Ham.* Q2 4.4.47-48; Oxford 2ᵉ 718J).[15] Indeed, how does Hamlet stand?

Laertes, I take it, has an I.D. all along—he is Polonius' (and his [absent] mother's) son, Ophelia's brother: he is the one who r-e-l-a-t-e-s:

POLONIUS This above all — to thine own self be true,
And it must follow, as the night the day,
Thou canst not then be false to any man.
Ham. 1.3.78-80

It is his role to relate (within the symbolic order) in just that way that defines Hamlet's failure to relate:

KING CLAUDIUS Laertes, was your father dear to you?
Or are you *like* the painting of a sorrow,
A face without a heart?
LAERTES   Why ask you this?
KING CLAUDIUS Not that I think you did not love your father...
Ham. 4.7.90-93 (emphasis added)

Of course not; of course, Laertes loved his father; there can be no question, etc. But that, of course, really is not the question. The question really is, how is it that Laertes *a-l-t-e-r-(e)-s* Hamlet's ego? how is it that Laertes' I.D. alters Hamlet's I? Fundamental to any answer we may offer will be the play's prior insight that the subject is not a subject except as anOther—

HAMLET I dare not confess that, lest I should compare
with him in excellence. But to know a man well were
to know himself[16]
Ham. Q2 5.2.30-32 (Oxford 2ᵉ 718N)—

even as the subject cannot speak without an (H)*oratio* ("speech") other to it:

HAMLET O God, Horatio, what a wounded name,
Things standing thus unknown, shall live behind me!
If thou didst ever hold me in thy heart,
Absent thee from felicity a while,
And in this harsh world draw thy breath in pain
To tell my story.
Ham. 5.2.296-301

Everywhere Hamlet turns, he confronts the reality of incest, which is hardly reducible to mere copulation—incest is also copying (fusion and confusion). And to grasp the import of incest as copying in *Hamlet*, it is necessary finally to confront one of the scandals of the play, or its indulgence in puns—"We must speak by the card, or equivocation will undo us" (*Ham.* 5.1.133-5). A pun is incestuous, the copulation of signifiers that should remain separate, producing a word containing imperfect copies of other words (Shoaf, *Duality* 60-71). Moreover, says Dr. Johnson (*Selections* 21-22):

> A quibble [i.e. pun] is to Shakespeare what luminous vapours are to the traveller; he follows it at all adventures, it is sure to lead him out of his way, and sure to engulf him in the mire. It has some malignant power over his mind, and its fascinations are irresistible. Whatever be the dignity or profundity of his disquisition, whether he be enlarging knowledge or exalting affection, whether he be amusing attention with incidents or enchaining it in suspense, let but a quibble spring up before him, and he leaves his work unfinished. A quibble is the golden apple for which he will always turn aside from his career, or stoop from his elevation. A quibble, poor and barren as it is, gave him such delight, that he was content to purchase it, by the sacrifice of reason, propriety, and truth. A quibble was to him the fatal Cleopatra for which he lost the world, and was content to lose it.

In many respects, this is an inexaggerably important piece of criticism (and not just of Shakespeare), but for my purposes what matters most in it is the demonizing of "quibbles" that culminates in the (predictable) demonizing of the woman (Cleopatra). You just know a pun has got to be (a) female:

> **HAMLET** Do you think I meant country matters?
> **OPHELIA** I think nothing, my lord.
> **HAMLET** That's a fair thought to lie between maids' legs.
> **OPHELIA** What is, my lord?
> **HAMLET** No thing.
> **OPHELIA** You are merry, my lord.
>
> *Ham.* 3.2.111-16

Hardly the least famous pun in English literature, "country matters" will do just nicely to make the point ("thing"): a pun like "c(o)unt(ry) mat(t)ers" is a no thing (Willbern, *Play* 125-42)—a "cunt mother," that is to say, irreducibly plural (cf. Irigaray's famous title, *Ce sexe qui n'en est pas un—This Sex Which Is Not One*). A pun like "c(o)unt(ry) mat(t)ers" scandalizes the symbolic order, which likes things hard and fast. And so Hamlet puns. This *m-e-t-a-l* Hamlet, who finds Ophelia "mettle more attractive" (*Ham.* 3.2.105), puns remorselessly throughout the play, even unto the very end—"The rest is silence" (*Ham.* 5.2.310)—and scandalizes just those who serve the symbolic order (and in turn are served by it):

> **HAMLET** ...I eat the air, promise-crammed. You cannot feed capons so.
> **KING CLAUDIUS** *I have nothing with this answer, Hamlet. These words are not mine.*
> **HAMLET** *No, nor mine now. (To Polonius) My lord, you played once i'th' university, you say.*
> **POLONIUS** That I did, my lord, and was accounted a good actor.
> **HAMLET** And what did you enact?
> **POLONIUS** I did enact Julius Caesar. I was killed i'th' Capitol. Brutus killed me.
> **HAMLET** It was a brute part of him to kill so capital a calf there.
> *Ham.* 3.2.90-102 (emphasis added)

"These words are not mine." Indeed. That is the question. Whose are the words? some "c-H-A-M-E-L-eon's"? The words "my desire" can be uttered by any one of hundreds of millions of speakers of English. And shall I labor under the illusion that my desire is special? Why, of course, I shall. So does everyone. So does Hamlet. Which, of course, is why he is (apparently) mad. To make words one's own is to appropriate them to meanings so idiotic (as well as idiolectal) as to sound mad:

> **POLONIUS** What is the matter, my lord?
> **HAMLET** Between who?
> **POLONIUS** I mean the matter you read, my lord.
> *Ham.* 2.2.196-8

But then madness has a way of sounding different:

> **POLONIUS** (*aside*) Though this be madness, yet there is method in't. — Will you walk out of the air, my lord?
> **HAMLET** Into my grave.
> **POLONIUS** Indeed, that is out o'th' air. (*Aside*) How *pregnant* sometimes his replies are! A happiness that often madness hits on, which reason and sanity could not so prosperously *be delivered of.*
> *Ham.* 2.2.207-13 (emphasis added)

Madness, punning, has a way of sounding like (a) woman: *pregnant* and *delivered of* meanings in which Reason and Sanity (the symbolic order) are not so pro(s)per-ous,[17] puns (two meanings in one sound) are the fee males must pay to speak:

> **HAMLET** Yet I,
> A dull and muddy-mettled rascal, peak
> Like John-a-dreams, *unpregnant of* my cause,
> And *can say nothing*...
>
> *Ham.* 2.2.568-71 (emphasis added)

Until he is pregnant, Hamlet "can say nothing." In order to speak, Hamlet must give birth:

> **KING CLAUDIUS** Love? His affections do not that way tend,
> Nor what he spake, though it lacked form a little,
> Was not *like* madness. There's *something in his soul*
> O'er which his melancholy *sits on brood*,
> And I do doubt *the hatch* and the disclose
> Will be some danger.
>
> *Ham.* 3.1.165-70 (emphasis added)

In order to be, Hamlet must be(come) female.[18] At the least, he must trope himself as female, and this he does by punning, for in his mad punning he participates in that two-in-one-ness that yokes madness, punning, and woman. All are improper (i.e., promiscuous, but also metaphoric[19]), and they prosper in pregnancy and delivery, in breeding (not to mention talkativeness). And we know what scandal attends such (s)excess: "Get thee to a nunnery. Why wouldst thou be a breeder of sinners?" (*Ham.* 3.1.122-3). Ophelia must be chastised, even if she should be chaste, "for the power of beauty will sooner transform honesty from what it is to a bawd than the force of honesty can translate beauty into his *likeness*" (*Ham.* 3.1.113-15; emphasis added). Ophelia must be (a) nun/none, threat to "unpregnant" Hamlet that she is.[20]

Surely, *Hamlet* rocks us so just because in its madness it teaches us what we pay for the (communal illusion of the) straight and true, the hard and fast, the pure and simple, etc.: we pay in reality—in the loss of reality—for copies of our desire proliferating in the symbolic order. The more copies of ourselves we make, the more copies of our desires proliferate, the more likely our secrets are to secrete (the play oozes with secretions and secrets alike).

HAMLET So, oft it chances in particular men
That, for some vicious mole of nature in them —...
Ham. Q2 1.4.7-8 (Oxford 2ᵉ 716B)

HAMLET Well said, old mole. Canst work i'th' earth so fast?
A worthy pioneer.
Ham. 1.5.164-5

Even before the mole begins to dig under his feet, Hamlet, such *m-e-t-a-l*, "[a]s Great Shapesphere puns it," knows the mole has already mined his fault(-line): "[He] Shall in the general censure take corruption / From that particular fault" (*Ham.* Q2 1.4.19-20 [Oxford 2ᵉ 716B]). The ghost is but a copy of the mole Hamlet has seen already within himself (cf. Holland 172), minor that he is: the mole in Hamlet is desire for his mother, and so the mole outside Hamlet is (the Ghost's) desire for his mother—Hamlet is frightened finally by Hamlet because finally Hamlet also desires Hamlet.[21]

Because the ghost is but a copy of the mole Hamlet has seen already within himself, we can almost hear him say, "would it were real," or, perhaps more precise, "would it were a true copy." Still, it would be a copy only and could not set him free. Not least of the many achievements in Shakespeare studies in our time has been the demonstration of the importance of *copia* to his writing (Cave, Parker, e.g.). It seems obvious now that we should understand Shakespearean rhetoric explicitly in terms of copiousness. The obvious evidence of copiousness is a copy (they are the same word [Skeat 111; Cave 3-9]). If something is rotten in the state of Denmark, this is surely, as countless others before me have noted, because Elsinore is over-ripe ([s]-*i-n- o-r- e-l-s-e*), teeming with and overrun by copies—too many Hamlets, in particular, for example. The mystery of the play, which no reading will ever plumb or exhaust, seems most spectral here, where it adumbrates Shakespeare's obsession with doubles, twins, mirrors, and copies. As Shakespeare's art is unimaginable without "quibbles," so too is it unimaginable without twins: both puns and twins are two much in the same plays; and that seems to have been just the way he liked it.

I don't know why. *Coincidentia oppositorum*? Plotinus ("All knowing comes by likeness")? Increases in capital (Halpern; Kamps)? "The habit of arguing *in utramque partem*"(Altman 34)? Doubtless many answers will come from many others.[22] But if I may, I will again adduce *syneciosis*, the "condition of being together at home with"—"a coupling or bringing together of contraries, but not in order to oppose them to one another (as in antithesis)" (Burton, *sub voce*). The "crosse-cople" (Puttenham's term for *syneciosis*) was, I think, a way Shakespeare followed to probe one of the most provocative issues in life and art alike and, predictably, as vexing as it is provocative—namely, coincidence. For him, one of the special properties of poetry seems to have been its challenge to the ordinary or accepted notion of coincidence. Poetry deepens if it does not also correct such a notion, exposing in it our efforts to "botch the words up fit to [our] own thoughts" (*Ham.* 4.5.10), to constrain and control, by calling them "coincidences," what are, in fact, complex connections of language and reality that typically disturb, even frighten us, because they confront us with the uncanny feeling of our otherness (*deja vous*, if you like).

Obviously, the uncanny does have a part to play here (Garber, *Ghost Writers* 103ff.). But by itself it is insufficient to tell the story—it implies that "it's all subjective," but that is not what Shakespeare is saying. Shakespeare is saying that it is also a property of the real "to have the engineer / Hoised with his own petard" (*Ham.* Q2 3.4.5-6 [Oxford 2ᵉ 717H])—blown up with his own bomb [lit., *fart*: see *OED* II *sub voce* "petard"]). It is a property of the real that we smell our own farts. We are "together at home with" our *likam* (body, likeness) in more ways than is dreamt of in our philosophy. There are connections within connections within connections. And if our home is *unheimlich*, *Hamlet* is the play that tells us so (and we must not be such Johnsonian purists as to regret petulantly that Shakespeare probably heard and felt the *home* in *hamlet* [in *Hamnet* his son's name as well]).[23] If Freud showed uncanny insight in realizing that *heimlich* ("the homely, the familiar") and *unheimlich* ("the uncanny") are actually just alike, not unlike (Freud, XVII: 219-52), Shakespeare, in this as in so much else, preceded him (and succeeds him) by his practice of *syneciosis*, the trope that "knows" that *heimlich* and *unheimlich* share a likeness: "O, 'tis most sweet / When in one line two crafts directly meet" (*Ham.* Q2 3.4.8-9 [Oxford 2ᵉ 717H]).

Hamlet is the most syneciotic of Shakespeare's plays because *Hamlet* is the play of the (m)other, the one whose genital is the original *Heimat*, the original *hamlet*, the place at once all too familiar and all too strange, utterly desirable and utterly revolting. Hamlet is most like his mother, and in that likeness and through it, Hamlet understands, exquisitely, "how a king may go a progress through the guts of a beggar" (*Ham.* 4.3.30-31). This is Shakespeare, yoking together by sapience the most hetero(homo)geneous of things.[24] Like the actor (he was also an actor), every time he performs, he twins himself, assumes a *syneciosis*, a "crosse-cople," between himself and the (other of his) character, and therein says to us (incestuous?), become a pun, "as you like it."

20
"To like his love":
The Violence of Volition in Illyria (Malvolio | Olivia | Viola/Cesario(n) —Or|si|no [Orison])

> To hear with eyes belongs to love's fine wit.
> Sonnet #23

In the Judeo-Christian tradition, the will is an enormous problem. It does not obey the intellect. It is fallen. It corrupts the mind. It is autonomous. It propels and compels the mind to revelation. It is divided against itself. It is devious. It can be perverse. It can be saintly. It can be immolated in the will of another, such as God's. It can rebel, against even God (taking vast numbers of the heavenly hosts with it). It can be broken. It can resist being broken even unto the cross. The will is a difficult subject.

The apostle of the will is St. Paul. The greatest doctor of the will in the West is St. Augustine.[1] Both teach the West to distrust the will. At the same time, both insist that something must be done with the will. Probably the archetypal decision is St. Paul's: "not I but Christ in me" (Galations 2:20, for example—and many versions thereof). But this decision, as we know, only reflects the founding decision of the Christian economy, or the absolute sacrifice of the will of the Son in and to the will of the Father. If something must be done with the will, in the Christian economy, the best and the highest thing to do with it is to give it up, sacrifice it, subject it to death—"Greater love hath no man than this, that a man lay down his life for his friends" (John 15:13). It is better to kill the will than suffer the will to kill its subject.

The paradoxes, the pains, and the undeniable triumphs of the will constitute one of the deep motives for Shakespeare's constant fascination and struggle with *like*ness in his dramas. Jacques Lacan provides preliminary access to why this should be so:

> Just as the senseless oppression of the superego lies at the root of the motivated imperatives of conscience, the passionate desire peculiar to man *to impress his image in reality* is the obscure basis of the rational mediations of the will.[2]

Humans are not only, to borrow a favorite image of the Renaissance, simians, copying what they see around them, they are also, at the same time, to borrow from Aristotle, "political animals," that insist on *being copied*—preferably, usually, by those who are (considered) inferior.[3] This, naturally, is what a royal court is all about: the high and the mighty and the wealthy postures and preens in the hope that he or she will become all the fashion, fashioning a self that others will desperately desire to copy.[4] This is power. And although it is sick, as we know, it is remarkably tenacious in its sickness, as we also know. By making you like me (in all senses that the phrase will bear), I acquire power over you; and no drug is more addictive or more lethal than power.

People by and large prefer to (be) like those who (are) like them because there is in this, at least potential, mutuality some promise of power-sharing. I (am) like you and thus give you some power over me; you (are) like me and thus give me some power over you. In all of Shakespeare's plays no character more exquisitely deconstructs this fiction of mutuality than Malvolio, whose striving for uniqueness and singularity (*TN* 2.5.146-7) may provoke our laughter but only at the expense of our comfort—as Olivia says: "He hath been most notoriously abused" (*TN* 5.1.375). Malvolio refuses the whirligig of social mutuality; and, however impure his motives, and however fitting the abuses he receives as comeuppance, the consequences of his *amour-propre* (*TN* 1.5.86) are profoundly instructive. He may be understood to be Hamlet without "that within which passeth show"—without, that is, Hamlet's searingly acute sense that without being (a)like there can be no being, however difficult being thus is. If Malvolio's "trappings and suits of woe" are ludicrous cross-garterings that elicit our scorn, at the same time, they teach us the unbearable knowledge that Hamlet (unlike Malvolio) tries to bear nonetheless, that "l'enfer, c'est les autres."[5]

For all its festiveness, *Twelfth Night* is a comedy with a darkness about it, a darkness in it. It is more than the surfeit and sickness of the first scene. Nor is it only the specter of death that to be sure haunts the play. It is also the violence of volition itself:

> For the good that I would I do not: but the evil which I would not, that I do. Now if I do that I would not, it is no more I that do it, but sin that dwelleth in me. I find then a law, that, when I would do good, evil is present with me. For I delight in the law of God after the inward man: But I see another law in my members, warring against the law of my mind, and bringing me into captivity to the law of sin which is in my members. O wretched man that I am! who shall deliver me from the body of this death?
>
> Romans 7:19-24

The divided and distracted will—or yes, or no (Or|si|no)—afflicts the characters (and the audience, too, I think) with a restlessness like that which also hounded St. Augustine: "Fecisti nos ad te, et inquietum est cor nostrum, donec requiescat in te."[6] Orsino in love is man in life: "my desires, like fell and cruel hounds,/... pursue me" (*TN* 1.1.21-22). And, if they catch him, they *will* tear him asunder, him their prey no matter what his prayer (Orison).

Will is also Shakespeare's name, and I think it is a mistake to underestimate or under-read the importance of this synonymy.[7] Will Shakespeare offers you what you will, as you like it, and he does so, I believe, because he wills himself to *will* through one of the most divided and vexed *Wills* that ever lived. I intuit in him more than just the Elizabethan habit of mind *in utramque partem*.[8] Nor do I think he is only a precocious anticipation of the Cartesian *cogito*, fleeing in doubt from doubt to the paradoxical certainty of doubt.[9] I think rather that he was a deeply religious individual in his youth who matured into an adult emotionally Catholic but socially and politically Protestant, always acutely if not tormentedly aware of the dualisms that bedevil both religion and society in the Christian west.[10] I believe that such a construction of his psychobiography enables us to account for his writings dramatic and non-dramatic alike, by helping us focus on Will Shakespeare's will.

This excursus on Shakespeare's name, on *will*, is not tangential to the argument at hand. For, in the famous scene where Malvolio attempts to construe the letter according to his desire, it is the will that Maria has omitted from the letter(s): M. O. A. I. <M A̶L̶V̶O̶L̶I̶O̶> L V L O=VO L L, or *vol*([*l*]untas [also (*l*)*lov*[e]]). It is the will that is compromised in Malvolio, and it is the will that he resigns in his delusion; his self-love costs him his will, his *free* will, in particular, and this, I propose, is why his character disturbs us so—can self-love so treacherously easily abolish the will, cancel its liberty? If so, what does it take to keep the will free?

I infer from Shakespeare's entire corpus that to keep the will free you must give up *keeping* at all. They who keep lose—King Lear being the most stunning and most excruciating example of this truth in the corpus.[11] Free will must be free *to* as well as free *from*: it must be free *to* those to whom you owe an obligation as well as free *from* those (persons or things) that seek to enslave you. The difficulty, we know, is learning to distinguish one and the other. The mistake, we need to learn, is assuming that complete fixation on the latter will save you. If there is no one in your life *to* whom your will is free, you have no hope of escaping the many *from* whom your will would be free. If you do not love at least one other with a *free* will, your will is already enslaved, to the most ruthless of all tyrants, yourself. And the world, as Lear so pitiably learns, will soon catch on and get in line to join the tyranny you have enthroned over yourself.

Hannah Arendt, following the definition of love she ascribes to Duns Scotus—"Amo: volo ut sis"—"I love [you]: I will that you be" (*Life* 2:144)—best enables us to understand the position: only by loving/willing another to be do you in any real sense certify your own being (hence Arendt's critique of Cartesianism's inevitable solipsism—Introduction note 35 and note 9 above). Such love/will Orsino and Olivia have yet to learn. Orsino is obviously less in love with Olivia than he is in love with love itself —consider, for example, his self-enamored sigh: "Love-thoughts lie rich when canopied with bowers" (*TN* 1.1.40).[12] And Olivia herself is hardly less guilty of self-indulgent posturing since "she hath abjured the sight/ And company of men" (*TN* 1.2.36-37) but is still surrounded by them. The postures of both rather prohibit than facilitate any meaningful relationship with another; and "what each wills" is more a narcissistic self-infatuation than an involvement with authentic solicitude. The will of each is turned inward. To turn the will of each outward will require Cesario/Viola, s/he who *cuts* (< *caedere*) and *violates*.[13]

Even at an elementary level, the precision of Shakespeare's language is impressive. Cesario/Viola cuts or separates Orsino and Olivia each from the pseudo-likeness he/she has adopted.[14] Both Orsino and Olivia alike fall in love with Cesario/Viola (and the homoeroticism of Orsino-Cesario is a way of acknowledging its superiority to autoeroticism, which Shakespeare consistently calls into question in his writings—see *Ven.* 157-74, esp., and note 12 this chapter). If the function of (m)othering is separation—i.e., cutting (as of the umbilical cord)—as inevitably it must be, then Cesario/Viola (m)others Orsino and Olivia, birthing them out of each's self-contained, autotelic or self-referential fantasy, and thrusting each into the reality of other-love, where willing the other to be is the supreme guarantor that you yourself are. And it must be emphasized that here as elsewhere Shakespeare possesses the courage to acknowledge that this dislocation is a violation (inseparable from violence) not only as of the birth trauma but also of the illusory self-containment that has not yet been actually won by becoming two.

It is in this way that we can appreciate the rich multiple-entendre of Cesario/Viola's dialogues with Olivia:

OLIVIA Stay. I prithee tell me what thou think'st of me.
VIOLA That *you do think you are not what you are.*
OLIVIA If I think so, I think the same of you.
VIOLA Then think you right, *I am not what I am.*
OLIVIA *I would you were as I would have you be.*
TN 3.1.136-40 (emphasis added)

"I would you were as I would have you be" is not the same thing as "amo: volo ut sis," but it is, so to speak, much closer to that ideal than Olivia used to be; it is still a kind of narcissism—I would you reflected *my image* of you—but it is only *a kind of* narcissism since it is directed outward, othered, and committed to an other's *being* other, if a projected other. When Cesario/Viola cuts and violates Olivia's self-contained and autotelic pseudo-likeness—"you do think you are not what you are" —Olivia emerges from that *not* into what she is, a woman in love with another, who desires that other to concede that he too thinks he is not what he is—"I think the same of you"—i.e., in love with her. Only Viola trumps this rebuttal with the truth (that is a lie): "I am not what I am." When Olivia then protests, which is all she can do in the face of such a confession, "I would you were as I would have you be," Viola bristles: "Would it be better, madam, than I am?/I wish it might, for now I am your fool" (*TN* 3.1.141-2). And from here, Olivia can only proceed, as if by an overpowering logic (of likeness) to express her real likeness, which is that of a woman in love with Cesario/Viola:

> ...Cesario, by the roses of the spring,
> By maidhood, honour, truth, and everything,
> I love thee so that, maugre all thy pride,
> *Nor wit nor reason can my passion hide.*
>
> *TN* 3.1.147-50 (emphasis added)

As Olivia thus (m)others into love(r) of Cesario, Viola, obeying the same logic, (m)others into (the former) Olivia (notice now the near identity of their names, but an *I*'s difference, and notice, too, that both names contain "lov[e]"):

> **VIOLA** By innocence I swear, and by my youth,
> I have one heart, one bosom, and one truth,
> And that no woman has, nor never none
> Shall mistress be of it save I alone
>
> *N* 3.1.155-8,

which is as much near to her true likeness as the new Olivia's likeness of love(r) is to hers. It is not that they have traded places; it is that they have inverted likenesses: Olivia is now in love (like Viola) with Cesario, as Viola, we know (*TN* 2.2.32), is in love with Orsino but as Cesario must (seem to) reject his love (like Olivia). And with this inversion Shakespeare can dramatize one of his deepest, most humane insights:

> **VIOLA** And so adieu, good madam. Never more
> Will I my master's tears to you deplore.
> **OLIVIA** Yet come again, for thou perhaps mayst move
> That heart which now abhors, *to like his love*.
> TN 3.1.159-62 (emphasis added)

No love until you *like* the love that would like to love you—that is, what you *will*.[15] And if, unconsciously, you feel compelled, as the parapraxis suggests, nonetheless to sound a word with *whores* in it ("abhors"), this is to say that the will, at least in part, recognizes itself, its desire, asserts itself, in the cut between the unconscious and conscious minds, and begins to insist that it have its day in the court of consciousness to affirm that it is not a whore, that it can indeed (will to) "like his love," whatever repression may have previously secreted in the mind.

If Feste is Olivia's "corrupter of words" (*TN* 3.1.35), enemy to repression (see especially his "catechiz[ing]" of her at *TN* 1.5.58ff.), Viola is the play's corrupter of likenesses, enemy to repression as well. Not only does she disguise herself, she also, like a successful fool, "corrupts" the pseudo-likenesses that she encounters among those whom she serves, coaxing them to know more and better than they realize. I hasten to say that I do not mean to imply that she consciously and deliberately intends or seeks these results. To the contrary, it seems clear that, considering herself as she does a "monster," and someone who disapproves of disguise as "a wickedness" (*TN* 2.2.34; 27), she would prefer any role (but especially that of Orsino's lover) to the one she is playing; moreover, if she were a fully conscious agent seeking to effect these changes, she would compromise just that freedom of the will in Olivia and Orsino that they must learn to exercise on their own. To such an extent, then, she is not a Feste, or a fool who must corrupt words deliberately and intentionally (see *TN* 3.1.56-67). Nonetheless, her speeches and actions have such an effect, a kind of salvific corruption, because she has put likeness into question, and, as Shakespeare clearly grasps, "made division" of herself, performing (a) Cesario(n upon herself):

> **ORSINO** One face, one voice, one habit, and two persons,
> A natural perspective, that is and is not.
> ...
> **ANTONIO** *How have you made division of yourself?*
> An apple cleft in two is *not more twin*
> Than these two creatures.
> TN 5.1.213-14; 220-2 (emphasis added)

In her Cesario(n birth), by which she becomes the brother of her brother, Viola embodies the outcome of Shakespeare's ongoing self-examination through twinship[16]: the human, to be one, must be two—"A natural perspective, that is and is not!"—for the individual herself is always already divided—like Cesario/Viola who can teach us Shakespeare's way. My identity is a disguise, not my true *like*ness: no one knows what *I* (am) like, only what I (am) *like*—this is why I must learn to *like your love*, you to *like my love*, or, to come to the crux of it, I must will your love as you must will my love, else no love will be. "But rather reason thus with reason fetter: / Love sought is good, but given unsought, is better" (*TN* 3.1.153-4). "Better," because so much rarer.

We can understand now why *Twelfth Night* quotes both *Venus and Adonis* and *The Rape of Lucrece* in the ways that it does. Compare

> "By law of nature thou art bound to breed,
> That thine may live when thou thyself art dead;
> And so in spite of death thou dost survive,
> In that thy likeness still is left alive."
>
> *Ven.* 171-4[17]

with

> Lady, you are the cruell'st she alive
> If you will lead these graces to the grave
> And *leave the world no copy*.
>
> *TN* 1.5.230-2 (emphasis added)

And recall that Olivia's seal is "a Lucrece" (*TN* 2.5.91) and that Maria has written to dupe Malvolio

> "I may command where I adore,
>   But silence *like a Lucrece knife*
> With bloodless stroke my heart doth gore.
>   M. O. A. I. doth sway my life."
>
> *TN* 2.5.103-6 (emphasis added)

Shakespeare quotes Venus to Adonis in Cesario's remark to Olivia, and he assimilates Olivia to Lucrece, so as to suggest the anxiety of *like*ness underlying Olivia's self-absorption in mourning. Both Adonis and Lucrece, although for very different reasons, resist *like*ning themselves to or with others, Adonis out of a narcissism Venus clearly recognizes and indicts (*Ven.* 161) and Lucrece out of a shame that forces her to accept that she alone must make a copy of herself (that is, example of herself) lest rumor repute her likeness as unchaste and faithless—Lucrece's suicide protects her copyright to her reputation (although not to her corpse[18]). But Olivia, obviously, has no such justification for her refusal of *like*ness, and her narcissism is just as potentially self-destructive as that of Adonis. To forestall an Adonisian or Lucretian end for her, Cesario/Viola attracts her into *like*ness first and foremost by means of her doubleness: Olivia learns to like his (Cesario's) love because it is also her (Viola's) love—we sense (and a great actress will find a way to convey this to us) that Olivia is attracted homoerotically as well as heteroerotically, that she intuits the feminine in Cesario/Viola and responds to it in her (e)motions toward love. Similarly, it seems quite obvious that Orsino is also attracted to Cesario homoerotically, even as he frequently responds to Viola's underlying femininity ("And all is semblative [i.e., *like*] a woman's part"—*TN* 1.4.34)—or yes, or no—and this is crucial for Shakespeare's purpose, the argument of and for likeness, which perforce premises doubleness. What you will is what you (are) like, and what you (are) like is what you will—or, as Sebastian says to Olivia in the dénouement, "nature to her bias [draws] in that" (*TN* 5.1.258).[19]

The difficulty of the will is, in fact, nature's bias in each man and each woman. Everyone is skewed, and everyone's cue is his or her will. To try to "straighten" the skew, to "correct" the bias—to seek an orthotic discursively applicable to each and to all—is the delusion we know today as totalitarianism (Arendt, *Origins* 465-6). Mutatis mutandis it is also the delusion of Malvolio, "sick of self-love" (*TN* 1.5.86) who, moreover, like every tyrant, would apply the orthotic to everyone but himself—everyone else should straighten up, especially Sir Toby (although Feste is hardly less culpable in Malvolio's eyes—*TN* 1.5.79-85).

Hence the overwhelming importance of forgery to the play, of the corruption of orthography. Maria can copy Olivia's hand to a very approximate likeness, and Malvolio will insist at the end that Olivia "[w]rite from it [the letter that Maria has forged], if [she] can, in hand or phrase" (*TN* 5.1.329)—i.e., prove that it is not her own hand. In a non-trivial sense, *Twelfth Night* is a play of and about "orthography." The playwright's "orthography" is different from the puritan's, from the totalitarianist's. The playwright's "orthography" includes and allows for "nature's bias," the will. When the playwright asks the fool for "ink, paper, and light" (*TN* 4.2.112-13), it is to "property" characters in senses neither Malvolio nor his tormenters can grasp (*TN* 4.2.93). Every character is biased by the playwright—character *is* bias, if you will. Every character is "propertied" with his or her props, her or his cues—what he will, what she will.[20] This is what it is to script a play, to write a character: it is not "straight writing," it is "biased" writing (frequently "queer" and "gay" writing), also often "foolish" writing, that forges an alterography that in turn corrects mere orthography. It is, in short, *play*-writing: "If this were played upon a stage, now, I could condemn it as an improbable fiction" (*TN* 3.4.125-6). Exactly. The feature of Shakespeare's writing I feel most able to distinguish is his bias or will toward *like*ness. He understood, as no other writer ever has, that every likeness is a disguise, a forgery, a swerve from the true, by which the individual subject, alone and mortal, tries to ascribe himself to a family, a group, a gender, a state, a church, a profession, a heaven (see, e.g., *AYL* 2.7.139-42). Shakespeare's *will*—his *voluntas*, his name, his desire, his intention, his devotion—makes division of itself repeatedly ("plays many parts," negatively capable), in poem after poem, play after play, so as to enable him to affirm "I have *one* heart, *one* bosom and *one* truth...*One* face, *one* voice, *one* habit" (*TN* 3.1.156 and 5.1.213; emphasis added). No writer more restlessly understands that fiction is a li(k)e that tells one('s) truth ("*[o]ne* thing expressing, leaves out difference"—Sonnet #105, line 8; emphasis added) and that, consequently, a "sentence is but a cheverel glove to a good wit, how quickly the wrong side may be turned outward" (*TN* 3.1.11-13). It is understandable that the glover's son (Honan 28-29) would before the end break his wand and drown his book, for if a sentence is "a cheverel glove to a *good* wit," what is the alterographer, the playwright, to do in this world of malvolion orthographers ("Marry...a kind of puritan"—*TN* 2.3.135), who will, he knows only too well, someday (try to) abolish difference and close his theater of likeness?

21
"That that likes not you pleases me best": The Agony of Reflection in *Troilus and Cressida*

Late in the play, as Diomedes is pressuring Cressida for her sex, he, Diomedes, complains against her, "I do not *like* this fooling" (*Tro.* 5.2.104; emphasis added). Troilus rejoins: "Nor I, by Pluto—but that that *likes* not you / Pleases me best" (*Tro.* 5.2.105-6; emphasis added). To expand: that which you do not like, that which is not like you, that which does not like you, pleases me best just because it reaffirms for me my "me" as different from (and superior to) your "you." This line encapsulates one of the most persistent concerns of the play, what I call the agony of reflection: very few of Shakespeare's plays so resolutely examine as *Troilus* does the human dependency upon seeing the self reflected in another in order to "ha(l)ve" a self at all.

If we were to ask Shakespeare to dramatize Plotinus's argument that "all knowing comes by likeness," we could hardly tax him to do better than the unforgettable exchange between Ulysses and Achilles in which the agony (and the agon) of reflection are inescapable:

> **ULYSSES** A strange fellow here
> Writes me that man, how dearly ever parted,
> How much in having, or without or in,
> Cannot make boast to have that which he hath,
> Nor feels not what he owes, but by reflection —
> As when his virtues, shining upon others,
> Heat them, and they retort that heat again
> To the first givers.
> **ACHILLES** This is not strange, Ulysses.
> The beauty that is borne here in the face
> The bearer knows not, but commends itself
> To others' eyes. Nor doth the eye itself,
> That most pure spirit of sense, behold itself,
> Not going from itself; but eye to eye opposed

> Salutes each other with each other's form.
> For speculation turns not to itself
> Till it hath travelled and is mirrored there
> Where it may see itself. This is not strange at all.
> **ULYSSES** I do not strain at the position —
> It is familiar — but at the author's drift;
> Who in his circumstance expressly proves
> That no man is the lord of anything,
> Though in and of him there be much consisting,
> Till he communicate his parts to others.
> Nor doth he of himself know them for aught
> Till he behold them formèd in th'applause
> Where they're extended.
>
> *Tro.* 3.3.90-115

To my mind, one of Shakespeare's most extraordinary achievements, this exchange is momentous for our understanding his theater of likeness. I only ha(l)ve a likeness—"no man is the lord of any thing"—by being reflected in another—"[t]ill he communicate his parts to others.../Till he behold them formèd in th'applause/Where they're extended." I am not unless you are. Given ordinary human viciousness, this condition leads understandably to "that that likes not you pleases me best."

In a famous moment, closely related, Thersites, "[a] slave whose gall coins slanders like a mint" (*Tro* 1.3.193), meditates upon Ajax:

> Why, a stalks up and down *like* a peacock — a
> stride and a stand; ruminates *like* an hostess that hath
> no arithmetic but her brain to set down her reckoning;
> ...
>   I said, "Good morrow, Ajax," and he replies,
> "Thanks, Agamemnon." *What think you of this man
> that takes me for the General?* He's grown a very *land-
> fish, languageless, a monster.* A plague of opinion! A
> man may wear it on both sides *like* a leather jerkin.
>
> *Tro.* 3.3.244-6 ; 253-7 (emphasis added)

Much in this speech repays close study. Theories of liminality, for example, find "land-fish, language-less, a monster" congenial to their arguments — indeed, the speech promises an entire anthropology (of vainglory, at any rate). Then, too, students of the rhetoric of sarcasm can hardly find a better, brief example of the mode (especially if sarcasm should mean something like "to tear flesh" [*OED* II *sub voce*]). But for understanding the theater

The Agony of Reflection in *Troilus and Cressida* 211

of likeness, I consider the reported exchange between Ajax and Thersites, with its consequent question—"What think you of this man that takes me for the general?"—to be very important, as important as other elements of the speech. Ajax is pretending a likeness that requires his pretense that he address Thersites in the likeness of Agamemnon. So to speak, this is how Ajax "warms up" for his new likeness as champion of the Greeks. No doubt, Ajax is as lumbering a dimwit as Thersites takes him to be (and we must always remember the pun on "jakes" [outhouse]), but Shakespeare can display in him, nonetheless, and with the surplus of sarcastic humor to punctuate the effect, the same agony of reflection that he observes in Achilles, Hector, or Troilus—all men who would ha(l)ve a likeness need another to ha(l)ve a likeness.

This reasoning leads us to an understanding of one of the most famous, as it is surely one of the most rhetorically complex, of all scenes ascribed to Shakespeare, the scene of Troilus, accompanied by Ulysses, with Thersites in the wings, observing Cressida with Diomedes in the Greek camp (*Tro.* 5.2). Object of much critical attention, this scene amounts to an essay in self-division, non-self-coincidence. In light of the work of the word *like* in the play and elsewhere in the canon, we see that it also amounts to a scene of the agony of reflection, the tortuous condition of depending on another's likeness to ha(l)ve a likeness. "Fear me not, sweet lord," says Troilus to Ulysses, who wonders about his emotional state as they watch Cressida dally with Diomedes, "I will not be myself, nor have cognition / Of what I feel" (*Tro.* 5.2.64-65), which, although meant as reassurance that he will not betray their hiding place, also admits that Troilus is losing the likeness that depended on Cressida, as if it were being flayed from off his surface like a skin of deceit. And when that skin, to call it such, is all but gone, Troilus can only cry out:

> This, she? No, this is Diomed's Cressida.
> ...
> *If there be rule in unity itself,*
> *This is not she. O madness of discourse,*
> ...
>   *This is and is not Cressid.*
> Within my soul there doth conduce a fight
> Of this strange nature, that a thing *inseparate*
> *Divides* more wider than the sky and earth,
> And yet *the spacious breadth of this division*
> *Admits no orifex* for a point as subtle
> As Ariachne's broken woof to enter.
> ...

> The *fractions* of her faith, orts of her love,
> The fragments, scraps, the bits and greasy relics
> Of her o'er-eaten faith, are bound to Diomed.
> **ULYSSES** May worthy Troilus e'en be *half attached*
> With that which here his passion doth express
>
>   *Tro.* 5.2.140; 144-5; 149-55; 161-5 (emphasis added)

Within the theater of likeness, reading must begin with the amazing precision, so Shakespearean, of Ulysses's question: although, in the first instance, it asks, can even half so raging an emotion actually be how it stands with you now, Troilus?, it also, simultaneously, reveals the exact pathology that Troilus suffers, "half attached"—the phrase not only estimating the quantity of his suffering ("passion") but also naming the ontology of his suffering, "*half* attached." Troilus is, indeed, *half* attached to Cressida (*his* Cressida, not Diomedes's) so as to ha(l)ve the likeness he has chosen: Troilus, the lover of Cressida. Now that that likeness is dissolved, he is but a *fraction* of himself, finding there is "no rule in unity itself" since "a thing inseparate/Divides more wider than the sky and earth." To like Cressida, Troilus suddenly and agonizingly discovers, is to be like Cressida, divided, and none of the fictions by which patriarchal fantasy maintains the illusion of masculine wholeness and integer-ness can resist the crumbling fragmentation of realizing the likeness you would ha(l)ve is another half as well as another's half; even when you project your fragmentation onto her, as Troilus so relentlessly and ruthlessly does, you still ha(l)ve to concede that "[w]ithin my soul there doth conduce a fight."

Troilus's heart-breaking discovery of the mad arithmetic of integrity (only half a man, as the saying goes) leads, as numerous feminist critics particularly have noted, to a fierce rejection of the feminine (mothers, especially) from his likeness and his liking—

> Let's leave the hermit pity with our mother
> And, when we have our armours buckled on,
> The venomed vengeance ride upon our swords,
> Spur them to ruthful work, rein them from ruth.
>
>   *Tro.* 5.3.47-50

Pity can stay with the women who can stay behind, far behind, for all Troilus cares. The extremity of his reaction bespeaks the masculinist misrecognition of his obsession with Cressida in the first place:

TROILUS... I stalk about her door,
Like a strange *soul upon the Stygian banks*
Staying for waftage. O be thou my *Charon*,
And give me swift transportance

...

Th'imaginary relish is so sweet
That it enchants my sense. What will it be
When that the wat'ry palates taste indeed
Love's thrice-repurèd nectar? *Death*, I fear me,
Swooning *destruction*, or some joy too fine,
Too subtle-potent, tuned too sharp in sweetness
For the capacity of my ruder powers.
I fear it much, and I do fear besides
That I shall *lose distinction in my joys*,

...

                                                  This is
the monstruosity in love, lady — that the will is infinite
and the execution confined; that the desire is boundless
and the act a slave to limit.
CRESSIDA They say all lovers swear more performance
than they are able, and yet reserve an ability that they
never perform: vowing more than the perfection of ten,
and discharging less than the tenth part of one. They
that have the voice of lions and the act of hares, are
they not monsters?
TROILUS Are there such? Such are not we. Praise us as
we are tasted; allow us as we prove. Our head shall
go bare *till merit crown it*.

                     Tro. 3.2.7-10; 17-25; 77-89 (emphasis added)

Parker (*Margins* 217ff.) has studied the figures of excess and disproportion in these and related speeches. I want to focus, additionally, on the figures of death that populate them, the figures of non-being, which repeatedly exceed the obvious punning on orgasm, the "petit mort." Troilus's misrecognition is to be measured, I propose, by his unconscious but nonetheless real recognition that he is investing his life in Cressida when he invests his liking and likeness in her:

My heart beats thicker than a feverous pulse,
And *all my powers do their bestowing lose*,
Like vassalage at unawares encount'ring
The eye of majesty.

                        Tro. 3.2.34-37 (emphasis added)

When his spying on Cressida and Diomedes proves her division, her non-integrity, it also proves his, since only a man so divided in himself already—"all my powers do their bestowing lose"—could behave "[*l*]*ike* a strange *soul upon the Stygian banks* / Staying for waftage," imagining "the monstruosity in love ... that the desire is boundless and the act a slave to limit." Only a self-deception so pure could finally come to power a disillusionment so raw. Like Lacan's obsessive, Troilus is already dead, unable to answer the question, "am I alive?" without an umbilicus to a(n) (m)othering likeness. When that umbilicus is severed, Troilus is, effectively, a mechanized corpse, intent on nothing but killing (*Tro.* 5.2.172-9).

If the theater of likeness shows us so clearly in *Troilus* the cost of ha(l)ving a likeness that serves for an identity, it thus, and just so, helps us to understand better Shakespeare's fascination in the play with the subjectivity of value:

> **HECTOR** Brother, she [Helen] is not worth what she doth cost
>   The holding.
> **TROILUS** What's aught but as 'tis valued?
> **HECTOR** But value dwells not in particular will.
> It holds his estimate and dignity
> As well wherein 'tis precious of itself
> As in the prizer. 'Tis mad idolatry
> To make the service greater than the god;
> And the will dotes that is inclinable
> To what infectiously itself affects
> Without some image of th' affected merit.
> **TROILUS...**
>   How may I avoid —
> Although my will distaste what it elected —
> The wife I chose?
>
> *Tro.* 2.2.50-59; 64-66

Obviously, significant irony emerges from this exchange when we pause to consider Troilus's own "mad idolatry" of Cressida, which "make[s] the service greater than the god" since Cressida is no god, by any definition. But, additionally, here Shakespeare continues his investigation of the agony of reflection: "value dwells not in particular will," that is, it does not reside exclusively in one, singular, perfectly isolated will; or, if it does, we consider it and its holder, just so, "mad"; for value "holds his estimate and dignity /As well wherein 'tis precious of itself/As in the prizer"—in other words, there is an object "out there," however tenuous "out there" may be, and value resides in both the prizer and the object prized, in the reflection of and between them. In his rebuttal of his brother, Troilus attempts to turn Hector's position to his own advantage by gradually insinuating the inestimable value that dwells in Helen herself, "[w]hose price hath launched above a thousand ships" (*Tro.* 2.2.81), so that he can conclude that Hector and others, who would abandon her, their "proper wisdoms rate [i.e., belittle their own wisdoms]/And ... /Beggar the estimation which [they] prized / Richer than sea and land" (*Tro.* 2.2.88-89; 90-91). But in doing so, Troilus reveals that he still believes "[w]hat is aught but as 'tis valued"—he still privileges the subjective position, the prizer's position ("why do you now/The issue of your proper wisdoms rate"), and in this belief, he will himself be "half attached" ultimately to his own valuelessness, or, to be precise, like-lessness, when Cressida no longer values him.

For, I take it, Shakespeare's *Troilus and Cressida* concludes as it does, in a disease-ridden collapse (*Tro.* Q 5.11 Oxford 2ᵉ 776AB) of all order and meaning, where "lechery eats itself" (*Tro.* 5.4.33), just so Shakespeare may emphasize Troilus's fate of like-lessness:

> And thou great-sized coward,
> *No space of earth shall sunder our two hates.*
> I'll *haunt thee like a wicked conscience* still,
> That mouldeth goblins swift as frenzy's thoughts.
> *Tro.* 5.11.26-29 (emphasis added)

Long before he dies, Troilus is no more. "Like a wicked conscience" that "mouldeth goblins swift as frenzy's thoughts," he has either rejected or lost the likenesses that were available to him for reflection and ha(l)ving; all that remains is to be the unheeded inner voice of one whom he hates and whom it is decreed he can never defeat. Too little too late, if indeed at all, did he understand the agony of reflection:

> Time hath, my lord,
> A wallet at his back, wherein he puts
> Alms for oblivion, a great-sized monster
> Of ingratitudes. Those scraps are good deeds past,
> Which are devoured as fast as they are made,
> Forgot as soon as done.
> ...
> For emulation hath a thousand sons
> That one by one pursue:
> ...
> For Time is like a fashionable host,

> That slightly shakes his parting guest by th' hand
> And, with his arms outstretched as he would fly,
> Grasps in the comer. Welcome ever smiles,
> And Farewell goes out sighing. O let not virtue seek
> Remuneration for the thing it was;
> For beauty, wit,
> High birth, vigour of bone, desert in service,
> Love, friendship, charity, are subjects all
> To envious and calumniating time.
> One touch of nature makes the whole world kin —
> That all with one consent praise new-born gauds,
> Though they are made and moulded of things past,
> And give to dust that is a little gilt
> More laud than gilt o'er-dusted.
> The present eye praises the present object.
>
> *Tro.* 3.3.139-144; 150-1; 159-74

If it is our lot to endure the agony of reflection — I am not unless you are — and if all our fantasies of independence take their beginning in denying any need for another, which is thus to give so much power over us to the other ("fashionable host"), then we are bound, Ulysses proposes, to a prison of presentism — "The present eye [I] praises the present object" — and all value is without avail arbitrary, subjective, temporary, and mutable, "alms for oblivion."

If this were Shakespeare's last play, the theater of likeness would end in the agony of reflection, the vicious cycle of seeing and being seen and seeing being seen, relentless visibility. It is not, however, his last play, and the theater of likeness will continue, to stage, I think, different ideas of reflection and value, but, in order to do so, it will have to give equal time to another idea, a very important one, that has vexed Shakespeare throughout his career — bastardy:

> **THERSITES** I am a bastard, too. I love bastards. I am
> bastard begot, bastard instructed, bastard in mind,
> bastard in valour, in everything illegitimate. One bear
> will not bite another, and wherefore should one
> bastard? Take heed: the quarrel's most ominous to us.
> If the son of a whore fight for a whore, he tempts
> judgement. Farewell, bastard.
>
> *Tro.* 5.8.8-14

Edmund is yet to be scripted, and value is yet to be put to the question on the heath, where visibility itself is made visible, beyond the agony of reflection, in the vision of

> the thing itself. Unaccommodated man ... no more but such a poor, bare, forked animal as thou art. Off, off, you lendings! Come, unbutton here.
>
> *Lr.* [1610] 3.4.100-3

—the end of reflection.

22
"Like as if that God/Owed not nor made not you": The Theater of Likeness in *The Book of Sir Thomas More*

After considerable deliberation, I have decided to include a brief discussion of the passages in *Sir Thomas More* in Shakespeare's hand (Scene 6 and, less securely, Scene 8). The principal motive of my discussion is the evidence emerging in these passages of exemplariness as Shakespeare understands and pursues it elsewhere in his writings. I hope to show, as efficiently as possible, that exemplariness and likeness function in More's famous speech pacifying the rebellion just as we would expect them to do from our now extensive familiarity with Shakespeare's theater of likeness.

More's speeches in Scene 6 contain 5 occurrences of *like*. First and foremost, the evocation of "pattern" in the speech we recognize from previous history plays in which the "mirrors for princes" tradition has figured along with other impulses of exemplariness:

> by this pattern
> Not one of you should live an agèd man;
> For other ruffians, as their fancies wrought,
> With selfsame hand, self reasons, and self right,
> Would shark on you.
>
> Scene 6.92-96 (Oxford 2ᵉ 821b)

Shakespeare, we know, thinks historiographically in terms of likenesses that invariably fall short of their ideal exemplars, produce consequences incompatible with their originals, or issue in copies the imitations of which have been only imprudently (because selfishly) foreseen. History is the history of copies, where copying is always fallible, mortal, interested, and incomplete. Next, the rhetoric of "[w]hen there is no addition but 'a rebel'/To qualify a rebel" (Scene 6.133-4 [Oxford 2ᵉ 821b]) is verifiably Shakespearean in the words *addition* and *qualify* which we recognize as words compatible with the theater of likeness—"when there is no [likeness or exemplar (lit., 'title of rank') to adduce] but a rebel/To [signify the likeness (the *qualitas*) of] a rebel." In other words, if we translate the lines into the theater of likeness, we feel immediately that the translation is faithful to Shakespeare. Similarly, the language of "[s]purn you *like* dogs, and *like* as if that God/Owed not nor made not you" (Scene 6.150-1 [Oxford 2ᵉ 822a]) is also faithful to Shakespeare in the measure to which we recognize the similarity to *Love's Labour's Lost* ("A speaks not *like* a man of God his making" [*LLL* 5.2.523; emphasis added]) and at the same time detect the familiarity that Shakespeare feels with the *imago et similitudo* tradition of Genesis (2:6). None of these instances by itself, I judge, would be sufficient to ground the case for Hand D as Shakespeare's, but all of them together seem to me to support the paleographical evidence defensibly.

If we turn our attention to Scene 8, we can, I think, discern again the theater of likeness, if at a greater remove. Obviously, the word *like* does not occur in these 21 lines (Oxford 2ᵉ 824b-825a). At the same time, More clearly speculates (mirrors for himself) within an understanding of exemplariness where he is thinking in terms of the model or pattern which he *should* follow although historical circumstance has now re-scripted that prescript:

> I, in my father's life,
> To take prerogative and tithe of knees
> From elder kinsmen, and him bind by my place
> To give the smooth and dexter way to me
> That owe it him by nature.
>
> Scene 8.8-12

Now that that prescript has lost its force, More reasons he must "physick" these things "by respect" (Scene 8.13) where our instruction from Portia in *The Merchant of Venice* helps us to hear the Shakespearean insistence on comparison, balancing, and weighing without which "[n]othing is good" (*MV* 5.1.99). In this flow of ideas and language, More's conclusion with a "maxim"("to be great / Is, when the thread of hazard is once spun,/A bottom great wound up, greatly undone" [Scene 8.19-21])—itself an utterly conventional move—nonetheless coheres with the theater of likeness and our expectations therefrom: this is just the way, in fact, Shakespeare would conclude the speech within the theater of likeness, and "[a] bottom great wound up, greatly undone" is fraught the way Shakespeare's language is always fraught, bearing more than we expect it to bear (as also in "More, the more thou hast ..." [Scene 8.14]).

I have tried, in this brief "inter-chapter," to suggest ways in which scholarly consensus arising from paleographic evidence finds support in the theater of likeness for Shakespeare's hand in *Sir Thomas More*. Certainly, the matter is vexed, and nothing of what I offer do I consider final. But I do think there is a preponderance of evidence from the theater of likeness tending in the direction of the consensus, and I hope that I have succeeded here in extracting and clarifying it.

23
"Like Doth Quit Like": The Measure of Likeness

> An imitation is artificial. It is not fortuitous as a true metaphor is.
>
> Both in nature and in metaphor identity is the vanishing-point of resemblance.
>
> Wallace Stevens, The Necessary Angel:
Essays on Reality and the Imagination

If we wish to see Shakespeare's "theater of likeness" in *Measure for Measure*, which is an obvious test case because an obviously difficult one, we will do best to begin at the end of the play where we find an instance of *like*ness that is powerfully instructive:

> **PROVOST** This is another prisoner that I saved,
> Who should have died when Claudio lost his head,
> As *like* almost to Claudio as himself.
> *He unmuffles Claudio*
> **DUKE** (*to Isabella*) If he be *like* your brother, for his sake
> Is he pardoned; and for your lovely sake
> Give me your hand, and say you will be mine.
> He is my brother too.
> MM 5.1.486-92 (emphasis added)

The point here, of course, is the irony. "As like almost" and "[i]f he be like" function first and foremost by ironic counterpoint: the clauses contravene or question likeness just because there can be no question in this instance —the figure *is* Claudio, not *like* him but *identical to* him. And the fiction that is served by this irony is the Duke's own "drama" of revelation that he is directing for the spectacle of his return to office and power. We must, in due course, take the measure of this drama within the drama since it will teach us much about Shakespeare's "theater of likeness."

But at this point we should consider that the irony in these passages from the end of *Measure for Measure* throws into relief the problem with *like*ness, expressed most clearly by Brutus in *Julius Caesar*: "That every *like* is not the *same*, O Caesar,/The heart of Brutus ernes [grieves] to think upon" (*JC* 2.2.128-9; emphasis added); expressed as well, perhaps more poignantly, by Isabella in her accusation of Angelo: "O, that it were *as like as* it is *true*!" (*MM* 5.1.104; emphasis added). Extraordinary conditions must obtain for like to be(come) the same, for (the) like to be like itself, coincident with itself, and at one with the truth. Shakespeare's entire dramatic output is an exploration of such conditions and their human cost. Every likeness entails necessarily some degree of *un*likeness, some element of difference (which is absent in the case of Claudio at the end of *Measure for Measure*); and in that space of variance, deceit and desire work their devious ways, even as life and love, too, find there their originality.

To close that space up, to confirm an entity as its likeness, is to challenge *as* with the ontic pretention of *is*, that change has been arrested, time suspended, and identity achieved. Truly the labor of saints and martyrs. To close oneself to a likeness (St. Paul, for example, to the likeness of Christ's death [Rom. 6.5]) is to abolish the self, to annihilate it (in the sense of mysticism's "dark night"), and become empty, so as to be filled or completed with the Holy Other (see, above, the Introduction page 12). Depressing, then, indeed, is it to realize that even saints, presumably the best of us, may not be truly empty, may be only look-alike saints, and still therefore harbor some secret room for desire (which is synonymous with time)—as does Angelo, for example, who is no angel. Although Escalus finds him "so severe that he hath forced me to tell him he is indeed Justice" (*MM* 3.1.509-11), Angelo is in fact *not* (identical to) Justice but only *like* Justice (at best):

> heaven hath my empty words,
> Whilst my invention, hearing not my tongue,
> Anchors on Isabel; God in my mouth,
> As if I did but only chew his name,
> And in my heart the strong and swelling evil
> Of my conception.
>
> *MM* 2.4.2-7[1]

The doubleness of the hypocrite or the wound of the non-self-coincident psyche, or perhaps both, here is no true emptiness—here lurks desire, tumescent, in a space full of the aching for time. In this space, where the player can act *like...?*, lurks the terror of hypocrisy *and* the promise of art alike. Every great saint has *acted* her role, *played* his part, to the utmost —the *realization* of His cross (such, for example, are the seemingly interminable narratives of hagiography). But, as Angelo makes vividly clear, the saint's role, his likeness, is not an eternal, timeless, unchanging script: "O cunning enemy, that, to catch a saint,/With saints dost bait thy hook!" (*MM* 2.2.185-6). It may be interrupted by greater forces—sex, for example.

If we follow the work of the word *like* in the play, it teaches us first and foremost that "[l]ike doth quit like" (*MM* 5.1.408) and *no more*. Duke Vincentio may decree to Angelo that "[i]n our remove be thou at full ourself" (*MM* 1.1.43), but the play exists to infirm this possibility completely. No one can "be at full" someone else; no one can with such "a figure / Be stamped" (*MM* 1.1.49-50); "[w]hat[ever] figure of us ... he will bear" (*MM* 1.1.16), the figure will not *be* the *one figured*. *Measure for Measure* at every turn proves Isabella wrong:

> Ignominy in ransom and free pardon
> Are of two houses; lawful mercy
> Is nothing kin to foul redemption.
>
> *MM* 2.4.112-14

Even if she *is a belle*, the power of her *is* does not guarantee purity (though, to judge by Angelo's lust, it guarantees beauty certainly enough).[2] To the contrary, as even Duke Vincentio's disguises and humors attest, "lawful mercy" must make common cause with many things that are foul, impure, questionable, hidden, dark, dangerous—"lawful mercy" and "foul redemption" prove very much like each other by the time the play has ended (we need only inquire of Lucio—*MM* 5.1.357 and 520-1, e.g.). And yet, crucially, "like doth quit like" *only*; like does not *become* like.

The word *quit* (Latin *quietus* < "to make rest, make quiet") has extraordinary resonance not only in Shakespeare but also in Chaucer, for example, in whose *Canterbury Tales*, as is well known, it plays a crucial role (Shoaf, *Currency* 166ff.). The notion of "requital" or "payback" arises from the basic idea of "quieting down" an opponent or condition such that he or it endures what the originally offended party endured. It is then a word suggesting a restoration of reciprocity, which can only obtain between *un*likes. Hence the Duke can say to Angelo at the end: "Well, Angelo, your evil quits you well./Look that you love your wife, her worth worth yours" (*MM* 5.1.495-6); and the profound implication is the incommensurability between his evil and his "payback"—he gets far more and far better than he deserves. (And note, again, the disturbing kinship between good and evil, as between "lawful mercy" and "foul redemption."). The point is reciprocity or, perhaps even better, mutuality: "Look that you love your wife; her *worth worth* yours" (emphasis added)—it's not that Mariana's worth balances Angelo's, nor is identical to his, but is *worth* his, is *hers* and stands next to and, if need be, over against his; she is *like* him because and as *different* from him. Herein lies a world of difference. Possibly the difference that makes Shakespeare Shakespeare.

From this vantage we can understand the by no means timid implication of the end of *Measure for Measure*.

> The very mercy of the law cries out
> Most audible, even from his proper tongue,
> "An Angelo for Claudio, death for death."
> Haste still pays haste, and leisure answers leisure;
> Like doth quit like, and measure still for measure.
> Then, Angelo, thy fault's thus manifested,
> Which, though thou wouldst deny, denies thee vantage.
> We do condemn thee to the very block
> Where Claudio stooped to death, and with like haste.
> Away with him.
>
> MM 5.1.404-13

We see that this is not yet right. It is not yet "like ... quit[ting] like." The implication that Angelo can be *identical to* Claudio and thus suffer *identically to* Claudio is the very flaw in the lex talionis—no eye is ever the same as the other eye, no tooth is ever the same as the other tooth, no life is ever the same as the other life. Each is only like the other (cf. *MM* 2.2.66-68). Is this not the scandal of Jesus of Nazareth? "Love thy neighbor *as* thyself" means your neighbor is not you—immense then the labor to love him as yourself (he may not even smell good). *Measure for Measure* does not end with the death of Angelo not only because Claudio is still alive but also because Shakespeare perceives the kinship between good and evil, that if the good will punish evil with evil, then evil triumphs. This, I believe, oppressed Shakespeare and drove his genius hard. Hence the Duke—"I find an apt remission in myself" (*MM* 5.1.497)—and hence also the precision of the Duke's observation

> By this Lord Angelo perceives he's safe.
> Methinks I see a *quick'ning* in his *eye*.
>
> MM 5.1.493-4 (emphasis added)

It is the lex talionis, an *eye* for an *eye*, that is dead, not quick, at the end of this play—even Lucio is spared (*MM* 5.1.518-19).

Surrogacy is central to the Judeo-Christian tradition. From Abraham and Isaac to God and Jesus, the sacrifice of the surrogate figures the ground of salvation—Jesus died for *our* sins (whoever in any generation "we" may be). *Measure for Measure* is a play that examines and, I think it is accurate to say, demystifies surrogacy—delegation and substitution repeatedly fail in the play and must be supplemented by disguise and subterfuge—and, in the process, foregrounds a question finally inescapable for Shakespeare: what of the surrogacy of the actor? which is also to say, what of the surrogacy of the playwright? Consider with me, at just this point, one of Shakespeare's more famous passages:

> But man, proud man,
> Dressed in a little brief authority,
> Most ignorant of what he's most assured,
> His *glassy essence, like* an angry ape
> Plays such fantastic tricks before high heaven
> As make the angels weep, who, with our spleens,
> Would all themselves laugh mortal.
>
> *MM* 2.2.120-6 (emphasis added)

Of a great many brilliant passages in his works that might be cited to the effect that "[a]ll the world's a stage,/And all the men and women merely players" (*AYL* 2.7.139-40), this is not the least and that because, I think, "like an angry ape" is preceded and complemented by "[h]is glassy essence." It is our "essence" like glass to reflect, to copy, to (be) like, to bespeak, the Other (see chapter 21, "The Agony of Reflection in *Troilus and Cressida*). We are like each other but also different from each other and therefore in need of each other to show each other what each looks like. What is it, then, to derive surrogacy from this elemental condition? Because I am like you, can I, must I, die for you? Because you are like me, can you, must you, die for me? Because you are like me but I do not like you, have I the right to exterminate you?—I'm white, you're black; I'm a Nazi, you're a Jew; I'm male, you're female? And what if all I should want to do is represent you? play you? act you? Can it be that the ape becomes "angry" only in the moment it apes?

For surrogacy, we know, is akin to dependency. And from dependency to hatred and anger is but a short journey, perhaps the twinkling of an eye. Claudio, we know, would make of his sister Isabella a surrogate, her maidenhead for his head:

> **CLAUDIO** Sweet sister, let me live.
> What sin you do to save a brother's life,
> Nature dispenses with the deed so far
> That it becomes a virtue.
>
> *MM* 3.1.134-7

And like an "angry ape" she reflects back to him the inwardmost horror of all surrogacy, or incest:

> **ISABELLA**   O, you beast!
> O faithless coward, O dishonest wretch,
> *Wilt thou be made a man out of my vice?*
> Is't not a kind of *incest* to take life
> From thine own sister's shame?
>
> MM 3.1.137-41 (emphasis added)

Every human sacrifice is a use of that which is interdicted to the user, or his own likeness as if it were not: this is why rituals of human sacrifice are so elaborately theatrical—the show must hide the violation. As men sacrificing another man use their likeness as if it were not, as if it were other, the father committing incest with his daughter uses his likeness as if it were not,[3] as if it were other. And the cries of neither can be heard in the night of our anger. Not even the Son of God could be recognized as the Son of Man. We must make (someone else) an ape to pretend that we ourselves are not apes. And this we know is the horror of every holocaust, whether originating in racism or sexism or political terrorism, that the victim is just like the perpetrator, a living being, reduced by the perpetrator to a thing so that the perpetrator can get off on pretending he is different from the victim, superior to her, more alive than he, richer than she, etc.

Isabella does not commit incest in *Measure for Measure* because Mariana substitutes for her in Angelo's clasp—surrogacy everywhere we look. But, in this case, surrogacy is not incest. This substitution is licit, licit because the partners are parts of a couple each as different from the other as like the other.[4]

> With Angelo tonight shall lie
> His old betrothèd but despisèd.
> So disguise shall, by th' disguisèd,
> Pay with falsehood false exacting,
> And perform an old contracting.
>
> MM 3.1.534-8[5]

The law can affirm and name this substitution because a differential relationship obtains; similarly, language can repeat the same—"So *disguise* shall, by th' *disguisèd*,/Pay with *false*hood *false* exacting"—because in fact there is a difference in each case. Angelo and Mariana, unrelated, can be married (*MM* 5.1.215-36), that is to say, joined by a coupling that is first and foremost verbal, contractual, conventional, and institutional ("affianced"), all of which insist that here the other is sanctioned to be used as if it were the like, rather than in incest where the like is (ab)used as if it were the other. Again, we can see, "like doth quit like," and *no more*. The Duke then is correct: "Shame to him whose cruel striking/Kills for faults of his own liking!" (*MM* 3.1.523-4); it is a shame, an abasement of humanity, to kill there where "like quit[ing] like" argues there can be no superiority, no precedence, no sanction to use the like as if the other—Angelo is just *like* Claudio and has no right therefore to *kill* him. "Twice treble shame on Angelo,/To weed my vice, and let his grow!" (*MM* 3.1.525-6), since, "like quit[ing] like," he should weed his first. "O, what may man within him hide,/Though angel on the outward side!" (*MM* 3.1.527-8)—my difference from you cannot depend on my hiding my likeness to you from you, for likeness will out (see the chapter on *King Lear* below and Cavell 122).

Measure for Measure is a play notable for its imagery of stamping, coining, and impressing. To be sure, Shakespeare employs this imagery frequently, in many works.[6] But it is especially significant in *Measure for Measure* because of the play's examination of *like*ness and surrogacy. In his first address to Angelo, Duke Vincentio says:

> Angelo,
> There is a kind of character in thy life
> That to th'observer doth thy history
> Fully unfold.
>
> *MM* 1.1.26-29

A few lines later Angelo protests

> Now good my lord,
> Let there be some more test made of my metal
> Before so noble and so great a figure
> Be stamped upon it.
>
> *MM* 1.1.47-50

In the next scene, Claudio will lament that

> The stealth of our most mutual entertainment
> With character too gross is writ on Juliet.
>
> *MM* 1.2.142-3

And, perhaps most tellingly from the present perspective, Angelo will rebut Isabella,

> Ha, fie, these filthy vices! It were as good
> To pardon him that hath from nature stolen
> A man already made, as to remit
> Their saucy sweetness that do coin God's image
> In stamps that are forbid.
>
> MM 2.4.42-46

I assume that these passages, especially the first two, participate in the deconstruction of surrogacy in the play since they point to the failure or the randomness and contingency of *transmitting a copy* from source to target. No character is ever stamped perfectly, and many are even "coined" "saucily" in "stamps that are forbid." Because to be is to be like, the being of every character has at best the character of that being, its *like*ness. There's the rub.

Hence the impressively precise use of *like* in the denouement between Isabella and Duke Vincentio.

> **ISABELLA** It is not truer he is Angelo
> Than this is all as true as it is strange.
> Nay, it is ten times true, for truth is truth
> To th'end of reck'ning.
> **DUKE**   Away with her.
> ...
> **ISABELLA** O prince, I conjure thee, ...
>   *Make not impossible*
> *That which but seems unlike.*
> ...
>   even so may Angelo,
> In all his dressings, *characts*, titles, forms,
> Be an arch-villain.
> ...
> **DUKE**   This is most *likely*!
> **ISABELLA** O, that it were as *like* as it is true!
>
> MM 5.1.43-46; 48; 51-2; 55-57; 103-4 (emphasis added)

Once again, the *is* of Isabella fails to secure ontological purity. In these exchanges the gap between *like*ness and truth, appearance and being, *as* and *is*, assaults us repeatedly and yet serves only to insist that to be is to be like—*O that it were as like as it is true*. Truth may be "truth/To th'end of reck'ning," but until it *appears like* the truth, it will not be seen, recognized, or affirmed—it will be invisible, even if she *is a belle*.[7] It is our lot and our sorrow that no matter what may be, it must also be like ... some other thing we know; only then can it be believed ("Truth may seem [i.e., be like] but cannot be" — "The Phoenix and the Turtle," line 62). Moreover, belief, etymologically, is itself "be like" —

> OTeut. *galaubian to believe, probably, "to hold estimable, valuable, pleasing, or satisfactory, to be satisfied with," f. galaub- "dear, pleasing"; cf. Goth. liuban, lauf, lubum, lubans, Teut. root *lub- , Aryan lubh-, to hold dear, to like, whence also LOVE, LIEF.
>
> OED II sub voce (double underlining added)

What I believe, you see, is what I (be)like and what I (be)like is who I am. There's the rub.

The sublimest example in the Judeo-Christian tradition of beliking one's being to absolute identity with the Other is the Passion of Jesus of Nazareth:

> and prayed, saying, O my Father, if it be possible, let this cup pass from me: nevertheless not as I will, but as thou wilt.
>
> Matt. 26:39

In this moment, as terrible as it is sublime, sublime because terrible, the Son of Man confesses his likeness to the Son of God, immolating his will in the will of the Holy Other. We are moved, whatever our faith, by the evident proof of what is required to ascend from beliking to being, from time to timelessness, from mortality to divinity, or *absolute* emptiness— "Nevertheless not as I will, but as thou wilt."

Angelo, however, is not empty. Angelo, a son of man, wants sex:

> **MARIANA**   ...and that [my husband] is Angelo,
> Who thinks he knows that he ne'er knew my body,
> But knows, he thinks, that he knows Isabel's.
>
> MM 5.1.198-200

The chiasms and reduplications are characteristic of Shakespeare's style, the style of the syneciotician (juxta-form and cruci-lingual), but now we see that they are also more, that they register the gap between *as* and *is*, thinking and knowing, *like*ness and truth ("Truth may seem but cannot be."). And as they do so, they tell us that often the truth must be served by the lie, the real by the apparent, right by wrong—we meet again, *pace* Isabella, the kinship between "lawful mercy" and "foul redemption."

Ultimately, Shakespeare says, being must be served by acting. This is no revelation; I am no oracle here. Whether we call it "metadrama" with Calderwood and others or "secondary Imagination" with Coleridge or "Werkimmanenten Deutung" with Burckhardt, we know that it is commonplace in Shakespeare studies to accept that, in Theseus's words in *A Midsummer Night's Dream*, from his comment about the rude mechanicals' play of *Pyramus and Thisbe*, "[o]ur sport shall be to take what they mistake" (*MND* 5.1.90)—acting, playing, is the mistake, the fiction, that provides us a chance to take, "construe" or "understand," but also "open ourselves to," being and truth. Here, too, of course (another commonplace), is why Shakespeare so often writes a play within the play: metadramatic reduplication enables ontological interrogation, the question of where truth and being lie (the obvious pun is no less important for being obvious).

From this vantage, we can, in a final step, turn to Duke Vincentio's drama within the drama of *Measure for Measure*. Throughout the fifth act, we know, he is directing a play, of revelation and restoration, unbeknownst to the principal actors, and so when, for example, he declares, "I protest I love the Duke as I love myself" (*MM* 5.1.338), Shakespeare places us on familiar ground, where illusory difference serves underlying identity, and vice-versa, with dramatic irony as the immediate result. But we have to do here with more than just dramatic irony or even "metadrama," I think. I can make my case by first quoting Angelo's capitulation:

> O my dread lord,
> I should be guiltier than my guiltiness
> To think I can be undiscernible,
> When I perceive your grace, *like power divine*,
> Hath looked upon my passes. Then, good prince,
> No longer session hold upon my shame,
> But let my trial be mine own confession.
> Immediate sentence then, and sequent death,
> Is all the grace I beg.
>
> *MM* 5.1.363-71 (emphasis added)

Duke Vincentio has indeed sought the *"like"*ness of "power divine"; he has sought and briefly obtained a copy of Boethius's God's eternal vision, wherein time is space, and past, present, and future are visible to him at once as extension in space (*Consolation* 5. Prose 6 [Green 115-19])—the Duke knows the past, he knows the present, and he knows at least the imminent future. Herein he is like the playwright, for whom also time is space (the stage is the spatialization of time). And Shakespeare, I assume, is interested not only in the drama of the Duke's divine-like dispensations (though they do, to be sure, make good drama), but also in the theory of likeness that this drama reflects. Only the divinity, only the author, know that "like doth [*only*] quit like." Only they know that surrogacy is licit only when it is sanctioned *as* licit, for the sanction acknowledges the preceding *il*licitness that can only be justly nullified by contract of mutuality—Jesus *does* agree: "Nevertheless not as I will, but as thou wilt." In the moment any of us should claim to own the truth with no illusion whatsoever, as if the truth were ab-solutely mine, in that moment the truth dies, murdered by illicit surrogacy—"Nevertheless not as thou wilt, but as I will": the end of the drama, as well as the end of truth, because the end of the audience to whom to pray, for whom to play.

24
"What didst not like?": Othello UnMoored

> Let husbands know
> Their wives have sense like them.
> *Othello* 4.3.92-93

Othello is a play awash in sea and nautical imagery.[1] My expression, "awash," is not facetious or precious. I hope to show that death by submersion is a major trope of the play's argument, and not just, for example, in an obvious case, such as the tempest that disperses the Turkish fleet (*Oth.* 2.1.17-24). Desdemona, the "land-carrack" (*Oth.* 1.2.50), sinks and drowns (on land) as Othello strangles her; Othello on her and his death-bed has reached, as he himself consciously says, the "very sea-mark of [his] utmost sail" (*Oth.* 5.2.275). Venice is a sea-faring state, itself subject to submersion, and Cyprus is an island surrounded by the sea. I propose, then, that *Othello, the Moor of Venice* is also *The (un)Mooring of Othello of Venice* and that Shakespeare exploits the polyvalence of "moor"[2] to examine and interrogate a certain understanding of eros and its effect on human beings. Eros freights human beings with more burden than they can bear and sinks human beings, so fraught, beneath the insupportable burden. Human beings perilously navigate tempestuous seas upon which no one is ever adequate "captain" because the identity of the "captain's captain" (*Oth.* 2.1.75) is always problematic. What if he should be a she?

We should pay heed to Cassio's effusion:

> She that I spake of, our great *captain's captain*,
> Left in the conduct of the bold Iago,
> Whose footing here anticipates our thoughts
> A sennight's speed. Great Jove, Othello guard,
> And swell his *sail* with thine own powerful *breath*,
> That he may *bless this bay with his tall ship*,
> Make love's quick pants in Desdemona's arms,

Give renewed fire to our extincted spirits
And bring all Cyprus comfort.

Oth. 2.1.75-83 (emphasis added)

Othello may be a captain of a Venetian ship, but of his own ship (presumably his body), he has himself a captain, named Desdemona. Othello may "bless this bay with his tall ship" and its swollen sail, but the ship of his body (and its sail) swell with a different breath than that of Jove—"quick pants in Desdemona's arms." Shakespeare insists on drawing eros and the sea into a proximity that will gradually become an inextricability. The sea-mark of Othello's utmost sail is sex.[3] He cannot go beyond it and so he dies upon it.

I kissed thee ere I killed thee. No way but this:
Killing myself, to die upon a kiss.

Oth. 5.2.368-9

As the Norton edition observes, "'die' in line 369 has the secondary sense of 'orgasm'" (2172). This sense is all the more important in light of what immediately follows:

LODOVICO (*to Iago*) O Spartan dog,
More fell than anguish, hunger, *or the sea,*
Look on the tragic loading of this bed.
This is thy work...

Oth. 5.2.371-4 (emphasis added)

Iago, "[m]ore fell ... [than] the sea" is responsible for "the tragic *loading* of this bed," where the "loading," or freight, is now the wreckage of those who ventured upon the sea "not wisely but too well" (*Oth.* 5.2.353), seeking a pleasure perhaps lawful (if barely, in Venice especially) but forbidden all the same since it provoked forces of resistance no less primal than anguish, hunger, and the very sea itself.

Immediately, then, the question arises, why did their pleasure provoke such forces? Obvious answers are, for all that they are obvious, still important: she is white, he black; she is a patrician's daughter, he a soldier-servant; she is young, he old; she is largely innocent of the world, he widely experienced—everywhere they seem opposite, and yet they are very alike. Their likeness it is that drowns them:

OTHELLO It gives me wonder great as my content
To see you here before me. O my soul's joy,

> *If after every tempest come such calms,*
> *May the winds blow till they have wakened death,*
> *And let the labouring barque climb hills of seas*
> *Olympus-high, and duck again as low*
> *As hell's from heaven.* If it were now to die
> 'Twere now to be most happy, for I fear
> *My soul hath her content so absolute*
> *That not another comfort like to this*
> *Succeeds in unknown fate.*
> **DESDEMONA**   The heavens forbid
> But that our loves and comforts should increase
> Even as our days do grow.
> Oth. 2.1.184-96 (emphasis added)

The content and the conténT of Othello's soul are all Desdemona, his "captain" ("head," *OED* II *sub voce*), and there is no likeness to the resulting comfort:

> **OTHELLO** Excellent wretch! Perdition catch my soul
> But I do love thee, and when I love thee not,
> Chaos is come again.
> Oth. 3.3.91-93

Being itself, which holds back chaos, depends on Desdemona whom Othello loves so much that he would (be) like her to the point of (con)fusion. Their love provokes such forces of resistance because it is an affront to the very ground of identity. The structure of difference on which identity depends dissolves in their relationship which threatens thus to become itself oceanic: hence Othello's exhortation of the elements—"If after every tempest come such calms ..." (*Oth.* 2.1.186)—amounts to competing with the sea which can threaten him with no death he is not perfectly happy, ready, and willing to die.[4]

Othello and Desdemona have overcome separation, the elemental condition of all beings, from the severing of the umbilical cord to the inhumation of the corpse, and would thus *be* the creation, their bed the omphalos of being. Not even the sea can compare to their fusion, and so it is that Shakespeare repeatedly invokes imagery of the sea to inscribe their passion, for no less a term can determine the termination of their likeness:

> **OTHELLO** Yield up, O love, thy crown and hearted throne
> To tyrannous hate! *Swell, bosom, with thy freight,*

> For 'tis of aspics' tongues.
> ...
> Like to the Pontic *Sea*,
> ...
> Even so my bloody thoughts with violent pace
> Shall ne'er look back, *ne'er ebb to humble love.*
>
> *Oth.* 3.3.452-4; 456; 460-2 (emphasis added)

Othello's "bloody thoughts" are *like* the sea and will "ne'er ebb to humble love"; the adjective ("humble") is exact, for pride is the name of such a likeness as would have erected a human couple to the center of being, making them unlike all other human beings.

So it is that Othello the Moor is finally moored in death and thus unMoored. It is as if Shakespeare had resolved to play out the full resonance of the word, tapping every resource of meaning in it, sounding its depth, and exploring the room it provides the mind for accommodating the more(s) of eros, the *amour* the Moor is doomed to feel. This resolution arises, I think, from Shakespeare's consistent meditation on *like* and likeness throughout his career as a playwright. No two lovers in his plays are both less alike and more alike at the same time than Othello and Desdemona, and this paradox fascinated him. The fascination brought him to one of the most revelatory (if not also revolutionary) speeches he ever wrote:

> **EMILIA** But I do think it is *their husbands' faults*
> If wives do fall. Say that they slack their duties,
> And pour our treasures into foreign laps,
> Or else break out in peevish jealousies,
> Throwing restraint upon us; or say they strike us,
> Or scant our former having in despite:
> Why, we have galls; and though we have some grace,
> Yet have we some revenge. *Let husbands know*
> *Their wives have sense like them.* They see, and smell,
> And have their palates both for sweet and sour,
> As husbands have. What is it that they do
> When they change us for others? Is it sport?
> I think it is. And doth affection breed it?
> I think it doth. Is't frailty that thus errs?
> It is so, too. And have not we affections,
> Desires for sport, and frailty, as men have?
> Then let them use us well, else let them know
> The ills we do, their ills instruct us so.
>
> *Oth.* 4.3.85-102 (emphasis added)[5]

It seems to me that a male suffering the "narcissistic wound" (Adelman, *Mothers* 169) of realizing his dependence on the female can be in a certain sense the most likely candidate for breaking through to the realization that women "have sense like" men. Moreover, it seems to me, there is a compelling logic to why he would make such a breakthrough in a play like *Othello*—it is a play about a woman and a man both hardly alike at all and yet profoundly alike at the same time, so that fusing them, as the sea imagery also suggests, leads to consequences within the unfolding of which canonical concepts of male and female must fall apart: if Desdemona loves Othello, then wives (may as well) have sense like their husbands— after all, Desdemona obviously behaves like a man in her dealings with her father and the patriarchy of Venice.

It is here that we can usefully meditate on their names, Othello and Desdemona. As we can infer from her behavior in Venice, Brabanzio's daughter is more properly named *Desdemona* rather than *Eudemona*, "unhappiness" or "ill fortune," rather than "happiness," or "blessing," or "prosperity" or "success."[6] The Greek prefix of destruction, δυσ, negates or destroys the value of the word to which it is affixed. In this case, that word is one of the most important in the ancient Greek philosophical vocabulary, above all in Aristotle. In the *Ethics*, *eudaemonia* is the highest condition to which humankind can aspire or attain, the condition of "happiness," in the fullest possible sense.[7] To possess a *daimon* that is *eu*, or favorably disposed toward one—that is, who "divides" or "allots" (the root senses of *daimon*) good fortune to one—is to be blessed and supremely so: if my "demon" is a spirit who relates to me in the manner denoted by *eu*, and I cooperate in my life with my "demon," then I am *happy*. But if my "demon" is *dys* (think of "dystopia" or "distrophy" or "disphemism," opposite of "euphemism"), then I am *un*happy and bound to misfortune, "allotted" a "lot" or "slice"[8] in life that is bad. Desdemona is so named, I suggest, by antiphrasis: so close does she come, although in a patriarchal world, to happiness as a woman—a happiness that, presumably, would be complete by her fusion with Othello—that she attracts, almost by uncanny fate, the opposite name, antiphrastically known by the negation of what she almost is *like*.

Similarly, with Othello's name, a kind of antiphrasis again. Joel Fineman famously speculated (*Effect*) that the name *Othello*, which we assume must be Shakespeare's invention, was invented by him from the Greek verb θελω meaning "to wish or will," where "will," Fineman implies, drew *Will* Shakespeare to the invention. *Pace* Fineman, I propose another Greek word as candidate for the invention: θῆλυσ, meaning "female" or "feminine" or, metaphorically, "soft," "gentle," "yielding," "weak." Transliterated the word is used today mainly in scientific contexts (see *OED* II *sub voce* "theelin"). If Shakespeare had encountered, in Homer or elsewhere (a scholiast, perhaps?), the Greek phrase ὁ θῆλυς...("the female..."), he could have, I conjecture, derived *Othello* from it. His motive, I further conjecture, would have been another antiphrasis: Othello, the Moor, the great general, is also "soft" and "gentle" (so certainly Desdemona found him) and subject thus to manipulation, even penetration, "yielding" and "weak," as Iago certainly found him, especially with his poison ("The Moor already changes with my poison"—*Othello* 3.3.329). The antiphrasis would thus also account for Othello's apparent uxoriousness by suggesting that, to the contrary, it was more his intrinsic "theelin-g" that drew him and bound him to Desdemona, which, tragically, nonetheless could not endure the onslaught of Iago's envy and malice. Finally, the antiphrasis would possibly help account for the homoeroticism that pervades the male relationships in the play.

Be that as it may, here is where clearly Iago enters into the argument. Iago's defining lines—"I am not what I am"; "Demand me nothing. What you know, you know" (*Oth.* 1.1.65; 5.2.309)—are the lines of a man without an identity.[9] Iago, whose name amounts to *I ago*, or "I act or perform or play" (< Latin *ago*: "to do or to act or to perform"), has no identity other than that of the character whose likeness he happens to be reflecting/performing in the given moment. As a character without an identity—an "ancient" or "ensign" (*Oth.* 1.1.32), i.e., one who *bears an identity for another*[10]—Iago is so placed that the (con)fused likeness of Othello-Desdemona can only be an intolerable irritant to him, a living condemnation of his likelessness:

> **IAGO** That Cassio loves her, I do well believe it.
> That she loves him, 'tis apt and of great credit.
> The Moor — *howbe't that I endure him not* —
> Is of a constant, loving, noble nature,
> And I dare think he'll prove to Desdemona
> A most dear husband. *Now I do love her too,*
> Not out of absolute lust — though *peradventure*
> *I stand accountant for as great a sin* —
> But partly led to diet my revenge
> For that I do suspect the lusty Moor
> Hath leapt into my seat, the thought whereof
> Doth, like a poisonous mineral, gnaw my inwards;
> And nothing can or shall *content my soul*
> *Till I am evened with him, wife for wife.*
> *Oth.* 2.1.285-98 (emphasis added)

Note first and foremost the obvious implication that Iago "loves"

Desdemona *because* Cassio and Othello love her, reflecting and echoing and acting their likenesses; and even if it were lust in him, his debt to that sin would be only "peradventure," not certain (because not real). Next, note the nearly exact echo in "content my soul" of Othello's "[m]y soul hath her content so absolute" (*Oth.* 2.1.192), further underscoring Iago's leeching of likeness from Othello. And, finally, note the tell-tale syntax as well as self-betraying content of "[t]ill I am evened with him, wife for wife," where "evened...wife for wife" is the very structure of non-identity, his likeness wholly contingent on Othello's, inseparable from his insatiable re*ven*ge.

Shakespeare also insists on Iago's leeching of likeness from those around him with different images. Significantly, for example, Iago boasts

> If consequence do but approve my dream,
> *My boat sails freely* both with wind and stream
> *Oth.* 2.3.58-59 (emphasis added),

and it should hardly surprise us that Iago speaks as if the sea were his element, too, as it is Othello's. But much more extensive an insistence on Iago's leeching of likeness is sustained through the ubiquitous imagery of eating, digesting, and excretion (see, inter alia, *Oth.* 1.3.347-9; 2.1.274; 3.3.136-8; 3.3.169-71; 3.3.396; 3.4.101-4; 4.1.195; 5.2.81-82). These instances, each in its way, suffuse the play with a pervasive and ominous sense of feeding or devouring, which leads to flesh assimilating flesh, or the conversion of one likeness into another. This conversion is most frightening in the case of Iago "diet[ing his] revenge" (*Oth.* 2.1.293). But, as we can readily see, it threatens in Othello, too, who becomes *like* Iago as he imagines dieting on the messes he will make of Desdemona (*Oth.* 4.1.195). As Iago leeches likeness from Othello, he inevitably and predictably injects Othello with his poison: "The Moor already changes with my poison" (*Oth.* 3.3.329), the poison of *being no self*, having no identity—"That's he *that was Othello*. Here I am" (*Oth.* 5.2.290; emphasis added; see also 3.3.362: "Othello's occupation's gone").[11] Iago's poison is so venomous that it empowers him even to speak of Othello as if Othello were he, Iago, himself:

> He's that he is. I may not breathe my censure
> What he might be. If what he might he is not,
> I would to heaven he were.
> *Oth.* 4.1.272-4

This is the tortured syntax of the *ensign*, he who is without an identity of his own, where the predicatelessness of the constative—"He's that he is" (that what?)—becomes Iago's means to assign the same lack of identity he himself suffers to Othello, and where the subjunctive riot of the verb *to be*—"what he might ... is not ... he were"—sustains and furthers the insinuation of Othello's Iago-like likelessness. But nowhere is this sick harvesting of another's identity more nauseating than in the instance of Othello's Iago-like parturition:

> **IAGO**   There are many events in the
> *womb* of time, which will be delivered.
> ...
> I ha't. It is *ingendered*. Hell and night
> Must bring this *monstrous birth* to the world's light.
>   *Oth.* 1.3.368-9; 395-6 (emphasis added)

> **OTHELLO**...to deny each article with oath
> Cannot remove nor choke *the strong conception*
> *That I do groan withal.* Thou art to die.
>   *Oth.* 5.2.59-61 (emphasis added)

Othello is pregnant by Iago (whom he has *married*, in effect [see *Oth.* 3.3.463-74]) to give monstrous birth to Desdemona's death—most seminal poison indeed.

Othello, I think, is the play in which Shakespeare tests with the strongest possible test the premise of his dauntingly difficult lyric, "The Phoenix and the Turtle" (see Burrow 82ff.). I would like to set certain passages from it in the context of *Othello* to put forward the hypothesis that Othello and Desdemona embody for Shakespeare the attempt and the failure at the ideal of eros imagined in the lyric. The demonstration, I think, is relatively simple. Consider first these lines from the lyric:

> Two distincts, division none.
> Number there in love was slain.
>
> Either was the other's mine.
>
> Property was thus appalled
> That the self was not the same.
>
> Reason, in itself confounded,
> Saw division grow together

"Love hath reason, reason none,
If what parts can so remain."
                    lines 27-28; 36-38; 41-42; 47-48 (emphasis added)

Now listen to various lines from the play:

OTHELLO   I had rather be a toad
And live upon the vapour of a dungeon
*Than keep a corner in the thing I love
For others' uses.*
                    Oth. 3.3.274-7 (emphasis added)

IAGO There's millions now alive
That nightly lie in those *unproper* beds
Which they dare swear peculiar.
                    Oth. 4.1.66-68 (emphasis added)

OTHELLO *But there where I have garnered up my heart,
Where either I must live or bear no life,
The fountain from the which my current runs
Or else dries up — to be discarded thence,
Or keep it as a cistern for foul toads
To knot and gender in!*
                    Oth. 4.2.59-64 (emphasis added)

The key issue is property. The "proper," the "own" ("L. *propri-us* one's own, special, particular, peculiar" — *OED* II *sub voce*) provokes the deepest anxiety of the patriarchy since paternity cannot (before the advent of DNA-testing) be proven — no man can be *certain* his son is his *own*.[12] His wife may have "a corner ... for others' uses" and the bed he "dare[s] swear peculiar" may admit "unproper" interlopers.[13] Hence those kinship systems that privilege the relationship between the maternal uncle and the sister's son (avunculate) — the maternal uncle cares for this nephew because he can be reasonably sure that his sister's son is at least partly his own blood; his own wife may be sleeping with who knows whom and her son may be anybody's, but his sister's son is at least partly *like* him (Murphy). The patriarch's ownership of his property is never secure because of the female, whose "duplicity" always undermines his "singleness" (think only of Brabanzio's "ownership" of Desdemona and its consequences). Hence the ideal of "The Phoenix and the Turtle": if "[e]ither [*were*] the other's mine," truly, property *would be* "appalled" since it would no longer make a difference, literally — the love thus celebrated would put an end to the doubleness of sexual difference and the self would not be the same as itself. And yet experience repeatedly proves that "[s]imple [cannot be] so well compounded." Even Othello and Desdemona with a love as pure as theirs cannot attain such well-compounded simplicity.

Even Othello and Desdemona are not the Phoenix and the Turtle. Nor are they Tristan and Isolde, though I conjecture that the ubiquitous sea imagery in the play derives in part from Shakespeare's awareness of the Tristan legend, which, in one version, offers, for example, the haunting pun on the bitterness ("amer") of love ("amer") in the sea ("mer") of being.[14] So also, I speculate, does the imagery of drugs or potions:

> **OTHELLO**   Yet, by your gracious patience,
> I will a round unvarnished tale deliver
> Of my whole course of love, what *drugs*, what charms,
> What conjuration and what mighty *magic* —
> For such proceeding I am charged withal —
> I won his daughter.
>

Oth. 1.3.89-94 (emphasis added)

Shakespeare has reimagined Tristan and Isolde and the Phoenix and the Turtle, as "an old black ram/... tupping [a] white ewe" (*Oth*. 1.1.88-9) so as, I believe, to strain his imagination to the utmost in contemplation of sexual division and its consequences for human being. Sexual division for Shakespeare is the founding crisis of human being, for from it emerges the theatre of likeness; and it is this theatre that enables Iago to destroy Othello.

Once we look, it is actually very easy to see:

> **IAGO** Ha! *I like not that.*
> **OTHELLO** What dost thou say?
> **IAGO** Nothing, my lord. Or if, I know not what.
> **OTHELLO** Was not that Cassio parted from my wife?
> **IAGO** Cassio, my lord? No, sure, I cannot think it,
> That he would steal away *so guilty-like*
> Seeing your coming.
> **OTHELLO**   I do believe 'twas he.
> ...
> **OTHELLO** "Think, my lord?" By heaven, thou echo'st me
> As if there were some monster in thy thought
> Too hideous to be shown! *Thou dost mean something.*
> I heard thee say even now thou *liked'st* not that,
> When Cassio left my wife. *What didst not like?*
>

Oth. 3.3.33-40; 110-14 (emphasis added)

Here, in brief, is a theater of likeness, and on its stage Iago can "mean something" simply by deploying (nothing but the word) *like*(ness)—"I like not that"…"so guilty-like"…"thou likedst not that"…"[w]hat didst not like?" Because of sexual division (just that, nothing more), when Cassio parts from Desdemona, Iago, a kind of pornographer, can invent a likeness (a play, in effect) that realizes the "monster in his thought," the monster, "green-eyed," that will destroy Othello, whose

> *unbookish* jealousy must *conster*
> Poor Cassio's smiles, gestures, and light behaviours
> Quite in the wrong.
> *Oth.* 4.1.100-2 (emphasis added)

Because Othello does not know how to read the book of *like*(nesses), he will (mis)construe a fiction to be reality, a *like*(ness) to be an identity, a lie to be the truth.

> **IAGO** The Moor is of a free and open nature,
> That thinks men honest that *but seem to be so,*
> And will as tenderly be led by th' nose
> As asses are.
> *Oth.* 1.3.391-4 (emphasis added)

All Iago need do is *act like* honest Iago, and Othello is ruined. Nowhere else in Shakespeare's plays do I find the theatre of likeness at once so succinctly and so terrifyingly in evidence. Ultimately because he cannot believe "wives have sense *like*" their husbands, Othello is seduced, betrayed, and destroyed, destroying as well, in the process, the person in the world he loves the most, who means the most to him. And sexual division as such impels his and Desdemona's tragedy.

To "believe" is to "be-like" (above, chapter 23 page 231). To believe is to invest one's likeness in whom one likes (by definition separate and divided from one). Iago's likenesses, however, interfere with and interrupt Othello's belief or beliking in Desdemona; they become, in effect, the script or book or play—the pornographic text—through which Othello construes his wife and her behavior. Almost literally pornographic, in fact, in Iago's viciously lurid portrayal of Cassio's alleged dream:

> **OTHELLO** Give me a living reason she's disloyal.
> **IAGO** I do not *like* the office,
> But sith I am entered in this cause so far,
> Pricked to't by foolish honesty and love,

> I will go on. I lay with Cassio lately,
> And being troubled with a raging tooth,
> I could not sleep. There are a kind of men
> So loose of soul that in their sleeps
> Will mutter their affairs. One of this kind is Cassio.
> In sleep I heard him say "Sweet Desdemona,
> Let us be wary, let us hide our loves,"
> And then, sir, would he grip and wring my hand,
> Cry "O, sweet creature!," then kiss me hard,
> As if he plucked up kisses by the roots,
> That grew upon my lips, lay his leg o'er my thigh,
> And sigh, and kiss, and then cry "Cursèd fate,
> That gave thee to the Moor!"
> **OTHELLO** O, monstrous, monstrous!
> **IAGO** Nay, this was but his dream.
> *Oth.* 3.3.414-32 (emphasis added)

We know, of course, that Iago *likes* the office "just fine." Othello's imagination corrupted by such graphic imagery, little wonder he sinks at last to his (in)famous expostulation:

> Was this fair paper, this most goodly book,
> Made to write "whore" upon?
> *Oth.* 4.2.73-74

He but continues and extends the pornographic script Iago's malice is prescribing, as if at this point he were all but Iago's scribe, his amanuensis.

And so, it seems to me, finally, one must comport oneself with awe before Othello's ultimate speech in Shakespeare's play, for it is a speech in which Othello authors *his own* script, dictating the "letter" that will report him to Venice and to the world:

> **OTHELLO** Soft you, *a word or two before you go*.
> I have done the state some service, and they know't.
> No more of that. I pray you, in your *letters*,
> When you shall these unlucky deeds *relate*,
> *Speak of me as I am*. Nothing extenuate,
> Nor set down aught in malice. *Then must you speak*
> Of one that loved not wisely but too well,
> Of one not easily jealous but, being wrought,
> Perplexed in the extreme; of one whose hand,

> Like the base Indian, threw a pearl away
> Richer than all his tribe; of one whose subdued eyes,
> Albeit unusèd to the melting mood,
> Drops [sic] tears as fast as the Arabian trees
> Their medicinable gum. *Set you down this,*
> And *say besides* that in Aleppo once,
> Where a malignant and a turbaned Turk
> Beat a Venetian and traduced the state,
> I took by th' throat the circumcisèd dog
> And smote him thus.
>   *He stabs himself*
> **LODOVICO** *O bloody period!*
> **GRAZIANO** All that is spoke is marred.
>   *Oth.* 5.2.347-67 (emphasis added)

Indeed, the *period* is bloody, but only Graziano, I suggest, need believe that "[a]ll that is spoke is marred." We may, rather, in awe—and, I daresay, with some sorrow—hear a man determine and declare how he shall be spoken of "as [he] is," according to *the likeness he chooses*. "Speak of me as I am"; "Then must you speak"; "Set you down this"; "And say besides": Othello *writes* his own epitaph; there is no more Iago-like prescript, only his script, period. Crucial, then, is the variant recorded in F, "Iudean" (Wells and Taylor, *Companion* 482). If we adopt this variant, Othello construes himself at the end of his life as Judas Iscariot, after Satan most heinous of the traitors recognized by Christianity. By this construal of likeness, which scripts his suicide, to be sure,[15] Othello also scripts Desdemona, or construes her, as Christ, "the pearl richer than all his tribe." This likeness I believe Othello intended (I believe, that is, Shakespeare revised *Indian* to *Iudean*) because, for the brief moment of his union with Desdemona, he was, he knows, black, but "far more fair than black" (*Oth.* 1.3.290): "I saw," Desdemona declared, "Othello's visage in his mind" (*Oth.* 1.3.252); and Othello knows—and what's more, scripts it as his final likeness—that he has betrayed and killed his savior.[16]

> **BRABANZIO** But words are words. I never yet did hear
> That the bruised heart was piercèd through the ear.
> *Oth.* 1.3.217-18

Shakespeare, it seems safe to say, lived in a world of words the rest of us will never inhabit. Still, I am troubled by the words Brabanzio utters just before he resigns himself to Desdemona's marriage; they seem to me troubling especially because Shakespeare is who he is. I feel I cannot conclude this chapter, then, without one final comment.

It is not just words, it is words *and ears*. Consider, in the lines cited above, "h*ear*" and "h*ear*t" and "p–*ear*–cèd" and "*ear*": something is calling out to us ("To hear with eyes belongs to love's fine wit" — Sonnet #23). We could say it this way. Brabanzio is mistaken. How else is the bruised heart "surgically lanced (and presumably cured)" (Norton, glossing "piercèd," 2112), *except* through the ear? (We are, we should perhaps remind ourselves, in a world *prior* to the advent of open-heart surgery, etc.) And when we have asked this question, have we not also surprised ourselves with the following, I think, inevitable realization, that *Othello* is *the* play in Shakespeare's canon about piercing the heart through the ear?

Without question, the meaning shifts. Iago pierces Othello's heart through his ear *not* for curing but for bruising. I don't deny that shift of meaning. But even with the shift, Brabanzio's declaration remains, I think, effectively a metacommentary on Shakespeare's art (if, it must be conceded, by the negation of the negation). Do we not *like* Shakespeare, are we not *like* him, just because he is *the* poet, we know, who teaches us how the "bruised heart is piercèd through the ear"? Is this not, for example, why all who take psychoanalysis seriously, either to promote it or to persecute it, agree that Shakespeare is the ur-script of the psychoanalytic project, the *talking cure* (Fineman, *Effect* 159)? Shakespeare of all poets who ever lived knows that there is no way to the heart but through the ear by means of language. (In a world prior to open-heart surgery, any other access to the heart must kill the heart.) And, if we follow this reasoning, do we not arrive at an exact understanding of why the play *Othello* breaks our hearts? Iago, like *Hamlet*'s Claudius, pours poison into Othello's ear — not medicine, not an antidote, but poison. Instead of the talking cure, Iago's is the talking *disease* — "Demand me nothing. What you know, you know./From this time forth I never will speak word" (*Oth.* 5.2.309-10) — his arrogance and assertion and mocking silence, all evidence that the disease has run its course and that he, the pathogen, is now superfluous, a mere waste product for excretion.

Othello is not, perhaps, a greater play than *Hamlet* or *King Lear* or *Macbeth*, but it is more important than they are, I venture to say, because it is the play that *proves* tragedy what it is, the annihilation of what makes us human, or our language. Shakespeare, I believe, would agree with Aeschylus, "words are the healers of a diseased temper."[17] But not when Iago utters them. Not when Lady Macbeth, Goneril and Regan, Claudius utter them. Then words amount to biological warfare, pestilential miasma, pouring through the porch of the ear, "murmuring hells of crime,"[18] until the heart can hear no more.[19]

25
"Hath lost me in your liking [lie, king]": *King Lear*

> If I speak like myself in
> this, let him be whipped that first finds it so.
> *Lr.* 1.4.146-7

> but I am bound
> Upon a wheel of fire, that mine own tears
> Do scald like molten lead.
> *Lr.* 4.6.39-41

> A most poor man, made tame to fortune's blows,
> Who by the art of known and feeling sorrows
> Am pregnant to good pity.
> *Lr.* 4.5.220-2

> *Ce sexe qui n'en est pas un*
> Luce Irigaray

The genital is a wound from which no one recovers. It is a fissure in being as well as in the body. It is as palpable in the male body as it is in the female body. Every genital, *pace* Irigaray, is "not one." Every genital has a tear, is in parts. Every "poor, bare, forked animal" (*Lr.* 3.4.101-2), otherwise "unaccommodated," (*Lr.* 3.4.100-1) is accommodated first by his or her genital, measured (< *modus*) at birth and *modi*fied as male or as female, in parts.[1] The real of *Lear* is the tragedy of learning too late that "'twas this flesh begot/Those pelican daughters" (*Lr.* 3.4.70-71). Their flesh is just alike, Lear's and his daughters', sexual flesh, parts of the same seed, tears from and in the same being, wounded.

The word *like* contributes importantly to the fable of human sexuality in *King Lear*. In the first part of this chapter, I will list and comment on various occurrences of the word in the play and then, after this survey, I will in the second part of the chapter venture an hypothesis about *King Lear* that I might summarize provisionally as follows. My likeness, when I settle on it (and it settles on me), is a prescript that in effect prescribes how I shall behave, for good or for ill; but *King Lear* is the play of all of Shakespeare's plays that deconstructs—more properly, *deaccommodates*—the very possibility of prescripts in human lives: when Edgar says, "[t]he weight of this sad time we must obey,/Speak what we feel, not what we ought to say" (*Lr.* 5.3.299-300), the very idea of a prescript ("what we ought to say") is voided, its place taken by the momentaneous script of feeling, in which "[r]ipeness is all" (*Lr.* 5.2.11; and cf. *Ham.* 5.2.168, "[t]he readiness is all").

Like and its various forms occur some 60 times in *King Lear*. But most significant perhaps is the work that the word does in the very beginning of the play—act 1, scene 1. Consider the following list, which includes just enough context to orient the reading (*Lr.* 1.1.103; 1.1.197-9; 1.1.207-12; 1.1.230-3; 1.1.268-70; emphasis added):

CORDELIA Sure, I shall never marry *like* my sisters.

LEAR If aught within that little seeming substance,
Or all of it, with our displeasure pieced,
And nothing more, may fitly *like* your grace,
She's there, and she is yours.

LEAR   For you, great King,
I would not from your love make such a stray
To match you where I hate, therefore beseech you
T'avert your *liking* a more worthier way
Than on a wretch whom nature is ashamed
Almost t'acknowledge hers.

CORDELIA But even the want of that for which I am richer —
A still-soliciting eye, and such a tongue
That I am glad I have not, though not to have it
Hath lost me in your *liking*.

CORDELIA Cordelia leaves you. I know you what you are,
And *like* a sister am most loath to call
Your faults as they are named.

In these passages, the word "like," as it does so often in other plays, connotes the burden of personal identity and its attendant crises, most especially the crisis of the child's likeness to the parent, which is so central to all of Shakespeare's work. In particular, the word in act 1, scene 1 establishes the dilemma of Cordelia as one of remaining faithful to her father without being like him or like her sisters. In struggling to "speak like [her] self" instead (*Lr.* 1.4.146), Cordelia will in a stroke tear herself from her parent and her siblings alike. "Lost in [their] liking," she ends in the arms of France, in his "liking," which presumably also is more to her liking. Cordelia, we can say with the help of this remarkable (and remarkably simple) word, can be *like* only a daughter or a sister or her husband's wife and nothing else, certainly nothing *like* what Lear wants her to be, a "nursery" (*Lr.* 1.1.124). Cordelia is not Lear's mother, nor is she Lear's wife, Lear's sister, Lear's servant, Lear's soldier, but his daughter: she therefore behaves like a daughter, and it costs her her life and like(ness).

No one in the world of *King Lear*, in short, can speak like himself or like herself with impunity. Cordelia immediately sees her plight—"What shall Cordelia *speak*? Love and *be silent*" (*Lr.* 1.1.62; emphasis added).² And the Fool understands as much almost innately (*Lr.* 1.4.146-7). Anyone who dares to speak like herself or like himself will suffer the fate of Cordelia or Kent or Edgar. Each in one way or another must "raze [her or his] likeness" (*Lr.* 1.4.4) else appearing in public may prove mortal (as eventually everyone learns):

KENT If but as well I other accents borrow
That can my speech defuse, my good intent
May carry through itself to that full issue
For which I *razed my likeness*.
Lr. 1.4.1-4 (emphasis added)

Cordelia razes her likeness to that of a French Queen; Kent, his to that of a wandering, masterless retainer; Edgar, his to that of Tom o' Bedlam. Such is the price of liking oneself enough to refuse to surrender one's likeness to a tyrant (lest I be lost in your lie, king).

In this sense, *King Lear* is the greatest of all of Shakespeare's plays in regard of the hopelessness of politics—in the world of politics (i.e., power), "[h]umanity must perforce prey on itself,/*Like* monsters of the deep" (*Lr.* [1605-6] Sc. 16.48-49; emphasis added). Also, in this sense, we can see why *King Lear* is a play obsessed in its language with the discourse of economics. "Off, off, you lendings!" (*Lr.* 3.4.102) is the cry of someone who has learned, if tragically too late, that what you (think you) own is instead the likeness (usually tyrannical) that owns you; and only "the thing itself ... unaccommodated man ... such a poor, bare, forked animal" (*Lr.* 3.4.98-100) can begin, in the absence of all artificial accommodations, to force "pomp" to "take physic":

> **LEAR**   Take physic, pomp,
> Expose thyself to feel what wretches feel,
> That thou mayst shake the superflux to them
> And show the heavens more just.
>
> Lr. 3.4.33-36

But after *King Lear*, we know only too well how very hard it is for pomp to strip itself to our universal likeness—a "poor, bare, forked animal"— where "[t]he art of our necessities[, being] strange,/... can make vile things precious" (*Lr.* 3.2.70-71; and cf. "Full oft 'tis seen/... our mere defects/Prove our *commodities*" [*Lr.* 4.1.19-21; emphasis added]). Pomp does not like to be shown this likeness. The truth would make free what pomp pretends to own:

> **GLOUCESTER** Let the superfluous and lust-dieted man
> That slaves your [heavens'] ordinance, that will not see
> Because he doth not feel, feel your power quickly.
> So distribution should undo excess,
> And each man have enough.
>
> Lr. 4.1.61-65

But the political world cannot tolerate the thought that "each man [might] have enough" any more than Lear in his dotage can tolerate the thought that Cordelia should love him "[a]ccording to [her] bond, no more nor less" (*Lr.* 1.1.93)—we are monsters of excess, and therein we are tragic.

When Albany comes to his senses regarding the monstrousness of Goneril, we learn from Oswald that

> What most he [Albany] should *dislike* seems pleasant to him;
> What *like*, offensive.
>
> Lr. 4.2.10-11 (emphasis added)

And this transvaluation of values in Albany, conveyed through the work of the word "like,"[3] besides suggesting to us why, at first, Lear "had more affected the Duke of Albany than Cornwall" (*Lr.* 1.1.1-2), also prompts us to perceive the loss of Lear in his daughter—"gon(e) Leir."[4] Lear is torn apart in Goneril ("Thou worse than any name," as Albany spits at her— [*Lr.* 5.3.147]). He/his name is also scattered in Regan, whose name tears the *rega*l from Lear; and, as well, his name is also scattered in Cor*de*l*ia*. It is commonplace that Shakespeare conveys much of his insight through puns, and proper names in his plays often provide extraordinary access to his meaning—Iago, for example, also spells *I ago* or "I act or perform." But the name Goneril, with its suggestion of sexually transmitted disease (*OED* II *sub voce* "gonnorhœa," the 16th-century evidence, esp.) as well as its repetition of Lear's name, seems especially ominous when we consider how unlike her husband, Albany, or her sister, Cordelia, she is. We are forced to admit the unfathomable mystery of likeness, even though we may hesitate to adopt Kent's explanation:

> **KENT**　　　　　　　It is the stars,
> The stars above us govern our conditions,
> Else one self mate and make could not beget
> Such different issues.
>
> *Lr.* [1605-6] Sc. 17.33-36

The problem is already there in Kent's language, although inaudible to him: there *never* was "*one self* mate and make" (emphasis added)—there were always two, necessarily, and where there are two, there will always be tears.

Because we are incomplete, because we are in need of another (who is always, first, our mother), we live our lives in pairs (at least) and are always subject to tears. In the beginning of the play, Lear tries, by the sheer force of his "sentence and...power" (*Lr.* 1.1.169), to legislate his way out of the human condition:

> 　　　　　　　　　Only we shall retain
> The name and all th'addition to a king. The sway,
> Revenue, execution of the rest,
> Belovèd sons, be yours.
>
> *Lr.* 1.1.135-8

In other words, Lear commits the very crime of which he a moment later accuses Kent—"com[ing] betwixt our sentence and our power" (*Lr.* 1.1.169)—by himself dividing sentence, or name, which he would retain, from power, which he alienates to Albany and Cornwall. He seeks, in a paroxysm of self-deception, to escape dependency by dependency, thinking to be independent in the very midst of a dependency far more onerous than the responsibilities of kingship. He is driven to this extreme of self-contradiction because, as his daughter Regan says, "he hath ever but slenderly known himself" (*Lr.* 1.1.292-3): I find the adverb, "slenderly," revealing—Lear's self-knowledge is *slender* just because he has never adequately acknowledged the other parts of himself that would make up a full or abundant self-knowledge. Of King Lear it is *im*possible to say "he hath ever *abundantly* known himself" because the many issues of himself that he is about now to tear apart from himself have never truly been a part of his life and his likeness. If it is the case that no man ever completely knows himself, then the tragedy of Lear is the more terrifying in that he has always practiced a moral and a spiritual anorexia (*anorexia* is the Greek privative prefix plus the Greek verb "to desire" [*OED* II *sub voce*]). Lear "hath ever but slenderly known" his desire.

Most particularly, sexual desire. For Lear, the genital has always been a wound that the other half of humanity suffers, women. But it is his tragedy and also his terrible glory to learn that he suffers it, too:

> **LEAR**   Let copulation thrive,
> For Gloucester's bastard son
> Was kinder to his father than my daughters
> Got 'tween the lawful sheets. To't luxury, pell-mell!,
> For I lack soldiers. Behold yon simp'ring dame,
> Whose face between her forks presages snow,
> That minces virtue, and does shake the head
> To hear of pleasure's name.
> The fitchew nor the soilèd horse goes to 't
> With a more riotous appetite. Down from the waist
> They're centaurs, though women all above.
> But to the girdle do the gods inherit;
> Beneath is all the fiend's. There's hell, there's darkness,
> there is the sulphurous pit, burning, scalding, stench,
> consumption. Fie, fie, fie; pah, pah! Give me an ounce
> of civet, good apothecary, sweeten my imagination.
> There's money for thee.
>
> Lr. 4.5.112–28

If, after this logorrhea of Lear's, Gloucester cries out, "O, let me kiss that hand!" (*Lr.* 4.5.128), it is of inexaggerable importance that Lear responds to him, "[l]et me wipe it first; it smells of mortality" (*Lr.* 4.5.129), for the first time in the play acknowledging that the stench of mortality contaminates his flesh, too. I take it that the references to odor and smelling in the play (*Lr.* 1.1.15; 4.5.103) culminate in this dawning awareness of Lear's that it is not only women's "fault" (error and pudendum) that smells (*Lr.* 1.1.15). That Lear should have to pass through such sordid imagination to come to his own odor of mortality is appalling—we may well pray, each of us, that s/he never has to descend into and assent to his or her body and its mortality through such a path—but that Lear can then go on, a few lines later, to exclaim,

> Thou rascal beadle, hold thy bloody hand.
> Why dost thou lash that whore? Strip thine own back.
> Thou hotly lusts to use her in that kind
> For which thou whip'st her.
>
> *Lr.* 4.5.156-9,

must chasten our too hasty conclusion: like Christ with the woman taken in adultery (John 8:1-11), Lear understands now the universality and the banality of lust—"Thou hotly lusts to use her in that kind/For which thou whip'st her" is more poisoned than "[h]e that is without sin among you, let him first cast a stone at her," but each is an equally profound testimony to our common animality. Tragically, though, Lear cannot like Christ kneel to write in the dirt a new script of the new law (John 8:6, 8), living as he does by the prescript of his own old law, to tear himself from which will require no less than the loss of everything he holds dear.

For I take it that at least one necessary response to Adelman's moving indictment of Lear and of Shakespeare as well (*Mothers* 128-9) is that the inexcusable sacrifice of Cordelia does nonetheless free Lear, if only for a moment, from the prescript that has bound him to the wheel of fire:

> Do not laugh at me,
> For as I am a man, I think this lady
> To be my child, Cordelia.
>
> *Lr.* 4.6.61-63

If I understand the feminist grievance, then "as I am a man" must be insupportably galling—what right has he to claim manhood at the cost of his daughter's life? Why must she be choked by hanging so that her voice should be swallowed in men's voices? Under what cock-eyed vision of justice can this sacrifice make even so much as the deluded sense of patriarchal ideology? And yet, Shakespeare, being Shakespeare, has Cordelia respond, "[a]nd so I am, I am" (*Lr.* 4.6.63), where no reader from Judeo-Christian culture can fail to hear the echo of the Tetragrammaton, "I am that I am" (Exodus 3:14).[5] However unbearable—and I confess that it troubles me, too—here Cordelia is represented to be *like* God, and because she is like God, Lear can imagine a new script:

> Come, let's away to prison.
> We two alone will sing like birds i'th'cage.
>
> *Lr.* 5.3.8-9

If the feminist hears in "we two al*one*" (emphasis added) the vicious, inexcusable abolition of Cordelia's subjectivity, I hear in "sing *like* birds i' the cage" (emphasis added), a difference in Lear that can only have arisen from "tears [that] / Do scald *like* molten lead" (*Lr.* 4.6.40-41; emphasis added), where the "*mol*ten *lea***d**" is necessarily the changing of ("molt," like a bird in a cage?) as well as the tearing of *Lear*—too late, yes, but may we presume to say, too little?

Arguably not. Edgar, who, after Hamlet, is the most female of Shakespeare's tragic heros (he is "*pregnant* to good pity"—*Lr.* 4.5.222; emphasis added), is precise in his instruction of us: "The worst is not/So long as we can say 'This is the worst'" (*Lr.* 4.1.27-28), for in that event we still are speaking by and from a prescript that dictates what we see in what we say. Only when language and breath are utterly destroyed will it be "the worst." Then death is the worst. But until death, life speaks, if only in paroxysms of repetition—"Never, never, never, never, never" (*Lr.* 5.3.284; see also 5.3.232, "Howl, howl, howl, howl!"). For life *would* write a new script,[6] and, like Posthumus in *Cymbeline*, who awakes with a new script lying on his breast—

> 'Tis still a dream, or else such stuff as madmen
> Tongue, and brain not; either both, or nothing,
> Or senseless speaking, or a speaking such
> As sense cannot untie. Be what it is,
> The action of my life is *like* it, which I'll keep,
> If but for sympathy.
>   (*Cym.* 5.5.239-44; emphasis added)—

we each of us would keep the new script, no matter how late it arrived and no matter how unintelligible, "if but for the sympathy," or likeness, to the action of his or her life.

And yet that likeness must entail a certain priority, must it not? A certain pre-text? No script is not also a prescript, surely? Every script has "always already" been written, right? This is essential Shakespeare, is it not? Holinshed and Ovid and Spenser and Chaucer, et al. Shakespeare never wrote anything that was not already written at least once, often twice or more. Everyone learns this even in an introductory course on "the Bard." But it is perhaps to miss the point.

Needed is a distinction between a pre-script and the prescriptive: Shakespeare is without peer in converting a pre-script into a new script by avoiding and evading the prescriptive, wherever it may lurk. If Shakespeare is the most innovative, the most creative, dramatist after the Greeks of 5th-century Athens, it is because he imagines the likeness of his language as the language of (un)likeness, juxta-form and cruci-lingual. This is, to be sure, Hamlet's "to hold as 'twere the mirror up to nature" (*Ham.* 3.2.21-22), but it is also something more and something else.

Keats's notion of "negative capability" suggests how we might define it (letter of 21, 27 [?] December 1817; emphasis added):

> at once it struck me what quality went to form a Man of Achievement, especially in Literature, and which Shakespeare possessed so enormously—*I mean Negative Capability, that is, when a man is capable of being in uncertainties, mysteries, doubts, without any irritable reaching after fact and reason*—Coleridge, for instance, would let go by a fine isolated verisimilitude caught from the Penetralium of mystery, from being incapable of remaining content with half-knowledge.

If Shakespeare is "capable of being in uncertainties, mysteries, doubts, without any irritable reaching after fact and reason," this also means that he is able to write *without prescription* as to the meanings of "uncertainties, mysteries, doubts," where prescription would be "fact and reason" irritably reached after. This is to say, then, that Shakespeare can be not only negatively capable, he can also *capably negate*—he can negate the accommodations, trappings and tropings of countless conventions, that circumscribe the real (with "fact and reason"), and he then can re-inscribe the real in the language of (un)likeness. Consider this example from *Venus and Adonis* (lines 592-600):

> And on his neck her yoking arms she throws.
>   She sinketh down, still hanging by his neck.
>   He on her belly falls, she on her back.
>
> Now is she in the very lists of love,
> Her champion mounted for the hot encounter.
> All is imaginary she doth prove.
> He will not manage her, although he mount her,
>   That worse than Tantalus' is her annoy,
>   To clip Elysium, and to lack her joy.

All accommodations of the sex act have here been negated, from the puritanical to the pornographic, so as to liken the sex act to a joust, with an unforgettable realization of coupling. I do not mean that there is no source for the imagery—the question of source is not to the point. To the point rather is *the nothing* that circumscribes the likeness that Shakespeare invents: this is as close to the *im*mediate as we can come in the mediated —we see her legs spread and the boy between them, we all but smell her vaginal secretions, and we feel her frustration at the missed orgasm. (Is it any wonder *Venus and Adonis* was so immensely popular [Burrow 7]?)

This it is to write without prescription. This it is that so many generations have recognized as Shakespeare's freedom in language. "Nothing will come of nothing" (*Lr.* 1.1.90) in Lear's world, perhaps, but in the real world of Shakespeare's art, of nothing—"The readiness is all"; "Ripeness is all"—comes the something of his singular likenesses. Readiness, like ripeness, is a condition of "nothing-ness": contentless (i.e., without prescription), it is a form of being (in love, I believe) that *reads* new meaning in the momentaneous script of feeling ("I see it feelingly"—*Lr.* 4.5.145), that, like writing in the sand, cannot be *pre*-scripted and cannot be copied. And like the law of love, it (ful)fills the law with the moment of love, thus canceling the prescript: "Go, and sin no more" (John 8:11).

Lear and Cordelia are denied this freedom: that is their tragedy. Nothing came of nothing for them, thanks to the "very foolish, fond old man" (*Lr.* 4.6.53), who learned too late that everyone, without exception, suffers the tears of sexuality. But it is, or can be, different for us. Unlike Lear, Shakespeare is a poet—a writer, not a dictator.

✾

> When they began to eat the meat, that was so tasteless they couldn't eat it. But Cap o' Rushes' father he tried first one dish and then another, and then he burst out crying.
> "What is the matter?" said the master's son to him.
> "Oh!" says he, "I had a daughter. And I asked her how much she loved me. And she said 'As much as fresh meat loves salt.' And I turned her from my door, for I thought she didn't love me. And now I see she loved me best of all. And she may be dead for aught I know."
> "No, father, here she is!" says Cap o' Rushes.
> (Aarne-Thompson 510; 923; Lindahl 240)

The first British scholar with whom I discussed *King Lear* was Nicholas Brooke, of the University of East Anglia, when I was a student there as a Marshall Scholar (between 1970 and 1972). He had recently undergone surgery for stomach cancer.

A notable Shakespearean who had commented on *King Lear* extensively, Brooke was also Head of English and American Studies at UEA and was dedicated to reform of many kinds in higher education. He was, above all, at this time, accessible, and frank.

I learned in my youth from Nicholas Brooke that in some sense a man with stomach cancer (especially virulent, in his case) is uniquely qualified to talk about *King Lear*. I have retained for more than 30 years now this sense that those dying under particularly gruesome conditions—most of the dear friends in my life have died of cancer—are, in the literal, painful sense, privileged (the word derives, in part, from the word *private*, hence *alone, deprived*) to speak of many things, especially works of art that strive to communicate human suffering. In contrast to such people, I have less right, less privilege, to comment on *King Lear*. This is not false humility or false consciousness (or conscience) on my part; it is what I believe ("be-like").

At my greater distance from the horror that seethes and spits in *King Lear*, I can in some sense only make a scholarly case. I have made that case in this chapter to the best of my ability, trying in particular to suggest that we can avoid Lear's "avoidance of love" (Cavell, *Disowning* 39-123):

> Lear and Gloucester are ... tragic... because they had covered their true isolation (the identity of their condition with the condition of other men) within hiddenness, silence, and position; the ways people do (122).

My belief ("be-like") in this avoidance of avoidance derives, simply, from the existence of a play written by a fellow human being, who was a poet—a writer, not a dictator—and who, like me, could read a fairy tale—and who, far beyond me, could see and show (θεα) what the fairy tale was really about. The worst is not.

26
"Do not assume my likeness": *Timon of Athens*—Misanthropy as Unlikeness

> I am Misanthropos, and hate mankind.
> *Tim.* 4.3.53

> Thou hast cast away thyself being like thyself.
> *Tim.* 4.3.221

The work of the word *like* in *Timon*[1] is especially instructive in that the fundamental question of the play, more transparent than in any other play perhaps, is, what is man like? Timon's misanthropy, in Shakespeare's vocabulary, is the fundamental issue of man's *like*ness, and man's *like*ness, in *Timon*, is inseparable from the dilemma—represented so frequently in Shakespeare—of choosing one's likeness or the always painful paradox of realizing I cannot (be) like myself unless I (am) also like others.

Timon's fate, we know, is to reach a point where he can in no way (be) like others:

> For he is set so only to himself
> That *nothing but himself* which looks *like* man
> Is friendly with him.
> *Tim.* 5.2.2-4 (emphasis added)

Timon is himself the only company he will keep. Anything else that looks like man he spurns since it must remind him that he also looks like man: "Thou hast cast away thyself being *like* thyself" (*Tim.* 4.3.221; emphasis added). This line is an exquisite realization of the theater of likeness. Division and reduplication, agency and yet non-self-coincidence, the subject that is also an object, the whole that is incontinently a fragment, the self that can be no self without some other, if only itself-as-other, in contradistinction to which to be a self—all are expressed in a single line of enduring Shakespearean psychological precision. When Apemantus ("Ape

Man") rails against Timon, "[d]o not assume my *likeness*" (*Tim.* 4.3.219; emphasis added), he asserts his own lifelong misanthropy, to be sure; but Shakespeare asks us to hear as well the syllables of the crisis of likeness: do not (be) like me—the obverse of which is always (be) like me.

Timon of Athens, I think, is a relatively simple play, or, perhaps better, a relatively pure play.[2] With notable lack of complication (no Iago here), the play presents us with the most human of all our double-binds: I must copy, but I must not copy. I want now to map the word *like* through the opening scenes of the play to demonstrate how the crisis of likeness emerges for Timon and for us.

The crisis of likeness announces itself very early in the play, in the fourth occurrence of the word:

> **JEWELLER** My lord, 'tis rated
> As those which sell would give; but you well know
> *Things of like value differing in the owners*
> *Are prizèd by their masters.* Believe't, dear lord,
> You mend the jewel by the wearing it.
>   *Tim.* 1.1.172-6 (emphasis added)

Although the syntax of these lines admits of a variety of constructions, they all cohere with the fundamental notion of the subjectivity of difference. The lines point to the dilemma of the substrate of likeness that can only be arbitrarily punctuated by differences. All humans are substantially alike but spend themselves furiously in arbitrary constructions of difference—theologically, the sin of pride; psychologically, the neurosis of separation (always threatening to become psychosis). Again, the relative purity of *Timon of Athens* commands our attention. Shakespeare's language is startlingly precise in its delineation of the crisis of likeness:

> **MERCHANT** A most *incomparable* man, *breathed*, as it were,
> To an untirable and continuate goodness.
> He *passes*.
>   *Tim.* 1.1.10-12 (emphasis added)

If "incomparable," then so by "breath"—report or rumor or fame—and thus in no way in substantial possession of his difference, which hinges on "goodness" that, if "untirable" and "continuate," by the very logic of "pass[ing]," can "pass" to "tirable" and "discontinuate" in human "breath" (as, in fact, it shortly does—"O my good lord, *the world is but a word*" [*Tim.* 2.2.149; emphasis added]).

If *Timon of Athens* is a play about wealth, abundance, and excess in its

Timon of Athens—Misanthropy as Unlikeness

topic, it is a play of leanness, spareness, and commanding exactitude in its language, and this I assign to Shakespeare, even when it may be Middleton composing. The line *"Like* madness is the glory of this *life" (Tim.* 1.2.130), where the initial *like* and the terminal *life* are separated and distended by the copulation of the extremes of human experience, madness and glory, makes us feel its spareness like a missile as well as a (dis)missive. Power here is in the service of something that beggars the slogans of ideology; primordial feeling urges itself upon us, even as it is the *"Ape* Man" who speaks:

> Hey-day, what a sweep of vanity comes this way!
> They dance? They are madwomen.
> Like madness is the glory of this life
> As this pomp shows to a little oil and root.
> We make ourselves fools to disport ourselves,
> And spend our flatteries to drink those men
> Upon whose age we void it up again
> With poisonous spite and envy.
> Who lives that's not depravèd or depraves?
> Who dies that bears not one spurn to their graves
> Of their friends' gift?
> I should fear those that dance before me now
> Would one day stamp upon me. 'T'as been done.
> Men shut their doors against a setting sun.
>
> *Tim.* 1.2.128-41[3]

It is important to listen to this entire speech not only because the Ape Man speaks, but because he who speaks is man who apes. The Ape Man apes us what we are like, and this is a sure Shakespearean stroke. Further, one of the more compelling stage directions extant in the canon, we might here pause to reflect, is *"Then comes, dropping after all, Apemantus, discontentedly,* **like** *himself" (Tim.* 1.2; bold emphasis added). The "Ape Man," the misanthrope, is "like himself," is actually directed to the stage as "like himself." A more compelling insistence that misanthropy in *Timon* is un/dis-like(ness) to/of others could hardly be invoked; and yet, at the same time, the invocation vibrates with contradictoriness—he who is, not only by definition but also by stage direction, "like himself" and presumably no other, condemns the *like*(ness) of all others, *as their Ape*(mantus):

> **TIMON** Thou art proud, Apemantus!
> **APEMANTUS** Of nothing so much as that *I am not like*
>   Timon.
>
> *Tim.* 1.1.192-4 (emphasis added)

But this is, inexorably, to have aped Timon so as to be able to be "not like Timon." The misanthrope who hates man is nonetheless and precisely therefore indissolubly linked to man, as by an umbilicus of (un)*like*(ness).

In the same scene, Timon asks Apemantus, "[h]ow *likest* thou this picture.... Wrought he not well that painted it?" (*Tim.* 1.1.199; 201; emphasis added). Apemantus replies: "He wrought better that made the painter, and yet he's but a filthy piece of work" (*Tim.* 1.1.202-3; emphasis added). Beyond even Thersites in *Troilus and Cressida* ("All the argument is a whore and a cuckold"—*Tro.* 2.3.71), Apemantus the "Ape Man" hates the human likeness, "a filthy piece of work"—to which nonetheless he is and must be Ape. If we ask why there is such hatred of the human likeness, we may answer with what the Ape well knows, though he can do nothing about it, that it is the human's *unlikeness* to nature:

> **LUCIUS' SERVANT** You must consider that *a prodigal course*
> *Is like the sun's,*
> *But not, like his, recoverable.*
> *Tim.* 3.4.14-16 (emphasis added)

> **TIMON** *But then renew I could not like the moon;*
> There were no suns to borrow of.
> *Tim.* 4.3.68-69 (emphasis added)

Supreme in all of nature in his ability to manipulate nature, man is nonetheless the victim of nature, unable finally to "recover" or "renew" *like* nature. Ultimately helpless in nature and against it, despite all his technologies, man can only hate nature, which is also, eo ipso, to hate himself, his kind, his likeness. The logic of misanthropy is exact (if circular): if I hate my kind, my likeness, I hate nature that produces it (and, to acknowledge the feminist case, females, in particular, for bearing it); or, if I hate nature for my mortality, then I hate my kind, my likeness, for being natural and therefore mortal—"and yet he's but a filthy piece of work," of which I myself, of course, am but an(other) Ape(mantus).

When Timon feeds his former "parasites" their banquet of warm water, he introduces it at length with castigating precision (*Tim.* 3.7.65-84), and, in particular, asserts that "[y]our diet shall be in all places alike." "Your diet shall be in all places *alike*" because Timon now knows, not that there are no differences, but that there is this one ineradicable *likeness*:

> Most smiling, smooth, detested *parasites*,
> Courteous destroyers, affable wolves, meek bears,

Timon of Athens — Misanthropy as Unlikeness

> You fools of fortune, trencher-friends, time's flies,
> Cap-and-knee slaves, vapours, and minute-jacks!
> *Tim* 3.7.93-96 (emphasis added)

All men are just alike, feeding on one another, "parasites."

I think that parasitism is the underlying figure of the theater of likeness in *Timon of Athens*. The figure is not unique to this play—*Othello* is at least one other instance of great and obvious import—but in *Timon* the figure has particular force. That force derives, I think, from the topic of food and eating, so integral to the plot of *Timon*, as it is to that of *Othello* as well. Indeed, in *Timon* the most elementary practice of the human is the alimentary, from banquets to root-grubbing. If all men are alike, they are alike because they eat, and their eating is parasitic.

We today reserve the word *parasite* to refer to a condition of disease, but it seems clear that in the world of *Timon of Athens*, the word is not to be so restricted: since all feeding destroys some host, all feeding is in this sense *parasitic*—all feeding is diseased (emphasis added throughout):

> **APEMANTUS** No, *I eat not lords.*
> **TIMON** An thou shouldst, thou'dst anger ladies.
> **APEMANTUS** O, *they eat lords. So they come by great bellies.*
> *Tim.* 1.1.208-10

> **APEMANTUS** O you gods, *what a number of men eats Timon, and he sees 'em not!* It grieves me to see *so many dip their meat in one man's blood*; and all the madness is, he cheers them up, too.
> *Tim.* 1.2.38-41

> **ALCIBIADES** So they were bleeding new, my lord; there's no *meat like* 'em [enemies]. I could wish my best friend at such a feast.
> *Tim.* 1.2.76-78

> **FLAMINIUS.** O you gods,
> I feel master's passion! This slave
> Unto this hour has *my lord's meat in him.*
> Why should it thrive and turn to nutriment,
> When *he is turned to poison*?
> O, may diseases only work upon't;
> And when he's sick to death, let not *that part of nature*
> *Which my lord paid for* be of any power
> To expel sickness, but prolong his hour.
> *Tim.* 3.1.54-62

FLAVIUS Why then preferred you not your sums and bills
When *your false masters ate of my lord's meat?*
Then they could smile and fawn upon his debts,
And *take down th'int'rest into their glutt'nous maws.*
Tim. 3.4.50-54

TIMON Keep it. I cannot eat it [gold].
Tim. 4.3.101

TIMON That nature, being sick of man's unkindness,
Should yet be *hungry*!
    He digs the earth
                      Common mother — thou
Whose womb unmeasurable and infinite breast
Teems and *feeds* all,
...
Yield him who all thy human sons do hate
From forth thy plenteous bosom, *one poor root.*
Tim. 4.3.177-8; 178-80; 186-7

That the whole life of Athens were in this!
Thus would I *eat it.*
    He bites the root
APEMANTUS *(offering food)* Here, I will mend *thy feast.*
TIMON First mend my company: take away thyself.
Tim. 4.3.284-6

TIMON   Where *feed'st* thou a-days, Apemantus?
APEMANTUS Where my stomach finds *meat*; or rather,
    where I *eat* it.
TIMON Would poison were obedient, and knew my mind!
APEMANTUS Where wouldst thou send it?
TIMON To sauce thy dishes.
Tim. 4.3.295-301

APEMANTUS   There's a medlar for thee;
    eat it.
TIMON *On what I hate I feed not.*
APEMANTUS Dost hate a medlar?
TIMON Ay, though it look *like* thee.
APEMANTUS An thou'dst hated meddlers sooner, thou
    shouldst have loved thyself better now.
Tim. 4.3.306-12

TIMON More things like men. *Eat*, Timon, and abhor them.
Tim. 4.3.400

TIMON Your greatest want is, *you want much of meat*.
Why should you want? Behold, the earth hath roots.
Within this mile break forth a hundred springs.
The oaks bear mast, the briers scarlet hips.
The bounteous housewife nature on each bush
Lays her full mess before you. Want? Why want?
Tim. 4.3.418-23

TIMON *You must eat men.*
...
                The earth's a thief,
That *feeds* and breeds by a composture stol'n
From gen'ral excrement. Each thing's a thief.
Tim. 4.3.427; 442-4

TIMON   ay, all I kept were knaves,
To serve in meat to villains.
Tim. 4.3.479-80

TIMON Most honest men. Why, how shall I requite you?
Can you *eat* roots and drink cold water? No.
Tim. 5.1.71-72

SECOND SENATOR If thy revenges *hunger for that food*
   Which nature loathes, take thou the destined tenth.
Tim. 5.5.32-33

The foregoing inventory, which is not exhaustive, is crucial, I think, just because it is so lengthy: from it, we see that feeding in *Timon of Athens* is, in effect, either parasitism or an exercise in and of disease, corruption, and death.

We also see in several items of the inventory how important to the play is the implication of cannibalism: "You must eat men." To be sure, the cannibalism is not literal, only implied, but, as implied, it underscores the "consumption" and "evacuation" of man's *likeness* in the play: "what a number of men eat Timon"—like eats like. Eating is, thus, multiply corrupt and not only an image but a fact as well of the crisis of likeness. When we eat, we as*simil*ate (make *like* us) what we eat, and so Flaminius can curse Lucullus,

> let not *that part of nature*
> *Which my lord paid for* be of any power
> To expel sickness, but prolong his hour.
> Tim. 3.1.60-62 (emphasis added)

and Flavius can exclaim,

> Why then preferred you not your sums and bills
> When *your false masters ate of my lord's meat?*
> Then they could smile and fawn upon his debts,
> And *take down th'int'rest into their glutt'nous maws.*
> Tim. 3.4.50-53 (emphasis added)

In both examples, the paradox of assimilation emerges starkly: what we make like us is no longer (like) itself *in us*—the men who ate Timon are not like Timon. Timon is their excrement, and for the rest of the play, he makes a present to them of their shit.

The perception of the relationship between money and shit is ancient.[4] Shakespeare relies on it obviously in *Timon*, as, for example, in the two speeches just quoted, where the imagery of paying and of interest is directly associated with alimentation and hence with waste. Thus, too, the medieval illumination convention of apes shitting money (Little 34) may well inform, though from a distance, Shakespeare's characterization of *Ape*-mantus. Be that as it may, if, as we have seen, *Timon of Athens* is a play about money and eating, it is also perforce a play about shit:

> **TIMON**   The earth's a thief,
> That *feeds* and breeds by a composture stol'n
> From gen'ral *excrement*.
> Tim. 4.3.442-4 (emphasis added)

As important as the word *excrement* here is the word *general*, for the most inward motive of the perception of money as shit is the acknowledgment of the *generality* or non-differentiation or, crucially, universal *like*ness, implicated in money and shit. As everything emerges from and returns to shit, so everything is reducible also to money—money can turn anything into something else because money can turn anything into itself:

> **TIMON** O, thou sweet king-killer, and dear divorce
> 'Twixt natural son and sire;
> ...

> *thou visible god,*
> *That sold'rest close impossibilities*
> *And mak'st them kiss,* that speak'st with every tongue
> To every purpose; O thou touch of hearts:
> Think thy slave man rebels, and by thy virtue
> Set them into confounding odds, that beasts
> May have the world in empire.
> *Tim.* 4.3.384-5; 389-95 (emphasis added)[5]

Timon is about comparison, almost pure as such, and presents a nearly transparent case for relief from comparison, likening. The play is about money as well, because it is about comparison. Money "equalizes" what is otherwise *unlike*—although at the deepest level, what is *unlike* is also *like*. All are alike animals, generally worse than the beasts (whose empire would, at least, know no hypocrisy), and each labors to distinguish himself, but each will submit to *like*(ness to) someone ("... solder'st close impossibilities/And makest them kiss"), in order to acquire more of what he thinks will distinguish him. All (are) like Timon, "soldered" to him (and therefore also "sold" to him), as long as his money promises to distinguish each of them (rich, richer, richest?), but (do) not like him when there is no more money. He's not worth shit then.

This, to follow Aristotle, is the "nonsense" of money (λῆρος—*Politics* 1.3.16 1257b10 [Sinclair 83]). Men affect to like one another when money promises differentiation, but this differentiation, which can only be the effect (the likeness) of money, comes "by [its] virtue/[That s]et[s] them into confounding odds" (*Tim.* 4.3.393-4); and they drop all pretense of liking one another when money vanishes, although they are then most alike in animal (i.e., inhumane) nature because the "confounding odds" are absent that kept them confounded *as men* seeking differentiation.

Money makes men like one another; money also makes men unlike one another and dislike one another. Money, when it is the difference, makes no difference (the "odds" are merely "confounding"), which is why so much money must be spent maintaining the illusion that it makes a difference. To be rich without the display of riches is not only to be a miser (hence also miserable), it is not even to be rich since only the display (or the rumored credit of display) makes one rich—money *is* "non-sense." Timon is not rich because he has money, he is rich because he is generous (looks and acts *like* he has money), and he is poor not when he has no money, but when he cannot and will not be generous. Hence the importance of all the gold he discovers and dispenses from his cave: it is crucial to the play's meaning that Timon have vast wealth at the end but be not rich because he is not generous; to the contrary, he loathes his kind (*genus, genera*). I can only be generous, however, when I (am) like my kind—everything else is politics, or, we may say, not inaccurately, shit.

In a theater of likeness about money and shit, it is inevitable that the inextricably intertwined problems of art and counterfeiting will arise:

> **TIMON** Good honest men. (*To Painter*) Thou draw'st a *counterfeit*
> Best in all Athens; thou'rt indeed the best;
> Thou *counterfeit'st* most lively.
> **PAINTER**   So so, my lord.
> **TIMON** E'en so, sir, as I say. (*To Poet*) And for thy fiction,
> Why, thy verse swells with stuff so fine and smooth
> That *thou art even natural in thine art*.
>   *Tim*. 5.1.78-83 (emphasis added)

We recognize this exchange as metadrama, of which, we know, there are many, many instances in Shakespeare's writings. But here we have more than self-reflexive, autotelic commentary on representation. As the sarcasm of "Good honest men!" suggests, we have here also metadrama as misanthropy as unlikeness, or rejection of representation as *nothing but counterfeit*. Timon's sarcasm, extending through "lively" and "stuff so fine and smooth" and "natural," insinuates that all likening is corrupt, counterfeit (unlike), no matter how "lively" or "natural," because motivated by greed. Not only is copying inherently difficult, requiring something like what we mean by "genius," it is also inevitably tainted by desire for gain. On top then of a conventional Platonic rejection of art as a copy of a copy, we also have Timon's rejection of art as alchemy, perhaps the most notorious fraud throughout the medieval and early modern eras:

> **TIMON** [*Striking Poet*] You are an *alchemist*; make gold of that.
> Out, rascal dogs!   *Exeunt* [*Poet and Painter one way, Timon into his cave*]
>   *Tim*. 5.1.114-15 (emphasis added)

Poetry as alchemy is a not improbable theoretical discourse, as Chaucer's *Canon's Yeoman's Tale* attests (Shoaf, *Chaucer's Body* chapter 3), but here we are well beneath theory, or at least beyond it, since Timon's obvious meaning is the rejection of all representation as counterfeiting merely—to copy is to lie, betray, deceive, pretend, etc.

Hence, finally, the extraordinary importance of the bitter diatribe between Timon and Apemantus at Timon's cave. It is an enactment of the crisis of likeness as copying:

APEMANTUS I was directed hither. *Men report
Thou dost affect my manners, and dost use them.*

...

> *Do not assume my likeness.*
> Tim. 4.3.199-200; 219 (emphasis added)

"Men report." "The world is but a word," as we have heard (*Tim.* 2.2.149). Apemantus has come to claim his "currency," his "unique" reputation as professional misanthrope, which, it appears, Timon now threatens to steal from him. But "[w]ere I like thee," Timon retorts, "I'd throw away myself" (*Tim.* 4.3.220). Timon does not want *his*, Apemantus', money either. Not to be out-cursed, Apemantus hurls back: "Thou hast cast away thyself *being like thyself*" (*Tim.* 4.3.221; emphasis added). Although I began by focusing on this line, I must return to it now that more information is in place.

First, note the important repetition with inversion between Timon and Apemantus:

TIMON Thou art proud, Apemantus!
APEMANTUS Of nothing so much as that I am not *like* Timon.
> Tim. 1.1.192-4 (emphasis added)

APEMANTUS Art thou proud yet?
TIMON Ay, *that I am not thee.*
> Tim. 4.3.278-9 (emphasis added)

The repetition suggests to us that both men protest too much. At a level not all that profound, each man already recognizes himself in the other despite differences that, as Timon insists (*Tim.* 4.3.250-77), are real enough. Each man starves for uniqueness, a nutrition impossible to attain, however, since uniqueness can only obtain by way of comparison or likeness: "All villains that do stand by thee are pure" (*Tim.* 4.3.363). Shakespeare's theater of likeness is first and foremost the recognition and acknowledgment that to be one you must be two, as well without as within ("Known unto these, and to myself disguised!"—*CE* 2.2.217). If singularity is what you want, you must be wanting, there is no help for it (only God is singular). Hence the inevitability of Timon's death; only death really separates us from others — but physically, not ethically, since all alike must die, and so, yet again, singularity is foiled. The play, in sum, startlingly enacts the ethical paradox, attended by psychic agony, that I cast away myself, being like myself (and cannot retrieve myself by myself).

Self-knowledge is self-alienation—"His semblable, yea, himself,

Timon disdains" (*Tim.* 4.3.22). Although Apemantus may argue that "[t]he middle of humanity thou never knewest, but the extremity of both ends" (*Tim.* 4.3.302-3), psychically speaking, there is no such "middle of humanity": either I know myself or I do not, and if "I" know "myself" then perforce I know that "I" cannot remotely begin to express my self, much less account for my "semblable." The radical non-self-coincidence of the conscious subject is the psychic reality informing Shakespeare's art—I am only as I (am) like others ("Known unto these, and to myself disguised!").

If I am Hamlet or Ophelia or Othello or Timon my lot, then, is tragic, for shall I be like Claudius or Goneril and Regan or Iago or Apemantus? Of course not. But, then, on second thought.... It is, in fact, not particularly easy, claiming and bearing an identity. Indeed, to have an identity, to "be somebody," as many of the plays teach us, is to be (like) some body (else).

27
"Writes them all alike": *Macbeth*

Imagine a film production of Shakespeare's play *Macbeth* in which identical male twins were cast in the roles of Macbeth and Lady Macbeth. The two siblings would be distinguished only by a minimal makeup: the one, cross-dressed as Lady Macbeth; the other wearing a distinct but narrow beard carefully trimmed. Their garments would be the same design and the same color, only slightly trimmed to mark her as feminine, him as masculine.

Now further imagine that a major digital design studio were contracted to generate the witches and the scenes in which the witches appear. The director would instruct the studio to digitize the witches so that every time a witch faced a character—Macbeth or Banquo, for example—that witch would look very similar though not identical to that character, almost but not quite a double of that character.

Finally, imagine that the principle set for Macbeth's castle would be so designed that various artifacts serving as accommodations and accoutrements (and entirely visible to the audience) would repeatedly show or imply the shape of a rib, perhaps going so far as a representation of a skeleton hanging on the wall (perhaps in a tapestry). Then, when Birnam Wood started marching toward Dunsinane, this rib motif would be repeated in each branch that the soldiers would be carrying since Birnam is "man rib" spelled backwards, the rib of Adam from which Eve was "created" serving thus as a visual leitmotif of the sickness of Macbeth's world, or "the ruthless excision of all female presence" (Adelman, *Mothers* 131) from a culture that therefore degenerates into war, savagery, and subhuman horror.

✤

Numerous students of Shakespeare have written about *Macbeth* with respect to the problematics of doubling and illusion in the play. If I revisit these problematics above, with a brief fantasy, it is out of a conviction that Shakespeare's use of the word "like" in *Macbeth* resembles his use of the word in other plays, and that analysis of "like" in *Macbeth* contributes helpful if not necessarily new insight into these problematics in the play. The burden that the word "like" carries and the work that it does are probably best suggested initially in a passage that many others have also addressed:

> **MACBETH** I pall in resolution, and begin
> To doubt th'equivocation of the fiend,
> That *lies like truth*. "Fear not till Birnam Wood
> Do come to Dunsinane" — and now a wood
> Comes toward Dunsinane.[1]
>
> *Mac.* 5.5.40-44

The clause "that lies like truth" is crucial for any reading of the play. But I will eventually argue that for Shakespeare the far more important concern lies in the phrase (which I postulate), "truths like lies." Nor do I shrink from the troubling homophony in my own prose, "*lies* in the phrase 'truths like *lies*'," since much of what I wish to argue is that it is this very (con)fusion that most delimits the meaning of the play *Macbeth*.[2]

Macbeth would eradicate from all discourse "juggling," "palter[ing]" (*Mac.* 5.10.19-20), equivocal, and double-crossing sound and sense—sound and sense that *palter*. In that desire lies (I did it again) his tyranny—a totalitarian desire for a totalizing language that would mirror his totalitarian rule of Scotland and history. It is just the measure of Shakespeare's peculiar genius that he understands that however ideal in theory a perfectly univocal language would be, in practice it would be an unspeakable horror.[3] A perfectly univocal language would spell the doom of any individuality since it would condemn every speaker to the reiteration of the same. Every discourse this side of eternity must endure equivocality, or the mixture of truth and lies, the likeness of truth to lies, which perforce includes *fictions*. If the truth cannot lie, as in fictions—parables, fables, exempla, fairy tales, all genres of indirection—the truth cannot speak. The tyrant would excise this "disease" from the truth—like Plato, banish the poets from the Republic (*Republic* 10.606D-607c [831-2]) —but poetry and poets always return knowing that the humorlessness of the tyrant is a sure mark of his evil. In "the iron bands of terror" (Arendt, *Origins* 473), totalitarianism eliminates even laughter. It is necessary then for the poet to preserve the likeness between truth and lies.[4] Otherwise, life would become "a tale / Told by an idiot, full of sound and fury,/ Signifying nothing" (*Mac.* 5.5.25-27) because to signify is necessarily to assert a proposition about reality that, since it is ab-out reality (separate and distinct from reality), must perforce admit that reality can contradict it (and thus also produce laughter, or, at least, a smile). To live in a life where reality cannot contradict truth-assertions is to live in a delusion—it is to be an *idiot*,[5] telling a tale full of sound and fury. This is why the tyrant, from Xerxes to Hitler to Saddam, so terrifies us: like Macbeth, he would impose his delusion (idiocy) on everyone, and the result, which is totalitarianism, is the abolition of significance, which is to say, the erasure of the human that cannot be without being different.

Macbeth is who one becomes when one tries to live in a language that is not dual ("my *single* state of man"—*Mac.* 1.3.139; emphasis added), just as Macbeth and Lady Son of Beth are the couple two become when they try to live in a sexuality that is not dual ("unsex me here"—*Mac.* 1.5.40): theirs is a marriage not of partners but of parts. By "dual" I mean a distinction from "double," such a distinction as I have argued for elsewhere, in my study of Milton, where duality or partnering is the antidote to doubleness or duplicity.[6] As Lady Son of Beth's personal namelessness so powerfully indicates, hers and Macbeth's relationship is not a true dual (not partners but parts) since she is denied independent identity, not even allowed a proper name—she is always only Lady *Mac*beth, where "mac" is Gaelic for "son of."[7] Their relationship rather is a duel at best (Shoaf, *Duality* 3-7), as their continual competition over who is the more ferocious of the two repeatedly witnesses (*Mac.* 1.5.15ff.; 1.5.37ff.; 1.5.59ff.; 1.7.35-59; 1.7.72-4; etc.). Their relationship, as their names hint, is an attempt at a univocal and unisexual marriage (parts, not partners), the evident failure of which bespeaks the impossibility of absolute identity—there is always only duality for us humans that is always on the verge of decaying into doubleness. And though we are right, like Macbeth, to fear the doubleness, we must, unlike Macbeth, refuse to replace it with univocality—we must rather seek unity through duality.[8]

Although Duncan laments that "[t]here's no art/To find the mind's construction in the face" (*Mac.* 1.4.11-12), only a few lines later Lady Macbeth chastises Macbeth,

> Your face, my thane, is as a book where men
> May read strange matters. To beguile the time,
> Look *like* the time;
>
> ...
>
>   look *like* the innocent flower,
> But be the serpent under't.
>   *Mac.* 1.5.61-65 (emphasis added),[9]

from which we may quickly infer that she is at best one-half of a being called "Macbeth," supplying as she does, at this point in the drama, the resolute and ferocious masculine half of the being (which, not improbably, resembles a domineering mother)—"fill me from the crown to the toe top-full/Of direst cruelty" (*Mac.* 1.5.41-42), she says only a few lines earlier. It follows, then, and we have to reflect only a moment to grasp this, that when, later in the drama, she walks in her sleep, compulsively washes her hands, and otherwise evinces mounting insanity, she is lapsing into the feminine half of the being Macbeth, while he, the other half, formerly having shown feminine reluctance (*Mac.* 1.7.1-28, e.g.), now continues in his descent into a brutal masculinity that knows nothing but war and murder. Shakespeare has succeeded terrifyingly in representing two humans neither of whom amounts to a whole being, each of whom must siphon identity from the other. Now the one, who should be a fierce warrior, is "too full o'th' milk of human kindness" (*Mac.* 1.5.16); now the other, who should be maternal, "would, while [the babe] was smiling in [her] face,/Have plucked [her] nipple from his boneless gums/And dashed the brains out" (*Mac.* 1.7.56-58). Never are there two people cooperating together in the dual of marital relationship; there are only two halves of a demented being (parts, not partners) competing fiercely in the duel of their common psychosis.[10]

For, as Macbeth insists, "I dare do all that may become a man;/*Who dares do more is none*" (*Mac.* 1.7.46-47; emphasis added). By this logic, Lady Macbeth is not only *not* a man but, in effect, since man is "naturally superior" to woman (according to Western misogyny), she is not even human, a monster instead, "excised" from the human race itself. When Macbeth again uses the same rhetoric,

> *What man dare, I dare.*
> ...
> Take any shape but that, and my firm nerves
> Shall never tremble. Or be alive again,
> And dare me to the desert with thy sword.
> If trembling I inhabit then, *protest me*
> *The baby of a girl.*
>
> Mac. 3.4.98; 101-5 (emphasis added),

the process of "excision" continues but with this peculiar torque, that when Macbeth ceases to be *man* he will be construed ("protested") as a girl's doll ("the baby of a girl"), not really female but a miniature imitation of a female, as if the female once excised were to return only as a drollery of itself, a puppet or caricature, so little is the duality of being ("male and female created He them"—Genesis 1:26-7) recognized let alone honored in the world of Macbeth. Even children, supposedly the justification for the female sex, make no difference:

SIWARD Had he [Siward's son] his hurts before?
ROSS Ay, on the front.
SIWARD Why then, God's soldier be he.
Had I as many sons as I have hairs
I would not wish them to a fairer death;
And so, his knell is knolled.
MALCOLM *He's worth more sorrow,*
And that I'll spend for him.
SIWARD *He's worth no more.*
                        Mac. 5.11.12-17 (emphasis added)

It is a fair question how many women would have to suffer to produce and then watch die as many sons as Siward has hairs on his body—this is no world not only for women but also for human being.

What world it is exactly we can more carefully measure by means of a passage peculiar but for all that of great importance to understanding the play:

MACBETH Ay, *in the catalogue ye go for men,*
As hounds and greyhounds, mongrels, spaniels, curs,
Shoughs, water-rugs, and demi-wolves are clept
All by *the name of dogs. The valued file*
Distinguishes the swift, the slow, the subtle,
The housekeeper, the hunter, *every one*
According to the gift which bounteous nature
Hath in him closed; whereby he does receive
Particular addition from the bill
That writes them all alike. And so of men.
Now, if you have a station in the file,
Not i'th' worst rank of manhood, say't.
                        Mac. 3.1.93-104 (emphasis added)

As with dogs, so with men, according to Macbeth: there is a "bill/That writes them all alike" and so they must be distinguished by "particular addition" in "the valued file." It is important to understand exactly what Macbeth is saying. All men are *alike* according to a certain bill. Each distinguishes himself in the general catalogue, the great lump of men, by a gift "which bounteous nature/Hath in him closed." It is then up to the individual man to distinguish himself. There is no intrinsic value in him—there is a gift, yes, but no value is intrinsically attached to the gift: only the "list specifying the value of the catalogued items" (Norton 2587) assigns value to the gift. The list is made up by someone else. The list is the result of subjective valuation. A man may have a great gift but if the cataloguer does not value it, it does not, as we say, count.[11] To count, a man must alter his likeness from every other man. He must, as we all know, compromise himself. Worse, he may in the course of history prostitute himself:

> And thence it is
> That *I to your assistance do make love,*
> Masking the business [the murder of Banquo] from the common eye
> For sundry weighty reasons.
> *Mac.* 3.1.124-7 (emphasis added)

In the world of Macbeth, in other words, every man is an island (I-land, more properly) detached from the main (cf. Donne, *Meditation* XVII). Not only is there no mutuality, not only is there no community, not only is there no social contract (even), there is nothing but a catalogue, a bill that writes all men alike, and thus the price of distinction can never be too high—a murder here, a rape there, an extortion here, some hypocrisy there, making love to someone's assistance yonder, whatever it takes to insert a mere life into the valued file.

That "file" is an anagram of "life" is no accident and that but for the *f* both are a *like* is even less an accident. A few lines before his speech to the murderers to whose assistance he makes love, Macbeth whines:

> Upon my head they placed a fruitless crown,
> And put a barren sceptre in my grip,
> Thence to be wrenched with an unlineal hand,
> No son of mine succeeding. If't be so,
> For Banquo's issue have I *filed* my mind,
> For them the gracious Duncan have I murdered,
> Put rancours in the vessel of my peace
> Only for them, and mine eternal jewel
> Given to the common enemy of man
> To make them kings, the seed of Banquo kings.
> *Mac.* 3.1.62-71 (emphasis added)

Obviously, the first meaning of "filed" here is "defiled," but I would argue that we must not suppress the "latent double"[12] in the word that betrays so much of Macbeth's unconscious terror—namely, his insecurity as to where in the *file* of men (and the life of man) he belongs, if he belongs in it at all. Macbeth has not only defiled his mind, he has also filed his mind in the catalogue of those who murder, usurp, and give their souls to the devil ("the common enemy of man"). And this because of an insecurity (cf. *Mac.*

3.5.32-3) running deeper than anyone before Shakespeare probably could have imagined.

If I compete with others of my sexual kind and fail, is it not her fault who got me who was inferior, no matter that they, the other men, were begotten of women, too? (Milton, we recall, ascribed his blindness to his mother [Kerrigan, *Complex* 82].) If I must die, is it not her fault (crime and pudendum)? Is it not her likeness? Why must I be like her? Who will deliver me from the body (*likam*) of this (woman) death (Romans 7:24)?

Certainly not they, the "secret, black, and midnight hags" (*Mac.* 4.1.64) themselves. Nor Scotland, which "cannot/Be called our mother, but our grave" (*Mac.* 4.3.166-7). Nor can it be Duncan's fantasy of motherless agriculture (cf. Adelman, *Mothers* 132):

> I have begun to plant thee [Macbeth], and will labour
> To make thee full of growing.
> *Mac.* 1.4.28-29

All such agriculture can do is, like Cadmus sowing the dragon's teeth (*Metamorphoses* 3.102-5), raise up warriors to internecine strife. No, there has to be something different. Difference itself.

Women, flesh-and-blood women, must be admitted into the world.

> **LADY MACBETH** Had he not resembled
> My father as he slept, I had done't.
> *Mac.* 2.2.12-13

For this instant—and it is only an instant, swallowed up in the next breath by gore—likeness ("resembled") shows us such hope as we have. We are alike. The daughter sees a likeness to her father. It stays her hand. It is true still that "[t]hriftless ambition ... will raven up/[Its] own life's means" (*Mac.* 2.4.28-29). We admit no sentimentality. But clearly our mutual likeness is our hope, and it depends on recognizing our differences—he resembled my father, says the daughter, having looked on her king. I infer that the daughter loved or, at least, feared her father. I infer that for this fragile instant, lost forever once passed, our likeness interceded. It then failed. That, I think, is a tragedy.

I would like to posit for the sake of argument that one possible definition of tragedy is the failure or lapse or corruption of our mutual likeness—and especially there where it should hold most, with fathers and sons and daughters and mothers and wives. One obvious merit of this provisional definition is how readily applicable it is to Shakespeare's tragedies. It is almost, from the vantage of this definition, as if we were looking at a "fundamental force" in his tragedies. But if so, this is only because, many will be ready to interject, it is a fundamental force in the great Athenian tragedies as well, and above all in *Oedipus Tyrannos*.

For the tragedy of Oedipus is that he is *too much* like his father Laius (likeness corrupted by excess), even to taking his place in his father's conjugal bed, and, as a consequence, becomes through his mother-wife too much like his children, who are also his siblings. In Aeschylus and Sophocles, in particular, tragedy is separation or, often worse, the failure of separation or, even worse yet, separation at the cost of death and abjection (I think of Orestes, in particular, as well as Oedipus). Freud and Lacan, modern doctors of desire, would almost certainly agree with Machiavelli that

> Nature has created men so that they desire everything, but are unable to attain it; desire being thus always greater than the faculty of acquiring, discontent with what they have and dissatisfaction with themselves result from it (Machiavelli, *Discourses* Chapter 37; Norton 2558).

Certainly, such a conclusion applies to Oedipus who will not rest from his desire to know, even though knowledge is doom. The absolute restlessness of desire is only exacerbated, it seems, by our mutual likeness, as if seeing oneself in one's (m)other were enough to drive a man to madness and on from there to readiness, which is all. Like Oedipus, Hamlet must know, whatever the cost. And what he comes to know, again like Oedipus, is himself as *not* his own: the condition of self-knowledge is self-alienation, self-othering that is not self-mothering, until (if at all) it is too late.

Clearly our mutual likeness is the ground of relationship (and discord) among us. Just as clearly, our mutual likeness can threaten us, at one extreme, with identification that we cannot tolerate (Hamlet, like Gertrude) or, at the other, with alienation that we cannot endure (Lear, by his daughters). Then relationship collapses and tragedy ensues. The two fragments that make up the being Macbeth are too alike to enjoy a relationship of marital wholeness and too disjointed to endure one apart from the other—"She should have died hereafter" (*Mac.* 5.5.16). Each is tragic in the measure to which mutual likeness is impossible for him, for her: together they feed each other's frenzies, apart they cannot function as individuals. So Macbeth would reduce all Scotland to his idiot's tale; so Lady Son of Beth would cleanse a stain no one can see (*Mac.* 5.1.30-38). Neither likes him- or herself enough to like each other enough to cooperate in a likeness of life or a life of likeness (reproduction).

Hence the overwhelming importance of Fleance, Banquo's son, such a threat to Macbeth. Fleance his son is also Banquo's likeness (not his creature, not his thing, not his doll), and in their mutual likeness lies the community of the future (*Mac.* 4.1.128-40) and the future of community, all because Banquo slept with a woman, his wife, and begot a son, their mutual likeness. Lady Macbeth may console herself and Macbeth that in Banquo and Fleance "nature's *copy*'s not eterne" (*Mac.* 3.2.39), but her very language betrays her and his despair: in Banquo and Fleance *nature* has a *copy*, whereas in the two of them no copy does nature have, now or ever; they have (re)produced no mutual likeness—they are not just childless, they are *likeless*.

For them St Augustine's "regio dissimilitudinis" (see the Introduction note 37) would be not just a trope of spiritual dryness and alienation: they actually dwell in such a land, where no one is like them and no one likes them. For them, no new beginning is possible, such as Hannah Arendt argues is the most powerful check against totalitarianism, for natality, as Arendt calls it (*Condition* 178)—the birth of a new being who can take different action from those who preceded him or her—is impossible in their world. Theirs is a world of fatality, not natality, a world of the prescripted, which is why the witches are so prominent in their world ("By the pricking of my thumbs,/Something wicked this way comes"—*Mac.* 4.1.61-62): Macbeth is bound to interpret his life always only according to someone else's script, even when the script is ambiguous, obscure, and ominous. The future may not be permitted simply to happen. It might be new.

Hence I infer that Lady Son of Beth's boast —

> I have given suck, and know
> How tender 'tis to love the babe that milks me.
> I would, while it was smiling in my face,
> Have plucked my nipple from his boneless gums
> And dashed the brains out, had I so sworn
> As you have done to this.
>
> *Mac.* 1.7.54-59

—is no more than a fantasy of her demented ambition.[13] I infer that she has never "given suck," and, further, when Macbeth says to her, "[b]ring forth men-children only,/For thy undaunted mettle should compose/Nothing but males" (*Mac.* 1.7.72-74), I infer that he speaks only hypothetically, conjecturally, and not out of any desire for a (future) male heir, such as Fleance. The witch knows "[s]omething wicked this way comes," by "the *prick*ing of *her* thumbs."

So allergic to the new are Macbeth and Lady Son of Beth that one is justified in the feeling that they have always been old, that they were effectively born old.

> **LADY MACBETH** Thy letters have transported me beyond
> This ignorant present, and I feel now
> The future in the instant.
>
> Mac. 1.5.55-57

—as if she had aged, before our very eyes but beyond human reckoning, collapsing "[t]he future in the instant." It is a just measure, then, of Shakespeare's insight into the tyrant's character that, following the report of Lady Son of Beth's death, Macbeth should moan,

> **MACBETH** *She should have died hereafter.*
> There *would have been a time* for such a word.
> Tomorrow, and tomorrow, and tomorrow
> Creeps in this petty pace from day to day
> To *the last syllable of recorded time*,
> And all our *yesterdays* have lighted fools
> The way to dusty death. Out, out, brief candle.
> Life's but a walking shadow, a poor player
> That struts and frets his *hour* upon the stage,
> And then is heard no more.
>
> Mac. 5.5.16-25 (emphasis added)

"Hereafter," "would have been," "tomorrow," "yesterday"—no(t) *now*. Macbeth and Lady Son of Beth have no now, acknowledge no now (it is but "this ignorant present"), and, consequently, Macbeth cannot but detest tomorrow. Tomorrow is an affront to him, its promise vain; and yesterday is the merest scroll of those vanities of creeping tomorrows, fit only to light a torch for fools on their way to death. Macbeth has no time—"There *would have been* a time." Macbeth has from the moment the witches accosted him had no time:

> **MACBETH** If it were done when 'tis done, then 'twere well
> It were done quickly. If th'assassination
> Could trammel up the consequence, and catch
> With his surcease success: that but this blow
> Might be the be-all and the end-all, here,
> But here upon this bank and shoal of time,
> We'd jump the life to come.
>
> Mac. 1.7.1-7

Moreover, from the moment of his birth, I infer, neither has he had any time. He neither could nor can wait for anything natural(ly). He murders even sleep, "great nature's *second* course,/Chief nourisher in life's feast" (*Mac.* 2.2.34; 37-38; emphasis added). He cannot wait for honors, for succession, for birth—he must have everything "now" (no time to wait for any "second course"), but this is a now only witches can inhabit with him (they know their victim well, do the witches). Hence the irony in the anagram of his first new title with which they hail him, Cawdor > -*c-o-w-a-r-d-*: for all his furious bravery, Macbeth is afraid of time, cowers before it and is a thrall to it. The tyrant (always a coward, in this sense) dwells in a simulacrum of God's "eternal now" ("the future in the instant") where he would see past, present and future as if they were all this present moment, "in the instant" (Boethius, *Consolation* 5. Pr 3ff.), but the tyrant "cannot [even] buckle his distempered cause/Within the belt of rule" (*Mac.* 5.2.15-16), much less see as God sees; and thus he surveys only "his hour upon the stage" and that, moreover, not as playwright but as actor merely, "poor player"—the written, not the writer; the creature, not the creator. He who would prescribe the new totally (totalizingly), as sole arbiter of its shape and value, finds himself at last in "this petty pace day by day" where every tomorrow is nothing but another tomorrow and "all our yesterdays" may as well have never been. He finds himself no(t) now. He finds himself out of time.[14]

28
"It is shaped, sir, like itself":
Antony and Cleopatra

> Here I am Antony,
> Yet cannot hold this visible shape.
> *Ant.* 4.15.13-14

> since my lord
> Is Antony again, I will be Cleopatra.
> *Ant.* 3.13.188-9

The word *like* occurs 69 times in *Antony and Cleopatra*. It does important work in many of these instances, but perhaps most important of all is the work that it does in act 2, scene 7, the drinking bout among the Roman leaders, during which Lepidus asks Mark Antony: "What manner o' thing is your crocodile?"

> ANTONY It is shaped, sir, like itself, and it is as broad as
>   it hath breadth. It is just so high as it is, and moves
>   with it own organs. It lives by that which nourisheth
>   it, and the elements once out of it, it transmigrates.
> LEPIDUS What colour is it of?
> ANTONY Of it own colour, too.
> LEPIDUS 'Tis a strange serpent.
> ANTONY 'Tis so, and the tears of it are wet.
>   *Ant.* 2.7.40-48

Mark Antony is speaking, and he too would be a crocodile, "shaped, sir, like [him]self." To grasp this apparent flippancy is to understand the crisis of self-coincidence or being "like oneself"—if I am like myself, where is this self I am like? Must I not be one in two, to be like my self? to like my self? Is this not already to feel the "beggary in the love that can be reckoned" (*Ant.* 1.1.15)? Love (including self-love) that is subject, in other words, to any form of numerical operation means that the love was *not* self-coincident, whole, complete, perfect, entire, *in*capable of addition, in the first place, but "beggared." "Number there in [Antony and Cleopatra's] love was [not] slain" ("The Phoenix and Turtle," line 28), and that is why Antony and Cleopatra must each commit self-slaughter.

Whatever the humor in Antony's tautology of the crocodile, Shakespeare uses the occasion—and we may fairly say that this is typical—to expose an extraordinary feature of Antony's psyche, or his derivativeness, with the consequent anxiety that repeatedly vexes him. Antony is not good at solitude. He depends upon, his identity derives from, association with others. When Cleopatra laments him in death, "[t]he odds is gone,/And there is nothing left remarkable/Beneath the visiting moon" (*Ant.* 4.16.68-70), she says more than she understands perhaps. Antony could only have been "the odds" by repeated, obligatory *comparison* with others: Antony, unlike Octavius Caesar, cannot stand alone.

This, to be sure, is not his opinion.

> **ANTONY** Let Rome in Tiber melt, and the wide arch
> Of the ranged empire fall. Here is *my space*.
> Kingdoms are clay. Our dungy earth *alike*
> Feeds beast as man. The nobleness of life
> Is to do thus; when such a *mutual pair*
> And such a *twain* can do't — in which I bind
> On pain of punishment the world to weet —
> We stand up peerless.
> **CLEOPATRA** [*aside*] Excellent falsehood!
> Why did he marry Fulvia and not love her?
> I'll seem the fool I am not. (*To Antony*) *Antony*
> *Will be himself.*
>
> *Ant.* 1.1.35-45 (emphasis added)

But, although he boasts (and threatens) that he "bind[s] ... the world to weet/We stand up peerless," the boast totters under the burden of its irony—only "we" are "peerless," while Antony alone, to the contrary, has many peers, (over) against whom he cannot "stand up." He is certainly right that "[o]ur dungy earth *alike*/Feeds beast as man," but his opinion on the "nobleness of life," however noble itself, binds *him*, as well as the world, to "*we* it."[1] And it is an open, aggravated question how "Antony/Will be *himself*."

My argument may appear infirm in light of the crucial exchange between Antony and the Egyptian soothsayer:

SOOTHSAYER Thy daemon, that thy spirit which keeps thee, is
Noble, courageous, high, *unmatchable*,
Where Caesar's is not. But *near him* thy angel
Becomes afeard, as being o'erpowered. *Therefore
Make space enough between you.*
...
If thou dost play with him at any game
Thou art sure to lose; and of that natural luck
He beats thee 'gainst the odds. *Thy lustre thickens
When he shines by.* I say again, thy spirit
Is all afraid to govern thee near him;
But he away, 'tis noble.
MARK ANTONY... be it art or hap,
He hath spoken true.

Ant. 2.3.17-21; 23-28; 30-31 (emphasis added)

The soothsayer clearly says that Antony's "daemon" is "unmatchable" — except when Caesar is nearby. If Antony were alone, or apart from Caesar, Antony would shine as singular, unique, (like) one of a kind, self-identical (a crocodile).

But, so far from undermining my argument, the soothsayer actually lends great credibility to it. What Antony cannot be is alone: he is inseparable from Caesar (part of the triumvirate) as he is inseparable indeed from all those in respect to whom he is, in Cleopatra's phrase, "the odds." Antony's tragedy is his enormous public(ity), the inescapable as it is the necessary consequence of his bravery ("His soldiership/Is *twice* the other *twain*" [*Ant.* 2.1.34-5; emphasis added]) and magnanimity ("He was not sad, for he would shine on those/That *make their looks by his*" [*Ant.* 1.5.54-5; emphasis added]). Antony's tragedy is his belonging-ness. And to whom he belongs, on them he depends, as do they on him (hence the importance of Enobarbus and his eventual suicide — "O Antony,/Nobler than my revolt is infamous,/Forgive me" [*Ant.* 4.10.17-19]). Antony's tragedy, in short, is being a third (triumvir) or a second (duumvir) or, simply, *a part of* rather than *apart from*. So much a part of the whole world is he that he can never finally be apart from the burden of the world upon him (hence the allusions to his "ancestor," Hercules [*Ant.* 1.3.84; 4.3.14; 4.13.44]; and see Shoaf, "*Certius exemplar*").

The play never rests from "paragon[ing]" Antony with others: "I will give thee bloody teeth/If thou with Caesar *paragon* again/*My man of men*" (*Ant.* 1.5.69-71; emphasis added), Cleopatra threatens Charmian. Everyone claims Antony as "my man of men," even Octavius, though he be merely politic in doing so:

> We could not stall together
> In the whole world. But yet let me lament,
> With tears as sovereign as the blood of hearts,
> That thou, my brother, my competitor
> In top of all design, my mate in empire,
> Friend and companion in the front of war,
> The arm of mine own body, and the heart
> Where mine his thoughts did kindle — that our stars,
> Unreconciliable, should divide
> Our equalness to this.
>
> *Ant.* 5.1.39-48

However hypocritical Octavius is in this speech, we also hear nonetheless the insistent language of "paragon[ing]," or likeness: Antony is a kind of monster of attraction, drawing to himself the awe and the envy alike of others about him. He is never a crocodile, "a thing, sir, like [him]self." As he says, only too truthfully, "[i]f I lose mine honour,/I lose myself" (*Ant.* 3.4.22-23), which is as much as also to say, "myself depends upon mine honour, that is but wind in others' mouths."

Camidius laments in the hour of defeat that, "[h]ad our general/Been what he knew himself, it had gone well" (*Ant.* 3.10.25-26), but Antony is "unqualitied/With very shame" (*Ant.* 3.11.44-45). The Norton edition, for example, glosses "unqualitied" as "lost his sense of self," and this gloss, I think, is helpful—Antony's self depends so drastically on others' opinions of him that shame must perforce lose him that self and he cannot be what he knows himself (if he knows at all). Cleopatra may face it out, "since my lord/Is Antony again, I will be Cleopatra" (*Ant.* 3.13.188-9), but Antony can be Antony again only when he "will oppose [Caesar's] fate" (*Ant.* 3.13.172):

> If he *mislike*
> My speech and what is done, tell him he has
> Hipparchus, my enfranchèd bondman, whom
> He may at pleasure whip, or hang, or torture,
> As he shall *like*, to quit me.
>
> *Ant.* 3.13.149-53 (emphasis added)

Unlike the crocodile, Antony *is* only "*as* [Caesar] shall like." He can never be quit of Caesar, except by dying.

So thorough is Antony's dependency on others' *like*ness, that twice we hear him "un-like" himself:

> *I wish I could be made so many men,*
> And all of you clapped up together in
> An Antony, that I might do you service
> So good as you have done.
>   *Ant.* 4.2.16-19 (emphasis added)

>   I thank you all,
> For doughty-handed are you, and have fought
> Not as you served the cause, but as't had been
> *Each man's like mine.*
>   *Ant.* 4.9.4-7 (emphasis added)

So far from being a crocodile, "a thing, sir, like [him]self," Antony is a thing fragmented or a thing "clapped up together," apparently condemned "to spend his fury/Upon himself" (*Ant.* 4.6.9-10) because that self is somehow everyman and no man at once. Hence, I take it, the enduring pathos of the suicides in the play. "[N]one but Antony should conquer Antony" (*Ant.* 4.16.17; cf. *JC* 5.5.56). "My resolution's placed, and I have nothing/ Of woman in me" (*Ant.* 5.2.234-5). Antony is "a thing ... like [him]self" only when he kills himself—although, even then, as he cries out, "I have done my work ill" (*Ant.* 4.15.105). Cleopatra, to secure herself, must unsex herself, although she has just a moment before this denial of woman in her commanded her women-servants to, "[s]how me ... like a queen" (*Ant.* 5.2.223). In this world, to be a self, even in the moment of ultimate *self-*assertion, is apparently not in the gift of mortals.

If "[h]ere [he is] Antony,/Yet cannot hold this visible shape" (*Ant.* 4.15.13-14), because his likeness is refracted through the myriad other "visible shape[s]" that "make their looks by his" (*Ant.* 1.5.55), Cleopatra is she, for her part, who "becomes" and who everything "becomes." The verb "become" does powerful work in the play (cf. Adelman, *Liar* 116, 144-5, 168). Used of both Antony and Cleopatra, it teaches us first that each protagonist is possessed not so much of a "visible shape" or stable likeness as of a character to perform or a role to play or a part to assume (*Ant.* 1.1.51; 1.4.21-24; 1.5.58-60; 1.1.6-10; 1.3.83-85; 1.3.96-98; 2.2.244-6; 2.5.19-20; 3.7.25-27; 3.12.34-36; 4.4.29-30; etc.). But the verb also teaches us, just by its applicability to both protagonists, that, in becoming, Antony is Cleopatra and Cleopatra is Antony, that Antony is the male Cleopatra ("glory of the father" in the two parts of her Greek name) and that Cleopatra is the female Antony, that gender in them is profoundly destabilized:

> From Alexandria
> This is the news: ... [Antony] is not more man*like*

> Than Cleopatra, nor the queen of Ptolemy
> More womanly than he.
>
> *Ant.* 1.4.3-7

In short, Antony and Cleopatra have become, and are, just alike.

Only in Shakespeare's theater of likeness can this simple declarative sentence declare its sentence. Antony and Cleopatra are not identical, they are not copies of each other, they are not versions of each other, they (are) *like* each other—each is the other's like. The work of the word *like* in Shakespeare helps us to see that this (would-be) Turtle and his (almost) Phoenix come very close to slaying number (lines 33-40):

> So between them love did shine
> That the turtle saw his right
> Flaming in the Phoenix' sight.
> Either was the other's mine.
>
> Property was thus appalled
> That the self was not the same.
> Single nature's double name
> Neither two nor one was called.

But because such like is possible only in language, never in reality, we also see and the more readily grasp the tragic point of Camidius' complaint, "[s]o our leader's led,/And we are women's men" (*Ant.* 3.7.69-70), and Scarus' bitter "passion" (*Ant.* 3.10.5):

> Yon riband-red nag of Egypt —
> ...
> *like a cow in June,*
> Hoists sails and flies.
> ...
> She once being luffed,
> The noble ruin of her magic, Antony,
> Claps on his sea-wing and, *like a doting mallard,*
> Leaving the fight in height, flies after her.
>
> *Ant.* 3.10.10; 14-15; 17-20 (emphasis added)

The reduction by simile of Antony and Cleopatra to the likenesses of a male duck and a cow unnervingly instruct the appalled audience in the scandalous result of a love so alike "[t]hat the self was not the same": it seems inhuman—the Phoenix and the Turtle are, after all, birds.

In their theater of likeness Antony and Cleopatra are neither duck nor cow. To the contrary, they are like to spurn the gods:

ANTONY   Egypt, ...
                         O'er my spirit
Thy full supremacy thou knew'st, and that
Thy beck might from the bidding of the gods
Command me.
                         Ant. 3.11.56; 58-61 (emphasis added)

If they were alone upon their stage, .., but there's the rub—who can be alone *if on a stage*? If Antony is "[t]he crown o'th' earth" (*Ant.* 4.16.65), if Cleopatra commands, "[p]ut on my crown ... I have/Immortal longings in me" (*Ant.* 5.2.275-6), then an audience can hardly be far away. The male Cleopatra, Antony, and the female Antony, Cleopatra ("boy"–ed, of course, on Shakespeare's stage [*Ant.* 5.2.216]), are wholly subject to their subjects. They may never *not* perform.

Hence, it seems to me, the mortal irony of Cleopatra's final performance:

> Come, thou mortal wretch,
> With thy sharp teeth this knot intrinsicate
> Of life at once untie.
>   *Ant.* 5.2.298-300

As surely as John Donne's "knotty Trinity" ("Holy Sonnet 16, line 3") is also the "not-y Trinity," full of nothing, because transcending any human intelligence, so Cleopatra's "knot intrinsicate/Of life" is also the "*not* intrinsicate of life," because the nothing of a life that cannot be lived without an audience. The mortal wretch is invited to "un*tie*" just because there is nothing to un*ite*—the audience (like "the odds") is gone. It is but the uttermost fantasy to ask, "[d]ost thou not see my baby at my breast,/ That sucks the nurse asleep?" (*Ant.* 5.2.304-5), for only in such fantasy can an asp be a baby. Caesar is profoundly right, if also predictably calculating, that in death, Cleopatra

> looks like sleep,
> As she would catch another Antony
> In her strong toil of grace
>   *Ant.* 5.2.340-2

—ever the actress, even in the "not intrinsicate of life": "No grave upon earth shall clip in it / A pair so famous" (*Ant.* 5.2.353-4; emphasis added).

29
"To join like likes": All's Will That Ends Ill

In a study devoted to the extraordinary work of the word *like* in Shakespeare's writings, some speeches, in particular, command attention—for example, Duke Vincentio's "Like doth quit like, measure still for measure," in *Measure for Measure* (5.1.408). Another of these speeches is Helen's first soliloquy in *All's Well That Ends Well*:

> What power is it which mounts my love so high,
> That makes me see and cannot feed mine eye?
> *The mightiest space in fortune nature brings*
> *To join like likes and kiss like native things.*
> Impossible be strange attempts to those
> That weigh their pains in sense and do suppose
> What hath been cannot be.
>   *AWW* 1.1.216-22 (emphasis added)

Here it is important, initially, to pay attention not to what the character is saying but to what the poet is doing.[1] The poet is feeling (out) a power he tested unrelentingly during the whole course of his career. It is the power of likeness. In this power he discerned one of the inescapables of human being, namely the question: what shall I (be) like? If Helen likes above her station, she is also *like* one above her station; she has chosen her likeness where she has found it (and where it has found her). The "power" that "mounts [her] love so high" and that "makes [her] see and cannot feed [her] eye[/I]" is the power— contingent, radical, unpredictable, and ineluctably carnal—of likeness, a power that, no matter how great the differences ("space") between two individuals' "fortune[s]" is, still occasions nature's enduring mystery, "[to cause them] to join like likes and kiss like native things," a feeding of I's as well as eyes.

Imperative before proceeding further with *All's Well* is to see the play's exact insistence on the problematic of likeness. This insistence is by way of the profound realization of incest in act 1, scene 3, lines 133-87, in the conversation between the Countess of Roussillon and Helen (emphasis added):

> **COUNTESS** Why not a mother? *When I said "a mother,"*
> *Methought you saw a serpent.*
> ...
> *[I] put you in the catalogue of those*
> *That were enwombèd mine.*
> ...
> **HELEN**   Pardon, madam.
> *The Count Roussillon cannot be my brother.*
> ...
> *He must not be my brother.*
> ...
> So I were not his sister. *Can 't no other*
> *But, I your daughter, he must be my brother?*
> **COUNTESS** Yes, Helen, you might be my daughter-in-law.
> God shield you mean it not! *"Daughter" and "mother"*
> *So strive upon your pulse.* What, pale again?
> ...
>   Now to all sense 'tis gross:
> You love my son.

In its economy—say, even, efficiency—this exchange is impressive. If Helen is Bertram's sister, then her passion is doomed, for her love is then incestuous—"Methought you saw a *serpent,*" the serpent (penile emblem) of incest. In this too-much likeness, this pestiferous resemblance, Helen would commit an abomination by "join[ing] like likes and kiss[ing] like native things" with her "brother." In her recoil from the "serpent," Helen (Shakespeare) dramatizes the vagaries and vicissitudes of desire, "wound [in the] ... goodly clew" (*AWW* 1.3.178), the tangled thread, of the symbolic of socio-cultural convention—the name (of the Father), "brother," debars Helen from the body of her beloved. She therefore must repel and repeal the name.[2] She must repel and repeal *both* names, "brother" and "sister." She must, in fact, embrace the apparently absolute social "space" (*AWW* 1.1.218) between Bertram and herself, even insist on it (*AWW* 1.3.150-5), however painful this must be, so as to separate and differentiate herself from Bertram (recall Myrrha: "Were I further off perchaunce I more myght win"—*Metamorphoses* 10.351), in order thus to be, in the realm of the Symbolic, a potential mate to breed with Bertram. To like, you must not be too like whom you like.

But hence the intolerable "clew" of our erotic relationships. To like you I must be like you (as we say, we must have something "in common") but not too much like you, for if we are too alike all we will do is get in each other's way, tangled thread. Therefore, all the more important to read what Shakespeare wrote: "... nature brings/To join like likes and kiss like native things." The joining is like *likes*, the kissing is like *native things*. That is to say, the joining is not of differences, not "like differents," but like *likes*. The kissing is not of aliens, not "like differents," but like *native things* — things of the same nativity, the same birth. In short, the joining resembles — alarmingly — nothing so much as incest. What are we to do? Do we have a clue?

※

Next the instances of *like* in the play need to be assembled and surveyed. They map, as they do so often in others of Shakespeare's plays, a way into the psychopathology of eros.

The word *like* or forms thereof occur 50 times in *All's Well*, as compared with, say, *Hamlet*, where it occurs some 90 times. This density of occurrence in a (sometimes denominated) "problem play" is another index to the crucial connection between these plays and the tragedies, written apparently many of them during the same period (1602-7). In both, Shakespeare is driven by what I consider irresistible psychic need to ask such questions as those I pose above. These plays are about the mystery, often terrifying, of likeness.

The very first occurrence of *like* in the play is highly instructive:

HELEN What was he [her father] *like*?
I have forgot him. My imagination
Carries no favour in't but Bertram's.
                     AWW 1.1.80-82 (emphasis added)

Helen, having forgotten her father, does not remember what he was *like*. She has no paternal likeness in her imagination. Or, if we choose to say that she protests too much and remembers very well what her father was *like* (*AWW* 1.1.80), only suppresses his likeness now in favor of Bertram's "favour," then we say effectively the same thing: namely, that difference has interrupted likeness ("I have forgot him") and Helen is ripe (in all senses) for *non-incestuous* intercourse — Helen is ready for that paradoxical otherness-likeness that is conventional heterosexual intercourse.

Hence, in the exquisite economy of Shakespeare's writing, the very next exchange, only a few lines later, between Paroles and Helen, is on *virginity*, or that which must be "lost" in, and for, conventional heterosexual intercourse.

298 "To join like likes"

>   **PAROLES** Are you meditating on virginity?
>   **HELEN** Ay.
>
>   *AWW* 1.1.109-10

In the lengthy exchange that ensues (lines 106-52), most important to my purpose, is the following moment:

>   **HELEN** How might one do, sir, to lose it [virginity] to her own *liking*?
>   **PAROLES** Let me see. Marry, ill, to *like* him that ne'er it *likes*.
>
>   *AWW* 1.1.148-50 (emphasis added)

It is important not to underread what Shakespeare has written here. Helen (not of Troy) proposes, by implication, to dispose of *her own* virginity, "to lose it to her own liking," where *liking* powerfully points the crisis unfolding. Meaning not only "predilection" or "election" but also "image" or "resemblance," *liking* amounts to Helen's declaration of independence, not only from the patriarchy but also from the tyranny of alienness—if the taker of her virginity must be different, he must be different to her *own liking*, bearing a "favour" she likes *and is like*. Hence, the extraordinary significance of Paroles' reply—"ill, to like him that ne'er it likes"—since, beyond anything he, Paroles, grasps, probably only echoing Helen as he does, it reinforces Helen's singularity, which will stand out again and again in the play (and which has dismayed generations of readers). This singularity consists in her relentless quest "to like him that ... likes" her virginity, to desire just him who desires her not only as much as, but also in the same way that, she desires him—that is, to and with the loss of that which she prizes the most, her maidenhead, where we understand the ring Bertram sacrifices for sex with Diana/Helen to be the nearest equivalent in a man's universe to the maidenhead Helen sacrifices when he deflowers her.

>   **BERTRAM** It [his ring] is an honour 'longing to our house,
>   Bequeathèd down from many ancestors,
>   Which were the greatest obloquy i'th' world
>   In me to lose.
>   **DIANA**   Mine *honour's such a ring*.
>   My chastity's the jewel of our house,
>   Bequeathèd down from many ancestors,
>   Which were the greatest obloquy i'th' world
>   In me to lose. Thus *your own proper wisdom*

> *Brings in the champion Honour on my part*
> Against your vain assault.
> **BERTRAM**   Here, take my ring.
> My house, mine honour, yea my life be thine,
> And I'll be bid by thee.
> AWW 4.2.43-54 (emphasis added)

Here, I think, will be found the real meaning of the notorious bed-trick, or Shakespeare's attempt to make a man *like* a woman in sexual intercourse of the first encounter, where exquisite loss is inevitable (and note that, presumably, Bertram has no expectation, and certainly no announced plan, of retrieving his family ring).

> **KING**   She hath that ring of yours.
> **BERTRAM** I think she has. Certain it is *I liked her*
> And boarded her i'th' wanton way of youth.
> AWW 5.3.212-14 (emphasis added)

Now *in extremis*, Bertram, though self-exculpating, must nevertheless admit "I liked her" even as he acknowledges he has lost "house, honour, yea, life." But his martyrdom—in the literal sense of "witness"[3]—is not yet complete; he has yet to witness one more clue to the care of eros:

> **KING** Is't real that I see?
> **HELEN**   No, my good lord,
> 'Tis but the shadow of a wife you see,
> *The name and not the thing.*
> **BERTRAM**   *Both, both. O, pardon!*
> **HELEN** O, my good lord, when I was *like* this maid
> *I found you wondrous kind.* There is your *ring*.
> And, look you, here's your letter. This it says:
> "When from my finger you can get this ring,
> And are by me with child," et cetera. This is done.
> Will you be mine now you are doubly won?
> AWW 5.3.308-16 (emphasis added)

"When I was *like* this maid"—that is, in bed with you, having intercourse—"I found you wondrous kind." Recall, also, just here, Helen's earlier insight,

> But O, strange men,
> *That can such sweet use make of what they hate.*
> AWW 4.4.21-22 (emphasis added)

"To join like likes"

Bertram has been deceived. But, deceived, he has witnessed how "wondrous kind" he is and what "sweet use [he can] make of what [he] hate[s]." Bertram has been led not to the cure but to the care of eros, its psychopathology as ever real (he *was* deceived) but not beyond care, if forever in this life beyond cure. When he begs pardon, he begs pardon of his wife in "both, both" name and thing; "doubly won," he will "love her dearly, ever ever dearly." She and he (are) like each other—

> **HELEN** If it appear not plain and prove untrue,
> Deadly divorce step between me and you.
> *AWW* 5.3.319-20

If the King of France has married Bertram "against his liking" (*AWW* 3.5.54), Helen nonetheless has chosen to "lose [her virginity] to her own liking," pleading with the Countess, her "mother," in particular, that if she, the Countess,

> Did ever in *so true a flame of liking*
> Wish chastely and love dearly, that [her] Dian
> Was both herself and Love, then give pity
> To [me]...
> *AWW* 1.3.207-10 (emphasis added)

"To join like likes and kiss like native things" requires a "true flame of liking," which is not the smoke(screen) of copying nor the all-consuming conflagration of alienness.

The King of France helps us toward knowledge of the "true flame of liking":

> **KING** 'Tis only title thou disdain'st in her, the which
> I can build up. Strange is it that our bloods,
> Of colour, weight, and heat, *poured all together*,
> Would quite *confound distinction*, yet stands off
> *In differences so mighty*. If she be
> All that is virtuous, save what thou *dislik'st* —
> "A poor physician's daughter" — thou *dislik'st*
> Of virtue for the name. But do not so.
> ...
> *The property by what it is should go,*
> *Not by the title.* She is young, wise, fair.
> In these to nature she's immediate heir,
> And these breed honour. That is honour's scorn

> Which challenges itself as honour's born
> *And is not like the sire;* honours thrive
> When rather from our acts we them derive
> Than our foregoers.
> ...
> If thou canst *like* this creature as a maid,
> I can create the rest.
>
>   AWW 2.3.118-25; 131-8; 143-4 (emphasis added)

Although this is, to be sure, very standard lore—we can find it everywhere, Cicero and Seneca, Boethius and Chaucer, Dante and Boccaccio, et al.[4]— Shakespeare varies it significantly with the work of *like*. We may infer from this work that a title is the merest likeness, arbitrary and contingent and negotiable, an epiphenomenon to an appearance (phenomenon) more immediate and substantial. But if this is so, note then the paradox. When the King "has create[d] the rest," he will have but added a title or titles, a likeness or likenesses, and still will be wide of the mark he holds up for approbation, "[t]he property by what it is should go,/Not by the title." Helen may be so virtuous that she *becomes* the likeness with which the King endows her, but such a pure Platonism in a world of shadows is debatable, indeed unlikely, as Bertram well knows when he concludes in the next line: "I cannot love her, nor will strive to do't" (*AWW* 2.3.146). To arouse a "true flame of liking" will ask more than an arbitrary instituting of likenesses, no matter how likely in the given case they seem. Bertram's "submi[ssion]/[Of his] fancy to [the King's] eyes" (*AWW* 2.3.168-9) is, we know, only an expediency until he can plot his extrication from marriage to Helen. She is not yet to his liking, and the King is lacking in the power to entitle her so.

Shakespeare would have us see that the likeness of liking depends on the liking of the likeness. It is impossible for me to *know* who you *are*, but it is reasonably easy for me to discern what and whom you (are) like so as to decide if I (am) like you. This, we should pause to observe, is why the character of Paroles is so important: "Simply the thing I am/Shall make me live" (*AWW* 4.3.334-5). After all his petty and bogus likenesses are stripped from him, "[d]amnable both-sides rogue" (*AWW* 4.3.227), "like a double-meaning prophesier" (*AWW* 4.3.102-3), Paroles (whose name means "words," that is, "titles"), imagines himself simply the thing he is. And, it seems, simply the thing he is elicits some care from Lafeu: "Though you are a fool and a knave, you shall eat. Go to, follow" (*AWW* 5.2.52-53). Immediately, though, we hear and understand that "fool" and "knave" are the new titles, the new words, that *Words* (Paroles) is *like*. And, predictably, when Lafeu next addresses him, it will be under even yet another new title:

> Mine eyes smell onions, I shall weep anon.
> (*To Paroles*) *Good Tom Drum*, lend me a handkerchief.
> So, I thank thee. Wait on me home, I'll make sport
> with thee. Let thy curtsies alone, they are scurvy ones.
> AWW 5.3.322-5 (emphasis added)

Newly christened *Tom Drum*, Paroles (and we) must concede that there is no such "[s]imply the thing [he is] / [that] shall make [him] live"—at most, it shall make him *like*.

This comes near the crux. Consider Bertram:

> This very day,
> Great Mars, I put myself into thy file.
> *Make me but like my thoughts,* and I shall prove
> A lover of thy drum, hater of love.
> AWW 3.3.8-11 (emphasis added)

To be "like [one's] thoughts" is perforce to be "file[d]" (also therefore "-l-i-f-e-[d]") under some category, or name, or title[5]; and the "true flame of liking" is inseparable from what life one wills to file under. Bertram wants to be, wills to be, a "lover of [Mars'] drum, hater of love"—such is what he wills to (be) like, as if he had also said "make me but like my will." "Simply the thing [he is]" is his will (meaning, in Shakespeare's lexicon, at least, desire, volition, penis, intention, want, lack, and freedom). And, as Shakespeare teaches us, all's will that ends ill.

✾

When Diana asks Helen, as they observe the troop pass by, "[i]s't not/A handsome gentleman (i.e., Bertram)?," Helen replies, "I like him well" (*AWW* 3.5.81-83). We must, I think, listen to Shakespeare. He may never have blotted a line (Ben Jonson [chapter 15 above note 2]), but I am not sure he ever wasted one either. Certainly not this one. Helen likes Bertram well. And, we may as well acknowledge, Helen likes Bertram's will. This line is not merely diegetic; it is importantly metatextual—it shows us the like of Helen.

As the King had said: "Virtue and she/Is her own dower" (*AWW* 2.3.144-5). Helen (once again, *not* of Troy) knows what she likes and what she is like. This is crucial, I believe, to removing the "problem" from the "play." Helen is one of Shakespeare's most important efforts at imagining and staging a woman who is like a man (*"vir-*tue *and she"*)—not disguised as man (not a Viola, for example), not acting like a man (Lady Macbeth, for example), but like a man while still, and insistently, a woman. Helen is Helen and never acts like a man, but she is like a man in that she pursues her goal, thinks her thoughts, feels her passions, chooses her way, negotiates her arrangements, contracts for her needs, employs her fellows, etc., just like a man. Throughout the play, Helen remains marked female, in the female's classification, but she consistently comports herself like a man—as if, that is to say, a woman were able and at liberty to do all that a man is able and at liberty to do. Helen can be *like* a man—not man-like, not a virago, not cross-dressed,[6] not disguised, not pretending, but like a *man* in the position that *she* holds, the place that *she* occupies. Helen does all the things a man does and remains a woman separate and different from men, who themselves, in turn, can, as a consequence of *her* likeness, assume *their* likenesses. "The web of our life is of a mingled yarn, good and ill together" (*AWW* 4.3.74-75); it is also a mingled yarn of female and male together, both of whom are good and ill by turns.

The king's "fistula" (*AWW* 1.1.32) is, not the key, but rather the key*hole*, that we must not flinch from analyzing if we would understand what Shakespeare is struggling to see and to say. A fistula is an "abcess (often anal)" (Norton 2184; see, further, *AWW* 1.3.239) that is excruciatingly painful and very difficult to cure.[7] Lafeu may be a Pandarus when he brings Helen to the King—"I am Cressid's uncle" (*AWW* 2.1.97)—but this is not, as it turns out, an episode of pimping, though sexual it surely is; to the contrary, we must acknowledge the staggering boldness of what Shakespeare attempts: Helen penetrates the king, Helen enters the king, introduces a foreign object into the king's body, *like a man* who introduces a foreign object into a woman's body, enters it, penetrates it.

> On's [Helen's father's] bed of death
> Many receipts he gave me, chiefly one
> Which, as the dearest *issue* of his practice,
> And of his old experience th'only *darling*,
> He bade me store up as a triple eye
> Safer than mine own two, more dear.
> *AWW* 2.1.103-8 (emphasis added)

Helen impregnates the king. Helen inseminates the king with her father's "dearest issue," his "only darling," his "third eye" (eyes and testicles are inseparable in Western erotic metaphoricity—think only of Oedipus Tyrannos). Thus she cures the king, she fills his hole. "A traitor you do look *like* [says Lafeu], but such traitors / His majesty seldom fears" (*AWW*

2.1.96-97; emphasis added); with reason, in this case, for by betraying the king's body to its female likeness—its penetrability, vulnerability, and receptivity—Helen (not of Troy) will introduce not a (w)hor(s)e into it, but a child ("issue," "darling") that will cure it. The traitor she looks like, I propose, is a woman who will enter a man's hole and make him whole, remaining herself the while always a woman.

That Shakespeare longed for such a "mingled yarn" of man and woman, I believe, is the compulsion behind his terrifying representations of sexuality that lies far deeper than the fear of "suffocating mothers" Adelman (*Mothers*) so brilliantly analyzes and explains. Shakespeare longed for a mother who is a father and a father who is a mother (so do I, I am not ashamed to confess); no less chaosmic a longing could have driven a man to write some 40 works of indescribable power over some 20 years, one every six months or so. This longing may be as beautifully and poignantly evident in the exchange between the king and Helen as it is anywhere in Shakespeare's writings:

> **HELEN** Inspirèd merit so by breath is barred.
> It is not so with him that all things knows
> As 'tis with us that square our guess by shows;
> But most it is presumption in us when
> The help of heaven we count the act of men.
> Dear sir, to my endeavours give consent.
> Of heaven, not me, make an experiment.
> I am not an impostor, that proclaim
> Myself against the level of mine aim,
> But know I think, and think I know most sure,
> My art is not past power, nor you past cure.
> ...
> **KING** Methinks in thee some blessèd spirit doth speak,
> His powerful sound within an organ weak;
> And what impossibility would slay
> In common sense, sense saves another way.
> Thy life is dear, for all that life can rate
> Worth name of life in thee hath estimate:
> Youth, beauty, wisdom, courage, all
> That happiness and prime can happy call.
> Thou this to hazard needs must intimate
> Skill infinite, or monstrous desperate.
> Sweet practiser, thy physic I will try,
> That ministers thine own death if I die.
>
> *AWW* 2.1.148-58; 175-86

I have no desire to mute the sexual pun in the last line; I simply insist that if the king and Helen "die" the "other way" (orgasm), they die that way, he like a woman while still a man, she, penetrating him with her "receipt," like a man while still a woman. Shakespeare struggles to imagine, within a culture that affords him no example, a true equality of the sexes.

✾

He fails, of course. So do we all. It will not happen. The cynic will insist, it cannot happen. But this is all the same not the end of Shakespeare's story.

For Adelman, as for others troubled by Shakespeare's representation of female sexuality, the bed-trick in *All's Well* is incontrovertible evidence of masculinist recoil and disgust at "female moisture": "He knows himself my bed [Diana's] he hath defiled" (*AWW* 5.3.302); "her riddle splits the sexual act into an imaginary defilement and a miraculous conception... Diana gets the taint and Helena gets the child" (Adelman, *Mothers* 85); and Bertram does not have to confront female sexuality. As far as it goes, the argument is powerful and true, powerful because true, since men, it is clear, do recoil (often in rage) from acknowledging their origin in "female moisture." But I propose that the argument does not go as far as Shakespeare did. The argument stops with will and thus ends ill.

Where else in Shakespeare does a woman speak *like* Helen, as Helen does, about human sexuality? Note that the work of the word *like* cautions against the nearly automatic rejoinder feminism would volley, "well, that's just masculinist ventriloquizing." The work of *like* suggests that, to the contrary, Shakespeare is seriously about imagining a woman like a man (but not man-like), and, if we are at all swayed by that word and its work, it will not do simply to infer nothing but "defilement" of sexuality from such passages as

> **HELEN**   Why then tonight
> Let us essay our plot, which if it speed
> Is wicked meaning in a lawful deed
> And lawful meaning in a wicked act,
> Where both not sin, and yet a sinful fact.
>
> *AWW* 3.7.43-47

or

> **HELEN**   But O, strange men,
> That can such sweet use make of what they hate,
> When saucy trusting of the cozened thoughts
> Defiles the pitchy night; so lust doth play
> With what it loathes, for that which is away.
>
> *AWW* 4.4.21-25

What is *also* happening in these speeches is that a woman is thinking *like* a man while remaining resolutely female. She wills *as* a woman to think *like* a man—and these are, to be sure, a (misogynistic) man's thoughts, especially "[t]hat can such sweet use make of what they hate." Helen's distinctiveness among Shakespeare's heroines, which makes her difficult for both male and female readers, is the expansiveness and elasticity of her will. She does not end ill because her all is not will though her will is all she can make it like.

Hence, finally, the exact (and exacting) point, *pace* Adelman, of Helen's last speech but two:

> **KING** Is there no exorcist
> Beguiles the truer office of mine eyes?
> Is't real that I see?
> **HELEN** No, my good lord,
> 'Tis but the shadow of a wife you see,
> The name and not the thing.
>
> *AWW* 5.3.306-10

Adelman contests "the distinction Helena makes between name and thing [that it] implies that the marriage is unconsummated even as her next words—'when I was like this maid, I found you wondrous kind' ...— insist on the fact of consummation" (*Mothers* 85). But this is to have read right over Bertram's exclamation intervening between these two speeches: "Both, both. O pardon!" (*AWW* 5.3.310). Until Bertram acknowledges her, she is, indeed, his wife only in "the name and not the thing," but in the instant he cries out "[b]oth, both[,] O pardon," and does acknowledge her, admitting his intercourse with her, she can, *like* his wife now in both "name *and thing*," say: "O, my good lord, when I was like this maid/I found you wondrous kind" (*AWW* 5.3.311-12). For Helen, all's well that ends well; until Bertram begs pardon, it cannot end well — and all's will that ends ill.

For readings of Shakespeare focused on "suffocating mothers," Helen's last line in *All's Well* must seem all but an *imprimatur* for their position: "O my dear mother, do I see you living?" (*AWW* 5.3.321). "*All's Well* analyzes male flight from a woman who has become nearly indistinguishable from the mother and the desperate measures necessary to render her safe and pure" (Adelman, *Mothers* 79). But the work of the word *like* suggests another reading, another idea. Likes attract, they do not repel. Now, for the first time, Helen can call the Countess *her* mother. Now, for the first time, because she is *not* "in the catalogue of those/That were enwombèd [hers]" (*AWW* 1.3.139-40), Helen can embrace the Countess like a mother

(I deliberately employ ambiguous syntax). And now, importantly, she can exclaim "[d]o I see you living?" because she, Helen, "one that [was] dead [but now] is quick" (*AWW* 5.3.305), "feels her young one kick" (*AWW* 5.3.304). Mother recognizes mother, "like doth quit like," because the difference that makes them alike is real at last.

30
"Thou show'st/Like one I loved indeed": *Pericles, Prince of Tyre*

All four of Shakespeare's romances, I want to argue, continue his lifelong fascination with copying and succession. Only now, these are folded into a narrower concern, which I'm going to tentatively call the problem of the he(i)r.

In this word I think we can usefully locate the crisis of likeness in the romances. The word *heir* is of uncertain origin, but Calvert Watkins postulates that it derives from an Indo-European root meaning, in the middle voice, "to be released," thus, effectively, abandoned or orphaned: the heir is the child or the adult who has been abandoned or lost by his parent who has died. (Every he(i)r is named Perdita, in one sense.) In this word, then, we can locate Shakespeare's obsession with maternity, understood now as the fear of abandonment by the mother, and we can also understand his fascination with succession as the likeness of the he(i)r to the parent, and, finally, we can catch perhaps the aging writer's increasing faith that likenesses can perdure across the generations to some beneficence — not all is lost all the time between parent and child, although the transmission is never anything but fraught with difficulty, especially when it is from father to daughter (hence my spelling *he(i)r*).[1]

The problem of the he(i)r is certainly most vivid in *The Winter's Tale* in the opening of which Leontes cannot stop obsessing about the likeness to him of his son, Mamillius (whom he subsequently, in effect, destroys). But the problem of the he(i)r is also palpable in the other three romances (as well as in the Sonnets). In *Pericles*, the issue is actually dual since Pericles mourns his father and loses both his wife and his daughter, to recover the two of them only beyond all expectation. In *Cymbeline*, the ancient king has lost both his sons and seems also to lose his daughter, so that he would have to accept as his he(i)r the issue of another man's body, a stepson. In *The Tempest*, the entire action in one sense is a question of the legitimate he(i)r to Milan, although certainly this can also be seen as a crisis of the relationship between siblings, as well as a movement toward securing succession by a marriage of properly endowed noble children, he(i)rs to their fathers' bodies. In each case, a crisis of likeness figures prominently and suggests that Shakespeare is still working within the theater of likeness to resolve erotic, political, and epistemological problems that haunted him all his adult life. And note also in each case, not to be slighted, that a daughter is indispensable to the resolution of the play: Marina, Perdita, Innogen, Miranda. I speculate that the real term of this list is Susanna Shakespeare, to whom, and her husband John Hall, Shakespeare would bequeath the bulk of his estate, and of whom it was written, in her epitaph on her tombstone (see Honan 400), that she was "witty above her sexe" and "some of Shakespeare was in that."

❈

Initially, to help support my case, a brief passage in the recognition scene in *Pericles* will do important work:

> **PERICLES**   I am Pericles
> Of Tyre. But tell me now my drowned queen's name
> As in the rest thou hast been god*like* perfect,
> [   ]
> The *heir* of kingdoms, and another *like*
> To Pericles thy father.
>   *Per.* Sc. 21.191-3; 195-6 (emphasis added)

First, note that I differ from Oxford 2ᵉ in my base text.² I do not include "So prove but true in that, thou art my daughter," after the line ending in "perfect"; and I retain Q1's *like* in preference to their reading *life* in "another like"; and I remove punctuation between "name" and "As." The text as Q1 transmits it very clearly links *heir* and *like*, and I believe more closely represents Shakespeare's concern—is the daughter *like* the father? is she *another* like the father? if so, she is his he(i)r. She in*her*its his kingdoms.

It is in this fashion, I suggest, that we can better grasp the meaning of the extraordinary, oft-discussed cry Pericles lifts to Marina a few lines earlier: "Thou that begett'st him that did thee beget" (*Per.* Sc. 21.183). As others note too, there is an implication of incest in this amazing line: in some sense, Pericles is "in" his daughter's body. But, in this "incest," which is *like* but also therefore *un*like the incest between the father Antiochus and his daughter (who, note well, is *un*named), Shakespeare reaches toward his mature understanding of the father-daughter relationship: the daughter can beget the father even as can the son, although the *like* will certainly be an*other*, *less* like the son (such as Shakespeare lost, Hamnet), but no less "like/To ... [the] father." In this "incest," however, and the structure of the recognition scene argues as much, the likeness of the daughter depends upon her *un*likeness; if Pericles emerges from Marina, he is, just so, separate from, apart from, different from her, even as the infant by birthing separates from the mother. His linking to her is not like the "liking" Antiochus "took with" his daughter:

> This king unto him took a fere
> Who died, and left a female *heir*
> So buxom, blithe, and full of face
> As heav'n had lent her all his grace,
> With whom the father *liking* took,
> And her to incest did provoke.
> *Per.* Sc. 1.21-26 (emphasis added)

In its structure, the entire play moves toward this new and regenerate understanding of the female *he(i)r* and the *like*: because the father is always already in his daughter—"some of Shakespeare was in that"—he must not insert his member into his daughter. If he recognizes and honors her difference, she can be his like. "All love the womb that their first being bred" (*Per.* Sc. 1.150), yes, but, just so, therefore, they cannot forget "their first being." A daughter cannot incant a pseudo-memory in which she re-members her father's being first (and thus his youth and potency) by serving as "an eater of her mother's flesh" (*Per.* Sc.1.173), for if she "eats" his member, which is her mother's flesh, she renders him "both a father and a son / By [his] uncomely claspings with [his] child" (*Per.* Sc. 1.170-1), corrupting thus the temporality and memoriality of in*her*iting through sexual division and reproduction—she (re)produces non-sense. If the father desires to be begotten by her whom he begot—to be reborn of her—then, like Pericles (and Cymbeline and Leontes and Prospero), he must lose her first. He must other her before she can mother him. All else is the lie against time that time dislikes.

The only lie against time humans can maintain is metaphor(ic). Time being irreversible in human flesh, language is our only defense against time, and, in language, metaphor is our most effective defense because it is a kind of incest—"divine," one might say—by which like couples with like and begets difference, or new meaning. One of Aristotle's examples is particularly helpful here. Speaking in the *Poetics* (21.1457b) of metaphor used "in the way of analogy," he writes (Golden and Hardison 130-1)

> When, of four terms, the second bears the same relation to the first as the fourth to the third; in which case the fourth may be

substituted for the second and the second for the fourth. And sometimes the proper term is also introduced besides its relative term. Thus a cup bears the same relation to Bacchus as a shield to Mars. A shield therefore may be called the cup of Mars and a cup the shield of Bacchus. Again evening being to day what old age is to life, the evening may be called the old age of the day and old age the evening of life.

The otherwise improbable likeness of cup to shield, when that likeness is analogized to Bacchus and Mars, yields a coupling that begets new meaning (Bacchus has a shield, Mars has a cup) just in the measure to which begetter and begotten exchange places: the cup begets the shield, the shield begets the cup; they give life and likeness to each other within the metaphor.

But a father and a daughter cannot exchange places in the same way: time debars it. And if actual, physical incest transpires anyway, genetics exacts a huge toll in a few generations with a weakened gene pool and deteriorating offspring. Time still wins. It always does.

> **PERICLES** Whereby I see that time's the king of men;
> He's both their parent and he is their grave,
> And gives them what he will, not what they crave.
>
> *Per.* Sc. 7.44-46

But in metaphor a father and a daughter can exchange places, can exchange the roles of begetter and begotten. The play is about just such exchange. The play is a dramatization of metaphor. This is visible most clearly in the recognition scene itself where the strategic positioning of *like* marks the unfolding of the cognitive process of likening so as to know and, finally, believe ("be-like"). In Scene 21, between lines 73 and 200, 127 lines, there are 13 occurrences of the word, one every 10 lines (*Per.* Sc. 21: 75; 91; 96; 98; 99; 107; 113-14; 123; 126; 127; 172; 193; [195 Q]; emphasis added):

> **MARINA** I am a maid,
> ...
>   gazed on *like* a comet.
> **PERICLES** Pray you, turn your eyes upon me.
> You're *like* something that — what countrywoman?
> ...
> **PERICLES** My dearest wife was *like* this maid,
> ...   as wand-*like* straight,
> ...   her eyes as jewel-*like*

> **MARINA**   If I should tell
> My history, it would seem *like* lies.
> **PERICLES**   Thou show'st
> *Like* one I loved indeed.
> **MARINA**   Some such thing I said,
> And said no more but what my circumstance
> Did warrant me was *likely*.
> **PERICLES**   Tell thy story.
> If thine considered prove the thousandth part
> Of my endurance, thou art a man, and I
> Have suffered *like* a girl. Yet thou dost look
> *Like* patience.
> **PERICLES**   Tell me if thou canst
> What this maid is, or what is *like* to be.
> **PERICLES**   I am Pericles
> Of Tyre. But tell me now my drowned queen's name
> As in the rest thou hast been god*like* perfect,
> The heir of kingdoms and another *like*
> To Pericles thy father.

Here Shakespeare shows us—brilliantly, I think—*like* becoming *be like* becoming *belief* ("be-like") as Pericles remembers, but does not re-member, without incest but with "incest," and is reborn, he and his daughter together now the metaphor named "Thou that begett'st him that did thee beget." This dramatization of cognition by likeness through metaphor culminates finally in Thaisa's recognition of her husband,

> O, my lord,
> Are you not Pericles? *Like* him you spake,
> *Like* him you are. Did you not name a tempest,
> A birth and death?
>
>   *Per.* Sc. 22.51-54 (emphasis added)

We only know, as Plotinus argues, through likeness. If, then, we would know, we must, so our lot has it, be separated enough, often not without immeasurable pain, from that we would know, so as to remember the likeness thereof—"Like him you spake,/Like him you are"—and thus know for the first time, the primordial time, know that we know.

So, too, then Pericles' remembering his father:

> **PERICLES** Yon king's to me *like* to my father's picture,
> Which tells me in what glory once he was —

Had princes sit *like* stars about his throne,
And he the sun for them to reverence.
None that beheld him but *like* lesser lights
Did vail their crowns to his supremacy;
Where now his son's a glow-worm in the night,
The which hath fire in darkness, none in light;
Whereby I see that time's the king of men;
He's both their parent and he is their grave,
And gives them what he will, not what they crave.
Per. Sc. 7.36-46 (emphasis added)

The work of the word *like* in this extraordinary aside is palpable: Pericles remembers by likeness to know "in what glory once [his father] was," at the toll, enormous, of his father's absence. If all knowing comes by likeness, all knowing, just so, is by indirection, difference, devi*a*tion, probating, distancing, separation—a repairing of the pair impaired by sexual pairing, the ground of all object-ifying in nature.

So fragile is every repair—the divorce courts blatantly attest it—that marriage, even before patriarchal phallologocentric anxieties of property and succession, must be in any culture, that is not machined beyond sexual division, the abyss of incertitude. Amniocentesis eliminates only a fraction of the guesswork. Marrying daughters and finding he(i)rs, then, comprise the insuperable risk of generational succession:

ANTIOCHUS (*aside*)
Heav'n, that I had thy head! He's found the
    meaning.
But I will gloze with him. — Young Prince of Tyre,
Though by the tenor of our strict edict,
Your exposition misinterpreting,
We might proceed to cancel of your days,
Yet hope, succeeding from so fair a tree
As your fair self, doth tune us otherwise.
Forty days longer we do respite you,
If by which time our secret be undone,
This mercy shows we'll joy in such a son.
Per. Sc. 1.152-61 (emphasis added)

KING SIMONIDES She tells me here she'll wed the stranger knight,
Or never more to view nor day nor light.
I *like* that well. Nay, how absolute she's in't,
Not minding whether I *dislike* or no!

Mistress, 'tis well, I do commend your choice,
And will no longer have it be delayed.
                    Per. Sc. 9.14-19 (emphasis added)

The man with a daughter must find a son, one whom he likes, ideally one whom he *is like*. Failure in such discovery can have fatal consequences. Shakespeare shows us clearly that Pericles is not like Antiochus, he is more like Simonides, in whom he sees the likeness of his father, and yet, at the same time, Shakespeare thus shows also, just as clearly, that Pericles *is* like Antiochus—"Thou that begett'st him that did thee beget," somehow "in" his daughter's body—and that he is further incestuous, in some sense, in that he is so like Simonides and so likes Simonides, who also likes him and is like him, that marrying Thaisa is also an incest in some sense. All knowing coming by likeness is eo ipso incestuous; and all coming knowing by likeness is eo ipso incestuous, too. As Beatrice observes, in *Much Ado*: "No, uncle, I'll none. Adam's sons are my brethren, and truly I hold it a sin to match in my kindred" (*Ado.* 2.1.56-58). Though Beatrice's witticism may be slyly mocking, it nonetheless teaches us a lot about its author, William Shakespeare, ever restless in his prosecution of the question, whom (am) I like? Eve's daughters are his sisters, and who among them shall he (be) like? What if he most is like his daughter Susanna? much less like Judith? What if, at the end of his life, perhaps as early as the birth of his granddaughter Elizabeth (1607), he recognizes and accepts that Eve's daughters are where his future li(k)es?

The play *Pericles* repeatedly shows traces of Shakespeare's lifelong concern with the *Fürstenspiegel* tradition (see chapter 7 on *Edward III*). The "Mirrors for Princes," or *specula principum*, were a crucial element of the high and late medieval political and jurisprudential culture surrounding monarchy. The most famous of these, Aegidius Romanus' *De regimine principum*, was a very influential book. Machiavelli's *Il Principe*, however early modern or Renaissance it may be, however post-medieval it may be, still stands in a long line of handbooks for educating and counseling the ruler. I have argued above that Shakespeare's *Edward III* shows strong influence of the *Fürstenspiegel* tradition; this influence, more diffuse perhaps, is nonetheless present also in both Henriads, especially the second, where Prince Hal's education is concerned, and if less distinct in *King John*, that may well be the exception that proves the rule. In *Pericles*, several passages importantly insist on the tradition: for example,

PERICLES [*lifting him up*]
Rise, prithee, rise. Sit down. Thou art no flatterer,

> I thank thee for it, and *the heav'ns forbid*
> *That kings should let their ears hear their faults hid.*
> Fit counsellor and servant for a prince,
> Who by thy wisdom mak'st a prince thy servant,
> What wouldst thou have me do?
>
> *Per.* Sc. 2.64-69 (emphasis added)

> **KING SIMONIDES** It's fit it should be so, *for princes are*
> *A model which heav'n makes like to itself.*
>
> *Per.* Sc. 6.10-11 (emphasis added)

> **KING SIMONIDES** O, attend, my daughter. *Princes in this*
> *Should live like gods above*, who freely give
> To everyone that come to honour them.
> And princes not so doing are *like* gnats
> Which make a sound but, killed, are wondered at.
>
> *Per.* Sc. 7.56-60 (emphasis added)

> **PERICLES**   My gentle babe Marina,
> Whom for she was born at sea I have named so,
> Here I charge your charity withal, and leave her
> The infant of your care, *beseeching you*
> *To give her princely training, that she may be*
> *Mannered as she is born.*
>
> *Per.* Sc. 13.12-17 (emphasis added)

It is the last of these passages with which we should be most concerned. Marina, not unlike perhaps Susanna Shakespeare Hall (or Elizabeth Tudor?), is to receive "princely training, that she may be/Mannered as she is born." Her gender is no impediment to her "princely training." I understand the rejoinder, "ha! she must be a *prince* and she must be *man*-nered." No doubt, neither Pericles nor Shakespeare is innocent of patriarchal incorrectness, but it remains true that her gender is no impediment to Marina's "princely training," even if it also remains true that her gender is subsumed by the dominant, hegemonic, colonizing masculinity that *man*-ners her. I can neither correct nor excuse this. But I will take the occasion to remind us of Elizabeth Tudor's comprehension of her similar lot (*Works* 335-46, esp. 337-8, 342):

> Of myself I must say this: I never was any greedy, scraping grasper, nor a strait, fast-holding Prince, nor yet a waster. My heart was never set on worldly goods, but only for my subjects'

good. What you bestow on me, I will not hoard it up, but receive it to bestow on you again. Yea, my own properties I account yours to be expended for your good, and your eyes shall see the bestowing of all for your good...The cares and trouble of a crown I cannot resemble more fitly than to the confections of a learned physician, perfumed with some aromatical savor, or to bitter pills gilded over, by which it is made acceptable or less offensive which indeed is bitter and unpleasant to take. And for my part, were it not for conscience' sake to discharge the duty which God hath laid upon me, and to maintain His glory, and keep you in safety; in mine own disposition, I should willingly resign the place I hold to any other, and glad to be free of the glory with the labors. For it is not my desire to be or reign longer than my life and reign shall be for your good. And though you have had and may have many mightier and wiser princes sitting in this seat, yet you never had nor shall have any that will love you better.

Here, in her Golden Speech, her last to Parliament (November 30, 1601), Elizabeth is canny, politic, self-seeking, manipulative, Machiavellian, expedient, theatrical, sexy, wary, clever, etc., etc. She is also one of the greatest Princes of the earth who ever lived. It is not her fault that she is female, no more than it is Susanna's that she is Shakespeare's daughter; and Shakespeare, nearing the end of his life, has come to know and acknowledge as much.

Barely two years earlier, or so we think, he had written Lear's spewing logorrhea against women and their sexuality (*Lr.* [1605-6] Sc. 20.106-24; and see, above, chapter 25 page 256), which ends with the terrifying "[i]t [Lear's hand] smells of mortality" (*Lr.* [1605-6] Sc. 20.128). I am aware that one can explain the difference between *Lear* in 1605 and *Pericles* in 1607 by collaboration, by foul papers, by stage conventions of various sorts, by popular demand, etc., etc. I think one can explain it also by Shakespeare. Gloucester may have asked Kent in his snide way, "[d]o you smell a fault?" (*Lr.* [1605-6] Sc. 1.16)—pudendum, fart ("faht"), fall, etc. (see V. Allen 310-17)—but Shakespeare nonetheless has learned that, much though patriarchal institutions may blame the female sex for the human condition, it is not the case.

I believe he learned this in no small part through his daughter and his granddaughter. I am thus unapologetically autobiographical, psychoanalytic, and authorial, none of which it is currently fashionable to be. Still, I *be like* (believe) this case, and I am not afraid to argue it. Although the history of *Pericles, Prince of Tyre* is exceedingly vexed, the textual transmission an insoluble tangle, and the collaboration uncertain, I think that we are all the same justified in believing that Shakespeare's voice, nay, possibly, his life, are in the play for us to observe. The playwright who lost his likeness Hamnet still has a likeness Susanna, his eldest, to whom I can imagine him saying, "[t]hou show'st / Like one I loved indeed" (*Per.* Sc. 21.113-14) and "there never came her like in [Stratford-upon-Avon]" (*Per.* Sc. 19.35-36). He had sufficient imagination—dare I also say, love, or, at least, liking?—to know that it was not her fault.

31
"What is like me formerly": Coriolanus's Core

> I had rather be their servant in my way
> Than sway with them in theirs.
> *Cor.* 2.1.200-1

> And he's as like to do't as any man
> I can imagine.
> *Cor.* 4.5.208-9

Coriolanus is a play very amenable to analysis by way of the work of the word *like*. *Coriolanus* is a play about a man who strives for absolute, perduring identity, a *core* of likeness. Hence, for example, the numerous instances where the language of the play insists on the "nature" of Coriolanus as if it were some kind of timeless, unchanging, essential *core* of the man (see especially *Cor.* 1.1.39-41; 2.3.187; 3.1.255-60; 3.2.13-14; 4.7.10-11; 4.7.41-43). To these must also be added, though they are more complex and require elaboration, the references to Coriolanus's name (most especially *Cor.* 5.1.11-15 and 5.6.90-1). *Coriolanus* is not only the tragedy of Caius Martius, it is also the tragedy of a man who would possess a core, possess it despite all that the world might say or do to negate it. Such a core, the play suggests, is already a corpse even though the greatest heart (*cor*) animate it: tauten a likeness to such torque of sameness and it *will* turn inhuman machine — "When he walks, he moves *like* an *engine*" (*Cor.* 5.4.18-19; emphasis added).

That Coriolanus is "like an engine," a machine, robot or automaton, is a commonplace of criticism of the play in recent decades. Moreover, criticism in the past 20 years or so has concentrated urgently on the political dimensions of the play, draining from it proof after proof of the neo-historicist/cultural-materialist ideology of post-marxism and its discontents. In addition, psychoanalytic criticism has been hardly less obsessed with probing to dissect the neurotic relationship between

Coriolanus and his mother, Volumnia, a woman whose very name sounds the mental disease of men disturbed by female *volume*, capacity that is also emptiness—that "nothing" so Shakespearean (Burckhardt; Willbern 1997) as to be effectively a mark of his mind.[1] But even in the midst of such enormous activity (and, I propose, anxiety, too) of criticism, the work of the word *like* in the play has much to offer still for our understanding. Shakespeare's last tragedy is also his most lucid examination of the tribulation of copying, the toil and toll of making likenesses, "in spite of death" (*Ven* 173).

Our most secure purchase on the work of *like* is first through the crucial instances of stage and acting imagery in the play.[2] Coriolanus knows that he is "a dull actor":

> **CORIOLANUS**   Like a dull actor now
> I have forgot my part.
>
> *Cor*.5.3.40-41

> **CORIOLANUS** You have put me now to such a part which never I shall discharge to th' life.
> ...
> **VOLUMNIA** To have my praise for this, perform a part
> Thou hast not done before.
>
> *Cor*. 3.2.105-6; 109-10

The perduring core of Coriolanus is allergic to acting or pretending or affectation — any performance that alters his form:

> **MENENIUS** Pray you, go fit you to the custom and
> Take to you, as your predecessors have,
> Your honour with your form.
> **CORIOLANUS**   It is a part
> That I shall blush in acting.
>
> *Cor*.2.2.143-6

The difficulty for Coriolanus is that there is such discrepancy between "honour" and "form": "honour" is bestowed by the populace,[3] but "form" is, or so he believes and so he insists, intrinsic, inherent, native, his own—

> While I remain above the ground you shall
> Hear from me still, and never of me aught
> But what is *like me formerly*.
>
> *Cor*. 4.1.52-54 (emphasis added)

Form may earn honor, but honor is not worth one's form. Hence, when Rome banishes him, he retorts, "I banish you" (*Cor.* 3.3.127), as if he were more Rome than Rome. Hence, too, when he honors his mother, he knows he is destroying his form:

> **CORIOLANUS** O my mother, mother, O!
> ...
> Most dangerously you have with [your son] prevailed,
> *If not most mortal to him.* But let it come.
> *Cor.* 5.3.186; 189-90 (emphasis added)

He knows he is destroying his like, of which there is no more in Rome.

To act or to play is to admit that one's core is subject to alteration, to a change of likes:

> **CORIOLANUS** Would you have me
> False to my nature? Rather say I play
> The man I am.
> *Cor.* 3.2.13-15

Coriolanus tries to cover the gap, "say I play/The man I am," but exposes it in the very attempt, conceding that he plays in the same breath that he lays claim to a nature ("the man I am") beyond playing. In a world where wholeness, singularity, integrity are just likenesses that can be played like any other likenesses, playing is as repugnant to Coriolanus as goodness is to Aaron (*Tit.* 5.3.188-9). Both bespeak a lapse in self-possession and self-coincidence. Neither Coriolanus nor Aaron consciously submits to such a lapse:

> **VOLUMNIA** If it be honour in your wars *to seem*
> *The same you are not*, which for your best ends
> You adopt your policy, how is it less or worse
> That it shall hold companionship in peace
> With honour, as in war, since that to both
> It stands in *like* request?
> *Cor.* 3.2.47-52 (emphasis added)

But there's the rub: it is not, Coriolanus knows full well, "in like request," for, "in [their] wars," two men can affirm, each to the other's core, that "[w]e hate *alike*" (*Cor.* 1.9.2; emphasis added), and that likeness alone justifies "to seem/The same you are not," for in that *alike* any lapse in self-coincidence is compensated by the other.

> **AUFIDIUS**   We hate *alike*.
> Not Afric owns a serpent I abhor
> More than thy fame and envy. Fix thy foot.
>
> *Cor.* 1.9.2-4

These two men are together alike whole, complete, perfect, and final: each does the other ab(w)hor(e), so as to win from that predatory abjection, so utterly sexual (as many before me have noted [e.g., Norton 942]), his sense that he is "absolute" (*Cor.* 3.2.40). That, moreover, the "fame and envy" should be assimilated to a "serpent" only hardens their "co(re)pulation" the more.[4]

If Coriolanus repudiates acting, or tries to do so, if he scorns any likening of himself demeaning to himself, it is because, psychoanalysis and its champions have taught us, Volumnia has s/mothered him (cf. Adelman, *Mothers* 38):

> I, considering how honour
> would become such a person — that it was no better
> than, picture-*like*, to hang by th' wall if renown made
> it not stir — was pleased to let him seek danger where
> he was *like* to find fame.
>
> *Cor.* 1.3.9-13 (emphasis added)

> Hear me profess
> sincerely: had I a dozen sons, each in my love *alike*,
> and none less dear than thine and my good Martius',
> I had rather had eleven die nobly for their country
> than one voluptuously surfeit out of action.
>
> *Cor.* 1.3.21-25 (emphasis added)

These passages teach us that Volumnia has one and only one likeness for her son and that she is determined to impose it upon him no matter the cost. One son or a dozen sons—all alike must reflect her likeness. Coriolanus exists to fill her volume (which will always be empty). In effect, then, "he" does not exist at all: *it* exists, the "engine" that occupies the body named Caius Martius Coriolanus. And on those occasions when *he* might emerge from *it* ("Wo Es war, soll Ich werden"[5]), Volumnia empties him again:

> **VOLUMNIA**   There's no man in the world
> More bound to's mother, yet here he lets me prate
> Like one i'th' stocks. Thou hast never in thy life
> Showed thy dear mother any courtesy,

> When she, poor hen, fond of no second brood,
> Has clucked thee to the wars and safely home,
> Loaden with honour.
> ...
> Come, let us go.
> This fellow had a Volscian to his mother.
> His wife is in Corioles, and this child
> Like him by chance.
>
> *Cor.* 5.3.159-65; 178-81

She takes his likeness from him, even the likeness of his son, now merely an accident, but, much more, she takes *her* likeness from him, the likeness of his mother as well, now one fit only for the stocks, not one fit to bear his like.[6]

The solitude of the obsessive, of the one condemned to autotelic self-sufficiency by the illusory sufficiency of the never-good-enough mother (cf. Winnicott 1954), marks Coriolanus (and now one *must* hear the "anus" in his name [cf. Goldberg]) as the monster of repetition that not good enough mothering makes of the child otherwise likely to express his freedom through disobedience or, worse, deviation (usually anal, especially in the particularly sensitive child who rebels against the violation of his orifices by the [m]other): if not bound in compulsion and obsession to repeat his mother's likeness, the child might become his own person, his mother then dismayed by the imperative of sex for the male to seek another not mother. So bound, Coriolanus is not deceived as to the monster he is: "... though I go alone, / Like to a lonely *dragon*...his fen" – *Cor.* 4.1.30-31 (emphasis added). And others recognize the worm as well:

> **AUFIDIUS** And shows good husbandry for the Volscian state,
> Fights *dragon-like*.
>
> *Cor.* 4.7.22-23 (emphasis added)

> **MENENIUS** There is differency between a grub and a
> butterfly, yet your butterfly was a grub. This Martius
> is grown from man to *dragon*. He has wings, he's more
> than a creeping thing.
>
> *Cor.* 5.4.11-14 (emphasis added)

The relation of the dragon to anality through the hoard that the worm always guards ("good husbandry") is obvious (from *Beowulf* to *The Hobbit*). Obvious, too, is that Shakespeare could well have known 16th-century uses of the word *fen* to mean "excrement."[7] But no less obvious is the play's suggestion that Coriolanus is the monster of retention and repetition who broods and fumes over the treasure, the (c)ore, that must never be evacuated or alienated: "I had rather be their servant in my way/Than sway with them in theirs" (*Cor.* 2.1.200-1), where the formal parsimony of "way/sway" is no less revealing than the content of the anally retentive (a)voidance of mixing with other human beings.[8]

And yet the (c)ore always circulates anew. The dragon is always defeated. As if he knew, though perhaps only subliminally, that he is *"like a thing / Made by some other deity than nature,/That shapes man better"* (*Cor.* 4.6.94-96; emphasis added), Coriolanus also knows that to be thus "shape[d] better" is to be *like* a monster:

> **CORIOLANUS** I had rather have one scratch my head i'th' sun
> When the alarum were struck than idly sit
> To hear my nothings *monstered*.
>
> *Cor.* 2.2.75-77 (emphasis added)

Proud he certainly is (and condemned for his pride), but we should also understand that the obverse of that pride, or his shame (and it is his mother's shame, in more senses than one), also drives Coriolanus to the extremest monstrosity of all, or his absolute aloneness ("a kind of nothing, titleless"—*Cor.* 5.1.13). Sicinius in scorn may demand,

> Where is this *viper*
> That would depopulate the city and
> *Be every man himself*?
>
> *Cor.* 3.1.263-5 (emphasis added)

but his scorn does not prevent us from hearing the tragic condition of Coriolanus, a "viper" (dragon) condemned to feel that he must "be every man himself." And this terrible burden, the burden of the compulsive who must make everything just so, like himself, we must not hesitate to consider, is his mother's volume: "If my son were my husband..." (*Cor.* 1.3.2) is a hollow counterfactual; inside the grammar is the incestuous truth—she too would hoard (and whore) the (c)ore of Coriolanus in her voluminousness.

Coriolanus is condemned to believe that he is not like others—he truly believes this—and therefore he does not like others. This play that so famously asks, "who does the wolf love"? (*Cor.* 2.1.7), might also ask "who does the dragon love?"

> **CORIOLANUS**   But out, affection!

> All bond and privilege of nature break;
> Let it be virtuous to be obstinate.
> ...
>   I'll never
> Be such a gosling to obey instinct, but stand
> As if a man were author of himself
> And knew no other kin.
> ...
> Not of a woman's tenderness to be
> Requires nor child nor woman's face to see.
>   *Cor.* 5.3.24-26; 34-37; 130-1

It is imperative to understand that, without for a moment exonerating Coriolanus of his pride or his shame or violence, we can and should also pity him. He is, all too literally, a "boy" (*Cor.* 5.6.103) in a world where a male may be a "son" (*Cor.* 1.3.2) or a "hare" (*Cor.* 1.9.7) or "fragments" (i.e., leftovers—*Cor.* 1.1.221) or a dragon but never human. Which is why his name is so crucial to the play's dynamic. He belongs to Mars ("Martius"), or he belongs to the city from whose penetrated gates he emerges triumphant with its name now his (cf. Adelman, *Mothers* 152); but when he attempts to be him "self," he is "a kind of nothing, titleless":

>   'Coriolanus'
> He would not answer to, forbade all names.
> He was a kind of nothing, titleless,
> Till he had forged himself a name o'th' fire
> Of burning Rome
>   *Cor.* 5.1.11-15 —

which forgery is never to be. The "kind of nothing" will end, rather, penetrated multiply by Volscian swords just because "he's as *like* to do't as any man I can imagine" (*Cor.* 4.5.208-9; emphasis added).

At the beginning and at the end of his career, Shakespeare writes tragedies of Romans, Titus and Coriolanus. His fascination with Rome (Kahn 1997), I would like to propose, emerges from his perception that Rome is a culture of copying, a culture of *like*ness.

Greece and the Greek language are a culture of discovery—eureka!, Archimedes cries. Greece is the seat of science, mathematics, logic, philosophy, the land of Pythagoras, Plato, Euclid, Aristotle. Greece is the origin of epic, Homer. Greece is also the stage of drama: Aeschylus, Sophocles, Euripides, Aristophanes. Scholarship may know more and better today. But Shakespeare would probably have thought roughly along such lines. Similarly, he would have understood Rome and Latin to be the culture of imitation (and emulation, *aemulatio*). He would have easily seen Rome to copy practically everything about and from Greece. Roman is Greek culture in (trans)*Latio*(n): "Graecia capta ferum victorem cepit et artis/intulit agresti Latio" (Captured Greece took captive her savage conqueror and brought civilization to rustic Latium—Horace, *Ep.* 2.1.156). And Rome, as I have already discussed, is a society built on strict imitation, of ancestors and traditions. Moreover, as we say, "when in Rome, do as the Romans do"—Rome copied also to be copied.

Latin is the supreme example of a literature that copies in order to assert its difference. Virgil is the consummate artist of this literature. "Secondary epic" is rightly and helpfully named (Lewis 33-51). It is useful, however commonplace, to know that the first half of the *Aeneid* is Odyssean and the second half Iliadic. When we have learned this and understood it, we are prepared to understand how Virgil was free to write one of the great stories of passion in world literature, the affair of Dido and Aeneas, and how he was free as well to make us feel for Turnus as we do at the end of book 12. In other words, it is not demeaning or degrading to call Latin the supreme example of a literature that copies; to the contrary, it is to recognize the genius of Latin, greatest of all recorded history's colonizing forces.

We have fairly strong evidence that Shakespeare taught Latin at some point in his early years (Honan 60-2). I favor this hypothesis, primarily because Shakespeare's ear is so finely attuned to roots and affixes in his English: he hears archaic sounds and their meanings in his language— Iago, or "I *act* or *perform* or *play*" (English *I* + Latin *ago*), being, to my mind, the most stunning example. But whether or not he actually taught Latin, he was much more attuned to Latin literature than appears on cursory view. Ovid pressures very much of what he writes. So does Seneca. And many others. One thing common to them all, including Shakespeare, is the craft (in all senses) to appropriate pre-scripts that are nonetheless not prescriptive of what they eventually write.

Finally, I can only speculate. But I do, then, speculate that Shakespeare drew powerfully from Latin senses of imitation and emulation, not just in sources and rhetoric, which we have known all along, but also in his poetics of likeness. If the word *like* occurs nearly 2400 times in his writings, if its appearances are so often crucially differential in work after work, it is because, to put it in terms he draws from Ovid's fable of Narcissus, "[t]hings growing to themselves are growth's abuse[—]

> Seeds spring from seeds, and beauty breedeth beauty:
> Thou was begot; to get it is thy duty.
> Upon the earth's increase why shouldst thou feed
> Unless the earth with thy increase be fed?
> By law of nature thou are bound to breed,
> That thine may live when thou thyself art dead;
> And so in spite of death though dost survive,
> In that thy *likeness* still is left alive."
>
> Ven. 166-74 (emphasis added)

Shakespeare was a man and a writer resolved that his "likeness still [be] left alive." I think this is, in part, because he lost Hamnet (Honan 235) — burying one's son fetches on hunger worse than that even Coriolanus suffers. But I also think that it was, finally—simply—"in spite of death."

32
"Almost as like as eggs":
The Winter's Tale

The Winter's Tale is the play in which Shakespeare most relentlessly pursues the issue of hereditary likeness so as to explore, through sexual conflict, its relation to poetic likeness. Leontes suffers paroxysms of doubt about his son's likeness to him. This doubt breeds lines on likeness prolifically. For example: "What? Hast smutched thy nose?/They say it is a copy out of mine" (*WT* 1.2.123-4). Then, again, when Paulina brings his daughter to Leontes, she declares:

> It is yours,
> And might we lay th'old proverb to your charge,
> So *like* you 'tis the worse. Behold, my lords,
> Although the print be little, the whole matter
> And copy of the father:
> ...
> And thou good goddess Nature, which hast made it
> So *like* to him that got it, if thou hast
> The ordering of the mind too, 'mongst all colours
> No yellow in't, lest she suspect, as he does,
> Her children not her husband's.
> *WT* 2.3.96-100; 104-8 (emphasis added)

The most important example, however, for the present argument, is actually one that returns us to Delphos. Leontes says to Mamillius:

> Thou want'st a rough pash and the shoots that I have,
> To be full *like* me. Yet they say we are
> *Almost as like as eggs*. Women say so,
> That will say anything. But were they false
> As o'er-dyed blacks, as wind, as waters, false
> As dice are to be wished by one that fixes

> No bourn 'twixt his and mine, *yet were it true*
> *To say this boy were like me.*
>
> WT 1.2.130-7 (emphasis added)

Recall now Montaigne's argument:

> The consequence we seeke to draw from the conference of events, is unsure, because they are ever dissemblable. No quality is so universall in this surface of things, as variety and diversity. The Greekes, the Latines, and wee use for the most expresse examples of similitude, *that of egs*. Some have nethelesse beene found, especially one in *Delphos*, that knew markes of difference betweene egges, and never tooke one for another. And having divers hennes, could rightly judge which had laid the egge. Dissimilitude doth of it selfe insinuate into our workes, no arte can come neere unto similitude. Resemblance doth not so much make one, as difference maketh another. Nature hath bound herselfe to make nothing that may not be dissemblable.
> "Of Experience," (Florio 322; Frame 815; emphasis added)

I am not concerned to argue that Montaigne is Shakespeare's source, but I am concerned to propose that the difference in eggs is a fertile difference indeed. Leontes sees a difference—else he would not protest so much the likeness he doubts. And the difference he sees is suggested by his simile, "false/As dice are to be wished by one that fixes/No bourn 'twixt his and mine." Leontes sees the difference of deceit—most particularly, of the counterfeit, that which looks identical to the original but in fact conceals its difference from the original, so as to replace the original. And he sees, his simile further suggests, why the counterfeit is so pernicious: it destroys the "bourn 'twixt his and mine."

Throughout his career, Shakespeare returns to the question of property, possession, the vexed problem of mine and thine (Parker, *Margins* 121-2, e.g.). In particular, he was fascinated by the various fictions by which the "bourn 'twixt his and mine" is established. The archetype of such fictions is clearly paternity: paternity is a legal fiction just because there is no "natural" evidence of "authorship" (until DNA-testing in the late 20th century)—the evidence of likeness being (this is the very crux of the matter) inadequate.[1] No degree of likeness is adequate finally and perfectly to allay the fear that difference has interposed itself in sexual relations.

Genealogical succession is always potentially counterfeit. But say there were such a degree of likeness. What then? Then, I think Shakespeare would answer, men would have only false dice to play with, only counterfeits.

Without difference — sexual, hereditary, verbal — there would be no reality in which likeness, fictional or otherwise, could function as a generator of meaning. As Wallace Stevens puts it: "Both in nature and in metaphor identity is the vanishing-point of resemblance" (*Angel* 72). If Mamillius were identical to Leontes — and I think Shakespeare chooses the female, "mammary" name to underscore the necessary difference between them — neither one of them would exist, even as the *statue* of Hermione, because it is identical to the *woman* Hermione, does not exist — it is a (momentary) counterfeit.

The lesson Leontes learns (at high cost) is the lesson of patience before the necessary insecurity of difference — for there to be a "bourn 'twixt his and mine," for there to be property of any sort, there must exist the risk of difference. Though the patriarchy may never rest in its relentless anxiety to control this risk —

> **LEONTES** That "once," I see, by your good father's speed
> Will come on very slowly. I am sorry,
> Most sorry, you [Florizel] have broken from his *liking*
> Where *you were tied in duty* [to marry according to the "good father's" wishes].
> WT 5.1.209-12 (emphasis added)

— we have read enough Shakespeare by now (in particular, *Lear* [1610] 1.1.233 — "[h]ath lost me [Cordelia] in your liking") to know that it is an anxiety that, like all anxiety, misrecognizes its impulse and miscalculates its response (most especially perhaps in the case of Lear). The risk remains, to look to like, if looking liking move, simply because not all are alike and there is everywhere more than *"his* liking" — "I love your majesty/ According to my bond, no more nor less" (*Lr.* [1610] 1.1.92-93).

The artist cannot afford to capitulate to an anxiety about difference. For there to be art, the artist must acknowledge and confess, through any and all devices at his disposal, that his art is different from whatever is construed to be the real — otherwise, he is a counterfeiter only. Nicholas of Cusa writes, helpfully,

> ars nostra formas accidentales, quae sunt similitudines naturalium, inducit in materiam, quam praesupponit.

> (our art induces in its materials, which it presupposes, accidental forms, which are the likenesses of natural [forms]).
> *Sermon* 16; Santinello 256 (my translation)

The forms are *accidental* ("fortuitous," as Wallace Stevens argues[2]), beyond conscious interference, and that is why they are art (and not artificial, or, worse, counterfeit). Art is always accidental, discovering in accidents(/ce) the coincidence that leads to the likeness of knowing.

When Hermione moves, namesake of Hermes as she is, the message she brings from the other is that nature is always more powerful than art. Art can do nothing that nature cannot overwhelm:

> Dissimilitude doth of it selfe insinuate into our workes, no arte can come neere unto similitude. Resemblance doth not so much make one, as difference maketh another. Nature hath bound herselfe to make nothing that may not be dissemblable (322; Frame 815).

But if nature will always overwhelm art, it is art's peculiar gift to acknowledge and confess this, too—after all, it is in a work of art that Shakespeare demonstrates the weakness and limitations of art. Or, to cast the same idea in Shakespeare's own words (which may depend upon Puttenham [Dobson and Wells, *Companion* 360] but are still audibly Shakespearean):

> Yet nature is made better by no mean
> But nature makes that mean. So over that art
> Which you say adds to nature is an art
> That nature makes. You see, sweet maid, we marry
> A gentler scion to the wildest stock,
> And make conceive a bark of baser kind
> By bud of nobler race. This is an art
> Which doth mend nature — change it rather; but
> The art itself is nature.
>   WT 4.4.89-97

The art itself is nature, nature is made better by no mean, or art, but nature makes that mean, or art. Again, we can profit from reading Cusanus:

> ars naturam imitatur, quantum potest, sed nunquam ad ipsius praecisionem poterit pervenire
>
> (art imitates nature, as far as it can, but it will never be able to attain to the precision of nature in its copies)
>   *De docta ignorantia* 2.1; Santinello 255 (my translation)

Nature is alone copious in precision (there are about 34,000 known species of spiders, for example), and art can never, as it were, "catch up": the condition of art is always "quantum potest"; but, like writing that is writing after, art is always *after* nature still, in all senses "after" will bear, because it is part of nature. As Mamillius is to Leontes, so art is to nature; and should nature or art ever go mad (or be pushed to madness?) and demand that each be identical to the other, then the life of man, as we know it, would cease: there would be no nature, there would be no art, there would be only the machine of identity—precision so precise that accidents(/ce) and hence coincidence would cease to be.[3]

Hence the statue must awaken. The statue must be seen to be a counterfeit. Otherwise nature has disappeared. But what we humans need, given what we humans are, is art *and* nature, and this need will continue until we are human no longer. Because of this need and because of the structures that condition it, we also need faith. "It is required/You do awake your faith" (*WT* 5.3.94-95), declares Paulina to Leontes before the statue. Faith is the obverse of counterfeiting; *legal* tender is creditable—you can have faith in it. You can believe ("be-like") that it is as current for you as it is for others, no unlawful aggrandizement hidden within it. Your faith in it, your trust or belief, is your willingness to be like it, to represent yourself by it when you buy with it: I am an honest person and I honestly represent my desire for such and such an object with this currency; in this currency I abide by the law of exchange that renders each his due according to the value of his currency.

Not for nothing, therefore, does Leontes cry out:

> O, she's warm!
> If this be *magic*, let it be *an art*
> *Lawful* as *eating*.
>
> *WT* 5.3.109-11 (emphasis added)

I have emphasized four words in this passage on which a very great deal depends—*magic, art, lawful, eating*. Leontes's first reaction is to assume magic. Magic is the agency that abolishes the distinction between art and nature (by distracting your attention from it). But, significantly, his faith leaves room for its obverse, doubt: "*If* this be magic." But if it is, let it not be magic after all, let it be rather art.[4] Let it be art that *is* art, not counterfeit, but lawful, current art that can pass as current in any exchange, art that I can believe in, be like. Indeed, let it be as lawful as eating is: as eating is to nature, let this art be to law. But no, that's not quite right. Eating is not lawful; eating is a primal necessity that all creatures obey. To call eating "lawful" is already to have coupled convention and nature, *nomos* and *physis*, the human and the non-human, thus to have acknowledged the likeness and the difference, syneciotically, that obtains between them, their mutuality (the primal necessity of eating is "together at home with" the notion of law). Hence, to say "[l]et it be an art lawful as eating" is not only to say, "let it not be counterfeit or false or a deceit," but also "let it be as full of justice in its domain as eating is in the domain of nature" (notice that "justice" is not the same thing as "right" or "license" or "liberty"). And since eating is primal, preceding art and law, this, then, is also to have said that nature makes the art in its justice. Nature teaches us that eating is so necessary it should be lawful; nature teaches us that art is so necessary, it should be lawful:

> Yet nature is made better by no mean
> But nature makes that mean.
> ...
>   This is an art
> Which does mend nature — change it rather; but
> The art itself is nature.
> WT 4.4.89-90; 95-97

Only nature creates the new—only (the art of) nature changes nature. Only nature can make the "art" of Hermione's "statue."[5] And thus Shakespeare informs us, after a lifetime of practice, that when the work of art comes to life, as on the stage, it is also, justly, a work of nature we are believing, be-liking, putting our faith in. It is art lawful as eating (and eating, communion, lawful as art, unlike the unlawful eating in the garden of Eden).

Shakespeare of all poets wrote least like him*self* (the artificial) and most *like* himself ("negative capability" Keats calls it), according to nature:

>   ...let your own
> discretion be your tutor. Suit the action to the word,
> the word to the action, with this special observance:
> that you o'erstep not the modesty of nature. For
> anything so overdone is from the purpose of playing,
> whose end, both at the first and now, was and is to
> hold as 'twere the mirror up to nature, to show virtue
> her own feature, scorn her own image, and the very
> age and body of the time his form and pressure.
> Ham. 3.2.16-24

The Norton edition, for example, glosses "the very age and body of the time his form and pressure" with "the true state of things at present, in shape ('form') and *likeness (as a stamp pressed in wax)*" (1708n6; emphasis added). I would hazard the following as a tentative, provisional conclusion to my years of work with the word *like* in Shakespeare's plays, that the word teaches us why we are im*press*ed by his art—we (be-) like it.[6]

33
"The Action of My Life is Like It": The Posthumus Theater of Likeness in *Cymbeline*

Shakespeare is quick to introduce the theater of likeness in *Cymbeline*:

> **FIRST GENTLEMAN**   [H]e that hath her —
> I mean that married her — alack, good man,
> And therefore banished! — is a creature such
> As, to seek through the regions of the earth
> For one his *like*, there would be something failing
> In him that should compare. I do not think
> So fair an outward and such stuff within
> Endows a man but he.
>
> Cym. 1.1.17-24

Posthumus Leonatus is without a *like* "through the regions of the earth." It is imperative for Shakespeare to establish Posthumus's singularity as quickly as possible, for his is the character that stamps the play, so I will argue, more than that of any other, even the unforgettable Innogen.[1] For Posthumus performs an understanding of likeness that may possibly be as close to Shakespeare's own as we will ever approach.

In act 5, scene 5, waiting in jail to die by hanging, Posthumus dreams and in his dream experiences an extraordinary vision. Upon awakening from this dream, he discovers a book by his side:

> A book? O rare one,
> Be not, as is our fangled world, a garment
> Nobler than that it covers. Let thy effects
> So follow to be most *unlike* our courtiers,
> As good as promise.
>   *He reads*
>   "Whenas a lion's whelp shall, to himself unknown,
>   without seeking find, and be embraced by a piece of

> tender air; and when from a stately cedar shall be
> lopped branches which, being dead many years, shall
> after revive, be jointed to the old stock, and freshly
> grow; then shall Posthumus end his miseries, Britain
> be fortunate and flourish in peace and plenty."
> 'Tis still a dream, or else such stuff as madmen
> Tongue, and brain not; either both, or nothing,
> Or senseless speaking, or a speaking such
> As sense cannot untie. Be what it is,
> *The action of my life is like it*, which I'll keep,
> If but for sympathy.
>
> Cym. 5.5.227-44 (emphasis added)

"The action of my life is like it" is a post-script by Posthumus. It is not a prescript. No one in his right mind would live his life as this book prescribes—"such stuff as madmen/Tongue and brain not." But Posthumus on the eve of his execution can see and say that it is his P.S.—this is what the action of my life sounded *like*. And I will keep this book, which the action of my life sounded like, "if but for sympathy," that is, according to the Norton edition's gloss, "if only for the similarity." Here in his mature command of his craft Shakespeare shares his mature understanding of likeness. Each of us seeks the likeness that will identify him or her, as well to him- or herself as to the world, but many of us learn, often only through immense suffering, that none of the prescriptive likenesses that precede us—parental, social, religious, political, etc.—is the likeness he or she most is like; all of these prescripts are pre-emptive, to some extent or other, of the likeness I like. If I live my life, for example, according to my father's likeness of me as a butcher—Shakespeare butchered, illegally, for his father, John, who was a glover and needed the skins for his trade—I may deprive myself of my likeness as a thespian—although, apparently, Shakespeare performed his butchering with some panache, showing already his true likeness (Aubrey 289; Honan 416).

I can only know my likeness posthumously. I must already be dead or on the verge of death. Or, as John Freccero (1988) would say of Dante and St. Augustine, I must die to my self, my old man (the Pauline "vetus homo"), through a conversion experience that leaves me a new man (the Pauline "novus homo"), who can read his past life as a whole text in retrospect. But, as soon as I put it in terms of Dante and Augustine, and orthodox Catholic Christianity, we can see the unique difference of Shakespeare, who, if emotionally Catholic, was perforce politically Protestant, since for him, consummate dramatist, every con*version* is a new likeness, a new version of the self, being tested in a world where the fashioning of likenesses, versions of the self, is but the *sprezzatura* of courtiers. No, for Shakespeare, the threat of death must be real—the hangman has to be waiting in the wings—otherwise, any one can fake it. And even then, as the case of Sir Walter Ralegh suggests, one cannot be so sure (Beer, *Ralegh* 82-108; Greenblatt, *Roles* 1-21).

But one can still learn a lot about the likes of a man who is about to die—Ralegh's speech from the scaffold tells us at least of enormous courage. One can read his posthumous likeness in that moment of exquisite non-indeterminacy (note that it is not determinacy but non-indeterminacy).[2] So, too, with Shakespeare's Posthumus. I am most interested, in the otherwise spirited and inspiring repartee between Posthumus and his Jailer (*Cym.* 5.5.245-300), in Posthumus's true likeness, as I think of it. Posthumus speaks as one who has come to know his likeness posthumously: "I tell thee, fellow, there are none want eyes to direct them the way I am going but such as wink and will not use them" (*Cym.* 5.5.279-81). None there are who want *I*'s to direct them the way I, Posthumus, am going but such as wink and will not use them: everyone who is to die, which is every one, has an *I* to death unless he winks. He has, in that moment of exquisite non-indeterminacy, his P.S.: he can posthumously accept the text that has befallen him—"The action of my life is like it, which I'll keep if but for sympathy"—or he can wink, and the ink will dry on a likeness not like his life. Thrown, as Heidegger says (*Being* 174, 219ff.) into a world not of his making, Dasein can be resolute to death or inauthentic to life. Being-unto-death, for a creature who *must* die, none excepted, gives meaning to life, it seems to me Shakespeare also learned, in just the measure to which, living thus posthumously, I am always prepared to write my post-script, which by definition is *mine*. Thus, surely the greatest example in the tragedies, Othello's post-script (*Oth.* 5.2.347-65, and, above, chapter 24 pages 246-7). As I have argued, though he learned only in the last possible moment, Othello nonetheless manages to write his post-script, and it is Othello in the end, not Iago, who dictates what his amanuenses will report to the Venetian state. Hence, the overwhelming importance of F's reading, "Iudean," as opposed to the Quarto's reading "Indian," since Othello is deliberately writing his post-script to conform his *I* to the likeness and the life of Judas Iscariot, who killed his savior and then hanged himself in despair. Such is Othello's choice—"The action of his life is like it"—and this is why it hurts us so much to watch it: *he* chooses this likeness, it is *his* post-script, however unfair (unlike?) it seems.

Posthumus is not the only character in *Cymbeline* to live his life and his likeness posthumously. Belarius does, too:

> Your pleasure was my mere offence, my punishment
> Itself, and all my treason. That I suffered
> Was all the harm I did.
> ...
> Their nurse Euriphile,
> Whom for the theft I wedded, stole these children
> Upon my banishment. I moved her to't,
> *Having receved the punishment before*
> *For that which I did then.* Beaten for loyalty
> Excited me to treason. Their dear loss,
> The more of you 'twas felt, the more it shaped
> Unto my end of stealing them.
>
> Cym. 5.6.335-7; 341-8 (emphasis added)

Unjustly punished by Cymbeline, Belarius authored his post-script, "[t]he action of my life is like it," and stole Cymbeline's sons in order to conform his life and *like*ness to that which he otherwise could not eschew, "which I'll keep/If but for sympathy."

Like Posthumus, like Belarius, Shakespeare too is *bela*ted. Every plot, every story, every source is a pre-script beliking him to a likeness he cannot simply acquiesce in—he must write his post-script (not Greene's, not Marlowe's, not Kyd's, not Fletcher's, but his). He cannot change the world of misogyny, but he can at least imagine a world in which Innogen is the "tender air" and *tender heir* who, perforce disinherited by brothers (*Cym.* 5.6.453), is still the heir if they fail, as Shakespeare well knew. He can imagine a world in which men feel guilt for their actions and, under the pressure of guilt, begin to change. He can imagine a world in which men at least acknowledge that

> it is place which lessens and sets off,
> And you may then revolve what tales I have told you
> Of courts, of princes, of the tricks in war;
> That service is not service, so being done,
> But being so allowed.
>
> Cym. 3.3.13-17

Above all, he can imagine a world of growth and its discontents.

This he does, in *Cymbeline*, through the arboreal imagery—trees, roots, leaves, branches, trunks. From the very beginning of the play, "I cannot delve him [Posthumus] to the root" (*Cym.* 1.1.28), to Belarius's reminiscence,

> Then was I as a tree
> Whose boughs did bend with fruit; but in one night
> A storm or robbery, call it what you will,
> Shook down my mellow hangings, nay, my leaves,
> And left me bare to weather
>
> *Cym.* 3.3.60-64,

to Arviragus's impassioned

> Grow patience,
> And let the stinking elder, grief, untwine
> His perishing root with the increasing vine.
>
> *Cym.* 4.2.60-62,

to the mysterious book Posthumus discovers, "when from a stately cedar shall be lopped branches which, being dead many years, shall after revive, be jointed to the old stock, and freshly grow" (*Cym.* 5.5.234-7), to Posthumus's extraordinary declaration to Innogen: "Hang there like fruit, my soul,/Till the tree die" (*Cym.* 5.6.263-4), to Cymbeline's unforgettable: "This fierce abridgement/Hath to it circumstantial branches which/ Distinction should be rich in" (*Cym.* 5.6.383-5), Shakespeare insists on the likeness and difference between trees and men. The difference is determinative. To grasp it the likeness is needed, but the difference is determinative. Men do not grow like trees. Men have only metaphoric roots; bipedal and ambulatory, they can not be rooted in the same way a tree is. Similarly, men have only metaphoric limbs, leaves, and vines. Men have no continuous growth rings; their likeness does not emerge from a root that exfoliates itself in one place spreading outward year after year the same but more. Men's growth is more catastrophic. Men are more often, and more terribly, uprooted. Violent events punctuate men's growth. Men are (to use Aristotelian categories) animal as well as vegetative, which is to say, locomotive and ever restless, ever rootless, and if philosophy calls mankind *arbor inversa* (his "root" or mind in the sky),[3] this, again, is only metaphoric. The desire the metaphor inscribes is the desire for place, "a local habitation and a name," but all mankind is displaced persons, no matter to which myth of our fall you subscribe. And Theseus is right about "airy nothing[s]" (*MND* 5.1.16).

A tree is almost the perfect likeness of a pre-script, its fruit emerging from an always discernible a priori. Men, in contrast, are creatures of the post-script, who ever live posthumously, retrospectively adjusting the ever restless psyche to another postulate of roots—o, do I belong here now? or do I, as usual, just long-to-be? *Cymbeline* is *the* play in Shakespeare's canon of the irreparable rootlessness of the human condition. Even Britain is Roman. No matter how deeply men may desire roots, they cannot be trees: "Hang there like fruit, my soul,/Till the tree die" is beautiful but also it is an "airy nothing." It cannot be, and Posthumus knows it, pre-scriptive. At best, it can be descriptive. Posthumus understands, better perhaps than any Shakespearean protagonist, the limits on human pre-scripts:

> Kneel not to me.
> The power that I have on you is to spare you,
> The malice towards you to forgive you. Live,
> And deal with others better.
>
> *Cym.* 5.6.418-21

The most powerful human pre-script is in fact the post-script, I forgive you: you do not have to conform your life any longer to this action that it was like, this pre-script that obligated you to me, perhaps it may have been by guilt; your life may now be like a different action, a different act, a different scene, a different script, a different play. "Live,/And deal with others better," like Jesus of Nazareth's "Go, and sin no more" (John 8:11), is the erasure of the writing, such writing as Jesus writes in the sand as he kneels before the woman taken in adultery, that has no legalistic claim against your likeness. But, as you will see, this is, then, just so, to be rootless.

And yet, someone is prepared to object, surely Posthumus Leonatus has always been Posthumus Leonatus, Belarius always Belarius, Innogen always Innogen, Arviragus always Arviragus, Guiderius always Guiderius, and Cymbeline always Cymbeline—he never changes. Surely, all the asides about breeding revealing itself, about the nature of nobility shining through (*Cym.* 3.3.79-98, e.g.), suggest that the very fiction or construct that the wealthy and the powerful insist on displaying to the masses is that of rootedness—we were always here and it has always been like this, do not think to revolt! Surely, this play inscribes Jacobean ideology of place and position by subversion and containment of the opposition. Surely, as the feminists argue, *Cymbeline* "seems able to reprove the most virulent forms of misogyny only when it simultaneously removes women from public power, transforms them into chaste, domesticated wives, and reaffirms the dominance of husbands" (Norton 2963); moreover, in the play, "Britain renews itself as women are disempowered or disappear. ... This is the dream of androgenesis, reproduction without union with women" (Norton 2962). Surely, Posthumus is the most prescriptive of monstrous masculinists in his notorious, perhaps even infamous, outburst of scathing misogyny:

> Is there no way for men to be, but women
> Must be half-workers? We are bastards all,
> And that most venerable man which I
> Did call my father was I know not where
> When I was stamped. Some coiner with his tools
> Made me a counterfeit;
> ...
>   I'll write against them [women],
> Detest them, curse them, yet 'tis greater skill
> In a true hate to pray they have their will.
>
> Cym. 2.5.1-6; 32-34

Surely, this play is replete with "a true hate," and nothing you can say about likenesses, post-scripts, and trees can change that.

Perhaps not. But my distress at these and other similar objections is their regular and predictable aversion to the specificity of Shakespeare's poetry. The very pregnancy of his poetry, which for me is the most inspiring feature of his access to the feminine within him, is bound in favor of an ideological scruple about the masculinism and patriarchalism of appropriating to his poetry any access to the feminine in him in the first place—he is in a jail from which neither vision nor book can liberate him.

But is it not possible to imagine that Shakespeare could both understand why Cymbeline would exclaim

>   O, what am I?
> A mother to the birth of three? Ne'er mother
> Rejoiced deliverance more.
>
> Cym.5.6.369-71

and recognize at the same time the posthumousness of the likeness? Even Cymbeline knows that this is "such stuff as madmen/Tongue, and brain not"—he is no mother—but "[t]he action of his life is like it," and he keeps it "if but for sympathy." If there are only men on stage at the end of *Cymbeline* (Innogen, of course, is a boy player), a common observation by feminism, is it not possible that Shakespeare could conclude that men are the ones in need of change, in need of posthumous likenesses, in need of (I will risk saying it) likening themselves to mothers and fruit-bearing trees? (Note that I am not essentializing women; I am instead referring to specific reproductive capacities.) It seems to me at least warrantable by a minimal humanity to allow Shakespeare the feeling in Cymbeline's response to Belarius:

> Thou weep'st, and speak'st.
> The service that you three have done is more
> *Unlike* than this thou tell'st. I lost my children.
> If these be they, I know not how to wish
> A pair of worthier sons.
>
> *Cym.* 5.6.353-7 (emphasis added)

For it is only, and possibly ever, through the *unlike* that we discover our like and likeness.

Which, finally, I take to be also the response, if not rebuttal, to the outcry against Posthumus's scathing misogyny. Scathing misogyny it surely is, but Posthumus *does change*:

> Let me make men know
> More valour in me than my habits show.
> Gods, put the strength o'th' Leonati in me.
> To shame the guise o'th' world, I will begin
> The fashion — less without and more within.
>
> *Cym.* 5.1.29-33

It is he who knows from the moment he thinks Innogen dead that he must live (his *like*ness) posthumously, always writing his postscript, "less without and more within"; and it is change, his growth, unlike a tree's growth in its massive dislocation, its catastrophic upheaval, that causes his character to stamp the play, to make the play posthumous—(writing) after writing.

More than Prospero's wand and book, more than Giulio Romano's statue, Posthumus's "fashion," I think, is Shakespeare's testament and legacy to the world: "less without and more within." It is the interiority, the ever unexpected inwardness, of his art that repeatedly takes our breath away and leaves us convinced that he is superior to all other English poets no matter how excellent in their craft they may be. It is to his art that we know we can always turn for "more within:"

> A book? O rare one,
> Be not, as is our fangled world, *a garment*
> *Nobler than that it covers*. Let thy effects
> So follow to be most *unlike* our courtiers,
> As good as promise.
>
> *Cym.* 5.5.227-31 (emphasis added)

Has any other writer ever made better on the promise that his book is "not

... a garment/Nobler than that it covers"? If we look, we always see "more within," even when we think we have seen it all—the inwordness of his writing chastens our presumption; and we feel, if we pause to think about it, that one very appropriate synonym for Keats's "negative capability" is "humility" (possibly what, also, the old king Cymbeline expresses when he exclaims "[a] mother to the birth of three"). Certainly, humility seems very pertinent when Posthumus's jailer, with whom he debated death in "an infinite mock," concludes, as he unfetters Posthumus to lead him away:

> I would we were all of one mind, and one mind good.
> O, there were desolation of jailers and gallowses! I speak against my present profit, but my wish hath a preferment in't.
>
> *Cym.* 5.5.296-300

We know, all of us, that we will never be "all of one mind," much less "one mind good"—such humility is beyond us. But we also know, if cynicism has not corroded the spirit within us entirely, that the "wish hath a preferment in 't." It is our loss (punishment for our pride) that we cannot say "[t]he action of [our lives] is like it"; but we keep Shakespeare's book anyway—"O rare one ... if but for sympathy." Some of us are even buried with it.

34
"Nor can imagination form a shape,/ Besides yourself, to like of": The End of Imagination in *The Tempest*

> Good wombs have borne bad sons.
> *Tmp.* 1.2.120

Like Chartres Cathedral, like Michelangelo's David, like the *Ninth Symphony*, like *Guernica*, *The Tempest* is one of the works of art by which we know what we are like:

> Our revels now are ended. These our actors,
> As I foretold you, were all spirits, and
> Are melted into air, into thin air;
> And *like* the baseless fabric of this vision,
> The cloud-capped towers, the gorgeous palaces,
> The solemn temples, the great globe itself,
> Yea, all which it inherit, shall dissolve;
> And, *like* this insubstantial pageant faded,
> Leave not a rack behind. We are such stuff
> As dreams are made on, and our little life
> Is rounded with a sleep.
> *Tmp.* 4.1.148-58 (emphasis added)

Such a reminder of our likeness is precious to us in just the measure to which we all too frequently, and frighteningly easily, forget it—The Thirty Years War, Ireland, the Holocaust. And yet, as cultural-materialist criticism has demonstrated in the past 25 years, *The Tempest* hardly excludes our other likeness. Colonialism, imperialism, eco-tyranny, etc., are also clearly evident in the play (Graff and Phelan). In many respects, the play is a devastatingly accurate and depressing representation of and commentary on human depravity. From this perspective, turned just slightly to a harsher light, the play is as dark as *Troilus and Cressida* or *Measure for Measure*. Look what brother does to brother. Look what he did to Caliban. Whatever we touch we spoil.

The Tempest manages to display its insights about our likeness with a remarkable calm; the oxymoron is deliberate, "calm tempest." This is owing, in part, and obviously, to the mastery of the mature artist, who knows his craft, what can and cannot be done with it (he cannot save Caliban). I think it is also owing to a resignation on the mature artist's part, represented, we know, by the fate of Prospero's book and wand (*Tmp.* 5.1.54-57), but much plainer and to the point, I believe, in the line I choose for the title of my chapter: "Nor can imagination form a shape/Besides yourself to like of" (*Tmp.* 3.1.56-57).

There is an end to imagination, and it is our like, *likam*, body and corpse. Imagination cannot form a shape besides our body to like of. (Technology may do so at some future date, by cloning or digitizing, but that will be no longer the *human* body, the *human* likeness—it will be a posthuman body cyborgized to a different likeness.) The end of imagination is the human body, the human likeness. (Hence Caliban's fate.) Finally, we must return to live in our bodies, which is also to die in them. Old Gonzalo speaks far more than he comprehends of Shakespeare's final understanding of likeness:

> in one voyage
> Did Claribel her husband find at Tunis,
> And Ferdinand her brother found a wife
> Where he himself was lost; Prospero his dukedom
> In a poor isle; *and all of us ourselves,*
> *When no man was his own.*
>   *Tmp.* 5.1.211-16 (emphasis added)

It is this discovery—"all of us [found] ourselves / When no man was his own"—that most interests Shakespeare and that signs the work most assuredly as his: how one comes to (find) oneself when one is not one's own. Looking back over the entire corpus, some 40 works, we see (it would be difficult not to see) a writer convinced that no one finds a likeness when she is her own or he is his own—no one *owns* his or her likeness ("Known unto these, and to myself disguised!" [*CE* 2.2.217]). It simply doesn't work like that. It works more like the plea in the Epilogue (lines 15-20) as Prospero takes his leave:

> And my ending is despair
> Unless I be relieved by prayer,
> Which pierces so, that it assaults
> Mercy itself, and frees all faults.
> As you from crimes would pardoned be,
> Let your indulgence set me free.

It works by mutuality or it works not at all.

Still, Shakespeare knows and never lets us forget the alternative, its common name, hatred. The people hate their rulers, the rulers hate the people, children hate parents, parents hate children, men hate women, women hate men, white hates black, west hates east, and so on ad nauseam. Nowhere in the canon do I see any shrinking from the fact. To the contrary, very few artists in our history have chronicled human hatred as William Shakespeare has done — just re-read *Othello* any time you doubt it. But at the same time, an ethic of mutuality is also palpable, indeed unavoidable, throughout the same canon. I will never know what I'm like just by looking in a mirror; I must look in you, as you look in me, to know my like(ness). "As you from crimes would pardoned be,/Let your indulgence set me free."

Our truest likeness, I conjecture Shakespeare to have believed, is forgiveness:

> **PROSPERO** Hast thou [Ariel], which art but air, a touch, a feeling
> Of their afflictions, and shall not myself,
> *One of their kind*, that relish all as sharply
> Passion as they, be kindlier moved than thou art?
> Though with their high wrongs I am struck to th' quick,
> Yet with my nobler reason 'gainst my fury
> Do I take part. *The rarer action is*
> *In virtue than in vengeance*. They being penitent,
> The sole drift of my purpose doth extend
> Not a frown further.
>
> *Tmp.* 5.1.21-30 (emphasis added)

It is, to be sure, the "rarer action"; there can be no disputing its rarity (and it exposes the divided self—"'gainst my fury/Do I take part"). But when it is the action taken, on those rare occasions, the first consequence is that we are not copies of each other. The first effect of forgiveness is difference, or, if you prefer, change: I set you free, you set me free, we go on each to a life of each's own.

> For you, most wicked sir, whom to call brother
> Would even infect my mouth, I do forgive
> Thy rankest fault, all of them, and require
> My dukedom of thee, which perforce I know
> Thou must restore.
>
> *Tmp.* 5.1.132-6

And thus Antonio is no longer a pseudo-Prospero, ruling as Prospero's malefic copy in Milan. Without something like this, call it by its etymology, "to give away [<*forgive*]," our "ending is despair."

This is not idealism, once you stop to think about it. If your end is life, then it is very practical politics, very workable politics, since it provides a chance for each to pursue each's likeness in a community of mutuality where all may benefit from the freedom of each. But if your end is death, vengeance is your better politics, to be sure. Vengeance will ensure a politics of scarcity so that a cabal of the few may triumph by exploiting the desire of all to live in a community.

> **PROSPERO**...[Antonio]...now...was
> The ivy which had hid my princely trunk
> And sucked my verdure out on't.
> ...
>   *like one*
> Who having into truth, by telling oft,
> Made such a sinner of his memory
> To credit his own lie, *he did believe*
> *He was indeed the Duke*. Out o'th' substitution,
> And executing th' outward face of royalty
> With all prerogative, hence his ambition growing —
> ...
> To have no screen between this *part he played*
> And him he played it for, he needs will be
> Absolute Milan. Me, poor man — my library
> Was dukedom large enough — of temporal royalties
> He thinks me now incapable; confederates,
> So dry he was for sway, wi'th' King of Naples.
>   *Tmp*. 1.2.85-87; 99-105; 107-1 (emphasis added)

I have quoted just enough of Prospero's recounting for Miranda their earlier fate that we may hear how vengeance works to deplete being and substitute copies—"he did believe / He was indeed the duke, out o' the substitution." The theater of likeness sees and shows that the crisis is one of copying: "this part he [Antonio] played"—Antonio copied his brother's role. But it is also, and in just this way, a crisis of likeness as the deficiency of likeness: "now he was/The ivy which had hid my princely trunk,/ And sucked my verdure out on't." Antonio is not Prospero's twin, he is Prospero's parasite; Shakespeare's imagery suggests not mere copying but parasitic depletion ("sucked my verdure out on't"). The distinction is inexaggerably important. By relinquishing his authority to a brother *too little like* him, Prospero helps to "beget" a parasite:

> in my false brother
> Awaked an evil nature; and my trust,
> *Like a good parent*, did *beget* of him
> A falsehood.
> *Tmp.* 1.2.92-95 (emphasis added)

Had the brothers been more alike, the one would not have become a parasite upon the other. In the precision of his imagery Shakespeare demonstrates that likeness, which is neither identity nor difference, is the ground of any community; but it is no guarantee of such community, even as, to quote Miranda, "[g]ood wombs have borne bad sons" (*Tmp.* 1.2.120)—a line, we may pause to observe, that sums up a very great deal of Shakespeare's art.[1]

Much is made in recent criticism of Prospero's apparent revulsion from female sexuality (see, among many, Menon 152-3), the "one thing" he will not name (*Tmp.* 1.2.267-8). To those for whom finally Shakespeare is a man who hates sex (or embodies a repressed sexuality of relentless, insistent gnawing), Prospero's attitude to Sycorax is infinitely telling. I am one who thinks Shakespeare hated division, not sex. I should acknowledge here, then, that, as I see it, Prospero's insistence that Ferdinand not break Miranda's "virgin-knot" (*Tmp.* 4.1.14-19; 51-54) is not revulsion from sex or the sex act but fear—a logical fear, I think — that if they couple here, on this island, in this atmosphere of magic and dark powers, a good womb will bear a bad son. The good womb (of Miranda) may bear a bad son anyway—after all, Prospero and Antonio are brothers (and who is the bad son?) — but if Ferdinand and Miranda wait for Hymen's blessing and until they have left the island, they will also have waited until Prospero has broken his wand and drowned his book, eschewing not only Venus and Cupid (*Tmp.* 4.1.91-101) but also the *doubt*ful prosperity of magic—"my trust/*Like* a good parent, did *beget* of him/A falsehood" (*Tmp.* 1.2.93-95; emphasis added).

Hence the terrible disturbance Caliban introduces into the play, as the offspring of Sycorax (whose is presumably not a "good womb") and thus a creature even less like Prospero than Antonio, Prospero's brother: he is "like/ A thing most brutish" whose "vile race/... had that in't which good natures/ [Can] not abide to be with" (*Tmp.* 1.2.358-62). Caliban is, obviously, *cannibal*, extremest form of parasite. Little more than talking animal, and that only by intervention of Prospero, he is Shakespeare's embodiment of unlikeness. "I have used thee," Prospero fumes, "[f]ilth as thou art, with human care," but the difference was insuperable; "and lodged thee/In mine own cell," where the one likeness, after hunger, most common to all creatures erupted, "till thou didst seek to violate/The honour of my child":

> **CALIBAN** O ho, O ho! Would't had been done!
> Thou didst prevent me; I had peopled else
> This isle with Calibans.
>
> *Tmp.* 1.2.351-53

He would have littered the island with copies of himself, his likeness. He has learned enough language not only to know how to curse (*Tmp.* 1.2.366-7) but also to estimate rightly the power of reproduction: when the isle had been peopled with Calibans, he would no longer have been unlike(d).

It is what we all want, to be like(d). None of us wants to be the alien, unlike(d). And yet, if anyone should accuse another of merely trying to be like the group or liked in the group, then furious indignation erupts and he or she instantly claims to be unique, individual, eccentric, etc., etc. We are nothing if not self-contradictory. Still, the majority of humans fear being unlike(d) and will admit it if they can. Even Caliban, hardly human, can, improbably, despite all appearances to the contrary, learn at least a bit of what it is to be like(d):

> **PROSPERO**   (*To Caliban*) Go, sirrah, to my cell.
> Take with you your companions. *As you look*
> *To have my pardon,* trim it handsomely.
> **CALIBAN** Ay, that I will; *and I'll be wise hereafter,*
> *And seek for grace.*
>
> *Tmp.* 5.1.295-9 (emphasis added)

Even Caliban can learn something of the theater of likeness and become more discreet in choosing a likeness to worship. Even Caliban can learn to "seek for grace," which is to like to be liked.

The precision of Shakespeare's language, even at its most exuberant (this is also true of Dante in my experience) is so astonishing that we often must pause for a very deep breath before we feel all that we have taken in. The hint that Caliban might be humanized, although only a hint (and hardly an excuse for colonialist imperialism), is all the same audible in Shakespeare's text and chastens our too easy assumption that his politics might be unilaterally alien(ating). His imagination, I think, is too expansive for that. He can imagine more in our likeness than all other but a very few artists:

The End of Imagination in *The Tempest* 353

MIRANDA O wonder!
How many goodly creatures are there here!
How beauteous mankind is! O brave new world
That has such people in't!

Tmp. 5.1.184-7

Oft-quoted though they be, these lines perhaps may be quoted again, in the present context, just to remind us of how much Shakespeare can imagine in our likeness. Certainly, he can imagine Antonio, the parasite, looking upon the sleeping king Alonso, saying, "[i]f he were that which now he's *like*—that's dead" (*Tmp.* 2.1.287), but he can also imagine Prospero saying to Alonso,

PROSPERO I rather think
You have not sought her [patience's] help, of whose soft grace
For the *like* loss I have her sovereign aid,
And rest myself content.
ALONSO You the *like* loss?

Tmp. 5.1.143-6 (emphasis added)

where, although the scene is nothing but Prospero's invention and neither loss is the case, still the invention serves to liken two who were once mortal enemies (*Tmp.* 1.2.121-2) but are now to be friends, like each other, by the marriage of their children. Such is the theater of likeness for Shakespeare in his final hour that he can imagine love at first sight, "[a]t the first sight/ They have changed eyes" (*Tmp.* 1.2.443-4), in homage to both Marlowe and Ovid, even as, at the same time, he acknowledges that if heterosexual love is to have any hope, it must begin in an exchange of I's. No one is his or her own. I am, as you like it.

What is it men in women do require?
The lineaments of Gratified Desire.
What is it women do in men require?
The lineaments of Gratified Desire.

"Several Questions Answered"
William Blake

35
"Said I for this the girl was like to him?": Is All True in *All Is True*?

For purposes of understanding Shakespeare's theater of likeness *Henry VIII* or *All Is True* is a very important play. One of the most controversial plays in the canon (it is included in the First Folio), it is important just where it is most controversial and resistant to critical categories—is it, for example, a history or a romance? Probably the next to the last play that Shakespeare undertook, he almost certainly collaborated on it with John Fletcher, and this collaboration has been the source of critical dispute for centuries. In this dispute, I find most convincing the arguments of those who assume that there was collaboration, that the play is not exclusively by Shakespeare, and I am convinced because, just as I would predict from studying Shakespeare's theater of likeness, the parts of the play that are, according to the best findings, his, are just those where the work of the word *like* is most audible—where, in short, it is his signature. Nowhere is this signature more evident, I think, than in act 5, scene 1 (the latest in the play we can see, we think, Shakespeare's collaboration):

> **OLD LADY** 'Tis a girl
> Promises boys hereafter. Sir, your queen
> Desires your visitation, *and to be*
> *Acquainted with this stranger. 'Tis as like you*
> *As cherry is to cherry.*
> **KING HENRY** Lovell —
> **LOVELL** Sir?
> **KING HENRY** Give her an hundred marks. I'll to the Queen. *Exit*
> **OLD LADY** An hundred marks...
> I will have more, or scold it out of him.
> *Said I for this the girl was like to him?*
> *All is True* 5.1.166-72; 174-5 (emphasis added)

Here is the theater of likeness we have come to recognize in Shakespeare's works: anxiety over the likeness of child to parent, the anxiety of genealogical succession, and the concomitant anxiety over epistemology, knowing by likeness—hence the incontestable importance of the second title that history records for the play, *All is True*, which generations of critics and scholars have recognized is deeply ironic (hence also the second question mark in the title to my chapter).

Not all is true in *All is True* if by "true" we mean to invoke a canon of verifiability, a post-Cartesian mathesis of certitude. All is true in *All is True* only within a canon of likeness, and that is why, predictably, there are many kinds of "true" in the play, not just one. In this regard, the play is, probably, as much romance as it is history (*Riverside* 1024), and, as in the romances, so in *All is True*, we find a surprisingly deep meditation on daughters, Elizabeth Tudor, of course, and probably also Elizabeth Stuart, if at a more distant remove. In a very real sense, Elizabeth Tudor is the term of the play, and if Fletcher wrote Cranmer's speech, still the spirit of the speech is Shakespeare's. Its truth is the truth of romance superimposed upon a different and various history that varies from that truth but without displacing it. It is truth like the truth that men and women would have liked to believe ("be-like").

In this way, it is an old truth or even old-fashioned truth. It is the truth as in Middle English *trawþe*, fidelity first and foremost to persons and those codes of honor by which persons relate to each other. It is now long since a commonplace that Early Modern England sees the dissolution of this old-fashioned *trawþe* in the turmoil of capital (Halpern, Howard, Kamps, e.g.). It is hardly necessary to repeat those arguments here. What does bear attention, however, is the way in which the word *like* marks the transition from *trawþe* to "truth." After long reading in 16th- and early 17th-century texts, I have found that *like* frequently appears just where the post-Cartesian world would expect *proof, approval, approbation* (*probation*) or, generally, empirical evidence presented to the parties as opposed to emotional accord between the parties.

Examples are in order. Consider, first, an extremely simple one, so simple as to be easy to overlook.

> **NORFOLK**   *Like* it your grace,
> The state takes notice of the private difference
> Betwixt you and the Cardinal.
>   *All Is True* 1.1.100-2

It is very easy to say, "well, this is just conventional politesse": "may it please your grace," "if your grace is amenable," etc., something like.[1] But what the language *does* say is, "is it like your grace": the conventional formula respects an understanding of truth as being like the one addressed with the truth.

Now consider more telling examples:

> I have been careful not to touch on matters of religion, knowing that he would greatly *dislike* persuasion to alter that religion he has been bred up in.

> For I will not stretch my commission to deal in such matters, and much less to put them at liberty and to deliver them into the town's hands. Being the Queen's subjects, and not required neither of this said town, I know not how it would have been *liked*, especially since part of that which they did counterfeit was Her Majesty's coin.
> Nicholl, Reckoning 197, 235 (emphasis added)

> I know the inconstancy of the people of England, how they ever *mislike* the present government and have their eyes fixed upon that person that is next to succeed.
> Elizabeth Tudor
(Bucholz and Key 125; emphasis added)

In these examples, it is obvious that the imperative is not verifiability, or proof, or even exactly approbation; here the imperative is that the subject *like* and *be like* the "truth" being communicated. Similarly, if Marlowe once was in "the gentle air of [Mr. Secretary Walsingham's] liking" (Nicholl, *Reckoning* 69), it is not that Marlowe had "proven" himself, or even most important that he had "proven" himself; it is rather far more important that Marlowe was someone whom Mr. Secretary Walsingham could like, be like, and be-like (i.e., believe). The truth was personal. Just how personal we may imagine when we recall now Catherine of Aragon's eloquent and moving self-defense in her effort to avoid being put off as Henry's wife:

> What friend of mine
> That had to him derived your anger did I
> *Continue in my liking*? Nay, gave notice
> He was from thence discharged?[2]
> All is True 2.4.29-32 (emphasis added)

And if this should be thought insufficient proof, remember then Cordelia's regret that her position has "lost [her] in [her father's] *liking*" (*Lr.* [1610]

358 "Said I for this the girl was like to him?"

1.1.233; emphasis added) and recall as well Leontes commiseration with Florizel: "I am sorry, ... you have broken from his liking / Where you were tied in duty" (*WT* 5.1.210-12).

Shakespeare lived and wrote on the cusp of the late-medieval world's yielding of *trawþe* to the Cartesian world of certitude and its dark other, doubt. The lexicon of *likeness* in his works is our archaeology of this seismic cultural change: when the "new Philosophy calls all into doubt" (Donne), it fractures the rhetoric of likeness into the mathesis of proof. The scientific revolution and laissez-faire capitalism emerge from the broken body (*likam*) of our image and likeness. When "God said, Let Newton be, and all was light," "Nature" and "Nature's laws" may no longer have lain "hid in night" (Pope, "Epitaph on Newton"), but truth, as distinct from laws, receded into shadows that break its body into so many tricks of that sear(ch)ing light. These comments, I hasten to insist, bespeak no nostalgia on my part for a pre-modern community, as if such could ever exist; they are rather, and only, an effort on my part to *prove* (I *do* live in a post-Cartesian world) that the word *like* is a powerful marker of the transition from the pre-modern to the modern—and thus perhaps as well of the transition from the human to the post-human.

✣

Shakespeare's signature *like*ness marks 5.1, as I have tried to show, in a way that connects *All is True* not only to his late romances but to his histories of the 1590s as well—the common concern with genealogical succession is audible. Moreover the occurrences of *like* in Katherine's pleas in 2.4 mark that scene as Shakespearean. The signature *like*ness, however, must win its case in 2.2 where only Hoy assumes Shakespeare's hand as dominant, with Fletcher's secondary; Hope, most recently among others, assigns 2.2 to Fletcher exclusively.

Here the telling evidence, I think, must be the crucial exchange between Norfolk and Suffolk regarding Wolsey's vaulting ambition. I quote only the most relevant passages:

NORFOLK 'Tis so.
This is the Cardinal's doing. The King-Cardinal,
That blind priest, *like* the eldest son of fortune,
Turns what he list. *The King will know him one day.*
SUFFOLK *Pray God he do. He'll never know himself else.*
...
SUFFOLK And free us from his [Wolsey's] slavery.
NORFOLK We had need pray,

> And heartily, for our deliverance,
> Or this imperious man will work us all
> From princes into pages. *All men's honours*
> *Lie like one lump before him,* to be fashioned
> Into what pitch he please.
> **SUFFOLK**   For me, my lords,
> I love him not, nor fear him — there's my creed.
> As I am made without him, so I'll stand,
> If the King please. His curses and his blessings
> Touch me *alike;* they're breath I not believe in.
> I knew him, and I know him; so I leave him
> To him that made him proud — the Pope.
>   *All is True* 2.2.18-22; 44-56 (emphasis added)

From the perspective of the theater of likeness, I would here, subject to robust correction, side more with Hoy than Hope on the grounds that the work of the word *like* in this exchange is Shakespearean work consistent with such work elsewhere in the canon. Even under robust correction conceding Fletcher's hand, I would propose for serious consideration still that Fletcher in that case is very much under the impress of Shakespeare in this particular, present exchange. To my ear, the confirmation is the additional, clear evocation of narcissism: "The King will know him [Wolsey] one day./**SUFFOLK** Pray God he do. *He'll never know himself else*" (emphasis added). If Fletcher wrote this, he certainly knew with whom he was collaborating, whom even he was copying. *All is True* is Shakespearean in spirit just because it is about how persons come to know themselves; and that is always by likeness and unlikeness, whether it is in *The Two Gentlemen of Verona* or *The Two Noble Kinsmen* or in any of the works intervening between them.

I would propose also that Fletcher, if it is his hand, is Shakespearean too in the lines,

> all men's honours
> Lie like one lump before him, to be fashioned
> Into what pitch he please,

since the epistemologically shrewd collocation *lie/like* and the pun in "pitch," in collocation with "fashioned," are just the sort of impresses Shakespeare left in the language. Finally, Suffolk's declaration that Wolsey's "curses and his blessings / Touch me *alike,*" although clearly more consonant with the vulgate English of the time, still shows a Shakespearean intimacy with the resonance of the word *like* in the English vocabulary of identity and difference.

There is apparent consensus that Fletcher wrote the Epilogue to *All is True*:

> 'Tis ten to one this play can never please
> All that are here. Some come to take their ease,
> And sleep an act or two; but those, we fear,
> We've frighted with our trumpets; so, 'tis clear,
> They'll say 'tis naught. Others to hear the city
> Abused extremely, and to cry "That's witty!" —
> Which we have not done neither; that, I fear,
> All the expected good we're like to hear
> For this play at this time is only in
> The merciful construction of good women,
> For such a one we showed 'em. If they smile,
> And say "'Twill do," I know within a while
>   All the best men are ours — for 'tis ill hap
>   If they hold when their ladies bid 'em clap.

I agree with this consensus, especially because of the rhyme, which is not Shakespearean, but I also find I cannot dismiss the pressure in

> All the expected good we're *like* to hear
> For this play at this time is only in
> The *merciful construction* of good women,
> For such a one we showed 'em (emphasis added),

where the syntax, admitting of "the expected good we are like," and the lexis "merciful construction" feel (I consciously choose this verb) Shakespearean to me—this is writing such as I have come to expect in the theater of likeness. Although Fletcher almost certainly wrote the lines, he wrote them, I believe, as a student of, perhaps an apprentice in, Shakespeare's theater of likeness, by association copying a mentor some 14 years his senior (and in reputation of very great stature), from whom he learned to "look to like, if looking liking move" (*Rom.* 1.3.99).

36
"And bear us like the time": The Crisis of Likeness in *The Two Noble Kinsmen*

The last play that Shakespeare undertook, according to our current knowledge, *TNK* is also a collaborative effort, again with John Fletcher. Within the theater of likeness the play and the collaboration both are very important for understanding Shakespeare's art and his gifts. In writing this final chapter, I have elected to subtitle it with the phrase that has motivated my study over the past quarter century, "the crisis of likeness," because I see in *TNK* clear evidence that Shakespeare at the end of his career still meditates on the crisis and its implications for the human condition, in which frequently our best, if not our only, option is to "bear us like the time" (*TNK* 5.6.136; by Shakespeare).[1]

Following respected attribution scholars, I assume that Shakespeare probably wrote a little less than half the play: "Act 1 ... Act 2, Scene 1; Act 3, Scenes 1 and 2; and ... most of Act 5 (Scene 4 excepted)"(Oxford 2ᵉ 1279). My discussion of *like* in the play—the word occurs around 60 times, roughly the average across the entire canon—finds that, in the scenes confidently ascribed to Shakespeare, it does work very like the work it does elsewhere in his writings and that, in the scenes ascribed to Fletcher, there is probable reason to assume that Fletcher is following his collaborator and mentor and clearly depending on his precedent (most especially, in *TNK* 2.2). Indeed, in *TNK* Shakespeare's signature *like* seems almost a pointer of the way to Fletcher, who time and again demonstrates that, although his own style is very different, he nevertheless understands his mentor's vision—

> **ARCITE** Why then would you deal so cunningly,
> So strangely, so *unlike* a noble kinsman,
> To love alone?
>   *TNK* 2.2.193-5; by Fletcher (emphasis added)

—that unique vision of the crisis of likeness in the human effort to negotiate being between identity and difference.

Shakespeare's vision of the crisis of likeness is clearly evident in Hippolyta's comment on the love between Theseus and Pirithous:

> Their knot of love,
> Tied, weaved, entangled with so true, so long,
> And with a finger of so deep a cunning,
> May be outworn, never undone. I think
> Theseus cannot be umpire to himself,
> Cleaving his conscience into twain and doing
> Each side *like* justice, which he loves best.
> *TNK* 1.3.41-47 (emphasis added)

That homoeroticism is evident in the play there can be no doubt, both male and female, but my concern lies less with the question of sexual orientation than with the characteristic Shakespearean effect of self-division, non-self-coincidence, dilemmatic likeness—"[c]leaving...[e]ach side *like* justice." We recognize Shakespeare's signature of likeness here and comprehend its coherence with the work of the word *like* throughout the canon. The struggle is, always, to distinguish, to differentiate and separate, somehow in a humane fashion, in the crucible of the otherwise inevitable violence that attends differentiation and separation—to desire, in other words, where the choice of desire can only diminish:

> O cousin,
> That we should things desire which do cost us
> The loss of our desire! That naught could buy
> Dear love, but loss of dear love!
> *TNK* 5.6.109-12; by Shakespeare

We know there can be no doubt that this is Shakespeare's voice because it is the voice that has guided us through the whole canon of works in which men and women struggle to escape the finitude of desire, the contingency of what I (am) like.

Sooner or later I must accept what I (am) like. This, Shakespeare time and again demonstrates, will hurt. Hence, immediately, Emilia's response to Hippolyta's anxiety:

> I was acquainted
> Once with a time when I enjoyed a playfellow;
> ...   when our count
> Was each eleven...

And she I sigh and spoke of were things innocent,
Loved for we did, and *like* the elements,
That know not what, nor why, yet do effect
Rare issues by their operance, our souls
Did so to one another. What she *liked*
Was then of me approved; what not, condemned —
No more arraignment. The flower that I would pluck
And put between my breasts — O then but beginning
To swell about the blossom — she would long
Till she had such another, and commit it
To the *like* innocent cradle, where, phoenix-*like*,
They died in perfume. On my head no toy
But was her pattern.
    ...   This rehearsal —
Which, seely innocence wots well, comes in
Like old emportment's bastard — has this end:
That the true love 'tween maid and maid may be
More than in sex individuall [Q's reading].
HIPPOLYTA   You're out of breath,
And this high-speeded pace is but to say
That you shall never, *like* the maid Flavina,
Love any that's called man.
EMILIA I am sure I shall not.
        TNK 1.3.49-50; 53-54; 60-72; 78-86 (emphasis added)

I have quoted at length here so that the six occurrences of *like* are sure to be heard in context, where there can be really no doubt that Shakespeare is writing, not only of possible homoeroticism, but also — and for the theater of likeness, more importantly — of the human dilemma of being between identity and difference. The two young girls, newly pubescent (*TNK* 1.3.67-8), share what sooner or later they will have to spare — and sparing it *will* seem less pleasant than adolescent sharing it, at least at first — and Shakespeare writes from a lifetime of wisdom of the beauty and the pathos (Flavina *does* die young) of what can only be transitory and ephemeral, given "sex individuall" (*TNK* 1.3.82; Q's spelling), at least as the patriarchy legislates "sex individuall."[2] Hence, too, I would propose, the Prologue (lines 1-8) to the play is probably more Shakespeare than Fletcher, at least in spirit:

New plays and maidenheads are near akin:
Much followed both, for both much money giv'n
If they stand sound and well. And a good play,

> Whose modest scenes blush on his marriage day
> And shake to lose his honour, is *like* her
> That after holy tie and first night's stir
> Yet still is modesty, and still retains
> More of the maid to sight than husband's pains.

I would argue for Shakespeare's work in these opening lines just because they set the stage for "sex individuall" as it will emerge in the play, within the theater of likeness, to be a cur(s)e no one can avoid, from the jailer's daughter to the princes of the land.

A similar argument I wish to make for 2.2, where everyone agrees Fletcher's hand is first clearly evident. In 2.2's 281 lines, there are 14 occurrences of the word *like* (*TNK* 2.2.12, 14, 18, 20, 22, 24, 28, 34, 50, 75, 99, 141, 231, 254), one every 20 lines, and one occurrence of *unlike* (*TNK* 2.2.194). This density does not, I think, argue against Fletcher's writing the scene—it is in his style, I agree; rather, I would propose that it shows how carefully he is collaborating with Shakespeare and following Shakespeare's lead in understanding the crisis of likeness in the play that they have together designed.[3] I believe this is most evident in the exchanges between Palamon and Arcite in the opening of act 2:

> **PALAMON**   O never
> Shall we two exercise, *like twins* of honour,
> Our arms again and feel our fiery horses
> *Like* proud seas under us.
> ...
> **ARCITE** No *figures of ourselves* shall we e'er see
> To glad our age, and, *like* young eagles, teach 'em
> Boldly to gaze against bright arms.
>   *TNK* 2.2.17-20; 33-35 (emphasis added)

This may be Fletcher's style, but it is Shakespeare's mind, especially in the anxiety over genealogical succession. And so much is even truer later in the scene when Arcite exclaims against Palamon,

> Why then would you deal so cunningly,
> So strangely, so *unlike* a noble kinsman,
> To love alone?
>   *TNK* 2.2.193-5 (emphasis added)

where the use of *unlike*, especially following Emilia's sudden infatuation with the flower narcissus (*TNK* 2.2.118-19), is consummately the lexicon and the thought of Shakespeare, however much it may be the style of Fletcher. The crisis of likeness in the form of narcissism is the direction now of the play, and Fletcher follows that direction, I think, out of respect for Shakespeare and, as well, out of a shrewd calculation that Shakespeare knows what he is doing.

Where in the play we are next confident of Shakespeare's work we see continuing marks of the theater of likeness. In 3.1, when Palamon and Arcite encounter each other in the forest, Palamon accosts Arcite,

> **PALAMON** Cozener Arcite, give me language such
> As thou hast showed me feat.
> **ARCITE**   Not finding in
> The circuit of my breast any gross stuff
> To *form me like* your blazon holds me to
> This gentleness of answer — 'tis your passion
> That thus mistakes, the which, to you being enemy,
> Cannot to me be kind.
>   *TNK* 3.1.45-51 (emphasis added)

This is Shakespeare's voice, distinctly, and *like* does expected work of calling attention to the crisis of identity and difference playing itself out between the two "cousins." When, a few lines later, Palamon continues to "doubt" (double—*TNK* 3.1.62) Arcite's honor and courage, Arcite replies

> **ARCITE**   Kinsman, you might as well
> Speak this and *act it in your glass* as to
> His ear which now disdains you.
>   *TNK* 3.1.70-72 (emphasis added),

we again hear distinctive Shakespearean lexis and cadence; and, we know where we are intellectually, too, in Shakespeare's understanding of narcissistic struggle to sort, separate, and claim a likeness that one can live with, and like with, and, perhaps, love with.

For numerous scenes from this point forward, Fletcher will script the play — he writes slightly more than half. When Shakespeare returns to complete the play ("Shakespeare was primarily responsible … for most of Act 5 [Scene 4 excepted]…" [Oxford 2^e 1279]), he writes exquisitely of the crisis of likeness as he has learned the toll that it exacts on humankind:

> A husband I have 'pointed,
> But do not know him. Out of two, I should
> Choose one and pray for his success, but I

> Am guiltless of election.
> ...   Therefore, most modest queen,
> He of the two pretenders that best loves me
> And has the truest title in't, let him
> Take off my wheaten garland.
>
> *TNK* 5.3.15-18; 21-24

To be "guiltless of election" all but the most hard-hearted of us would eagerly like; not to have to choose, where choice must condemn, would be a liberty almost unimaginable.[4] But if barely imaginable, it is never available to humans in their mortal condition. I must choose whom I (am) like. I cannot have it, "[w]ere they metamorphosed/Both into one!" (*TNK* 5.5.84-85), not only because

> There were no woman [or person]
> Worth so composed a man: their single share,
> Their nobleness peculiar to them, gives
> The prejudice of disparity, value's shortness,
> To any lady [or person] breathing —
>
> *TNK* 5.5.85-89,

but also because "sex individuall" is also "sex dividual" and prohibits such overcoming of division—"Two distincts, division none" belong only to the Phoenix and the Turtle (line 27 and see Introduction 5-6). We are, Shakespeare so exquisitely understood, creatures of no "*single* share"; we are, as Montaigne also grasped, always "somehow double" (*Essais* 9; see, above, chapter 4 page 49):

> for he that was thus good,
> Encountered yet his better. I have heard
> Two emulous Philomels beat the ear o'th' night
> With their contentious throats, now one the higher,
> Anon the other, then again the first,
> And by and by out-breasted, that the sense
> Could not be judge between 'em — so it fared
> Good space between these kinsmen, till heavens did
> Make hardly one the winner.
>
> *TNK* 5.5.122-130

That "the sense/[Cannot] judge between 'em" is sometimes comic, sometimes tragic, sometimes both (Fletcher and his principal collaborator Beaumont are renowned in the then new genre of tragicomedy, for which

Fletcher actually provided a definition—Vickers, *Criticism* 502-3). But it is always a contingency of the body and its *like*ness, whether Philomels or Theban cousins.

Over Arcite's body Theseus will declare: "His part is played, and, though it were too short,/He did it well" (*TNK* 5.6.102-3). By this point in the master's theater of likeness we should be at liberty to paraphrase Shakespeare's "[h]is part is played" as "[h]is like(ness) is known..." Moreover, by now we also should be at liberty to confess that that is all we know or can know, his (or her) likeness. We are privy to no more:

> O you heavenly charmers,
> What things you make of us! For what we lack
> We laugh, for what we have, are sorry; still
> Are children in some kind. Let us be thankful
> For that which is, and with you leave dispute
> That are above our question. *Let's go off*
> *And bear us like the time.*
>
> *TNK* 5.6.131-7 (emphasis added)

Notes

Introduction

1. There is a significant body of work on exemplariness in late medieval and early modern England. My own introduction began with my teacher, the late Judson Boyce Allen, whose title *The Ethical Poetic of the Later Middle Ages*, I consider to be an excellent starting point for study of the topic. See also Lyons. A convenient test of the significance of exemplariness in the period is to read Marguerite de Navarre's *Heptameron* (1559) which repeatedly includes at the end of a tale critical commentary on the examples featured in the tale, their point and their efficacy and their role in human interaction—a meta-exemplarity, in effect; see especially Day 1, Story 5 (100-1) and Lyons 116-17 esp. Further, consult the helpful essay by Kinney, and Mack 32, 90-91.
2. Cited by Gilles Deleuze in "The Schizophrenic and Language," 324-39, at 327.
3. The bibliography is vast. I include in the next paragraph a very short list of titles. But Shakespeare himself provides a typically memorable as well as concise example, in *All Is True* (from a part of the play ascribed to him):

> Things done well,
> And with a care, exempt themselves from fear;
> *Things done without example, in their issue*
> *Are to be fear'd.*
>
> 1.2.89-92 (emphasis added)

Though in context referring to a wildly unpopular tax levied by Wolsey, without precedent, the idea extends actually through the very fabric of early modern codes of conduct—without a precedent likeness, behavior is always potentially anomalous and to that extent threatening (even as, thinkers of the period are coming to realize, a precedent likeness at the same time is no guarantee of desirable behavior).

See also, for the *Fürstenspiegel* tradition, Aegidius Romanus, Giles of Rome (d. 1316), *De Regimine principum* (ca. 1280, extant in more than 300 MSS); Christine de Pisan, *Treasure of the City of Ladies and Book of the Body Politic*; Sir Thomas Elyot, *The Book Named the Governor*; Niccoló Machiavelli, *The Prince*; for conduct or civility books, see Erasmus, "On Good Manners for Boys," Baldassare Castiglione, *The Courtier*—a crucial historical study of these materials, justly celebrated, is Norbert Elias, *The Civilizing Process*; on Plotinus, see Pierre Hadot, 33-34, 67; on Ficino's translation and transmission of Plotinus to early modern culture, see Allen *Ficino*; *imitatio Christi* is a phrase most generally associated with the name of Thomas à Kempis, and with the *Devotio moderna* and the Brethren of the Common Life from the end of the 14th century onward, but it is an idea inescapable in the Gospels, and the career of St. Paul is unthinkable without it—one of the greatest witnesses to the idea is the (tradition of the) crucifixion of St. Peter *upside down*, a copy of Jesus's crucifixion, but not a counterfeit (Michelangelo's great painting, "Martyrdom of St Peter" [1546-50] is in the Cappella Paolina, Palazzi Pontifici, Vatican—[http://www.kfki.hu/~arthp/html/m/michelan/2paintin/5peter.html, last accessed 07.15.03]).

4. At this point, consider that the root of "example," "sample," etc. is the IE verb meaning to "take, distribute" which generates, among other words, the Latin verb *emere*, "to buy, select for purchase"—an example is something you put your money on, so to speak. Similarly, something that is *exempt* (from the same root) is something "bought out of" ("taken from") the competition or the context. Now, also, recall Henry VIII:

> Things done well,
> And with a care, *exempt* themselves from fear;
> Things done without *example*, in their issue
> Are to be fear'd.
> *All Is True* 1.2.89-92 (emphasis added)

Shakespeare's ear (see below, n 25), at all times acutely tuned, hears that things done with *example* are *exempt* from fear. We, in turn, learn not to underestimate the deliberateness informing the theater of likeness.

5. See, also, the (in)famous *The Anatomy of Abuses* by Philip Stubbes, the more instructive for its very extremism, excerpted conveniently in McDonald 340-1, esp. 341.

Here, too, it is imperative to note, though the subject is too vast to treat in any detail in this book, the constant anxiety in Early Modern England over idolatry in the theater; see, esp., O'Connell 36-62, and, more generally, Besançon's remarkable study. The theater poses the threat of idolatry just because the theater is the sight/site of likeness.

At the same time, however, it would be a mistake to restrict this condition to the theater alone. If we read Horace, as practically everyone in Early Modern Europe did, we see that copying likeness is, in fact, structural to poetry as such: "Si vis me flere, dolendum est/Primum ipsi tibi" (If you want me to weep, first you must be grieving yourself—*Ars poetica* 102); see, further, the dated but still useful commentary by Spingarn 30-37; for an exhaustive Lacanian analysis of likeness in early modern rhetoricians and grammarians, see Sharon-Zisser's writing on what she calls the "similaic copula" (167-276).

6. Consider, too, Philip Massinger, *The Roman Actor: A Traegedy* (1629), which, its title notwithstanding, makes a similar point:

> if done to the life,
> As if they saw their dangers and their glories,
> And did partake with them in their rewards,
> All that have any spark of Roman in them,

> The slothful arts laid by, contend to be
> *Like* those they see presented.
>
> 1.3.90-94 (my emphasis)

Cited in Vickers, *Criticism* 551; see, further, Vickers's Introduction 50-55, on emulation and "inflaming" by example.

7. After *Henry V*, Shakespeare writes no histories again until *Henry VIII* (*All Is True*), which is only debatably a history play and a collaboration, as well, with John Fletcher. I am of the opinion shared by some that *All Is True* is, in fact, more romance than history, and I hope to show in my chapter on the play that it does indeed, in the parts we can assign to Shakespeare, provoke issues of fathers, daughters, and inheritance that are consistent with concerns of his late romances.

8. Cf. Empson 218-49, esp. 226 and 246. The fineness of Empson's argument is the way in which he shows just that Iago "feels himself really 'honest' as the kind of man who can see through nonsense" (224). Without this pernicious illusion of self-satisfaction, it would not hurt nearly as much as it does to see Iago "dragging Othello into his own state of mind" (246) — as I would put it, making Othello *like* him.

9. *OED* II *sub voce* "theater," "*n*.: a. Gr. θέατρον, a place for viewing, esp. a theatre, f. θεᾶσθαι to behold (cf. θέα sight, view, θεατής a spectator)."

10. *OED* II *sub voce* "theory¹," "a. Gr. θεωρία a looking at, viewing, contemplation, speculation, theory, also a sight, a spectacle, abstr. n. f. θεωρός...spectator, looker on, f. stem θεα — of θεᾶσται to look on, view, contemplate."

11. Here, I would like to acknowledge reading in Baudrillard I undertook some 20 years ago; although I claim no fluency in his theory or discourse, I know I have been influenced by his understanding of the simulacrum.

12. It may perhaps help, and it cannot hurt, to remind ourselves here of Aristophanes' moving speech in Plato's *Symposium* (excerpts from 189e-191d; 542-4):

> ... for in the beginning we were nothing like we are now. For one thing, the race was divided intro three, that is to say, besides the two sexes, male and female, which we have at present, there was a third which partook of the nature of both, and for which we still have a name, though the creature itself is forgotten. For though "hermaphrodite" is only used nowadays as a term of contempt, there really was a man-woman in those days, a being which was half male and half female. And secondly, gentlemen, each of these beings was globular in shape, with rounded back and sides, four arms and four legs, and two [190a] faces, both the same, on a cylindrical neck, and one head, with one face one side and one the other, and four ears, and two lots of privates, and all the other parts to match. ...[190b] And such, gentlemen, were their strength and energy and such their arrogance, that they actually tried...to scale the heights of heaven and set upon the gods...[190c] Zeus offered a solution. I think I can see my way, he said, to put an end to this disturbance by weakening these people without destroying them. What I propose to do

is to cut them all in half, thus killing two birds with one stone, for each one will be only half as strong, and there'll be twice as many of them, which will suit us very nicely. They can walk about, upright, on their two legs, and if, said Zeus, I have any more trouble with them, I shall split them again, and they'll have to hop about on one. ...[191a] Now, when the work of bisection was complete it left each half with a desperate yearning for the other, and they ran together and flung their arms around each other's necks, and asked for nothing better than to be rolled into one. So much so, that they began to die of [191b] hunger and general inertia, for neither would do anything without the other. And whenever one half was left alone by the death of its mate, it wandered about questing and clasping in the hope of finding a spare half-woman—or a whole woman, as we should call her nowadays—or half a man. And so the race was dying out. Fortunately, however, Zeus felt so sorry for them that he devised another scheme. He moved their privates round to the front, for of course they had originally been on the outside—which was now the back—and they had begotten and conceived not upon each other, but, [191c] like the grasshoppers, upon the earth. So now, as I say, he moved their members round to the front and made them propagate among themselves, the male begetting upon the female—the idea being that if...a man should chance upon a woman, conception would take place and the race would be continued, while if man should conjugate with man, he might at least obtain such satisfaction as would allow him to turn his attention and his energies to the everyday affairs of life. ...So you see, gentlemen, [191d] how...this love is always trying to redintegrate [sic] our former nature, to make two into one, and to bridge the gulf between one human being and another.

13. Hence those kinship systems that privilege the relationship between the maternal uncle and the sister's son (avunculate)—the maternal uncle cares for this nephew because he can be reasonably sure that his sister's son is at least in part his own blood; his own wife may be sleeping with who knows whom and her son may be anybody's, but his sister's son is at least to some extent *like* him. See "A Kinship Glossary: Symbols, Terms, and Concepts," compiled by Michael Dean Murphy: http://www.as.ua.edu/ant/Faculty/murphy/436/kinship.htm. Last accessed 07.14.03.

14. See, respectively, Holden 77-78 (but see also, Honan 80); Duncan-Jones 224-6; and Holden 249-52.

15. Among a great many sources, one may consult Levin, *Heart*, and Levin *Reign*, esp. 80-103, "Plots, Conspiracies, and the Succession"; and Boehrer.

16. As in Richard Crookback but also Henry VI, notoriously unlike his illustrious, famous father, Henry V.

17. Holden writes (166):

Beyond the personal grief ... Shakespeare had been robbed of a direct line of descent. ... all four of them [he and his three brothers] would be dead, with no surviving male issue, within fifteen years of their father. There was now no Fleance to stretch the Shakespeare line to the crack of doom. Now it would die ... with its most famous son.

These are *not* trivial biographical data. To the contrary, they are of indispensable importance for understanding Shakespeare's theater of likeness. A man's son is (or ought to be) his likeness. Take this away, and the crisis of likeness erupts, practically everywhere. Think only of Henry VIII.

But it may also help to listen to Ben Jonson:

> Rest in soft peace, and asked, say, "Here doth lie
> Ben Jonson his best piece of poetry."
> For whose sake henceforth all his vows be such
> As what he *loves* may never *like* too much.
> "On My First Son"
(McDonald, Companion 295; emphasis added)

18. See, further, Howard and Rackin 127-30.
19. For studies of Shakespeare's style, I have found especially helpful Stewart, esp. chapters 2-3; Burrow; McDonald, *Arts*; and Elam. Of course, the bibliography is endless, but there are certain areas of consensus, those I list in particular. I also want to acknowledge the help I have found in Hope, *Grammar*.
20. In addition to Fineman, Heather Dubrow has also discussed the importance of *syneciosis* to understanding Shakespeare's poetry, especially *The Rape of Lucrece*—see esp. 80-83.
21. Note at this point that in classical rhetoric συνοικείωσις is *conciliatio*, "a manner of argumentation . . . by which an argument of the opposing party is exploited for the benefit of one's own party" (see Lausberg 346). "Therefore I lie with her, and she with me,/And in our faults by lies we flattered be" (Sonnet #138): the "lying" that one might oppose to Shakespeare and his lady Shakespeare turns to his own advantage, "conciliating" (the irony is deep) the opponent who would confront him with his "lying" even as he "conciliates" two different senses of "lie."

Conciliation, I suggest, is a powerful idea for understanding the art of Shakespeare. It is not compromise, anything but. It is "couplement" that yields profound insight into otherwise occulted relationships: "I pall in resolution, and begin/To doubt th'equivocation of the fiend,/That lies like truth" (*Mac.* 5.5.40-42)—Shakespeare *conciliates* the words "lies" and "truth" (so that they are "together at home with" each other) in such a way that we see, as we could not otherwise do, into the murderous compulsiveness that torments "Bellona's bridegroom" (*Mac.* 1.2.54) as he struggles with the fiend (who lies, but lies like truth, fiendishly).

Consider, further, in this regard Mueller's conclusions about Lyly's style:

> Thus the syntax and semantics of these clauses with redoubled superlatives bespeak not simply "the precarious closeness of extremes," as Barish says...but something more awesomely mysterious: the co-existence of extremes in an identity or

> interdependency relation whose nature is never clarified yet constantly reaffirmed (405).

When, in my own critical terminology, I describe Shakespeare's writing as juxta-form and cruci-lingual, I am also recognizing its imbeddedness in this late Elizabethan rhetoric; although his writing issues in a style far more inclusive and humane than Lyly's, his juxtapositions and "crosse(-cople)s" "bespeak...the co-existence of extremes in an identity or interdependency relation whose nature is never clarified yet constantly reaffirmed."

22. Harry Berger, Jr., has argued, notably, that "the Shakespeare play, as a text to be interpreted by readers, provides a critique of the play as script—that is, as the basis of performance" (99 et alibi). From this fruitful idea, I draw some corroboration of my own theory that all theater is theory: no particular theatrical performance ever exhausts the theoretical potential of the textual form of the play—the play can always generate a *different likeness* of itself (cf. the *Othello* of Olivier and Finlay with that of Fishburne and Branagh, for example).

23. I know how controversial the issue of ritual in Greek drama is; I want to observe merely that we can see at least some motive of the sacred in its earliest manifestations. For my reading in and understanding of Greek drama and its Latin exemplars, I thank my teacher in the 1970s, Frederick M. Ahl, who bestowed exemplary generosity on me in conversation after conversation about the literature and its poetry.

24. See Janson; see also *RII* 2.1.23-24.

25. Honan provides an excellent view (45):

> Memory-work was endless. At Leicester's Free Grammar School—which cannot have been much unlike Stratford's—each morning's lesson was repeated by pupils next day "without booke." On Fridays, the week's lessons had to be known by heart, "perfectlie." From the age of 7 until about 15, William memorized Latin almost daily. Unlike the meandering, fuzzy, verbose English language—so unfixed and variable, so quickly changing that Chaucer was almost unintelligible after 200 years—Latin was lucid and precise. For a millennium and a half it had been the pre-eminent language of Europe,... In the 1570s the literary prestige of Latin was immense. The sound of a language—far more than its syntax or vocabulary—appealed to Elizabethans, and William's memorizing of Latin would, above all, train his ear. With a good memory, he would later be able to synthesize in his work a very great deal of verbal material that he had heard or read. Experience with the preciseness of Latin would help him to express himself with point, logic, and lucid continuity, and save him from larding his English writing with bombast, "inkhorn" terms, or exotic and high-sounding words adopted simply for show.

See also Ong, *Rite*; Brink 101-2; and Kintgen 44-45 especially, where he quotes Auden ("In Memory of W.B. Yeats"): "The words of a dead man are modified in the guts of the living." Consult, further, the opening pages of Mack, "Rhetoric in the Grammar School."

26. Honan (60) writes:

> In the seventeenth century, John Aubrey ... [noted] "He understood Latine pretty well ... for he had been in his younger yeares a Schoolmaster in the Countrey." This is a fairly well authenticated report ... not particularly surprising, unlikely, or merely gossipy.

See also Wells, *Time* 37-38:

> Shakespeare was, I suspect, our first great literary commuter. ... He had the good sense to maintain a household many miles away [from London]. We know little about the contents of New Place, but my guess is that it contained a comfortable, book-lined study situated in the quietest part of the house to which Shakespeare retreated from London at every possible opportunity. ...

27. The famous quote is Horace's, *Ep.* 2.1.156. See, further, Kahn, *Roman* 11ff., and 135 esp., on "aemulatio."

28. On the Spartan "agōgē," *The Oxford Classical Dictionary* includes in its entry (41):

> The Spartan public upbringing. The classical agōgē, supervised by the *paidonomos* ("boy-herdsman"), embraced males aged 7-29. ... There were three general stages, *paides, paidiskoi,* and *hēbōntes,* probably representing ages 7-17, 18-19, and 20-29; several individual year-classes were separately named. The *paides* were trained in austerity, obedience, and mock battles by older youths within companies (*ilai*), subdivided into herds (*agelai*) of age-mates with their own internal leadership. At age 12 they entered an institutionalized pederastic relationship with a young adult (see HOMOSEXUALITY).

Consult, further, Leitao 143-69.

29. My text of Ovid is the Loeb; here 10.252. See the recent collection of essays by Taylor, *Ovid,* esp. his Introduction, 1-12, and the first essay, "Myths Exploited...," by Maslen 15-30.

30. In making this statement, I remain aware of the significance of Aristotle to early modern European culture—despite the rejection of his logic and dialectic by humanists and of his philosophy generally by radical scientific thinkers such as Lord Bacon. Most especially, I depend in my own thinking on his famous opinion (*Poetics* 22.1459a6-7) that

> by far the most important matter is to have skill in the use of metaphor. The skill alone it is not possible to obtain from another; and it is, in itself, a sign of genius. *For the ability to construct good metaphors implies the ability to see essential similarities.*
>
> Golden and Hardison 132 (emphasis added)
>
> polu de megiston to metaphorikon einai. monon gar touto oute par' allou esti labein euphuïas te sêmeion esti: to gar eu metapherein to to homoion theôrein estin.

"To see essential similarities"—to theorize likenesses (to homoion theôrein estin) — is indeed the "sign of genius" if Shakespeare is our exemplary test case.

But the evidence that I have seen, both in the canon and in the context of the canon, suggests that, at least in his theater of likeness, Shakespeare is more Platonic than Aristotelian—i.e., suspicious of mimesis (using the term in the widest generic sense) even as he is profoundly and inevitably attracted to it.

31. Many would cite, e.g., Greene, but this is but one among innumerable, and it is important to acknowledge here that the bibliography on this topic in the modern languages exceeds any individual's aspiration to comprehensiveness. Just so, I am not writing a book on *imitatio*.

32. Nor is it a theater of *as* or the *same* or *copy* or *image*. The word *as* is far less avoidable in English than is *like* or *image* (153 times) or *same* (219 times) or *copy* (14 times); it occurs over 6000 times in the canon. But predominantly it differs from *like* in the crucial feature that *as* is a quantifier without respect to the specificity of substance: this gallon of milk is as heavy as this sliver of lead—milk is not *like* lead. Similarly, if one says that X is the same as Y, X and Y are no longer a*like* (they are the same); likewise, with *copy*, although here semantic specificity is harder to (pre-)determine. In sum, likeness is its own, separate condition.

These distinctions are not semantic quibbles but a crucial part of the vocabulary of Western aesthetics—see Halliwell. It is imperative to remember, even though the book I am writing is not a work of professional philosophy, that the topic of the book touches on a complex of issues inseparable from the very thought of Western philosophy—what is the relationship between (to use conventional if therefore problematic terms for it) the original and its copy? I cannot answer this question as a professional philosopher nor is that my aim; my aim is rather to engage with Shakespeare's choice, increasingly deliberate over his career, I think, of the word *like* (some 2,400 times) to convey his theory of theater (and the theater of his theory of our "image and likeness"). *Like* is his word, a signature of his.

Still, I have not ignored *copy*, *same*, or *as* in the course of my book; I regularly call attention to moments where they are significant to the theater of likeness—"As flies to wanton boys are we to th'gods;/They kill us for their sport" (*Lr.* [1610] 4.1.37-38), or, so telling,

> PAULINA   It is yours,
> And might we lay th'old proverb to your charge,
> So *like* you 'tis the worse. Behold, my lords,
> Although the print be little, the whole matter
> And *copy* of the father: eye, nose, lip,
> The trick of's frown, his forehead, nay, the valley,
> The pretty dimples of his chin and cheek, his smiles,
> The very mould and frame of hand, nail, finger.
> And thou good goddess Nature, which hast made it
> So *like* to him that got it, if thou hast
> The ordering of the mind too, 'mongst all colours

No yellow in't, lest she suspect, as he does,
Her children not her husband's.
                           WT 2.3.96-108 (emphasis added)

33. See Liddell-Scott, *sub voce*. See, also, *Phaedo* 103e; *Republic* 596a; *Parmenides* 132a; in *Plato: The Collected Dialogues*, 85, 820, 926, respectively.
34. See below n. 37.
35. My understanding of Cartesianism is indebted to Hannah Arendt. See *The Life of the Mind* 1: *Thinking* 48-49; 2: *Willing* 151; 181.
36. Nicholas of Cusa, *De docta ignorantia* 2.1 (Santinello 230); my translation. Cf. Montaigne, "Of Experience" (Frame 817; 819).
37. *Confessions* 7.10.16; see O'Donnell's extensive commentary at http://www.stoa.org/hippo/comm7.html#CB7C10S16, lemma **in regione dissimilitudinis**. O'Donnell notes also that

> A. quotes Plotinus expressly at civ. 9.17, "ubi est illud Plotini, 43 ubi ait, 'fugiendum est igitur ad carissimam patriam, et ibi pater, et ibi omnia. quae igitur, inquit, classis aut fuga? *similem deo fieri.*' si ergo deo quanto similior, tanto fit quisque propinquior: nulla est ab illo alia longinquitas quam eius dissimilitudo."

I quote a translation of the *City of God* passage cited by O'Donnell as follows:

> What has become of that saying of Plotinus, "We must flee to our beloved country. There the Father is, and there is everything. Where shall we take ship? How can we flee? By becoming like God." If man comes near to God in proportion as he grows *more like him*, then *unlikeness to God is the only separation from him*...
>   Trans. Bettenson 364 (emphasis mine in the translation)

Of most importance here is the clear evidence that the Latin Christian tradition was thoroughly familiar with the Plotinian argument, whether or not immediate knowledge of Greek was available. It was also familiar with the moving parallel to *Aeneid* 4.347, Aeneas pleading with the enraged Dido: "Hic amor, haec patria est" ("There [Italy] is my love, there my country"). It is unlikely that Shakespeare knew the theological arguments first-hand, although his early contact with recusancy suggests that we should not rule out the possibility altogether, but it is equally likely that the moral tenor of the theology would have been part of his intellectual climate, by no means alien to him. See, further, my arguments in chapter 27, "'Writes them all alike': *Macbeth*."

38. Many examples might be adduced, but the most vivid and convincing is the surging consumerism of early modern England—see Halpern 245. As Halpern observes, "the aristocracy felt emasculated by conversion from a military to a consuming class," and this, in part, I assume and posit, because consumerism immediately insists on *un*likeness by the vicious and insidious compulsion it feeds to differentiate and distinguish: since the aristocracy are almost uniformly *alike* (even inbred in some cases), only conspicuous consumption of material products at an ever increasing rate (impoverishing not a few,

"emasculating" them) can maintain the illusion of unlikeness or (artificial) uniqueness (see further chapter 26, "'Do not assume my likeness': *Timon of Athens*, Misanthropy as Unlikeness"). The Renaissance proverb—"We are all Adams sons, silk onely distinguisheth us" (cited in Stallybrass and Jones 270)—positions our understanding: our likeness drives us to pursue different likeness (we must feel the full force of the oxymoron, "different likeness"); and Shakespeare's theater of likeness exposes this compulsion and its co-pathologies with prodigious insight, using likeness to portray likeness in the land of unlikeness where no likeness is ever adequate to an identity, to that which we call (out for), perhaps desperately, the individual (cf. Stallybrass and Jones 32 and 275-6).

39. Here I speculate, but would not wish to assert beyond speculation, that Shakespeare, in his sacramentalism, as I call it, participates in an attitude perhaps best represented by Cusa's thinking of the "coincidentia oppositorum" (as in *De docta ignorantia*). More than the "epidemic of paradoxes" (see Colie), a postulate of the "coincidence of opposites" respects both the syneciotic, "conciliative" (n. 21) character of Shakespeare's style and, at the same time, his enormous regard for nature, where apparently random coincidence again and again shows hidden coin(tense)cidence. Nothing in the purview of his art was too small for Shakespeare to miss its connectedness or, perhaps better, its belongingness: the microscopy of his sight answered to the macroscopy of his vision—"coincidentia oppositorum" (juxta-form and cruci-lingual). See, further, Barish, esp. 111.

40. I conjecture that "kenotic" might serve as one useful synonym for Keats's famous insight into Shakespeare's "negative capability": Shakespeare's "negative capability" is also his "kenotic writing." In a sense, Shakespeare "empties" himself to assume the "likeness" of his characters. Self-emptying fairly describes what Shakespeare does: there is a self there, but it empties itself ... to be (like) Iago, Romeo, Brutus, Hamlet, Rosalind, Beatrice, et al.

How? Language. He soaked in language. If he could say it, he could imagine it. Note: *not* if he could imagine it, he could say it, but the other way round. That's the trick of the *Sonnets*, for example: "I lie with my love"—okay, let's see where that goes; how far can I run with that? If he could say it, he could see it (theory/theater) and show it (theater/theory). Cf. Fineman, "Anecdote" 74.

Chronology

1. Norton expresses the matter well (69):

    [I]f we now see Shakespeare's dramaturgy in the context of his contemporaries and of a collective artistic practice, readers continue to have little difficulty recognizing that most of the plays attached to his name tower over those of his rivals.

    See also Erne 34-35.

Chapter 1

1. Oxford 2ᵉ dates the inception of Shakespeare's sonnet writing to 1593; obviously, this dating and Burrow's cautious proposals are compatible. My own intuition suggests to me that Shakespeare probably wrote sonnets earlier than age 28. But most important is the larger picture in which we see the mutual inter-relationship between poems and plays in the emergent early theater of likeness.
2. Francisco Patrizi (d. 1597) argues that "Cognitio nihil est aliud, quam Coitio quaedam cum suo cognobili" (Cassirer 134) — "cognition is nothing other than a certain coitus with its knowable (thing)." I think this trope is of considerable importance to understanding Shakespeare's theater of likeness (I do not claim it is a source — Shakespeare would not have needed a source for the idea).
3. Fineman writes (81):

   > (It follows as a corollary, though one that is not very relevant to my argument, that Shakespeare's characters are psychologically authentic only to the extent, which may, of course, be considerable, that natural humans reenact the literary representation of human nature).

   To my argument, this "corollary" is not only "relevant" but important; the theater of likeness assumes "that natural humans reenact the literary representation of human nature." It is not just that we are simian-like (Introduction n. 24); it is that we are storiers of our own likenesses (see chapter 33 below page 339, on Sir Walter Ralegh's famous performance before his death on the scaffold). "The universe is made up of stories, not atoms" (Muriel Rukeyser), may not be a true story but it is nevertheless the story of the truth, of cognition that is coitus like love.
4. And, to be sure, this "you" may be only the second-person singular pronoun, nothing more (that is the nature of linguistic "shifters"); but, as a psychiatrist would then observe, there is more than a passing chance that some pathology is gnawing on an I thus unknowing of itself.
5. Hence Fineman: "Language manages noticeably to redouble with a difference the complementary similarities of a figurality based on likeness" (37); also "[i]f idealizing language articulates the difference that the likeness of its Nature would normally excise, it will find itself specifically subverted by the difference that it speaks" (119).
6. The reader looking to assess the difference of my position from Fineman's may compare this analysis of Sonnet #105 with his at 140-3.

   Fineman explicitly claims his interest is in "the 'languageness' of language ... that distinguishes all [Shakespeare's] sonnets and gives them their peculiar literary quality" (27). My interest is in the language of likeness. For part of the way, these are the same phenomenon. The language of likeness leads eventually to the likeness of language, its "languageness," on which Fineman concentrates, the copula. But the likeness of language, I think, leads to another theory and another theater, the couple, that is not exhausted in the "languageness" of language, a reference to (and reverence for) the body, *likam*.

Chapter 2

1. Recall *A Lover's Complaint* (lines 293-4, Oxford 2ᵉ 801b):

   O cleft effect! Cold modesty, hot wrath,
   Both fire from hence and chill extincture hath.

   Shakespeare is unsurpassed in the representation of the "cleft effect" of love and in lovers.
2. "One touch of nature makes the whole world kin" (*Tro.* 3.3.169).
3. The supreme instance of this monitoring in the canon is the rude mechanicals in *MND*, especially Bottom. Not the fairies but the Athenian workers provide the surety that this is a comedy, that it cannot be *like* a tragedy (and all the more so in that the rude mechanicals attempt to play a tragedy).
4. In the contrary tragic theater of likeness, for example, in *Titus Andronicus*, the sons of Tamora will perform this likeness against Lavinia, "like soldiers," raping and mutilating her "'gainst the nature of love."

   By this analysis, we see, and will discuss at length many times later, that tragic likeness is likeness that has melted into the real, polluting it beyond any hope of separation, division, and subsequent reflection. In tragic likeness, examples are irresistibly prescriptive, which is why they seem like fate; and the fatality Shakespearean tragic protagonists suffer is less *hamartia* than powerlessness against that which has been already written or spoken—"Come not between the dragon and his wrath" (*Lr.* [1610] 1.1.122):

   That thou hast sought to make us break our vows,
   Which we durst never yet, and with strained pride
   To come betwixt our sentence and our power,
   Which nor our nature nor our place can bear,
   Our potency made good take thy reward.
   Lr. [1610] 1.1.167-71

   This is aw(e)ful. It is absolutism unchecked by any interruption of feeling. And, just so, the rupture Lear will feel as a consequence will sunder him from the *real*; his absolutism having poisoned the real, the real turns into Lear (real > < Lear), submerging him in his own poison—mad, sick, old, naked, and, above all, unyielding.

   From this perspective, we can suggest that the genius of the comedic, by contrast, is interruption ("timing," as a pro would say)—the gift of stopping before it is too late, before a pratfall becomes the fall, before pain becomes permanent.

Chapter 3

1. "The most heterogeneous ideas are yoked by violence together" — Samuel Johnson, *Lives* 1:20.
2. Here I speculate that *kills* in line 166 is a choice of diction influenced by *like* at the end of line 165 — "To hear with eyes belongs to love's fine wit" (Sonnet #23.14).

Chapter 4

1. I will adopt this conventional designation for the four plays — *The First Part of the Contention of the Two Famous Houses of York and Lancaster* (1590-1), *The True Tragedy of Richard Duke of York and the Good King Henry the Sixth* (1591), *The First Part of Henry the Sixth* (1592), and *The Tragedy of King Richard the Third* (1592-3). I prefer it to the First Tetralogy, also commonly used for the four plays.
2. Elizabeth's famous self-characterization in her Armada speech to her troops at Tilbury, Essex, August 9, 1588 — *Collected Works* 326.
3. The original of Nietzsche's argument follows:

    ... jedes Wort wird sofort dadurch Begriff, dass es eben nicht für das einmalige ganz und gar individualisirte Urerlebniss, dem es sein Entstehen verdankt, etwa als Erinnerung dienen soll, sondern zugleich für zahllose, mehr oder weniger ähnliche, d. h. streng genommen niemals gleiche, also auf lauter ungleiche Fälle passen muss. Jeder Begriff entsteht durch Gleichsetzen des Nicht-Gleichen. So gewiss nie ein Blatt einem anderen ganz gleich ist, so gewiss ist der Begriff Blatt durch beliebiges Fallenlassen dieser individuellen Verschiedenheiten, durch ein Vergessen des Unterscheidenden gebildet...

    Über Wahrheit und Lüge im aussermoralischen Sinne

4. The original of Nietzsche's argument follows:

    Was ist also Wahrheit? Ein bewegliches Heer von Metaphern, Metonymien, anthropomorphismen, kurz eine Summe von menschlichen Relationen, die, poetisch und rhetorisch gesteigert, übertragen, geschmückt wurden, und die nach langem Gebrauch einem Volke fest, canonisch und verbindlich dünken: die Wahrheiten sind Illusionen, von denen man vergessen hat, dass sie welche sind, Metaphern, die abgenutzt und sinnlich kraftlos geworden sind, Münzen, die ihr Bild verloren haben und nun als Metall, nicht mehr als Münzen, in Betracht kommen. ...denn bis jetzt haben wir nur von der Verpflichtung gehört, die die Gesellschaft, um zu existiren, stellt, wahrhaft zu sein, d. h. die usuellen Metaphern zu brauchen, also moralisch ausgedrückt: von der Verpflichtung nach einer festen Convention zu lügen, schaarenweise in einem für alle verbindlichen Stile zu lügen. Nun vergisst freilich der Mensch, dass es so mit ihm steht; er lügt also in der bezeichneten Weise unbewusst und nach hundertjährigen Gewöhnungen—und kommt eben durch diese Unbewusstheit, eben durch dies Vergessen zum Gefühl der Wahrheit.

5. According to Cummins (97-98),

> The *Craft of Venery* deduces the etymology of the French word *sanglier* from his [the boar's] unsociable nature: '"Why clepe ye borre synguler?" "For he is the furst yere a *pigge,* the while he sokythe his dame, and when his dame hathe left him, then is he called at that yere *suklyng,* the whiche is called yn ffrenche *sorayne*. The IIIde yere they ben called *hogastrys,* and when he is of age of IIII yere, he schall departyn out of companye by kynde of age and schal gone alone. And when he is alone, he schall then be called *synguler* for the causes fore seid."

Cummins also cites Psalm (79) 80 (.14), where the boar is called *singularis ferus*. "Exterminavit eam aper de silva et singularis ferus depastus est eam 14 The boar out of the wood hath laid it waste: and a singular wild beast hath devoured it" (276-7).

6. My position resembles less that of Adelman (*Mothers* 9) or Bloom (*Anxiety* xxxv) and more that of Greenblatt (Norton 509).

7. We know that the theaters were closed because of a particularly virulent outbreak of Plague during these years, and we assume that Shakespeare was writing, in great part, to secure patronage and thus income during a lean hour. He was wildly successful in his endeavor since *Ven.* was an instant "hit." But it is interesting to consider, I think, that the commercial success did not represent a suspension of the psychic quest.

Chapter 5

1. The Editors of the *Textual Companion* write a very long statement (113a-115b) of the case for collaboration in *Titus*, principally in Act 1; Peele's hand is apparently uncertain, however. Recognizing that this is a very thorny problem, I must admit I nevertheless find the play to be Shakespeare's, no serious doubt in my mind.
2. The reader consulting this chapter in isolation may wish to consider the final paragraph of the preceding chapter as an orientation.
3. Significantly, the list begins with Act 2—i.e., after the act which may have been largely Peele's work (Oxford 2ᵉ 155).
4. This discrepancy, it is probably true to say, has been one of the dominant notes of the past 25 years of criticism, in Greenblatt, Maus, and a host of others.
5. *OED* II *sub voce,* "It.; lit. 'charge,' 'loading,' f. *caricare* to charge, load, exaggerate."
6. I propose that we have here one key to one of the most vexed cruces in English

literary history. Hamlet has no viable, applicable story; all stories around him that he can see are corrupt or suspicious or vested. He has, therefore, no alternative but to write *his* story—for him, no pre-script(ion) at all. For him, "[t]he readiness is all," and it is just that, *all*. Hence the (in)famous delay, until readiness is ready.

7. This is why forgery or counterfeiting is so important to literary theory: non-mutation or non-deviation suggests an absence of creative intention, the presence of malicious intention, or, if not that, then of mechanical replication; see, in particular, Hugh Kenner, *The Counterfeiters*.
8. I speculate—I can do no more—that this lesson was for Shakespeare inseparable from his likeness to Marlowe, which he had to mut(il)ate. Cf. Bloom, *Anxiety* xxix.
9. I avoid "generative" because I do not wish to imply that Shakespeare is somehow androgynous—I do not believe that it would be helpful to think of him as an androgyne.
10. Norton 371 comments on the possibility of excluding *Titus* from the canon.
11. I comment further on this matter in my chapter on *Coriolanus*.

Chapter 6

1. For just a few examples, see Hendricks and N. Vickers.
2. Oxford 2^e notes also (237) that

   > The writing of the poem seems to have been a formative experience for Shakespeare. In it he not only laid the basis for his later plays on Roman history, but also explored themes that were to figure prominently in his later work.

3. We need to remember that in EME "will" is also slang for the genitalia — see esp. Fineman 1987.
4. See the entry under Zeuxis in the *Oxford Classical Dictionary*, where we also read that he was reputed to have said that, had he painted the boy with the grapes better, the birds would have been too frightened to try to peck them—the illusion of verisimilitude is always just that.

Chapter 7

1. The Oxford editors disagree: "We believe ... that Shakespeare was responsible only for Scene 2...and Scene 3...and for Scene 12...and possibly Scene 13, and that one or more other authors wrote the rest of the play" (257).
2. It will perhaps help to reflect further here on 16th-c. understandings of the "mirrors."

   > Its ["A Mirror for Magistrates"] aim is medieval, whether we take the statement of its editor, Baldwin, in the address to the nobility—"here as in a loking glass, you shal se if any vice be in you, how the like hath ben punished in other heretofore, wherby admonished, I trust

it will be a good occasione to move to the amendment"—or that in the address to the reader—"which might be as a mirour for al men as well nobles as others to shewe the slipery deceiptes of the wavering lady, and the due rewarde of all kinde of vices."

> *The Cambridge History of English and American Literature*
> Volume III. *Renascence and Reformation* IX.
> "A Mirror for Magistrates." § 1. The original design.

On "mirrors for princes" in late medieval England, see Ferster; on mirrors more generally, see Grabes; Garber (*Ghost Writers* 116) discusses mirror as "example" and cites *HV* 2.Prol. 6, "the mirror of all Christian kings."

3. See, further, in confirmation *HV* 3.1.17-30 (emphasis added):

> On, on, you noblest English,
> Whose blood is fet from fathers of war-proof,
> Fathers that *like* so many *Alexanders*
> Have in these parts from morn till even fought,
> And sheathed their swords for lack of argument.
> Dishonour not your mothers; now attest
> That those whom you called fathers did beget you.
> *Be copy now* to men of grosser blood,
> And teach them how to war. And you, good yeoman,
> Whose limbs were made in England, *show* us here
> The mettle of your pasture; let us swear
> That you are worth your breeding — which I doubt not,
> For there is none of you so mean and base
> That hath not noble lustre in your eyes.

The theater of likeness would expect just here, in this play, just such an evocation of the "mirrors for princes"; but it also accounts for the ironies provoked by "famous victories"—see chapter 10, "'I cannot tell vat is 'like me': Inventing a Likeness in The Second Henriad."

Chapter 8

1. This passage, in *TNK*, is assigned confidently to Shakespeare, not Fletcher.
2. The word "gossip" was originally "god-relative" referring to a child's sponsor at baptism (*OED* II *sub voce*):

> [OE. *godsibb* masc. (f. *god* god + *sib(b* adj., akin, related: see sib *a*.) = ON. *guð-sefe* masc., *guð-sifja* fem., OSw. *guzsowir* masc., *guÞziff*, *gudzsöff* fem. ...] **1** One who has contracted spiritual affinity with another by acting as a sponsor at a baptism. **a** In relation to the person baptized: A godfather or godmother; a sponsor.

3. I draw on the following account:

> "Pholus (Pholos). A Centaur, son of Silenus and the nymph Melia. In the performance of his fourth task, which was to bring the

Erymanthian boar alive to Eurystheus, Heracles (q.v.) took his road through Pholoë, where he was hospitably entertained by Pholus. The Centaur set before his guest roast meat, though *he himself fared on raw*. Heracles asking for wine, his host said he feared to open the jar, which was *the common property of the Centaurs*; but, when pressed by the hero, he consented to unclose it for him. The fragrance of the wine spread over the mountain, and soon brought all the Centaurs, armed with stones and pine sticks, to the cave of Pholus. The first who ventured to enter were driven back by Heracles with burning brands: he hunted the remainder with his arrows to Malea. When Heracles returned to Pholoë from this pursuit, *he found Pholus lying dead along with several others*; for, having drawn the arrow out of the body of one of them, while he was wondering how so small a thing could destroy such large beings, it dropped out of his hand and stuck in his foot, and he died immediately (Apollod.ii.5.4 foll.)" (emphasis added).

From http://www.perseus.tufts.edu/ (06.04.03 last access)

Chapter 9

1. I accept the assignments in Oxford 2^e.
2. Regarding the lost *Love's Labour's Won*, I will take this occasion to conjecture — what else can one do? — that it was probably also topical.
3. The locution "speaks not like a man" occurs nowhere else in the canon that I can find.
4. Hence also the subversive counterpoint between the nobility plot and the *commedia dell'arte* subplot. Shakespeare exposes the one with the other: "Here is like to be a good presence of Worthies" (*LLL* 5.2.529; emphasis added) cuts in the direction of the nobles as well as the non-noble players.

Chapter 10

1. This chapter is the first essay I wrote and published in my project ("'For there is figures in all things'"). Except for rearrangement of parts of it, I have left it unmodified, and I have simplified notation wherever I could.
2. I refer, obviously, to Saussurean ideas even as I am aware of numerous attacks on de Saussure from many different ideological poles.
3. Note that the character who makes this crucial response to Henry V is named *Will*iams — as if Shakespeare, pluralizing his own given name, inserts himself into his play to expose the problematic of Henry's multiple identities. See, further, on Shakespeare's use of his name, Will, Fineman (1987, 1991) and Willbern.
4. "Elizabeth's godson, Sir John Harington, suggested that the queen's success

5. Richard's narcissism, which I assume is obvious not only here but throughout the play, differs from that of Richard III (whom I have called the "disfigured Narcissus") just in the measure to which Richard is so obviously a poet, a man of poetic temperament rather than political or martial temperament (though he is no coward, as the end of the play shows). Richard II's self-love is never mixed quite so thoroughly with self-loathing as is Richard III's; this is part of the innocence or naiveté of Richard II, that renders him unfit to rule but also endows him with prodigious discursive powers. He is very much a "figured Narcissus," and this accounts in part for our sense of loss when he dies—someone beautiful has vanished from the world (see, further, *RII* 3.3.67-70) and we grieve at the disappearance of the difference.
6. See chapter 7 on *Edward III*.
7. This also is Shakespeare's "perjured eye" (Sonnet #152), the eye/I that can only know its li(k)e.
8. And the words also mirror earlier occurrences of themselves in the play:

> God pardon all oaths that are broke to me.
> God keep all vows unbroke are made to thee.
> Make me, that *nothing* have, with *nothing* grieved,
> And thou with all *pleased*, that hast all achieved.
> *RII* 4.1.204-7 (emphasis added)

Shakespeare's ear is unerring: time and again, he shows that Richard failed to grasp the difference in likeness and the likeness in difference until it was too late. The king may boast, "[w]e were not born to sue, but to command" (*RII* 1.1.196), but the king cannot command the meaning (the likeness) of "nothing" (and see, further, John of Gaunt's ultimately vain warning to the same effect—*RII* 1.3.219-25).

Consider, further, as well, the notable crux at *RII* 2.2.30-32:

> **QUEEN** I cannot but be sad: so heavy-sad
> As thought — on thinking on no thought I think —
> Makes me with heavy nothing faint and shrink.

Hearing Shakespeare sound syneciotic changes on "nothing" in the play, I would paraphrase:

> I cannot but be sad, so heavy-sad, since thought, although I think that I am thinking on no thought, makes me, just so, with that heavy nothing (of thinking that I am thinking on no thought, nothing) still faint and shrink.

In this play, "nothing" is an influential player, nothing less than a differentiating power.

9. Percy's wife explains very clearly why Henry V had to eliminate his likeness Hotspur:

> by his [Hotspur's] light
> Did all the chivalry of England move
> To do brave acts. He was indeed the *glass*
> Wherein the noble youth did dress themselves.
> He had no legs that practised not his gait;
> And speaking thick, which nature made his blemish,
> Became the accents of the valiant;
> For those that could speak low and tardily
> Would turn their own perfection to abuse
> *To seem like him.* So that in speech, in gait,
> In diet, in affections of delight,
> In military rules, humours of blood,
> *He was the mark and glass, copy and book,*
> *That fashioned others.*
>
> 2HIV 2.3.19-32 (emphasis added)

The threat of this likeness, that all copy Hotspur "to seem like him" rather than Hal, future Henry V, is the more pressing just in the measure to which Hotspur was a "mirror for princes" long before Hal. Hotspur was a known commodity in a venerable tradition who could not be discredited without being defeated and, finally, slain.

10. Notice here the pressing insistence in the Second Henriad on succession and inheritance.
11. Cf. Hal's dream with that of Richard, as he departs from his wife for the last time:

> Join not with grief, fair woman, do not so,
> To make my end too sudden. Learn, good soul,
> To think our former state a happy *dream,*
> From which awaked, the truth of what we are
> Shows us but this. I am sworn brother, sweet,
>   To grim necessity, and he and I
>   Will keep a league till death.
>
> RII 5.1.16-22 (emphasis added)

Chapter 11

1. I adopt and adapt Hegel's "concrete universal" (*Lectures on the History of Philosophy* 2.2.3 "IDEA OF A CONCRETE UNIVERSAL UNITY") to my purposes, which include not only a concern with "the one and the many," but also a suspicion that Shakespeare's tragedies examine the exigencies and the costs of human inversion of the Incarnation, flesh attempting to become Word (most evident in *King Lear*) as a defense against the vicissitudes of history and

the inexorableness of time; such an attempt is not only bound to fail, it is also bound to self-deception, that self-deception that is always tragic and yet that, when released, issues in peace—"The readiness is all."

2. See *Being and Time*, § H175, on "the they:" "Under the mask of 'for-one-another,' an 'against-one-another' is in play," which is always tending toward death, the death of Dasein before the death of Dasein's body.

3. In one of the, for me, most powerful moments in Western literature, Telemachus tells Athena, who is in disguise, that Penelope claims he is Odysseus's son, but "I don't know, for who knows for sure his own begetting?" (*Odyssey* 1.216). "Thrown," as Heidegger expresses it, into a world remorselessly prior to him or her, each person must dis/cover "his own begetting" or accept without question what others prescribe. It seems to me that Shakespeare's theater of likeness is the theater (and the theory) of resisting mere acceptance of the likeness that one has been told is one's own, even when the cost, as so often, is life itself.

4. Wallace Stevens: "In reality as in metaphor, identity is the vanishing point of resemblance" (*Angel* 79).

5. Inasmuch as we here deal with a crisis of categorizing and the effort to use comparison for categorizing without pejoration, which is extremely difficult to do, we see Shakespeare in a line that includes also his great predecessor Chaucer:

> But nathelees, whil I have tyme and space,
> Er that I ferther in this tale pace,
> Me thynketh it acordaunt to resoun
> To telle yow al the condicioun
> Of ech of hem, so as it semed me,
> And whiche they weren, and of what degree.
>
> *Canterbury Tales* I A 35-40

For my argument that the *Canterbury Tales* and the *General Prologue*, especially, are usefully thought of also as the "Category Tales," see Shoaf, *Chaucer's Body* 134-7.

6. *OED* II *sub voce*: "f. *inter* between, within + *legìre* to bring together, gather, pick out, choose, catch up, catch with the eye, read."

7. Wells and Taylor, *Companion* (294), observe:

> 2.1.86/817 word] Q2; name Q1. Many editors follow Q1, but there is no adequate reason to suspect that Q2 is corrupt. The error is probably one of memorial substitution in Q1 under the influence of repeated "name." Even if the variant arises through misreading, corruption from "word" to "name" is, in the context, more likely than the reverse.

I find this argument sensible and would not dispute the reading they choose. At the same time, given the thesis I am pursuing, I think I owe it to myself and my reader to acknowledge that Q1 records "name."

8. See the *Roman de la Rose* 4293ff.: "Love is hateful peace and loving hate ... love is a sin touched by pardon but a pardon stained by sin" (trans. Dahlberg

94-95); and Petrarch's sonnet 132: "S' amor non è" ("If not love, then what is this that I feel..."; trans. Cook 192-3). No doubt, many other sources intervene as well from which Shakespeare draws to write Romeo's speech; these two, however, are especially influential in the *fin'amors* tradition.

Chapter 12

1. I base "consimilibus" upon Aubrey's "consimility" in his entry under Francis Beaumont: "there was a wonderful consimility of phansey between him and Mr. John Fletcher..." (43).
2. Scheid and Svenbro's study of tropes of weaving in Western literature has been very important to my thinking on Shakespeare's theater of likeness.

Chapter 13

1. Who, recall, was branded bastard by legal proceedings, which were later nullified and the slander revoked. See Levin (2003) 7. I speculate that *King John* may be more about Elizabeth than at first we appreciate—how *do* you know the child is like the father? Mary Tudor spread the rumor that "Elizabeth physically resembled Mark Smeaton, reputed to be one of Anne Boleyn's lovers, more than Henry VIII" (Levin, *Reign* 10).

Chapter 14

1. See, above, Preface pages xviii-xix.
   Here, I would take occasion to cite Ulpian Fulwel's moral interlude, *Like Will To Like* (1568), in which the word *like* occurs over 300 times. The interlude also uses the idea of like attracted to like to develop continuous satire of human failing as the devil pursues his likeness among men and women.

   > THE PROLOGUE
   > Cicero in his book De Amicitia these woords dooth expresse,
   > Saying nothing is more desirous then like is unto like;
   > Whose woords are most true and of a certainty doubtles:
   > For the vertuous doo not the vertuous company mislike.
   > But the vicious dooth the vertuous company eschue:
   > And like wil unto like, this is most true.
   > ...
   >
   > Where like to like is matched so
   > That vertue must of force decay:
   > There God with vengeance, plagues and woe
   > By iudgement iust must needs repay.
   > For like to like, the worldlings cry,

> Although both like doo grace defye.
> And where as Sathan planted hath
> In vicious mindes a sinful trade,
> There like to like dooth walke this path,
> By which to him like they are made.

The interlude and its context in late Elizabethan culture merit extended study.

2. It may be that we must think even harder about how deep the irony runs in Portia's eye-opening question: "Which is the merchant here, and which the Jew?" (*MV* 4.1.171).

3. Here may be found one explanation for Portia's remarkable castigation of Bassanio's oath:

> **BASSANIO** Portia, forgive me this enforcèd wrong,
> And in the hearing of these many friends
> I swear to thee, even by thine own fair eyes,
> Wherein I see myself —
> **PORTIA**   Mark you but that?
> *In both my eyes he doubly sees himself,*
> *In each eye one. Swear by your double self,*
> And there's an oath of credit.
>
> MV 5.1.240-6 (emphasis added)

Bassanio will not be "respective" until he no longer "doubly sees himself," until he is no longer a "double self." He must, so to speak, cease being Bassanio and/as Antonio and become Bassanio-Portia (her *portion* in him): only when he sees from this perspective will he become "respective," seeing singly, not doubly.

Chapter 15

1. Oxford 2ᵉ restores Sir John Oldcastle as the character's name (481). Since it is not material to my argument, I retain Falstaff for greater ease of recognition.

2. Which is how I understand Ben Jonson's famous complaint that Shakespeare never blotted a line:

> I remember, the players have often mentioned it as an honour to Shakespeare that in his writing (whatsoever he penned) he never blotted out line. My answer hath been, would he had blotted a thousand. Which they thought a malevolent speech. . .
>
> Timber, or Discoveries (1630)

Had Shakespeare prodigally "blotted a thousand," he would have also assassinated the prodigy that he is.

Chapter 16

1. It is important to register the solecism in Don Pedro's "you are like an honourable father": he may mean she "looks like" her father or he may mean she "behaves like" her father or he may mean "she has the defining characteristics, moral as well as physical," of her father; but all of these meanings mean just that he cannot mean she *is* "like her father"—anatomically, it is impossible, and there is all the difference (it might as well be) in the world. Because she can never *be* "like her father" in the way a son could *be* "like his father," she cannot be trusted to bear her father's likeness, although she could, in fact, bear it, morally as well as physiologically (a grandson), far more honorably than could, for example, a son profligate, dissolute, or otherwise corrupt from a father upright and decent. Here is where sexual division is so cruel, that a good daughter is simply not *like* a son, good or otherwise. Is it possibly significant that, as the historical evidence hints (Honan 400), Shakespeare related well to Susannah, who, in turn, was said to have her father's wit? Are all of Shakespeare's early plays a prelude to Lear and Cordelia? A prelude to learning that a daughter is as good as a son however unlike a son?
2. I should make a point of noting that I see the conversions of Beatrice and Benedick not as shallow and expedient but as inevitable extensions of the likenesses already at work.

Chapter 17

1. The actual text in the Folio is entitled *The Tragedy of Julius Caesar*.
2. I acknowledge another way of comprehending Caesar's uniqueness.

> **ANTONY** Pardon me, Julius. Here wast thou bayed, brave hart;
> Here didst thou fall, and here thy hunters stand
> Signed in thy spoil and crimsoned in thy lethe.
> *O world, thou wast the forest to this hart;*
> *And this indeed, O world, the heart of thee.*
> How *like* a deer strucken by many princes
> Dost thou here lie!
> JC 3.1.205-11 (emphasis added)

It is possible to think of Caesar as "*like* a deer," as *so very much nature*, that the world was forest to his hart and he was heart to the world. The pun, which is venerable (it is found also in Chaucer's *Book of the Duchess*, for example [1313]), serves Shakespeare as a way of removing Caesar from the order of things, of installing him outside the boundaries of culture. But whether we think of him as para-natural or as inner-natural, the point is Caesar's difference, distinguishing him from everyone else without exception.

3. My sense of Shakespeare's career as a writer is strongly influenced by the evidence that he was frequently divided between the monologic and the

dialogic. Recall, for example, Sonnet #105 (7-8):

> Therefore my verse, to constancy confined,
> *One thing expressing, leaves out difference.*

Like Dante and Milton, as I understand them, he was attracted to what we might call "monarchical meaning" and yet at the same time profoundly distrusted it and the emotions that it arouses—they are the makings and the markings and the marrings of totalitarianism.

4. It is imperative in this moment to hear what Brutus is saying, the *name* of honor. Of all likenesses a man may pursue, honor is perhaps the most fraught because it is essentially and substantially "the *name* of honor"—no matter how honorable a man may be, if he lose the name of honor, he is not honorable:

> What
> is honour? A word. What is in that word "honour"?
> What is that "honour"? Air. A trim reckoning! Who
> hath it? He that died o' Wednesday. Doth he feel it?
> No. Doth he hear it? No. 'Tis insensible then? Yea, to
> the dead. But will it not live with the living? No. Why?
> *Detraction will not suffer it.* Therefore I'll none of it.
> Honour is a mere scutcheon. And so ends my catechism.
>
> 1HIV 5.1. 133-40 (emphasis added)

"What is honour? A word." The likeness of honor is non-negotiable; the very definition of *honor* is "non-negotiability," the singular, undivided, constant word, with which therefore Falstaff will have nothing to do—hang your life on a word? "Detraction [i.e., slander] will not suffer it."

Yet, in fact, men do hang their lives on a word. And herein is why the tragedy of Brutus is so important to Shakespeare's theater of likeness: it prepares the stage for the understanding of tragedy as the elimination of options, the reduction of one's likeness to absolute singularity—no room in Rome for Brutus.

5. Cf. Antipholus of Syracuse: "Known unto these, and to myself disguised!" (*Err.* 2.2.217).

Chapter 18

1. Milton also shares Shakespeare's anxiety over sorting. In Book 8 of *Paradise Lost*, Adam argues with God (383-84; 389-92; emphasis added),

> "Among unequals what societie
> *Can sort*
> ...   Of fellowship I speak
> Such as I seek, fit to participate
> All rational delight, wherein the brute
> Cannot be human *consort*"

Both writers, I suggest, are reacting, out of a kind of preternatural sympathy, to the cultural cataclysm through which they lived of method-ism: whether we cite Ramus or Descartes or a host of other thinkers on the eve of the Scientific Revolution, we find method moving toward scientific method and the resulting breakdown and decay of older protocols of categorizing or sorting the world and the human in the world—I *can* sort with *what* consort? See not only Ong but also Burckhardt.

2. "*Twelfth Night* would prove to be, in the view of many critics, both the most perfect and in some sense the last of the great festive comedies"—Norton 1762.

3. My reflection of Derrida is obvious, but I hope to distort the reflection in useful ways as my work progresses—see, e.g., *Dissemination* 208-26.

4. *OED* II *sub voce*:

> Gr., κωμῳδία n. of practice f. κωμῳδός comedian; a compound, either of κῶμος revel, merry-making, or of its probable source, κώμη village + ἀοιδός singer, minstrel, f. ἀείδ-ειν to sing (cf. ode). The κωμῳδός was thus originally either the "bard of the revels" or the "village-bard."

As the village-bard, the comedian is the singer of the collective and the families that comprise it:

> 'Tis Hymen peoples every *town*.
>   High wedlock then be honourèd.
> Honour, high honour and renown
>   To Hymen, god of every *town*.
>
> AYL 5.4.141-4 (emphasis added)

Hymen's is the voice of the comedian, and Shakespeare, gifted in this voice though he be, is nonetheless beginning to find it incapable of saying what he needs to say.

5. Thus, note the exciting and exacting precision of Shakespeare's language: Hymen speaks,

> Good Duke, receive thy daughter;
> Hymen from heaven brought her,
>   Yea, brought her hither,
> That thou mightst join her hand with his
> Whose heart within his bosom is.
> **ROSALIND** (*to the Duke*) *To you I give myself, for I am yours.*
> (*To Orlando*) *To you I give myself, for I am yours.*
> **DUKE SENIOR** If there be truth in sight, you are my *daughter*.
> **ORLANDO** If there be truth in sight, you are *my Rosalind*.
>
> AYL 5.4.109-17 (emphasis added)

Rosalind is here *connected*, she is *inserted into* the net of relationships, she acknowledges those to whom she belongs, but are "my daughter" and "my Rosalind" Rosalind? Comedy does not answer this question, which is why, I think, Shakespeare was compelled to experiment with tragedy.

6. See also

    > Then is there mirth in heaven
    > When earthly things made even
    >   Atone together.
    >
    > *AYL* 5.4.106-8

7. I know that *divinity* and *division* have different roots; I also know that Shakespeare could hear what he was saying.

Chapter 19

1. For this version of my argument, I have simplified notation wherever possible; full notation can be found in Shoaf, "Like Mother."
2. Here, as throughout my study, I follow the text established in Oxford 2ᵉ. I think that the complexity of transmission in the case of *Hamlet*, however, warrants my citing the Oxford editorial statement at some length (681):

    > It is our belief that Shakespeare wrote *Hamlet* about 1600, and revised it later; that the 1604 edition was printed from his original papers; that the Folio represents the revised version; and that the 1603 edition represents a very imperfect report of an abridged version of the revision. So our text is based on the Folio; passages present in the 1604 quarto but absent from the Folio are printed as Additional Passages because we believe that, however fine they may be in themselves, Shakespeare decided that the play as a whole would be better without them.

    Hence, when I cite passages present in the 1604 quarto, I give full reference not only to the quarto but to the pages in Oxford 2ᵉ where the Additional Passages are printed—e.g., *Ham*. Q2 4.4.47-48; Oxford 2ᵉ 718K.
3. I will represent anagrams in this form: I am concerned to represent letters in all their insistence and (seeming) impertinence.
4. Notice now the excruciating irony of Hamlet's Hercules proportion—

    Claudius / Hamlet
    ≠
    Old Hamlet / Hercules.

    Hercules, as Shakespeare would have known, was the victim of a *woman*, Hera, throughout his life ("Gr. Ἡρακλῆς(-κλέης), Hera, wife of Zeus + κλέος glory, renown, lit. 'having or showing the glory of Hera'—*OED* II *sub voce*"). In other words, all four men are, tragically, just a*like*, showing the glory of Her(a).
5. I follow Lacan ("Jouissance") to understand and represent the overturning of the generality of the woman in Hamlet's emerging self-consciousness: the illusion of the woman is gradually fading before the reality of this particular woman, Gertrude.

    On the importance to understanding *Hamlet* of the wordplay between

Latin *mater* and English *matter* (which derives from *mater*), see Ferguson, esp. 294-5; see also Parker, *Margins* 254, 263.

6. F1 continues Hamlet's speech just quoted, crucially from my perspective, with

> **HAMLET** Sir, in this Audience,
> Let my disclaiming from a purpos'd euill,
> Free me so farre in your most generous thoughts,
> That I have shot mine Arrow o're the house,
> And hurt my *Mother*.
>
> 5.2.177-81 (in F's orthography)

Q1 and Q2 have "brother," which may in the end be a better reading, but I wish to observe that the textual history of the play includes, if only as an error, the agony as well as the irony of Hamlet's renewed "sanity."

7. As others have noted, the rhetorical device most frequent in *Hamlet* that bears the burden of splitting/doubling is hendiadys; see Holland 167:

> ... one of the tragedy's two characteristic figures of speech: hendiadys, which means expressing a single idea by two nouns or adjectives parted by a conjunction: "the sensible and true avouch of mine own eyes," "the gross and scope of mine opinion."

The word *like* can be understood to spawn perverse hendiadys: splitting where there should be no division—"love *like* love."

On the other hand is isocolon (Ferguson, "Letters" 293): "balanced clauses joined by 'and'," which is the rhetorical device favored by Claudius:

> ... the principle of similarity...governs Claudius's syntax...Claudius's isocolonic style is also characteristically oxymoronic: opposites are smoothly joined by syntax and sound, as for instance in these lines from his opening speech:
>
>> Therefore our sometime sister, now our queen,
>> Th'imperial jointress to this warlike state,
>> Have we, as 'twere with a defeated joy,
>> With an auspicious and a dropping eye,
>> With mirth in funeral and with dirge in marriage,
>> In equal scale weighing delight and dole,
>> Taken to wife
>
> I.ii.8-14

8. Dutch, Danish, and Swedish forms of the word mean "corpse." See Skeat, *sub voce*; also Ayto 295. For a discussion of Shakespeare's neologism "incorpsed" (*Ham.* 4.7.72), see Ferguson, "Letters" 301ff.

9. And to the "tragedy" of *Hamlet*: the notorious difficulty of the play's genre, even its scandal, can be compassed, at least partially, just here: *Hamlet* is obviously *like* "revenge tragedy" and, just as obviously, it is not—*Hamlet*, like Hamlet, is trying to break free from its likeness to predecessors.

10. Cf. Lacan's rich meditation on separation ("*Separare*, séparer, ici se termine en *se parere*, s'engendrer soi-même...") in "Position de l'inconscient" (*Écrits* 843).

11. On "close" in the play, see Parker, *Margins*, 254-5, who also notes the play with "closet" (254).
12. Which was not stirring at the beginning—

    BERNARDO Have you had quiet guard?
    FRANCISCO Not a mouse stirring.

    Ham. 1.1.7-8

    Here it is pertinent to note that repetition in *Hamlet* is often a smear of words, a certain stain, that spreads across the play even as rottenness spreads through Elsinore and Denmark; and *like*(ness) itself (known otherwise as the "body") is the (name of the) contagion. See, also, Parker, *Margins* 218: "Words themselves are coupled in this play with a sense of pestilent breeding. ..."
13. Cf. Freud's famous if cryptic utterance, "Wo Es war, soll Ich werden" (*SE* XXII:80), where "Es" is Freud's German for "Id," the "it" of the unconscious.
14. Cf. Cavell, *Disowning*:

    To exist is to take your existence upon you, to enact it, as if the basis of human existence is theater, even melodrama.... Hamlet's extreme sense of theater I take as his ceaseless perception of theater, say show, as an inescapable or metaphysical mark of the human condition.... His bar—his lack of 'advancement' into the world—is expressed in one's sense (my sense) of him as the Ghost of the play that bears his and his father's name, a sense that his refusal of participation in the world is his haunting of the world. (As if he is a figure in a play.) He overcomes his refusal only in announcing his death. (*Disowning* 187-8).

15. The syntax admits of a confession of guilt (cf. Adelman, *Mothers* 246n4).
16. And consider also Hamlet at *Ham.* 5.2.78-9: "For by the image of my cause I see/The portraiture of his."
17. From one perspective, the problematics of the "proper" and "property" are among the oldest contests in Western philosophy. Plato is concerned with it, for example, in the *Cratylus*. Heidegger addresses it especially in the essay "Logos (Heraclitus, Fragment B 50)." See also, for historical overview, Parker, *Ladies* 36ff.
18. I think it difficult to exaggerate how important Claudius' intuition here is: he recognizes, if only subliminally, the woman in Hamlet, the *egg-bearer*, and thus all the more pointed his earlier exclamation: "I like him not, nor *stands it safe with us*" (*Ham.* 3.3.1; emphasis added).
19. In the Latin rhetorical tradition, *improprie* is one word used to mean "metaphorically"; another, equally suggestive, is *abusive* (reflecting the Greek *catachresis*, "against usage")—see Shoaf, *Currency* 33-34 and notes 24-27.
20. Lest my irony be lost in the monotone of ideologizing, let me insist that I ventriloquize—I personally do not believe Ophelia deserves chastisement, even as, I know, my commentary here perforce chastises her all over again.
21. Hence the notorious crux, in this speech peculiar to Q2 (namely, "the dram of eale"), is amenable to a certain emendation:

> **HAMLET** So, oft it chances in particular men
> That, for some vicious mole of nature in them — ...
> The dram of [z]eale
> Doth all the noble substance over-daub
> To his own scandal.
>
> *Ham.* Q2 1.4.7-8; 20-22 (Oxford 2ᵉ 716B)
> Wells and Taylor, *Companion* 410

I would paraphrase the text to say, with my emendation of "eale" to "[z]eale": "the tiny amount (eighth of an ounce) of *excess desire* ([z]eale) does all the noble substance smear over to his own scandal."

This construction and paraphrase track and continue the logic of the earlier part of Hamlet's speech where "o'ergrowth" and "o'erleavens" suggest a failure of proportion between the "vicious mole" (a blemish) and the "virtues else ... as pure as grace" (*Ham.* Q2 1.4.17 [Oxford 2ᵉ 716B]); in other words, my emendation "[z]eale" here would suggest exactly that excess (desire) only a "dram" of which, a tiny bit of which, would be enough to swell so as to smear over the "noble substance," which, in turn, would be enough for "scandal."

This, of course, is only conjecture.

22. Here it is relevant, not to mention proper, that I acknowledge these other scholars precisely by remarking that their copiousness empowers my ability to copy from them, as I learn from them, but also that my copying from them, to develop my own theses, attests to and legitimates their copiousness. The genealogy of learning is familial—and most of its crises are like those of a (more or less dysfunctional) family (in which incest is not unheard of). Have we here, I permit myself to wonder, one reason why *Hamlet* is the site of such immense scholarly and critical activity? Here, in this play, if anywhere, sons and daughters must *separare* in order to *se parere* (and my macaronic French and English is itself evidence of the crisis [see above n. 10]). Indeed, now perhaps, just so, is the time for me to acknowledge my likeness, and unlikeness, to Shell, who writes brilliantly of likeness and the lex talionis in Shakespeare (117-36, in particular); but not only did I develop my ideas before reading his work (the obligatory if petulant plea of professionalism), also I differ from him in my insistence on the uncanny sign of *like*(ness), even as I depend on him to explain so well "the movement ... from substitution and likeness to identification" (136).

23. These are the same name. See Honan 90.

24. I deliberately adapt Dr. Johnson's famous characterization of the "metaphysicals" so as to leverage my own alternative account of Shakespearean rhetoric. See Johnson, *Lives* 1:20:

> Wit...may be more rigorously and philosophically considered as a kind of discordia concors; a combination of dissimilar images, or discovery of occult resemblances in things apparently unlike. Of wit, thus defined, [the metaphysical poets] have more than enough. The most heterogeneous ideas are yoked by violence together.

Chapter 20

1. See, esp., Arendt, *Love*, and *Life* 2:84-110.
2. *Écrits*, trans. Sheridan 22 (emphasis added).
3. See Janson 1-5; Aristotle, *Metaphysics* 1.1.
4. Greenblatt's *Renaissance Self-Fashioning* is rarely far from my side as I try to imagine the difference between *like*ness and fashion(ing), a difference that has everything to do with early modern interiority.
5. "Hell is others" — Jean-Paul Sartre, *Huis Clos*.
6. "You have made us for yourself, and unquiet is the heart within us until it rests in you — *Confessions* 1.1 (translation mine).
7. The crucial evidence is found in Sonnets #134-6, #143, and in "A Lover's Complaint," lines 126-33.
8. I depend here not only on Altman's fine study but also, more generally, on Cassirer, Fish, Ong, and others who have engaged the question of method in 16th- and early 17th-century Europe. Whether we consider Ramus, or Milton, or, somewhat later, Locke, we are always looking at the real though elusive moment when rhetoric (which is always and everywhere involved in ethics) ceded method for the understanding of nature to science (which is always and everywhere involved in experience/experimentation) — it would take centuries for us to learn again that science is also rhetorical. Perhaps Bacon was the last to feel the obligatory connection between rhetoric and science (see, e.g., *The Advancement of Learning* 2 [ed. Vickers 190ff.]).
9. I follow Arendt's critique of the Cartesian solipsism — *Life*, 1:48-49; 2:151; 181. As I would put it, to pass from the *cogito* directly to the *ego* is to indulge a dangerous oblivion to the contumacy of mind — to forget how stubborn the self can be.
10. I rely on Honan's biography, which seems to me both judicious and forthright in its assessment of Shakespeare's relationship to the Catholic ambience of Stratford and environs during his youth — see, e.g., 6-7, 51-2, 78-79.
11. See also Sonnet 16: "To give away yourself keeps yourself still" (line 13).
12. Here note also the importance of the explicit allusion to the Actaeon myth (*TN* 1.1.17-22). It is not only the problem of the gaze nor only the dismemberment of Actaeon's body that are invoked, but also the violation of sexual intercourse per se. Few myths more graphically distinguish sterile erotic fascination (like Orsino's) from fertile copulation — even homoerotic copulation produces more love than the solitary masturbatory gaze that tears the body asunder. Moreover, I think Shakespeare would have been drawn to Ovid's concluding remarks on the fate of Actaeon:

   > Rumor in ambiguo est; aliis uiolentior aequo
   > Visa dea est, alii laudant dignamque seuera
   > Virginitate uocant; *pars inuenit utraque causas.*
   > *Metamorphoses* 3.253-5 (emphasis added)

   > As the tale spread views varied; some believed
   > Diana's violence unjust; some praised it,

> As proper to her chaste virginity.
> *Both sides found reason for their point of view.*
>
> (trans. Melville 58)

Or yes, or no: Or I si I no. The raw dilemma of auto-eroticism is its indecideability, its inconclusiveness, non-commitment, and vacillation (the hounds that tear it asunder as it wanders in the forest). Unless Orsino belongs to a lover, "rumor in ambiguo est" if his "desires, like fell and cruel hounds" (*TN* 1.1.21) dismember him: he would fall victim to his name, not just a "bear" ("orsino" < Italian: "bear-like") but also in(complete)human, prey with no hope of prayer (Orison).

13. See *OED* II *sub voce* (emphasis added):

    > 1540 R. JONAS tr. Roesslin's Byrth of Mankynde I. ix. fol. liii, "They that are borne after this fashion be called *cesares*, for because they *be cut out* of theyr mothers belly, whervpon also the noble Romane *cesar* the j. of that name in Rome toke his name."

14. It is crucial to recall here also that when Malvolio first reads the forged letter, he unwittingly spells "cut" (*TN* 2.5.85-87):

    > These be her very c's, her u's, and her t's, and
    > thus makes she her great P's.

    In addition to the innuendo regarding the female genitals (c u [n] t), we must also consider the possibility that Shakespeare has here another way of suggesting the general effect Cesario/Viola will have on those with whom she comes into contact. No one escapes the cut; everyone is cut one way or another.

15. And Shakespeare understands completely the perversion of this precondition—merely recall Tarquin's threat to Lucrece: "Unless thou yoke thy *liking* to my will" (*Luc.* 1633; emphasis added).

16. On Shakespeare's twins, Hamnet and Judith, see Honan 90, 231, 235, 321, and 389-96. I think that Shakespeare's own twins contributed significantly to his anxiety of twinship, doubling, crossing, (il)legitimacy, and *lik(en)ing*; the death of Hamnet by age 11, furthermore, may have exacerbated the anxiety, an anxiety I see most explosive and delirious in the actions of Leontes in *The Winter's Tale*.

17. See also Sonnets #10-18. Here, as elsewhere and often in Shakespeare's works, hetero- and homoeroticism are preferable to autoeroticism. At this stage in my studies, I speculate, provisionally and tentatively, that we see in this preference the emotionally Catholic individual (Introduction) who desires above all *to (re)produce*; as I understand his work, Shakespeare recoils from sterility in all its forms—sterility appalls him as the failure of human nature. Fertility, however, does insist on human *nature*—that the human is part of nature— and hence also Shakespeare's fitful misogyny: just because the overcoming of sterility necessitates passing through female sexuality, the mat(t)er of nature, Shakespeare for much of his adult life struggles, often cataclysmically (as in *Lear*), with the deeply contradictory imperative (to some extent, certainly, a

fantasy), "be natural < > transcend nature" : "connect with woman" < > "repel woman."

18. *RL* 1850-2:

> They did conclude to bear dead Lucrece thence,
> To show her bleeding body thorough Rome,
> And so to publish Tarquin's foul offence.

And see further chapter 6, page 67.

19. Or, as Maria says, under the forgery of Olivia,

> Thy [Malvolio's] fates open their
> hands, let thy blood and spirit embrace them, and *to
> inure thyself to what thou art like to be,* cast thy
> humble slough, and appear fresh. Be opposite with a
> kinsman, surly with servants. Let thy tongue tang
> arguments of state; put thyself into the trick of
> singularity. She thus advises thee that sighs for thee.
>
> *TN* 2.5.141-7 (emphasis added)

Here as elsewhere, Maria is almost empathic: she knows exactly what words will seduce ill will (< Malvolio), "a kind of puritan" (*TN* 2.3.135) — *inure* or "work" (< French *oeuvre*) yourself to your like(ness), for that is *what you will* (opposite, surly, tang[y] tongue, the trick of singularity).

20. Cf. Calderwood, *The Properties of* Othello. Here also I would acknowledge Berger, Fineman, and others who argue that characters are effects rather than causes of discourse (in Fineman's memorable phrase, "characteristic Shakespearean subjectivity effects"): characters become "who" they "are" as we believe, "be-like," their properties which are their effects upon us — "the *result* of a particular interpretive dialogue between reader, actor, director, or spectator, and the text" (Berger, *Trifles* 213; my emphasis). Believing/be-liking them, we invest our likeness in their likeness and thus they become "real" for us — they are like us as we be-like them.

I remain nonetheless edgy about the problem of agency inseparable from this position. Although Berger does a good job in many parts of *Trifles* addressing this problem (esp. 226-7), it seems to me far from certain that we fully grasp the relation between agency and subjectivity effect.

Chapter 23

1. Shakespeare underscores and measures Angelo's infelicitous remorse, self-accusation of clinging hypocrisy, with the evocation of the Sarum Use:

> God, be in my head, and in my understanding;
> God, be in my eyes, and in my looking;
> *God, be in my mouth,* and in my speaking.
> God, *be in my heart*, and *in my thinking.*
> God, be at my end, and at my departing.
>
> Sarum Primer, 1558 CE (emphasis added)

2. On the name Isabelle,

> **ISABEL** (f) Most likely a medieval Spanish form of ELIZABETH ... **ELIZABETH** (f) "oath of God" (Hebrew). In the Old Testament this was the name of the wife of Aaron. In the New Testament this was the mother of John the Baptist.... From "Behind the Name: The Etymology and History of First Names."
>
> http://www.behindthename.com/nmc/eng7.html
> Last accessed 04/02/04

3. Cf. Ovid's brilliant dramatization of this in the tale of Myrrha's incest with her father Cinyras—*Metamorphoses* 10.
4. See Shoaf *Duality*, passim, where I develop at length the argument for the viability of *part*nership—"Sole partner and sole part of all these joyes" (*Paradise Lost* 4.411), as Adam says to Eve in his first speech in the poem.
5. Here I follow Oxford 2^e, but I acknowledge the textual issue the editors address at pages 870-1.
6. Most notably, perhaps, in *King Lear* [1610] 4.6.83-84.
7. Recall once more *The Madness of King George III* on the necessity of seeming—above, Introduction page 2.

Chapter 24

1. I would like to thank Kazumi Shimodate for making available to me a copy of his 1989 essay.
2. *OED* II *sub voce*: "moor n 1—the primitive sense of the n. would be 'dead' or barren land; Moor n 2—a native of *Mauretania*; moor v 1—to secure (a ship, boat, or other floating object) in a particular place by means of chains or ropes, which are either fastened to the shore or to anchors."
3. It is crucial to note that lines 273-9 in Act 5 Scene 2, which contain this nautical figure ("my journey's end ... my butt / And very sea-mark of my utmost sail"), are not in Q, only in F: I conjecture that they comprise one of Shakespeare's brilliant revisions.
4. Consider, further,

> But that I love the gentle Desdemona
> I would not my unhousèd free condition
> Put into circumscription and confine
> For the seas' worth.
>
> *Oth.* 1.2.25-28

Shakespeare insists that Othello thinks of himself always in terms of the sea—the sea is his element.

5. I quote this speech in its entirety for several reasons. Not least of them, however, is that the speech does not occur in Q (Wells and Taylor, *Companion* 488); I think it is a revision in F on which Shakespeare worked as he thought more deeply about *Othello*'s place in his theater of likeness. "It seems that Shakespeare partially revised his play...building up Emilia's role in the

closing scenes" (Oxford 2ᵉ 873). It is possible—I am aware I can never prove it—that the addition of Emilia's speech is in part a response to the work of *like* in 3.3; see below pages 242-4.

6. See *The Oxford Classical Dictionary*, 3ʳᵈ ed., *sub voce* "daimōn." See also Fineman, "The Sound of 'O'" 145, citing Cinthio who also understands Desdemona to mean "the unfortunate one."

7. "… happiness … is what we state the end of human nature to be" (*Ethics* 10.6).

8. Μοῖρα, the Greek for "fate," means that which is "sectioned," "cut," "divided," a "part"—see The Perseus Project, http://www.perseus.tufts.edu, *sub voce* III.

9. Cf. W. H. Auden, "The Joker in the Pack," 246-72.

10. I list the essential information from the *OED* II *sub voce* "ancient" n²:

    ancient … Forms: 6 **ancyent, ansyant, ancientt, auncient(e, -chient,** 67 **antesign,** 68 **antient,** 7 **aucyent,** 8 **anshent,** 6 **ancient.** [a corruption of ensign *n.*, early forms of which, like *ensyne, enseygne*, were confounded with *ancien, ancyen*, the contemporary forms of *ancient*, with which they thus became formally identified from 16th to 18th c. Also spelt by pseudo-etymology *antesign.*] **1** An ensign, standard, or flag: *pl.* insignia, colours. **2** A standard-bearer, an "ensign." (The full name was ***ancient-bearer:***...

11. We may compare Iago now to Satan:

    > Nor hope to be my self less miserable
    > By what I seek, but *others to make such*
    > *As I* …
    >
    > *Paradise Lost* 9.126-8 (emphasis added)

    I imagine Milton inventing Satan remembered Iago.

12. See also Stephen Daedalus's astonishing meditation on this problem in "Scylla and Charybdis":

    > Fatherhood, in the sense of conscious begetting, is unknown to man. It is a mystical estate, an apostolic succession, from only begetter to only begotten. On that mystery and not on the madonna which the cunning Italian intellect flung to the mob of Europe the church is founded and founded irremovably because founded, like the world, macro- and microcosm, upon the void. Upon incertitude, upon unlikelihood. Amor matris, subjective and objective genitive, may be the only true thing in life. Paternity may be a legal fiction. Who is the father of any son that any son should love him or he any son?
    > http://www.online-literature.com/james_joyce/ulysses/9/

    And see, again, chapter 11 above note 3.

13. Shakespeare's language in Iago's sarcasm repays very close attention:

    > **IAGO**   There's millions now alive
    > That nightly *lie* in those *unproper* beds
    > Which they dare swear pecu*liar*.
    >
    > *Oth.* 4.1.66-68 (emphasis added)

Shakespeare could hardly have been ignorant of the origin of *peculiar* in Latin *pecus*, "property in cattle, private property, that which is one's own" (*OED* II *sub voce*): for Iago, all matters relating to wives are cow-like (at best). But, equally, Shakespeare could hardly have failed to hear and see *liar* within *peculiar*; hence, almost certainly, he also heard and saw in Iago's sarcasm something like: millions now alive nightly *lie* (prevaricate, mendacity) in those beds neither proper nor truly their own property even though they dare swear they are *peculiar* but thereby show they are "cow-liar-like," not only they the beds but also they themselves—such is the evil influence upon them of whores (which all wives are, naturally, for Iago). If we add to the rich cascade of sound *wear* in *swear*, we can also hear and see Iago saying: the beds (and, by implication, the men) wear cow-liar lies and are thereby cow-liar-like.

14. The relevant passage reads, in Judith Shoaf's translation:

> "[God's] grace come to me—
> [Bitterness*] so holds me—
> [How can I] please my heart
> [While embarked] on the sea*?
> [Had I known] what the sea/love was like —
> [That it would be] so bitter* —
> [Never would] I have placed myself
> [on a ship....]"

Shoaf comments: "Here there is a clear double entendre. The starred terms indicate the play on *l'amer* or *amer* (the act of loving), *la mer* (the sea), and *l'amer* or *amer*, bitterness/gall (or the adjective bitter)." See, further, the bibliography assembled at her website—http://www.clas.ufl.edu/users/jshoaf/Carlisle.htm.

15. Judas hanged himself—see Matthew 27:3-5:

> 3: When Judas, his betrayer, saw that he was condemned, he repented and brought back the thirty pieces of silver to the chief priests and the elders, 4: saying, "I have sinned in betraying innocent blood." They said, "What is that to us? See to it yourself." 5: And throwing down the pieces of silver in the temple, he departed; and he went and hanged himself.

16. I should acknowledge here that my reading of Othello's final speech differs markedly from Calderwood's (*Properties*) which I finally find unconvincing. I would go so far as to suggest, in fact, that, in contrast to Iago ("I am not what I am" [1.1.65]), Othello in the end is more like St. Paul ("By the grace of God I am what I am" —I Cor 15.10), just in the measure to which the contrast, the difference of the likeness between Iago and Othello, powers Othello's will to admit that he has thrown "a pearl away/Richer than all his tribe." Othello is not saved, but we all know that he is not Iago either.

17. "orgêês nosousêês eisin iatroi logoi" —*Prometheus Unbound* 380.
18. Cf. T. S. Eliot, *Four Quartets*, "The Dry Salvages," Section 3.
19. This concluding meditation on *ear* is in part also a homage to the memory of Joel Fineman, who, just before his death, was working on an essay entitled

"Shakespeare's Ear" — the essay, incomplete, is found on pages 222-31 of *The Subjectivity Effect*. Consider esp. 231n5: "people don't want to read nowadays, substituting thematic reaction for reading." Everything I do as a scholar and a critic begins in *resistance* to such substitution.

Chapter 25

1. I accept the arguments of Oxford 2ᵉ for printing and studying two versions of *King Lear* (909, *The History of King Lear*, and 1153, *The Tragedy of King Lear*). But I am confident that for examining the theater of likeness in the two versions, I can move freely between them without violence to either's individuality ("Each version has its own integrity" — 1153). As theater of likeness, the two plays share a mutual vision, which, if anything, the version of 1610 brings more sharply into focus, chiefly by insisting even more sharply on Cordelia's unlikeness to her sisters and her father.
   In this chapter, then, I omit the identifier [1610] since all citations will be from The Tragedy unless otherwise noted.
2. Significantly, I believe, the Tragedy alters the History's "What shall Cordelia do" to "What shall Cordelia *speak*."
3. Notice the difference between the Tragedy — "What most he should dislike seems pleasant to him;/What like, offensive" — and the History — "What he should most *defy* seems pleasant to him;/What like, offensive" — a difference charged, I think, with Shakespeare's restless sensitivity to the work of the word *like* in his dramatic lexicon.
4. For the spelling "Leir," see the title *The True Chronicle History of King Leir*.
5. Notice that it is the Tragedy that adds the second "I am."
6. Is this not, as we today can claim, the meaning of the genome, the information code of life, that keeps on writing after?

Chapter 26

1. On the vexed issue of collaboration in *Timon*, see Jonathan Hope (*Authorship* 151):

   > The results of my study of *Timon of Athens* give broad support to the position of Lake (1975:279-86), who finds evidence for a non-Shakespearean presence in sections of the play, possibly with subsequent Shakespearean revision of those sections. This is mainly provided by scene 1.02, which is unlikely to be by Shakespeare, and tests on the conventional division given by Lake (which ascribes to Middleton scenes 1.02, 3.01, 3.02, 3.03, 3.04, 3.05, 3.06, 4.02b, 4.03b). These tests show that the "Middleton" scenes are not quite as Middletonian as might be expected if he were the author of all of them.
   >   The main conclusions to be drawn from this are that there is

almost certainly a non-Shakespearean presence in *Timon of Athens*, but that it has not yet been precisely isolated, either because subsequent Shakespearean revision has blurred the evidence, or because more careful work is needed.

For purposes of my study, I assume that the Shakespearean "presence" predominates in *Timon* (Hope, e.g. finds it possible that "Shakespeare prepared the final copy text of the play" [*Authorship* 104]); and I further assume that this predominance justifies my inferences from the word *like* in the play. Put more precisely, I believe that the work of *like* in the play is Shakespearean even if Middleton authored various scenes—i.e., Middleton was following Shakespeare's like as well as his lead (see also Hope, *Authorship* 103).

2. I mean "pure" in its ideology, not in its text or textual transmission, which is mired in difficulty (see preceding note).

3. If it is objected that we have here just more, interminable, misogyny, I would not contest the objection—Apemantus is without doubt a misogynist. But I would propose that finally misanthropy per se is the greater determinant of the speech's meaning and effect: the target is not women but mankind. And I think this is true throughout:

> **APEMANTUS** What things in the world canst thou nearest compare to thy flatterers?
> **TIMON** *Women nearest;* but men, *men are the things themselves.*
>
> *Tim.*4.3.320-3 (emphasis added)

4. Freud 1:243, 273; 5:403; 9:168, 173-4, 12:187-90; 17:72-74, 76, 82, 128, 130-2; Little 34, 53, 164, 178; Laporte, esp. chapters 1 and 6.

5. See also

> This yellow slave
> Will knit and break religions, bless th'accursed,
> Make the hoar leprosy adored, place thieves,
> And give them title, knee, and approbation
> With senators on the bench. This is it
> That makes the wappered widow wed again.
> She whom the spittle house and ulcerous sores
> Would cast the gorge at, this embalms and spices
> To th' April day again. *Come, damnèd earth,*
> *Thou common whore of mankind, that puts odds*
> Among the route of nations.
>
> *Tim.* 4.3.34-44 (emphasis added)

Chapter 27

1. I note especially here the usefulness to me of Greenblatt's Introduction to *Macbeth* in Norton (2555-62).

2. My insistence on "lies" partly follows Shakespeare's lead in *Macbeth* 2.3, the scene between the Porter and Macduff, where the intricate punning on "lie" (*Mac.* 2.3.35-40) alerts the reader to the unruliness of the word (and words).
3. In my argument here, I depend on Arendt, *Origins*, and on her teacher, Heidegger, especially "The Question Concerning Technology," for my understanding of the need to preserve the human from ideology, not just political but also religious ideology.
4. As perhaps even Plato himself does, at the end of the same book of the *Republic*, with the myth of Er?
5. See the *OED* II *sub voce*:

   Gr. ἰδιώτης private person, common man, plebeian, one without professional knowledge, "layman"; and so, ignorant, ill-informed person, f. ἴδιος private, own, peculiar.

6. See especially "Milton's Numbers," in *Duality*, xxiii:

   TWO: Must itself be two, or divided into
   THE DUAL: One + One = One — mating, whole, principle of human creativity, structure of the psyche and of language; Christ, "true image of the Father," and God are the perfect dual.
   THE DOUBLE: One + One = Two — duplicity, confusion, division, reiteration, doubt [*doub-*] (fear), copying, imitation, Narcissus, the failure of self-coincidence — the Devil.

7. *OED* II *sub voce*:

   Irish and Gaelic *mac*:–OCeltic **makko-s*, cogn. w. Welsh *mab*:–OWelsh *map*:–OCeltic **makwo-s*.] The Gaelic word for 'son'....

8. Shakespeare's irony, when Macbeth declares, "[b]ut yet I'll make assurance double sure" (*Mac.* 4.1.99), is layered and intricate in the measure to which Macbeth, we surmise, hardly hears all that he is saying in "*double* sure."
9. See the final chapter on *TNK*, for a discussion of the contrast between "look like the time" and *TNK*'s conclusion, "bear us like the time."
10. Recall that Macbeth is "Bellona's bridegroom" (*Mac.* 1.2.54), an epithet of far-reaching implication for understanding the entire play — Macbeth is not married to Lady Son of Beth only, or even in the first place.
11. See *TC* 2.2.51-9, and my comments in chapter 21.
12. Wallace Stevens, "It Must Be Abstract," VIII, in the first section of *Notes Toward A Supreme Fiction* (387).
13. Since, as the play abundantly testifies, the two of them have no son between them (they are parts, not partners), Lady Macbeth's boast can only refer to a previous marriage, a pregnancy out of wedlock, or be a fantasy of her dementia. I infer the latter as most consistent with the fused dementia into which the two of them are precipitously plunging.
14. A speculation is in order here, perhaps even obligatory. It is universally known that the text of *Macbeth* is problematic; in particular, there is general agreement "that it has been shortened" (Wells and Taylor, *Companion* 543), and we know from Forman (1610) only "that the Folio text represents accurately *in most respects* the play as acted in Shakespeare's lifetime" (543; my emphasis).

Is it possible that if *Macbeth* is so much shorter than the other major tragedies, Shakespeare is responsible for as much? The promptbook from which F derives and which reflects his rough draft may also reflect his understanding that time is a luxury that cannot be afforded in the world of Macbeth or the play of *Macbeth*.

Chapter 28

1. The *ploce* on "ee" emphasizes, I think, Shakespeare's suggestion that Antony tries to assert in language what cannot be secured in reality.

Chapter 29

1. The character is saying that class and breeding debar her from joining with Bertram "like likes and kiss[ing him] like native things"; but Shakespeare, as we will see, hardly restricts the lines to this information alone.
2. Cf. Ovid's Myrrha, guilty of incest with her father Cinyras, as she agonizes over names:

   > were not Cinyras my father than,
   > Iwis I myght obtaine to lye with him. But now bycause he is
   > Myne owne, he cannot bee myne owne. *The neerenesse of our kin*
   > *Dooth hurt me. Were I further off perchaunce I more myght win.*
   > And if I wist that I therby this wickednesse myght shunne,
   > I would forsake my native soyle and farre from Cyprus runne.
   > This evill heate dooth hold mee backe, that beeing present still
   > I may but talke with Cinyras and looke on him my fill,
   > And touch, and kisse him, if no more may further graunted bee.
   > Why wicked wench, and canst thou hope for further? doost not see
   > How by *thy fault thou doost confound the ryghts of name and kin?*
   > And wilt thou make thy mother bee a Cucqueane by thy sin?
   > Wilt thou thy fathers leman bee? *wilt thou bee both the mother*
   > *And suster of thy chyld? shall he bee both thy sonne and brother?*
   >   *Metamorphoses* 10.348-61; trans. Golding (emphasis added)

   I think it at least worth consideration that Myrrha is among Shakespeare's studies for Helen in the first part of *All's Well*.
3. *OED* II *sub voce*, from the Greek μάρτυρ ("f. Aryan root *smer- [whence Skr. smar] to remember"). Note, too, that "Bertram" is the anagram, with the "B" struck, "marter," or even "B[e] marter."
4. Chaucer's version is especially moving, given that it is uttered by the Loathly Lady in the *Wife of Bath's Tale—CT* III D 1146-76.
5. See chapter 27, on *Macbeth*, and Shakespeare's work with "file" (which is also "life" and "like" but for the "f/k") in *Macbeth* 3.1.65-71 and 3.1.93-109.
6. I am aware that Helen would have been played by a boy actor: I posit that,

in fact, this circumstance further promoted and energized Shakespeare's experiment—the boy actor could play *like* a woman playing *like* a man with just that complication of *like*ness that would have underwritten the experiment; he must, for illusion's sake, remain in the *like*ness of her even as "she" acts *like* a man, the female thus not absorbed in the male by reason of the exigencies of theater.

7. See, further, Citrome's essay, which is, in part, a study of fistula.

Chapter 30

1. I pause at this point to share with my reader my sense of poignancy at the dedication of *V&A*:

   > But if the first *heir* of my invention prove deformed, I shall be sorry it had so noble a godfather, and never after ear so barren a land for fear it yield me still so bad a harvest (Oxford 2ᵉ 224; emphasis added).

   Nor can I leave this sentence without remarking the choice of the older English word for *plow*, or *ear* (rhyming six words later with *fear*) as exquisite Shakespearean sensitivity to his language and his craft (and see also chapter 24, n. 19).

2. I acknowledge, of necessity, the excruciating difficulty of the textual history of *Pericles*, in particular the involvement of Wilkins in the first nine scenes. I find largely convincing the arguments of Taylor, Jackson, Warren, and others who have in recent decades devoted their attention to it. But my own, cautious but real, sense of the play as Shakespeare's theater of likeness is best grounded in the recognition in the *Textual Companion* that (557; emphasis added):

   > for a collaborative play Wilkins may not even have possessed, afterwards, his own foul papers. A fair copy would need to be made for use by the company; Shakespeare, as the senior collaborator, may have made this copy himself (thus enabling him to smooth any joins between the two shares, or *to revise his partner's work as he saw fit*)...

   Like in the play is Shakespeare's signature.

Chapter 31

1. See the overview in Bliss; consult also the annotated bibliography by Huffman, et al.
2. Noticed by many different critics—see the citations in Adelman (*Mothers*), 152-3 and 326n56, who herself also discusses the imagery.
3. And therefore is a kind of popularity. Consider, thus, also, Menenius' remark, "Martius Caius Coriolanus, whom/We met here both to thank and to remember/With *honours like himself* (*Cor.* 2.2.46-48; emphasis added), which begs the question what honors might be *like* him; and more, were there honors

like him, who then would "he" be? what would be his core? Consult, further, Adelman (*Mothers*), 153, 155.

4. Note here also the closely related passage (Menenius speaks): "This is *unlikely./* He and Aufidius can no more atone/Than violent'st contrariety" (*Cor.* 4.6.74-76; emphasis added), the irony of which is gross: it is, just the contrary, most *likely* that "violent'st contariety [can] atone" since the very extremity of the violence bespeaks the dependence of each contrary faction upon the other. Coriolanus and Aufidius are effectively twins—"were I anything but what I am,/I would wish me only he" (*Cor.* 1.1.231-2)—as others have also noted, and the perfidy of this twinship is suppressed but at the same time exhibited in the name *Aufidius,* not *Perfidius,* since Aufidius will practice perfidy upon Coriolanus as the only way to cancel the at*on*ement; predictably, this perfidy is followed by remorse, "[m]y rage is gone,/And I am struck with sorrow" (*Cor.* 5.6.147-8), says Aufidius, just as we would expect of someone who has betrayed and destroyed part of himself.

5. Freud's beautiful summation (see above chapter 19 n. 13), "where it was shall I come to be," "where the unconscious motivations of my libidinal body were shall a conscious self emerge into knowledge of his or her being and the vicissitudes of that being," is especially applicable to Coriolanus, I feel, just because he is so cruelly and ruthlessly (b)locked in the *it* his mother has botched into being—for him no "soll ich werden" is possible.

6. Note here Volumnia's not particularly veiled threat: "This is a poor epitome of yours,/Which by th' interpretation of full time/May show *like* all yourself" (*Cor.* 5.3.68-70). Not only is she caustically implying that Coriolanus's impending attack on Rome will forestall this "show like all [him]self," she also more than hints that she herself would forestall it, "*may* show like all yourself." Coriolanus, I assume, being her son, cannot *not* hear this threat.

7. OED II *sub voce* "excrement" 2:

> Mud, clay, dirt, mire, filth. Also, excrement. 1513 Douglas *Æneis* iii. iv. 17 The vile belleis of thai cursit schrewis Aboundis of fen maist abhominable. 1535 Stewart *Cron. Scot.* III. 440 The loving in ane mannis mouth, Maid of him self, stinkis lyke ony fen Into the eiris of all vther men.

8. Freud comments on the bipolarity of the anal, a sphincter that both retains and eliminates—see Laplanche and Pontalis 35-6.

Chapter 32

1. Hence the cruel irony of Mamillius's death—he was so obviously *like* his father.
2. Cf. Stevens (*Angel*) 73 (emphasis added): "An imitation is artificial. It is *not fortuitous* as a true metaphor is." See also Percy, esp. 70-73.
3. Science-fiction has most keenly and disturbingly imagined such a future — I think, e.g., of Asimov's *Foundation* trilogy, in which "psychohistory" and its predictions function because difference has been all but eliminated (except in

"The Mule," precisely the deviant).

By the same token, surrealism was an early movement wholly revolting against such a future, which its practitioners could already foresee, perhaps not without clairvoyance.

4. Obviously, he does not want it to be *magic*, for it is his body that is restored as well, when Hermione's is also, and magic would only compromise this wonder.

5. Similarly with Giulio Romano the Italian sculptor credited with her statue (*WT* 5.2.96); as a real Italian sculptor (b. ca. 1499, Roma; d. 1546, Mantova) *and* as Shakespeare's *Romeo* and *Juliet*, he provides an example of an "art lawful as eating"—the same syneciosis of nature and convention. See, further, Fineman, *Eye* 307.

6. Readers will recognize the relationship between my position and Burckhardt's "Werkimmanente Deutung" (285ff.). I acknowledge as much here: I agree with him that "the starting point for all interpretation is piety and the best method is the one which most favors it" (313). But, then, Heminge and Condell may already have said as much: "And if then you doe not like him, surely you are in some manifest danger, not to understand him" (*The First Folio*, "To the Reader").

Chapter 33

1. "Tennyson himself died in 1892, a memorable death with, according to an account by his son, Shakespeare's *Cymbeline* open before him at the lines he loved: 'Hang there like fruit, my soul, / Till the tree die'"—http://www.litencyc.com/php/speople.php?rec=true&UID=4349 (last accessed 04.28.03). These are words of Posthumus to Innogen (*Cym.* 5.6.263-4) on whom Tennyson doted. I think the remarkable figure also influenced Milton, to some extent, although Scripture obviously was the greater warrant:

   > So maist thou live, till like ripe Fruit thou drop
   > Into thy Mothers lap, or be with ease
   > Gatherd, not harshly pluckt, for death mature:
   > This is old age.
   >
   > *Paradise Lost* 11.535-58

2. Just so, succeeding generations produced multiple readings of Ralegh's death — Beer 109ff.

3. See Boncompagno (before 1243),

   > 8.1.6 De dispositione cerebri humani.
   >
   > Homo dicitur microcosmus, idest minor mundus, et dicitur arbor inversa, quoniam a philosophis asseritur habere in superiori parte radices.
   >
   > Concerning the disposition of the human brain. Man is called microcosm, i.e., lesser world, and is also called inverted tree because

philosophy asserts that he has his roots in the upper part [of his body, or his brain] (my translation).

Chapter 34

1. At this point, not only for validating my argument but also for illuminating the time-frame of Shakespeare's career, it is imperative to recall, from his first tragedy, *Titus Andronicus*, Lavinia's anguished plea to her tormentors: "Yet every mother breeds not sons a*like*" (*TA* 2.3.146). Early as well as late, late as well as early, Shakespeare broods on the sorrows of breeding.

Chapter 35

1. And see, further,

   Lord Chancellor Thus far,
   My most dread sovereign, may it *like* your grace
   To let my tongue excuse all.
   All Is True 5.2.181-3 (emphasis added)

   Messenger An't *like* your grace…
   All Is True 4.2.101 (emphasis added)

2. Hope assigns 2.4 to Shakespeare (*Authorship* 150). Remember also Katherine's plea in the same speech:

   I have been to you a true and humble wife,
   At all times to your will conformable,
   Ever in fear to kindle your dislike,
   Yea, subject to your countenance, glad or sorry
   As I saw it inclined.
   All is True 2.4.21-25 (emphasis added)

Chapter 36

1. When Lady Macbeth counsels her husband to "[l]ook like the time" (*Mac.* 1.5.63), she does so precisely to teach him "[to] beguile the time" (*Mac.* 1.5.62). This expediency is not the decorum that Theseus recommends, but Shakespeare does not shrink from seeing and showing that they are nonetheless similar, so closely are guile and grace "at home with each other" (*syneciosis*), cross-coupled.

2. I accept Q's reading here. According to the Norton edition (3216): "Q has 'individual,' which in the seventeenth century could mean the indivisible unity of male and female, and hence may be correct." This reading more starkly emphasizes the dilemma in question.

3. Also, one could follow Vickers's line of reasoning here: "But of course, even within a straightforward joint authorship, one contributor may insert short segments of verse into the other's scenes, or even touch up passages, as several scholars have suggested for this play [*viz. The Two Noble Kinsmen*]" —Vickers, *Co-author* 431.

4. Stevens (*Collected Poems* 403),

> He had to choose. But it was not a choice
> Between excluding things. It was not a choice
> Between, but of.
> "Notes Toward a Supreme Fiction"

Works Consulted

Aarne, Antti, and Stith Thompson. *The Types of the Folktale*. Folklore Fellows Communications 184. Helsinki: Academia Scientarum Fennica, 1961.
Adelman, Janet. *The Common Liar: An Essay on* Antony and Cleopatra. New Haven: Yale UP, 1973.
———. *Suffocating Mothers: Fantasies of Maternal Origin in Shakespeare's Plays, "Hamlet" to the "Tempest"*. New York: Routledge, 1992.
Aeschylus. *Prometheus Unbound*. The Perseus Project, http://www.perseus.tufts.edu. Last accessed 09.03.01.
Alighieri, Dante. *La Commedia*. http://etcweb.princeton.edu/dante/index.html. Last accessed 02.15.05.
Allen, David G., and Robert White. *The Work of Dissimilitude: Essays from the Sixth Citadel Conference on Medieval and Renaissance Literature*. Newark: U of Delaware P, 1992.
Allen, Judson Boyce. *The Ethical Poetic of the Later Middle Ages*. Toronto: U of Toronto P, 1982.
Allen, Michael J. B. *Marsilio Ficino: His Theology, His Philosophy, His Legacy*. Ed. Michael J. B. Allen and Valery Rees with Martin Davies. Leiden: Brill, 2002.
Allen, Valerie. "Broken Air." *Exemplaria* 16.2 (2004): 305-22.
Altman, Joel B. *The Tudor Play of Mind: Rhetorical Inquiry and the Development of Elizabethan Drama*. Berkeley: U of California P, 1978.
Anonymous. *The Chronicle History of King Leir*. Ed. Sir Sidney Lee. London: Chatto & Windus, 1909.
Arendt, Hannah. *The Human Condition*. Chicago: U of Chicago P, 1958.
———. *Love and Saint Augustine*. Edited and with an interpretive essay by Joanna Vecchiarelli Scott and Judith Chelius Stark. Chicago: U of Chicago P, 1996.
———. *The Life of the Mind*. 2 vols. New York: Harcourt Brace Jovanovich, 1973.
———. *The Origins of Totalitarianism*. New York: World Publishing Co., 1972.
Aristotle. *Metaphysics*. Trans. Hugh Lawson-Tancred. New York: Penguin, 1998.
———. *Nicomachean Ethics*. Trans. W. D. Ross. Oxford: Oxford UP, 1952.
———. *Poetics*. Trans. Leon Golden and O. B. Hardison, Jr., *Classical and Medieval Literary Criticism: Translations and Interpretations*. Ed. Alex Preminger, O. B. Hardison, Jr., Kevin Kerrane. New York: F. Ungar Pub. Co., 1974.

_____. *Politics*. Trans. T. A. Sinclair. New York: Penguin, 1992.
Aubrey, John. *Brief Lives*. Ed. John Buchanan-Brown. New York: Penguin, 2000.
Auden, W. H. *The Dyer's Hand*. New York: Vintage, 1990.
Auerbach, Erich. *Mimesis: The Representation of Reality in Western Literature*. Trans. Willard R. Trask. New York, 1953.
Aughterson, Kate. Ed. *The English Renaissance: An Anthology of Sources and Documents*. London: Routledge, 1998.
Augustine. St. Aurelius. See St. Augustine.
Ayto, John. *Dictionary of Word Origins*. New York: Arcade, 1991.
Bacon, Francis. *The Advancement of Learning*. In *Francis Bacon: The Major Works*. Ed. Brian Vickers. Oxford: Oxford UP, 1996. 120-299.
Bainbridge, David. *The X in Sex: How the X Chromosome Controls Our Lives*. Cambridge, MA: Harvard UP, 2004.
Barber, C. L. *Shakespeare's Festive Comedy*. Princeton: Princeton UP, 1959.
_____. See Wheeler, Richard P.
Barnard, John, and D. F. McKenzie, with the assistance of Maureen Bell. *The Cambridge History of the Book in England*. Vol 1V: 1557-1695. Cambridge: Cambridge UP, 2002.
Barish, Jonas. "The Uniqueness of Renaissance Drama." *Comparative Drama* 11 (1977): 103-112.
Baudrillard, Jean. *Simulations (Foreign Agents)*. Paris: Semiotext(e), 1983.
Beer, Anna R. *Sir Walter Ralegh and his Readers in the Seventeenth Century: Speaking to the People*. New York: St. Martin's P, 1997.
Bennett, Alan. *The Madness of George III* [stage play]. New York: Random House, 1995.
Berger, Jr., Harry. *Making Trifles of Terror: Redistributing Complicities in Shakespeare*. Stanford: Stanford UP, 1997.
Besançon, Alain. *The Forbidden Image: An Intellectual History of Iconoclasm*. Trans. Janet Marie Todd. Chicago: U of Chicago P, 2001.
Bible. King James Version. Electronic Text Center, U of Virginia Library. http://etext.virginia.edu/kjv.browse.html. Last accessed 08.11.01.
_____. Revised Standard Version. Electronic Text Center, U of Virginia Library. http://etext.virginia,edu/rvs.browse.html. Last accessed 08.11.01.
Blake, William. *The Complete Poetry and Prose of William Blake*. Ed. David V. Erdman. New York: Anchor, 1982.
Bliss, Lee. "What Hath a Quarter-Century of *Coriolanus* Criticism Wrought?" *Shakespearean International Yearbook* 2 (2002): 63-75.
Bloom, Harold. *A Map of Misreading*. Oxford: Oxford UP, 1975.
_____. *Shakespeare: The Invention of the Human*. New York: Riverhead Books, 1998.
_____. *The Anxiety of Influence: A Theory of Poetry*. 2nd ed. Oxford: Oxford UP, 1997.
Boccaccio, Giovanni. *Decameron*. Trans. Guido Waldman. Oxford: Oxford UP, 1993.
Boehrer, Bruce T. *Monarchy and Incest in Renaissance England: Literature, Culture, Kinship, and Kingship*. Philadelphia: U of Pennsylvania P, 1992.
Boethius. *The Consolation of Philosophy*. Trans. Richard H. Green. Indianapolis:

Bobbs-Merrill, 1962.
Boncompagno (1194-1243). *Rhetorica novissima.* http://lettere.unipv.it/scrineum/wight/rn8.html. Page ed. by Steven M. Wight. Last accessed 04.05.04.
Brecht, Bertolt. *Die Dreigroschenoper: nach John Gays "The Beggar's Opera."* Berlin: Suhrkamp, 1994.
Brink, Jean R. "Literacy and Education." In Hattaway. 95-105.
Bronfen, Elisabeth. *Over Her Dead Body: Death, Femininity and the Aesthetic.* New York: Routledge, 1992.
Bronson, Bertrand H., with Jean M. O'Meara. New Haven: Yale UP, 1986.
Bruns, Gerald. L. *Inventions — Writing, Textuality, and Understanding in Literary History.* New Haven: Yale UP, 1982.
Bucholz, Robert, and Newton Key. *Early Modern England 1485-1714.* Oxford: Blackwell, 2004.
Burckhardt, Sigurd. *Shakespearean Meanings.* Princeton: Princeton UP, 1968.
Burke, Kenneth. *A Grammar of Motives.* New York: Prentice-Hall, 1945.
Burton, Gideon. "The Forest of Rhetoric: *silva rhetoricae.*" http://humanities.byu.edu.rhetoric/. Last accessed 04.26.04.
Calderwood, James L. *Metadrama in Shakespeare's Henriad: Richard II to Henry V.* Berkeley: U of California P, 1979.
———. *To Be and Not to Be: Negation and Metadrama in Hamlet.* New York: Columbia UP, 1983.
———. *The Properties of Othello.* Amherst: U of Massachusetts P, 1989.
Callaghan, Dympna C. Ed. *A Feminist Companion to Shakespeare.* Oxford: Blackwell, 2000.
The Cambridge History of English and American Literature in 18 Volumes (1907–21). Vol. 3. *Renascence and Reformation.* http://www.bartleby.com/213/0901.html. Last accessed 07.02.03.
Cassirer, Ernst. *The Individual and the Cosmos in Renaissance Philosophy.* New York: Harper & Row, 1964.
Castiglione, Baldassare. *The Courtier* (translated into English by Sir Thomas Hoby and published in 1561).
Cave, Terence. *The Cornucopian Text: Problems of Writing in the French Renaissance.* Oxford, 1979.
Cavell, Stanley. *Disowning Knowledge in Six Plays of Shakespeare.* Cambridge: Cambridge UP, 1987.
———. "The Avoidance of Love: A Reading of *King Lear.*" In *Disowning Knowledge.* 39-124.
———. "*Coriolanus* and Interpretations of Politics." In *Disowning Knowledge.* 143-78.
Chaucer, Geoffrey. http://etext.virginia.edu/mideng.browse.html. Last accessed 12.02.04.
Christine de Pisan. *Treasure of the City of Ladies* and *Book of the Body Politic.* In *The Selected Writings of Christine De Pizan: New Translations, Criticism.* Ed. Renate Blumenfeld-Kosinski. Trans. Renate Blumenfeld-Kosinski and Kevin Brownlee. New York: Norton, 1997. 116-54; 201-15.
Citrome, Jeremy. "Bodies that Splatter: Surgery, Chivalry, and the Body in the *Practica* of John Arderne." *Exemplaria* 13 (2001): 137-72.

Colie, Rosalie L. *Paradoxia epidemica: The Renaissance Tradition of Paradox.* Princeton: Princeton UP, 1966.
Culler, Jonathan. Ed. *On Puns: The Foundation of Letters.* London: Basil Blackwell, 1988.
Cummins, John. *The Hound and the Hawk: The Art of Medieval Hunting.* London: Phoenix, 2001.
Deleuze, Gilles. "The Schizophrenic and Language: Surface and Depth in Lewis Carroll and A. Antonin Artaud." In Kurzweil and Phillips. 324-39.
de Meun, Jean, and Guillaume de Lorris. *Le Roman de la Rose.* Ed. Félix Lecoy. 3 vols. Paris: Champion, 1966-74. Trans. Charles Dahlberg. Princeton: Princeton UP, 1971.
De Margreta, Grazia, Maureen Quilligan, and Peter Stallybrass. Ed. *Subject and Object in Renaissance Culture.* Cambridge: Cambridge UP, 1996.
de Montaigne, Michel. *Essais.* Trans. John Florio. London, 1910.
———. *The Complete Essays of Montaigne.* Trans. Donald M. Frame. Stanford: Stanford UP, 1958.
de Navarre, Marguerite. *The Heptameron.* Trans. P. A. Chilton. Harmondsworth: Penguin, 1984.
de Saussure, Ferdinand. *Course in General Linguistics.* Ed. Charles Bally and Albert Sechehaye, in collaboration with Albert Riedlinger. Trans. Wade Baskin. New York: McGraw-Hill, 1966.
Derrida, Jacques. "White Mythology: Metaphor in the Text of Philosophy." *New Literary History* 6 (1974): 5-74.
———. *Dissemination.* Trans. Barbara Johnson. Chicago: U of Chicago P, 1981.
Dobson, Michael, and Stanley Wells. Ed. *The Oxford Companion to Shakespeare.* Oxford: Oxford UP, 2001.
Donne, John. *John Donne: The Complete Poetry of John Donne.* Ed. John T. Shawcross. New York: Doubleday, 1967.
Duncan-Jones, Katherine. *Ungentle Shakespeare: Scenes from His Life.* London: Thomson Learning, 2001.
Dutton, Richard, Alison Gail Findlay, Richard L. Wilson. Ed. *Lancastrian Shakespeare: Region, Religion and Patronage.* Manchester: Manchester UP, 2004.
———. *Lancastrian Shakespeare: Theatre and Religion.* Manchester: Manchester UP, 2004.
Elam, Keir. *Shakespeare's Universe of Discourse: Language-games in the Comedies.* Cambridge: Cambridge UP, 1984.
Elias, Norbert. *The Civilizing Process.* Trans. Edmund Jephcott. 2 vols. New York: Urizen Books, 1981-82.
Eliot, T. S. *Collected Poems, 1909-1962.* New York: Harcourt, 1963.
Elyot, Sir Thomas. *The Book Named the Governor.* London: Dent, 1907.
Empson, William. *The Structure of Complex Words.* Cambridge, MA: Harvard UP, 1989.
Erasmus, Desiderius. *The Education of a Christian Prince.* Trans. Neil M. Cheshire and Michael J. Heath; with the Panegyric for Archduke Philip of Austria, trans. Lisa Jardine. Ed. Lisa Jardine. Cambridge, U.K.: Cambridge UP, 1997.
———. *Fürstenerziehung (Institutio Principis Christiani).* Ed. A. J. Gail. Paderborn: F. Schöningh, 1968.
———. *Literary and Educational Writings.* Volume 1: *Antibarbari/Parabolae;* Volume

2: *De copia / De ratione studii*. Ed. Craig R. Thompson. Toronto: U of Toronto P, 1978.
———. "On Good Manners for Boys." *Collected Works* 25 (1985): 269-89.
Erne, Lukas. *Shakespeare as Literary Dramatist*. Cambridge, U.K.: Cambridge UP, 2003.
Evans, Dylan. *An Introductory Dictionary of Lacanian Psychoanalysis*. London: Routledge, 1996.
Famous Victories of Henry V, The. The Oldcastle Controversy: Sir John Oldcastle, Part I and the Famous Victories of Henry V. Ed. Peter Corbin and Douglas Sedge. Manchester: Manchester UP, 1991.
Felperin, Howard. "'Tongue-Tied Our Queen?': The Deconstruction of Presence in *The Winter's Tale*." In Hartman and Parker. 3-18.
Ferguson, Margaret W. "*Hamlet*: Letters and Spirits." In Hartman and Parker. 292-309.
———. "St. Augustine's Region of Unlikeness: The Crossing of Exile and Language." *Georgia Review* 29 (1975): 842-64.
Ferster, Judith. *Fictions of Advice: The Literature and Politics of Counsel in Late Medieval England*. Philadelphia: U of Pennsylvania P, 1996.
Fineman, Joel. "Fratricide and Cuckoldry: Shakespeare's Doubles." In Schwartz and Kahn. 70-109.
———. "The History of the Anecdote: Fiction and Fiction." In Veeser. 49-76.
———. *Shakespeare's Perjured Eye*. Berkeley: U of California P, 1986.
———. "Shakespeare's Will: The Temporality of Rape." *Representations* 20 (1987): 25-76.
———. "The Sound of 'O' in *Othello*: The Real of the Tragedy of Desire." In *The Subjectivity Effect*. 143-64.
———. *The Subjectivity Effect in Western Literary Tradition: Essays Toward the Release of Shakespeare's Will*. Cambridge, Mass.: MIT, 1991.
Fish, Stanley E. *Surprised by Sin: The Reader in* Paradise Lost. Berkeley: U of California P, 1971.
Fleming, James Dougal. "Prevent Is Not Prevent: Rape and Rhetoric in *The Tempest*." *Exemplaria* 15 (2003): 451-72.
Forey, Madeleine. Ed. *Ovid's Metamorphoses, by Arthur Golding*. Baltimore: Johns Hopkins UP, 2002.
Forster, E. M. *Howards End*. Ed. Alistair M. Duckworth. Boston: Bedford Books, 1997.
Foucault, Michel. *Discipline and Punish: The Birth of the Prison*. Trans. Alan Sheridan. New York: Vintage, 1979.
———. *The Order of Things*. New York: Vintage Books, 1973.
Frame, Donald M. Trans. *The Complete Essays of Montaigne*. Stanford: Stanford UP, 1958.
Freccero, John. *Dante: The Poetics of Conversion*. Ed. Rachel Jacoff. Cambridge, MA: Harvard UP, 1988.
Freud, Sigmund. *The Standard Edition of the Complete Psychological Works of Sigmund Freud*. 24 vols. Trans. under the general editorship of James Strachey. London: Hogarth P and the Institute of Psycho-Analysis, 1953-1974.
Fulwell, Ulpian. *Like Will to Like*. John Allde, 1568. Accessible at http://www.umm.

maine.edu/faculty/necastro/drama/wtl.txt. Last accessed 07.22.03.

Garber, Marjorie. "*Hamlet*: Giving Up the Ghost." *Shakespeare's Ghost Writers*. London: Methuen & Co., 1987. Rpt. Wofford. 297-331.

———. *Shakespeare's Ghost Writers*. London: Methuen & Co., 1987.

Gibaldi, Joseph. Ed. *MLA Handbook for Writers of Research Papers*. 6th ed. New York: MLA, 2003.

Girard, René. *A Theater of Envy: William Shakespeare*. 1991; rpt. South Bend, IN: St. Augustine's Press, 2004.

Goldberg, Jonathan. "The Anus in *Coriolanus*." In Mazzio and Trevor. 260-71.

Golding, Arthur. See Forey.

Grabes, Herbert. *The Mutable Glass: Mirror-imagery in Titles and Texts of the Middle Ages and the English Renaissance*. Cambridge: Cambridge UP, 1982.

Graff, Gerald, and James Phelan. *William Shakespeare: The Tempest: A Case Study in Critical Controversy*. Boston: St. Martin's, 2000.

Greenblatt, Stephen. *Renaissance Self-fashioning: From More to Shakespeare*. Chicago: U of Chicago P, 1980.

———. *Sir Walter Ralegh: The Renaissance Man and his Roles*. New Haven: Yale UP, 1973.

Greene, Thomas M. *The Light in Troy: Imitation and Discovery in Renaissance Poetry*. New Haven: Yale UP, 1982.

Hadot, Pierre. *Plotinus, or the Simplicity of Vision*. Trans. Michael Chase. Chicago: U of Chicago P, 1993.

Halliwell, Stephen. *The Aesthetics of Mimesis: Ancient Texts and Modern Problems*. Princeton: Princeton UP, 2002.

Halpern, Richard. *The Poetics of Primitive Accumulation: English Renaissance Culture and the Genealogy of Capital*. Ithaca: Cornell UP, 1991.

Hartman, Geoffrey H. See Parker, Patricia.

Hattaway, Michael. Ed. *A Companion to English Renaissance Literature and Culture*. Oxford: Blackwell, 2000.

Hegel, G. W. F. *Lectures on the History of Philosophy*. The lectures of 1825-1826. Ed. Robert F. Brown. Trans. R.F. Brown and J.M. Stewart with the assistance of H.S. Harris. Berkeley: U of California P, 1990.

Heidegger, Martin. *Being and Time*. Trans. John Macquarrie and Edward Robinson. New York: Harper, 1962.

———. "Logos (Heraclitus, Fragment B 50)." *Early Greek Thinking: The Dawn of Western Philosophy*. Trans. David Farrell Krell and Frank A. Capuzzi. San Francisco: Harper and Row, 1975. 59-78.

———. *The Question Concerning Technology and Other Essays*. Trans. William Lovitt. New York: Harper and Row, 1977.

Holden, Anthony. *William Shakespeare: An Illustrated Biography*. London: Little, Brown, & Co., 2002.

Hendricks, Margo. "'A word, sweet Lucrece': Confession, Feminism, and *The Rape of Lucrece*." In Callaghan. 103-18.

Hirschfeld, Heather Anne. *Joint Enterprises: Collaborative Drama and the Institutionalization of the English Renaissance Theater*. Amherst: U of Massachusetts P, 2004.

Holland, Norman N. *The Shakespearean Imagination*. New York: Macmillan, 1964.
Homer. *The Odyssey*. www.perseus.org. Last accessed 07.15.04.
Honan, Park. *Shakespeare: A Life*. New York: Oxford UP, 1998.
Hope, Jonathan. *Shakespeare's Grammar*. London: Thomson Learning, 2003.
_____. *The Authorship of Shakespeare's Plays: A Socio-linguistic Study*. Cambridge: Cambridge UP, 1994.
Horace. *Ars poetica*. O. B. Hardison, Jr. and Leon Golden, *Horace for Students of Literature: The Ars Poetica and Its Tradition*. Gainesville: UP of Florida, 1995.
_____. *Epodes*. Trans. David West. Oxford: Oxford UP, 1997.
Hornblower, Simon, and Antony Spawforth. Ed. *The Oxford Classical Dictionary*. 3rd ed. Oxford: Oxford UP, 1996.
Howard, Jean, and Phyllis Rackin. *Engendering a Nation: A Feminist Account of Shakespeare's English Histories*. New York: Routledge, 1997.
_____. *The Stage and Social Struggle in Early Modern England*. London: Routledge, 1994.
Huffman, Clifford Chalmers, and John W. Velz. Ed. *The Rape of Lucrece, Titus Andronicus, Julius Caesar, Antony and Cleopatra, and Coriolanus: An Annotated Bibliography of Shakespeare Studies, 1910-2000*. Pegasus Shakespeare Bibliographies. Fairview, NC: Pegasus Press, 2002.
Hunter, Lynette. "Books for Daily Life: Household, Husbandry, Behaviour." In Barnard, et al. 514-32.
Hurley, Susan, and Nick Chater. *Perspectives on Imitation: From Neuroscience to Social Science*. 2 vols. Cambridge, MA: MIT P, 2005.
Irigaray, Luce. *Ce sexe qui n'en est pas un*. Trans. Catherine Porter with Carolyn Burke. Ithaca: Cornell UP, 1985.
Jackson, MacDonald P. *Defining Shakespeare: 'Pericles' as Test Case*. Oxford: OUP, 2003.
Jacobus, Lee A. *Shakespeare and the Dialectic of Certainty*. New York: St. Martin's, 1992.
Janson, H. W. *Apes and Ape Lore in the Middle Ages and the Renaissance*. London: Warburg Institute, U of London, 1952.
Johnson, Samuel. "Cowley." In *Lives of the English Poets*. Ed. G. Birkbeck Hill. 3 vols. Oxford: Clarendon, 1905.
_____. "Preface (1765) to Shakespeare." *Selections from Johnson on Shakespeare*. Ed. Bertrand H. Bronson with Jean M. O'Meara. New Haven: Yale UP, 1986.
Jones, Ann Rosalind, and Peter Stallybrass. *Renaissance Clothing and the Materials of Memory*. Cambridge: Cambridge UP, 2000.
Jones, John. *Shakespeare at Work*. Oxford: Clarendon, 1995.
Jonson, Ben. *Ben Jonson*. Ed. C. H. Herford and Percy Simpson and Evelyn Simpson. Oxford: Clarendon, 1925-63. 11 v.
Jost, Walter, and Wendy Olmsted. Ed. *A Companion to Rhetoric and Rhetorical Criticism*. Malden, MA: Blackwell, 2004.
Joyce, James. *Finnegans Wake*. http://www.trentu.ca/jjoyce/fw-295.htm. Last accessed 02.19.05.
_____. *Ulysses*. http://www.online-literature.com/james joyce/ulysses/. Last accessed 02.19.05.

Kahn, Coppélia, with Murray M. Schwartz. Ed. *Representing Shakespeare: New Psychoanalytic Essays*. Baltimore: Johns Hopkins UP, 1980.

———. *Roman Shakespeare: Warriors, Wounds, and Women*. London: Routledge, 1997.

Kamps, Ivo. Ed. *Materialist Shakespeare: A History*. London: Verso, 1995.

Keats, John. *The Letters of John Keats, 1814-1821*. 2 vols. Ed. Hyder Edward Rollins. Cambridge, MA: Harvard UP, 1958.

Keenan, Hugh T. Ed. *Typology and English Medieval Literature*. Georgia State Literary Studies 7. New York: AMS, 1992.

Kenner, Hugh. *The Counterfeiters: An Historical Comedy*. Bloomington: Indiana UP, 1968.

Kerrigan, William. *Hamlet's Perfection*. Baltimore: The Johns Hopkins UP, 1994.

———. *The Sacred Complex: On the Psychogenesis of "Paradise Lost."* Cambridge, MA: Harvard UP, 1983.

Kilgour, Maggie. *From Communion to Cannibalism*. Princeton: Princeton UP, 1990.

Kinney, Arthur F. "Continental Poetics." In Jost and Olmsted. 80-95.

———. And David W. Swain. *Tudor England: An Encyclopedia*. New York: Garland, 2001.

Kintgen, Eugene R. *Reading in Tudor England*. Pittsburgh: U of Pittsburgh P, 1996.

Kodera, Sergius. "Narcissus, Divine Gazes and Bloody Mirrors: The Concept of Matter in Ficino." In Allen, *Ficino*. 285-306.

Kurzweil, Edith, and William Phillips. Ed. *Literature and Psychoanalysis*. New York: Columbia UP, 1983.

Lacan, Jacques. "Desire and the Interpretation of Desire in *Hamlet*." *Literature and Psychoanalysis, The Question of Reading: Otherwise*. Ed. Shoshana Felman. *Yale French Studies*, 55-56 (1977): 11-52.

———. "Discussion de l'article de S. Leclaire et J. Laplanche: l'inconscient: une étude psychanalytique." *L'Inconscient* (VIth Colloque de Bonneval). Desclée De Brower, 1966.

———. *Écrits*. Paris: Éditions du Seuil, 1966. Trans. Alan Sheridan. *Écrits: A Selection*. New York: Norton, 1977.

———. "God and the Jouissance of T̶h̶e̶ Woman" and "A Love Letter." *Encore: Le séminaire XX* (1972-73). Paris: Éditions du Seuil, 1975. 61-82. Trans. Jacqueline Rose. *Feminine Sexuality: Jacques Lacan and the École Freudienne*. Ed. Juliet Mitchell and Jacqueline Rose. New York: Norton, 1982. 137-61.

———. "Position de l'inconscient." *Écrits*. 829-50.

———. *Le Séminaire, Livre XVII. L'envers de la psychanalyse, 1969-70*. Ed. Jacques-Alain Miller. Paris: Seuil, 1991.

Laplanche, J., and J.-B. Pontalis. *The Language of Psychoanalysis*. Trans. Donald Nicholson-Smith. New York: Norton, 1973.

Laporte, Dominique. *History of Shit*. Cambridge: MIT, 2002.

Laqueur, Thomas W. *Solitary Sex: A Cultural History of Masturbation*. Cambridge, MA: Zone Books, 2004.

Lausberg, Heinrich. *Handbook of Literary Rhetoric: A Foundation for Literary Study*. Foreword by George A. Kennedy. Trans. Matthew T. Bliss, Annemiek Jansen, David E. Orton. Ed. David E. Orton & R. Dean Anderson. Leiden: Brill, 1998.

Lear, Jonathan. *Happiness, Death, and the Remainder of Life*. Cambridge, MA: Harvard UP, 2000.

———. *Love and its Place in Nature: A Philosophical Interpretation of Freudian Psychoanalysis*. New York: Farrar Straus Giroux, 1990.

———. *Open-minded: Working Out the Logic of the Soul*. Cambridge, MA: Harvard UP, 1998.

Leitao, David. "The Legend of the Sacred Band." In Nussbaum and Sihvola. 143-69.

Lemaire, Anika. *Jacques Lacan*. Trans. David Macey. London: Routledge & Kegan Paul, 1977.

Levin, Carole. "Elizabeth I." In Kinney and Swain. 223-6.

———. *The Heart and Stomach of a King: Elizabeth I and the Politics of Sex and Power*. Philadelphia: U of Pennsylvania P, 1994.

———. *The Reign of Elizabeth I*. London: Palgrave, 2003.

Lewis, C. S. *A Preface to* Paradise Lost. Oxford: Oxford UP, 1942.

Liddell, Henry George, and Robert Scott. *A Greek-English Lexicon*. Accessible at http://www.perseus.org.

Lindahl, Carl, John McNamara, and John Lindow. *Medieval Folklore: A Guide to Myths, Legends, Tales, Beliefs, and Customs*. Oxford: Oxford UP, 2002.

Little, Lester K. *Religious Poverty and the Profit Economy in Medieval Europe*. Ithaca: Cornell UP, 1978.

Lupton, Julia Reinhard, and Kenneth Reinhard. *After Oedipus: Shakespeare in Psychoanalysis*. Ithaca: Cornell UP, 1993.

Lyons, John D. *Exemplum: The Rhetoric of Example in Early Modern France and Italy*. Princeton: Princeton UP, 1989.

Macdonald, Russ. *Shakespeare and the Arts of Language*. Oxford: Oxford UP, 2001.

———. *The Bedford Companion to Shakespeare: An Introduction with Documents*. Boston: Bedford Books of St. Martin's, 1996.

Machiavelli, Niccoló. *The Prince*. http://www.gutenberg.org/etext/1232.Last accessed 02.19.05.

Mack, Peter. *Elizabethan Rhetoric: Theory and Practice*. Cambridge: Cambridge UP, 2002.

McNeely, Trevor. *Proteus Unmasked: Sixteenth-Century Rhetoric and the Art of Shakespeare*. Philadelphia: Lehigh UP, 2004.

Marlowe, Christopher. *Hero and Leander*. In *The Penguin Book of Renaissance Verse 1509-1659*. Sel. David Norbrook. Ed. H. R. Woudhuysen. London: Penguin, 1993. 266-90.

Marotti, Arthur F. "Shakespeare and Catholicism." In Dutton. *Theatre and Religion*. 218-41.

Maslin, R.W. "Myths Exploited: The Metamorphoses [sic] of Ovid in Early Elizabethan England." In Taylor, *Shakespeare's Ovid*. 15-30.

Maus, Katharine Eisaman. *Inwardness and Theater in the English Renaissance*. Chicago: U of Chicago P, 1995.

May, Steven W. *Sir Walter Ralegh*. Boston: Twayne, 1989.

Mazzio, Carla, and Douglas Trevor. *Historicism, Psychoanalysis, and Early Modern Culture*. New York: Routledge, 2000.

Meier, Christian. *Caesar*. Trans. David McLintock. London: Harper Collins, 1995.

Menon, Madhavi. *Wanton Words: Rhetoric and Sexuality in English Renaissance Drama.* Toronto: U of Toronto Press, 2004.
Michelangelo's "Martyrdom of St Peter" [1546-50], Cappella Paolina, Palazzi Pontifici, Vatican. http://www.kfki.hu/~arthp/html/m/michelan/2paintin/5peter.html. Last accessed 07.15.2003.
Milton, John. *Paradise Lost.* http://www.dartmouth.edu/~milton/. Last accessed 02.15.05.
Mueller, Janel M. *The Native Tongue and the Word: Developments in English Prose Style 1380-1580.* Chicago: U of Chicago P, 1984.
Murphy, Michael Dean. Compiler. "A Kinship Glossary: Symbols, Terms, and Concepts." http://www.as.ua.edu/ant/Faculty/murphy/436/kinship.htm. Last accessed 07.14.2003.
Nicholas of Cusa. *De docta ignorantia. Nicholas of Cusa: Selected Spiritual Writings.* Trans. H. Lawrence Bond. New York: Paulist, 1997.
Nicholl, Charles. *The Reckoning: The Murder of Christopher Marlowe.* Chicago: U of Chicago P, 1995.
Nietzsche, Friedrich. *Über Wahrheit und Lüge im aussermoralischen Sinne.* In *Kritische Studienausgabe.* Vol. I. Ed. Giorgio Colli and Mazzino Montinari. München: de Gruyter, 1999.
Nussbaum, Martha, and Juha Sihvola. *The Sleep of Reason: Erotic Experience and Sexual Ethics in Ancient Greece and Rome.* Chicago: U of Chicago P, 2002.
O'Connell, Michael. *The Idolatrous Eye: Iconoclasm and Theater in Early-Modern England.* New York: Oxford UP, 2000.
Olmsted, Wendy. See Jost, Walter.
Ong, Walter J. "Latin Language Study as a Renaissance Puberty Rite." *Studies in Philology* 56 (1959): 103-24.
_____. *Ramus, Method, and the Decay of Dialogue: From the Art of Discourse to the Art of Reason.* Cambridge, MA: Harvard UP, 1958.
Ovid. *Metamorphoses.* Ed. and trans. Frank J. Miller. Cambridge, MA: Harvard UP, 1916.
_____. *Metamorphoses.* Trans. A. D. Melville. Oxford: Oxford UP, 1986.
Oxford English Dictionary. 2nd ed. Ed. J. A. Simpson, Edmund S. Weiner. Oxford: Oxford UP, 1989.
Parker, Patricia. "*All's Well That Ends Well*: Increase and Multiply." In *Creative Imitation: New Essays on Renaissance Literature in Honor of Thomas M. Greene.* Ed. David Quint, et al. Binghamton, N.Y.: Medieval & Renaissance Texts & Studies, 1992. 355-90. Later version in *Shakespeare from the Margins* 185-217.
_____. *Literary Fat Ladies: Rhetoric, Gender, Property.* London: Methuen, 1987.
_____. And Geoffrey H. Hartman. Ed. *Shakespeare and the Question of Theory.* New York: Methuen, 1985.
_____. *Shakespeare from the Margins: Language, Culture, Context.* Chicago: U of Chicago P, 1996.
Pascal, Blaise. *Oeuvres completes.* Ed. Michel Le Guern. Paris: Gallimard, 1998.
_____. *Pensées.* Trans. A. J. Krailsheimer. Harmondsworth, Penguin, 1995.
_____. *Pensées.* Trans. H. F. Stewart. New York: Pantheon, 1950.

Paster, Gail Kern. *The Body Embarrassed: Drama and the Disciplines of Shame in Early Modern England*. Ithaca, N.Y.: Cornell UP, 1993.
Percy, Walker. "Metaphor as Mistake." In *The Message in the Bottle: How Queer Man Is, How Queer Language Is, and What One Has to do with the Other*. New York: Farrar, Straus and Giroux, 1975. 64-82.
Perloff, Marjorie. *Wittgenstein's Ladder*. Chicago: U of Chicago P, 1996.
Petrarch, Francesco. *Petrarch's Songbook: Rerum Vulgarium Fragmenta: A Verse Translation*. Trans. James Wyatt Cook. Asheville: Pegasus, 1995.
Phillips, William. See Kurzweil, Edith.
Plato. *Meno*. Trans. W. K. C. Guthrie. *Plato: The Collected Dialogues*. Ed. Edith Hamilton and Huntington Cairns. Bollingen Series LXXI. Princeton: Princeton UP, 1961. 353-84.
———. *Republic*. Trans. Paul Shorey. *Plato: The Collected Dialogues*. Ed. Edith Hamilton and Huntington Cairns. 575-844.
———. *Symposium*. Trans. Michael Joyce. *Plato: The Collected Dialogues*. Ed. Edith Hamilton and Huntington Cairns. 526-74.
Plotinus. *The Enneads*. Trans. Stephen MacKenna. 2nd ed. London: Faber, 1956.
Pope, Alexander. "Epitaph on Newton." http://members.aol.com/Philosdog/Newton.html. Last accessed 05.09.05.
Puttenham, George. *The Art of English Poesie*, 1589. Menston, Yorkshire: Scolar, 1968. Also http://etext.lib.virginia.edu/toc/modeng/public/PutPoes.html. Last accessed 04.12.04.
Rabkin, Norman. *Shakespeare and the Problem of Meaning*. Chicago: U of Chicago P, 1981.
Rackin, Phyllis. See Howard, Jean.
Reinhard, Kenneth. See Lupton, Julia Reinhard.
Rose, Jacqueline. See Mitchell, Juliet.
Rubin, Gayle. "The Traffic in Women: Notes on the 'Political Economy' of Sex." In *Toward an Anthropology of Women*. Ed. Rayna R. Reiter. New York: Monthly Review, 1975. 157-210.
Santinello, Giovanni. *Il pensiero di Nicolo Cusano nella sua prospettiva estetica*. Padua: Liviana, 1958.
Sartre, Jean-Paul. *Huis clos*. Ed. Jacques Hardréé and George B. Daniel. New York: Appleton-Century-Crofts, 1962.
Sarum, Use of. http://www.spiritwalk.org/prayer.htm. Last accessed 04.28.05.
Saul, Nigel. *Richard II*. New Haven: Yale UP, 1997.
Scheid, John, and Jesper Svenbro. *The Craft of Zeus: Myths of Weaving and Fabric*. Trans. Carol Volk. Cambridge, MA: Harvard UP, 1996.
Schwartz, Murray M. See Kahn, Coppélia.
Serres, Michel. *Hermes: Literature, Science, Philosophy*. Ed. Josué V. Harari and David E Bell. Baltimore: Johns Hopkins UP, 1983.
———. *The Parasite*. Trans. Lawrence Scheher. Baltimore: Johns Hopkins UP, 1981.
Shakespeare, William. *The Oxford Shakespeare*. 2nd ed. Oxford: Oxford UP, 2005.
———. *The Norton Shakespeare, Based on the Oxford Edition*. Ed. Stephen Greenblatt, et al. New York: W.W. Norton, 1997.
———. *The Riverside Shakespeare*. 2nd ed. Ed. G. B. Evans, et al. Cambridge, MA:

Houghton Mifflin, 1997.

———. *The Complete Sonnets and Poems*. Ed. Colin Burrow. Oxford: Oxford UP, 2002.

———. *Edward III*. Ed. Giorgio Melchiori, Brian Gibbons, and A. R. Braunmuller. Cambridge: Cambridge UP, 1998.

———. *Shakespeare's Edward III*. Ed. Eric Sams. New Haven: Yale UP, 1996.

Shannon, Laurie. *Sovereign Amity: Figures of Friendship in Shakespearean Contexts*. Chicago: U of Chicago P, 2002.

Sharon-Zisser, Shirley. *The Risks of Simile in Renaissance Rhetoric*. New York: Peter Lang, 2000.

Shell, Marc. *The End of Kinship: "Measure for Measure," Incest, and the Ideal of Universal Siblinghood*. Stanford: Stanford UP, 1988.

Shimodate, Kazumi. "Ebb to Humble Love: An Approach to *Othello* through Water Imagery." *Eigo eibungaku Kenkyujo Kito/Journal of the English Institute* 1989, 1-26.

Shoaf, R. Allen. "'Certius exemplar sapientis viri': Rhetorical Subversion and Subversive Rhetoric in *Pharsalia* IX." *Philological Quarterly* 57 (1978): 143-54.

———. *Chaucer's Body: The Anxiety of Circulation in the* Canterbury Tales. Gainesville: UP of Florida, 2001.

———. *Dante, Chaucer, and the Currency of the Word: Money, Images, and Reference in Late Medieval Poetry*. Norman, Oklahoma: Pilgrim Books, 1983. www.clas.ufl.edu/rashoaf/currency/dccw.html

———. "'For there is figures in all things': Juxtology in Shakespeare, Spenser, and Milton." In Allen and White. 266-85. http://web.clas.ufl.edu/users/rashoaf/shake/jux.htm

———. "*Hamlet*: Like Mother, Like Son." *Journal X* 4.1 (1999): 71-90.

———. *Milton, Poet of Duality: A Study of Semiosis in the Poetry and the Prose*. 1985. Rpt. Gainesville: The UP of Florida, 1993. http://www.clas.ufl.edu/users/rashoaf/duality/front/toc.htm

———. "*Troilus and Criseyde*: The Falcon in the Mew." In Keenan. 149-68.

———. "The Play of Puns in Late Middle English Poetry: Concerning Juxtology." In Culler. 44-61.

———. *The Testament of Love, by Thomas Usk*. TEAMS Middle English Texts Series (METS). Kalamazoo: Medieval Institute Publications, 1998. http://www.clas.ufl.edu.users/rashoaf/folia/html

Sidney, Sir Philip. *A Defense of Poetry*. 1595. In Vickers, *Criticism* 336-91.

Siegel, Muffy E. A. "*Like*: The Discourse Particle and Semantics." *Journal of Semantics* 19.1 (2002): 35-71.

Sihvola, Juha. See Nussbaum, Martha.

Skeat, Walter W. *A Concise Etymological Dictionary of the English Language*. New York: Perigree, 1980.

Skura, Meredith. *Shakespeare the Actor and the Purposes of Playing*. Chicago: U of Chicago P, 1993.

Smith, Bruce R. *Homosexual Desire in Shakespeare's England: A Cultural Poetics*. Chicago: U of Chicago P, 1991.

———. *The Acoustic World of Early Modern England: Attending to the O-factor.* Chicago: U of Chicago P, 1999.
Sophocles. *Oedipus the King.* Ed. Thomas Gould. Englewood Cliffs, N.J.: Prentice-Hall, 1970.
Spevack, Marvin. *A Complete and Systematic Concordance to the Works of Shakespeare.* 9 vols. Hildesheim: Georg Olms, 1968-1980.
Spingarn, Joel E. *Literary Criticism in the Renaissance.* 2nd ed. New York: Harcourt, 1963.
St. Augustine. *City of God.* Trans. Henry Bettenson. Harmondsworth: Penguin, 1972.
———. *Confessions 7.10.16. The Confessions of Augustine: An Electronic Edition* at http://www.stoa.org/hippo/. Based on the Oxford edition (© 1992) by James J. O'Donnell. Last accessed 07.16.2003.
Stallybrass, Peter. See Jones, Ann Rosalind.
Stevens, Wallace. *The Collected Poems of Wallace Stevens.* New York: Alfred A. Knopf, 1967.
———. *The Necessary Angel: Essays on Reality and the Imagination.* New York: Vintage, 1965.
Stewart, Garrett. *Reading Voices: Literature and the Phonotext.* Berkeley: U of California P, 1990.
Streuver, Nancy S. "Metaphoric Morals: Ethical Implications of Cusa's Use of Figure." In *Archéologie du signe.* Ed. Lucie Brind'Amour and Eugene Vance. Toronto: PIMS, 1983. 305-34.
Suetonius. *Lives of the Twelve Caesars.* Trans. Robert Graves. 1957. Rpt. New York: Penguin, 2003.
Swain, Donald W. See Kinney, Arthur, F.
Taylor, A. B. Ed. *Shakespeare's Ovid: The* Metamorphoses *in the Plays and Poems.* Cambridge: Cambridge UP, 2000.
Taylor, Mark. *Shakespeare's Imitations.* Newark: U of Delaware P/Associated University P, 2002.
Thomas of Britain. *The Carlisle Fragment of Thomas's Tristan.* Trans. Judy Shoaf. http://www.clas.ufl.edu/users/jshoaf/Carlisle.htm. Last accessed 07.20.03.
Tudor, Elizabeth. *Elizabeth I Collected Works.* Ed. Leah S. Marcus, Janel Mueller, and Mary Beth Rose. Chicago: U of Chicago P, 2002.
Veeser, H. Aram. Ed. *The New Historicism.* New York: Routledge, 1989.
Vickers, Brian. *English Renaissance Literary Criticism.* Oxford: Clarendon, 1999.
———. *Shakespeare, Co-author: A Historical Study of Five Collaborative Plays.* New York: Oxford UP, 2002.
Vickers, Nancy J. "'The blazon of sweet beauty's best': Shakespeare's Lucrece." In Parker and Hartman. 95-115.
Virgil. *Aeneid.* Trans. H. Rushton Fairclough. 2nd ed. 2 vols. Ed. G. P. Goold. Cambridge, MA: Harvard UP, 1999.
"Voice of the Shuttle." http://vos.ucsb.edu/myth.asp. Last accessed 04.10.04.
Warren, Roger. Editor. *Pericles.* Oxford: Oxford UP, 2003.
Watkins, Calvert. *The American Heritage Dictionary of Indo-European Roots.* 2nd ed. Boston: Houghton Mifflin Company, 2000.

Wells, Stanley, and Lena Cowen Orlin. *Shakespeare: An Oxford Guide*. New York: Oxford UP, 2003.

———. *Shakespeare: For all Time*. Oxford: Oxford UP, 2003.

———. And Gary Taylor, with John Jowett, and William Montgomery. *William Shakespeare, A Textual Companion*. Oxford: Clarendon, 1987.

Wheeler, Richard P., and C. L. Barber. *The Whole Journey: Shakespeare's Power of Development*. Berkeley: U of California P, 1989.

White, Robert. See Allen, David G.

Willbern, David. *Poetic Will: Shakespeare and the Play of Language*. Philadelphia: U of Pennsylvania P, 1997.

———. "Shakespeare's Nothing." In Schwartz and Kahn. 244-63.

Williams, Gordon. *A Glossary of Shakespeare's Sexual Language*. London: Athlone, 1997.

Winnicott, D. W. "Transitional Objects and Transitional Phenomena." *The International Journal of Psycho-analysis* 34 (1953): 89-97.

Wittgenstein, Ludwig. "Remarks on Frazer's *Golden Bough*." In *Philosophical Occasions 1912-1951*. Ed. James C. Klage and Alfred Nordmann. Indianapolis: Hackett P., 1993.

Wofford, Susanne. Ed. *William Shakespeare, "Hamlet."* Case Studies in Contemporary Criticism. Boston: Bedford Books, 1994.

Woolf, Virginia. *To the Lighthouse*. London: Hogarth, 1990.

Index of Names and Topics

Adelman, Janet, 239, 304, 306
Adonis, 14, 43, 45, 47, 49-52, 75, 115, 205, 206, 260
Aeschylus, 249
Alimentation, 270
Altman, Joel B., 1, 398
Anagram, 23, 24, 30, 39, 40, 50, 108, 114, 155, 280, 285, 394
Antithesis, 197
Anus, 6, 323
Anxiety, 5, 23, 37, 205, 320, 331, 356, 362, 364, 382, 383, 392, 399
Arendt, Hannah, 202, 283, 377
Aubrey, John, 375
Augustine, St., 11, 199, 201, 283, 338
Autoeroticism, 202

Bacon, Francis, 375, 398
Bastard, 53, 125-27, 129, 216, 343, 363
Believing (< "be-liking"), 231, 400
Be-like, 245, 261, 313, 333, 356, 357, 400
Berger, Harry, Jr., 374, 400
Bias, 125-6, 206-7
Birth, 4, 61, 82, 216, 242, 285, 311
Bloom, Harold, 382, 383
Boar, 48, 50, 51, 382
Body, 4-8, 16, 17, 37, 48, 102, 138, 146, 147, 153, 163, 190, 191, 236, 309, 310, 334, 348, 409, 410
Boy player, 343
Brooke, Nicholas, 260, 261
Burckhardt, Sigurd, 232

Cannibal, -ism, 62, 146, 269, 351
Canon, of Shakespeare, 5, 25, 69
Cartesian, -ism, 10, 201, 202, 356, 358, 377, 398
Catharsis, 165
Catholic, -ism, 11, 12, 90, 338, 399
Cavell, Stanley, 10, 11, 105, 147, 155, 156, 191, 192, 229, 261, 396
Certitude, 105
Chaucer, Geoffrey, 39, 225, 272, 388, 391
"Cleft effect," 380
Coincidence, 198, 332
Comedy, 28, 35, 75, 76, 79, 89, 115, 152, 156, 161, 162, 178, 180, 187, 192, 393
Comparison, 94, 102, 112, 131, 140, 220, 271, 388
Conciliatio, 373
Confusion, 57, 80, 82, 100, 178, 193, 406
Copiousness, 143, 197, 397
Copy, 1-5, 9, 18, 59, 60, 62, 72, 73, 107, 155, 193, 194, 196, 197, 200, 205, 206, 219, 283, 292, 326, 329, 349, 350, 376
Copying, 1, 2, 4, 5, 18, 59, 60, 62, 72, 193, 200, 219, 300, 309, 320, 350, 359, 370, 396, 405
Counterfeit, 15, 16, 70, 80, 111, 136, 137, 272, 330-4, 343, 370
"Couplement," 10, 21, 22, 373
Couples, 33, 10, 20-22, 80, 102, 153, 238, 373, 411
Coupling, 8, 22, 100, 104, 197, 228, 312
Cross-dressing, 177

"Crosse-cople," 7, 16, 21, 81, 197, 198, 374
Cusa, Nicholas of (Cusanus), 11, 331, 377

Daughter, 7, 44, 58, 89, 119, 136, 139, 183, 184, 253, 254, 256, 257, 281, 282, 296, 309-313, 317, 391
Derivativeness, 74, 288
Descartes, René, 393
Disguise, 23, 29, 35, 96, 128, 204, 205, 207, 225, 227, 228, 388
Division, 5-7, 29, 85, 117, 141, 162, 185, 186, 204, 211, 214, 242, 244, 245, 263, 311, 366, 380, 391, 394, 404, 406
Donne, John, 11, 293
Double, 5, 30, 49, 76, 78, 79, 95, 101, 102, 117, 123, 154, 156, 275-7, 390, 405
Doubleness, 224
Doubling, 28, 30, 76, 93, 192, 399
Doubt, 6, 11, 20, 45, 57, 61, 155, 156, 196, 197, 201, 259, 329, 330, 358, 362, 363, 388, 389, 404, 406
Dual, 15, 112, 277, 278, 309, 406
Dubrow, Heather, 373

Ear, 31, 86, 88, 89, 120, 146, 248, 316, 326, 359, 365, 366, 370, 386, 403, 408
Eating, 241, 267, 269, 333, 334
Education, 46, 260, 315
Eggs, 329, 330, 332, 334
Elizabeth I, 7, 44, 97, 129, 172, 316, 317, 356, 357, 381, 385, 389, 401
Eros, 235, 236, 238, 299, 300
Example, 1-3, 57, 58, 64, 65, 67, 72, 73, 97, 98, 100, 132, 201, 202, 224, 225, 326, 329, 330, 355-7, 369-71, 391
Excrement, 269, 270
Exemplariness, 1, 3, 5, 7, 46, 57, 58, 63, 65-67, 69, 72, 74, 99, 369

Fart, 198
Father, 4, 43-46, 59, 60, 87, 88, 118, 119, 126, 127, 149-51, 187, 189-91, 193, 281, 282, 303, 304, 309-15, 331, 384, 389, 391

Feeding, 241, 267, 269
Fiction, 47, 96-98, 103, 113, 123, 126, 143, 156, 200, 207, 223, 232, 245, 330
Fineman, Joel, xxi, 7, 373, 378, 379, 383, 385, 400, 410
Fletcher, John, 340, 356, 358-61, 363-6, 384
Food, 122, 123, 132, 267-9
Forgive, -ness, 27, 135, 289, 342, 350, 389
Freud, Sigmund, 198, 396, 405, 409
Fürstenspiegel tradition, 45, 63, 69, 70, 72, 73, 315, 369

Garber, Marjorie, 198
Gender, 48, 97, 131, 133, 135, 137, 139, 141, 207, 243, 291, 316
Genital, 7, 119, 198, 251, 256
Girard, René, 166
Glass, 2, 17, 64, 71, 98, 173, 227, 365, 386, 387
Glove, glover, 207
Grammar, 324, 370, 373, 374
Greenblatt, Stephen, xxi, 398

Hamnet, 318, 399
Hathaway, Anne, 6
Hear, 51, 79-82, 86, 88, 89, 91, 144, 145, 153, 155, 156, 168-70, 186-90, 197-9, 247, 248, 256-8, 290
Heidegger, Martin, 133, 339, 388, 396
Heir, 7, 309, 310, 313, 340
Heracles, 83, 289, 385, 394
Historiography, 46, 74
History, 3, 4, 6, 14, 43-47, 49, 63, 74, 86, 90, 95, 106, 219, 355, 356
Homoeroticism, 140, 202, 362, 363
Honan, Park, 372, 374
Howard, Jean, 6, 177
Hunt, 50, 51, 279, 385, 391
Husband, 7, 40, 76, 78-80, 82, 118, 135, 151, 154, 155, 191, 231, 235, 238-40, 245, 364, 365
Hymen, 177, 178-80, 181, 183, 185, 351, 392-3

Identity, 19, 31, 57, 75, 101, 107, 115,

126, 192, 205, 214, 237, 240-2, 274, 373, 374
"Image and likeness," 12, 138, 358, 376
Imagination, 16, 87, 121, 158, 163, 186, 223, 244, 246, 256, 297, 347-9, 351
Imitation, 4, 10, 62, 219, 223, 326, 406, 409
Improper, 196
Incest, 187, 191-3, 228, 229, 296, 297, 311, 313, 401, 407
Inheritance, 11, 387
Inwardness, 55, 179, 344
Inwordness, 110, 111, 345

Jesus, 82, 226, 231, 370
Johnson, Samuel, 85, 170, 194, 397
Jonson, Ben, 373, 390
Joyce, James, xviii, 8, 22, 61, 114, 178, 187, 402
Juxta-form ("juxtological"), 21, 30, 81, 100, 104, 108, 231, 259, 374

Keats, John, 60, 378
Kenosis, 12, 224 (empty)
Kenotic, 23, 378

Lacan, Jacques, 186, 199, 370
Latin, 12, 23, 240, 326
Law, 21, 64, 71, 79, 118, 119, 122, 123, 134, 135, 137, 141, 152, 153, 200, 257, 260, 333, 334, 358
Legitimacy, 7, 125, 127, 129, 399
"Lover's Complaint, A," 380

Madness, 135, 190, 191, 195, 196, 211, 265, 267, 282, 401
Marlowe, Christopher, 55, 159-61, 340, 353, 357, 383
Marriage, 76, 78, 82, 102, 104, 141, 152, 153, 178, 180, 277, 306, 310, 353, 395, 406
Mask, 280, 388
Mate, 35, 37, 39-41, 290
Mating, 36, 37
Memory, 374
Metamorphoses, 10, 49, 281, 296, 398, 407
Metamorphosis, 23, 25-27, 29, 31, 33, 90

Metaphor, 21, 47, 125, 223, 311-13, 388, 409
Milton, John, 2, 8, 30, 112, 138, 277, 392, 398, 401
Mimesis, 79, 376
Mirrors, 45-47, 49, 63, 64, 70, 72, 73, 74, 95, 98-100, 102, 173, 174, 259, 276, 315, 334, 349, 383, 384, 386
Misogamy, 153
Misogyny, 278, 342
Model, 1, 61-62, 63, 100, 220, 316
Montaigne, Michel de, 11, 44, 49, 95, 96, 330, 366, 377
Mother, 5, 6, 44, 49, 60, 82, 106, 107, 189-91, 193, 197, 212, 281, 296, 304-7, 320-4, 409
Mutuality, 8, 91, 139, 140, 200, 280, 334, 349, 350
Myrrha, 296, 407

Narcissism, 72, 203, 205-6, 359, 365, 386
Narcissus, vii, xviii, xx, 23, 25, 26, 30, 49-50, 326, 364, 386, 406
Natality, 283
Nothing, 7, 155-6, 259-60

Ovid, 10, 25, 49, 353, 375, 398, 401

Parker, Patricia, 330
Partners, 15, 28, 228, 277, 278, 401, 406
Parturition, 82
Philomela, 10
"Phoenix and Turtle, The," 5, 138, 185, 244, 288, 292, 293, 366
Plato, 10, 11, 160, 276, 301, 371, 376
Playing, 72, 123, 192, 232, 321
Playwright, 73, 166, 178, 227, 232, 238, 285, 318
Playwriting, 55, 207
Plotinus, 209, 313, 377
Poet, 16, 18, 21, 22, 46, 47, 108, 116, 163, 168-70, 172, 248, 260-1, 272, 276, 334, 344, 386
Poetics, 326
Poetry, 39, 50, 61, 75, 99, 109, 146, 177, 180, 198, 272, 276, 343, 370, 373
Politics, 253, 350

Pornography, 245, 246
Pregnancy, pregnant, 195, 196, 242, 251, 258, 343
Prescript, 4, 8, 45, 46, 55, 59, 73, 74, 85-87, 91, 106, 129, 139, 172, 191, 220, 257, 258, 260, 341, 342, 383
Prescriptiveness, 1, 4, 74, 91
Property, 5, 119, 198, 242, 243, 292, 300, 301, 317, 330, 331, 396, 400, 402, 403
Psychoanalysis, 132, 322
Pun, punning, 1, 26, 50, 85, 103, 111, 113, 114, 128, 132, 133, 170, 172, 194-7, 211, 213, 340
Puritan, 259, 400

Qualify, 219
Quality, 11, 61, 95, 107, 131, 138, 171, 259, 330
Queer, 206

Race, 57, 371
Rackin, Phyllis, 373
Readiness, 92, 182, 190, 260, 282, 383
Reading, 7, 66, 306
Reflection, 33, 70, 71, 173, 209, 215-17, 380
Representation, 28, 53, 55, 57, 70, 158, 272, 275, 305, 347, 380
Reproduction, 59, 311
Respect, 131, 133, 139, 140
Revenge, 48, 59, 113, 132, 238, 240, 241
Rhetoric, 1, 2, 8, 9, 35, 39, 49, 85, 117, 210, 219, 278, 326, 358, 397
Romances, 7, 60, 309, 355, 356
Rome, 54, 57, 58, 62, 67, 169, 288, 321, 325, 369, 392, 399

Science, 325, 398
Script, 8, 73, 74, 85-87, 139, 172, 206, 245-7, 257, 258, 283, 342, 365
Season, 131, 135, 139
Seeds, 17, 51, 65, 251, 280, 327
Separation, 190, 202, 237, 314
Sex, 5-7, 16, 17, 70, 104, 126, 137, 156, 209, 231, 236, 305, 363, 364, 366, 371
Shame, 2, 16, 19, 29, 49, 58, 64, 65, 113, 205, 228, 229, 232, 290, 324, 325, 344

Shit, 270-2
Simian, 9, 200, 379
Simile, 21, 93, 292, 330, 377
Similitude, 11, 95, 330, 332
Singular, 48, 50, 51, 102, 103, 111, 112, 214, 289, 392
Skin, 1, 5, 128, 182
Son, 6-7, 43-44, 53, 59-60, 70, 372-3
Sorting, 109, 178-80, 392
St. Paul, 7, 82, 199, 224, 370, 403
Stevens, Wallace, 177, 223, 331, 388, 406
Succession, 6, 7, 43, 44, 52, 72, 76, 101, 102, 104, 125, 129, 188, 285, 309, 310, 330, 356, 358
Surrogacy, 226-30, 233
Susanna Shakespeare (Hall), 7, 310, 316, 391
Syneciosis, 8, 16, 19, 21, 81, 104, 197, 198, 373, 410
Syneciotician, 10, 92, 100, 104, 231

Theory, 5, 8-10, 41, 52, 75, 177, 232, 276, 371, 374, 376, 379
Theory, theater (sharing same Greek root), 5, 8-10, 378, 379
Time, 3-5, 8, 17, 33, 170, 171, 173, 174, 215, 216, 230, 231, 284, 297, 311, 312, 362, 376, 406, 411
Tragedy, 14, 28, 53, 58, 59, 60, 62, 76, 105, 107, 161, 162, 165, 166, 168, 172, 175, 181, 182, 236, 253, 254, 256, 257, 261, 281, 282, 289, 319, 320, 366, 380, 392-5, 404
Translation, 11, 220, 331, 332, 369, 377
Trawpe, 356
Twins, 76, 80, 116, 350, 364, 399, 409
Type, 67

Uncanny, 24, 43, 117, 129, 198, 397
"Unlikeness, land of," 11, 77, 122, 378

Violence, 36, 162, 325, 381, 397, 398, 404
Virgil, 326

Wall, 117-119, 122, 169, 275
Wells, Stanley, 375
Wife, 6, 30, 37, 39, 53, 122, 141, 155, 156,

191, 240, 241, 243-5, 253, 299, 300, 306, 387
Will (Shakespeare's name), 201
Womb, 17, 107, 347, 351

Wordplay, 170, 394
Work of art, 67

Yoke, 36, 381, 397